FLORA ANDAMAN ISLANDS

FLORA ANDAMAN ISLANDS

C. E. PARKINSON

GYAN

Published by

Gyan Publishing House
5, Ansari Road
Daryaganj, New Delhi-110002
Phone: 011-47034999, 9811692060
E-mail: books@gyanbooks.com

Distribution Network
gyanbooks.com
India, USA, Canada, UK, Australia

ISBN: 978-93-7447-321-4 (PB)

First Published, 1923

2nd Impression 2026

Printed at: Gyan Press, Delhi.

FLORA ANDAMAN ISLANDS
Author: C. E. PARKINSON

FOREST FLORA OF THE ANDAMAN ISLANDS

C.E. PARKINSON

1923

FOREWORD.

Mr. Parkinson has asked me to write a foreword for his book and I take the opportunity of making a few remarks on the general question of the preparation of forest floras, the importance of which it is believed is frequently not sufficiently realised.

The greatly increased value of many woods and other forest products which, a few years ago, were practically worthless, combined with the steadily growing intensity of our forest management during recent years, have made it clear that an efficient forest officer in India now ought to possess a more detailed knowledge of the vegetation constituting the forests in his charge than that which was considered necessary in earlier days. It has also become increasingly evident during recent years that the classical detailed Floras hitherto available in India, indispensable though these undoubtedly are, do not sufficiently facilitate the successful identification of species by the average forest officer.

There has been a tendency in the past to think that a forest officer who studies and tries to know well the plants in his forest is gradually becoming "only a botanist" and is therefore decreasing in value as a practical forest officer. This idea appears to be due to a misunderstanding, on the one hand, regarding the lines of work which fall within the legitimate scope of the science of botany and, on the other hand, as to the kind of botany which an efficient forest officer ought to know.

For the production of a really satisfactory Forest Flora, for instance, it is not always realised that two distinct classes of work are essential, *viz.* :—

(1) herbarium work, comprising a study of the herbarium specimens, plates and original descriptions on which the species and other subsidiary taxonomic groups of systematic botanists are primarily based and which are the authority for the various specific and varietal names which have been published. Without this study it is impossible to decide what name is the correct one for any particular species or other group ;

(2) what is usually called field work which comprises a study of the living plants in the forest, of the various characters which enable us to recognize them in the forest at different seasons of the year and of the range of variation which they exhibit. Such work forms a necessary part of forest

botany and constitutes an important branch of botanical science.

It is only exceptionally that forest officers experience the necessity, or have the opportunity, for doing much work of class (1) but, on the other hand, it is often not sufficiently realized that a more or less considerable knowledge of field botany should form an essential part of the equipment of every efficient forest officer in India.

It is also not always understood that, apart from its value in practical forestry, advanced work of class (2), supplemented when necessary by experimental cultures, is of great importance from a purely scientific point of view, inasmuch as it is essential for correctly defining the boundaries of specific groups and for deciding such questions as to whether a group should be classified as a species or variety and the best way of dealing with so-called "intermediates" and forms of hybrid origin.

For many years, the writer has urged the importance of making the utmost use of the botanical knowledge possessed by officers of the Forest Department, in the preparation of small local forest floras,([1]) the primary object of which is to facilitate the work of identification of species by forest officers and to disseminate widely through all ranks of the Department a good practical knowledge of our forest plants. With the object of accelerating this work a scheme for the preparation of *descriptive lists* of species was drawn up in 1913 which subsequently received the sanction of the Government of India. ([2])

The primary principle on which this scheme was based is indicated in the following extract:—

"There is a tendency on the part of some Forest Officers to believe that the correct definition of species necessarily depends on abstruse technical characters which the ordinary man can neither hope to recognize nor understand. In most good species, however, minute botanical characters (which are naturally of most value to the systematic botanist working in a herbarium with as a rule only scanty material) can be correlated with other and more obvious characters which serve to distinguish the species in the field and which are naturally of primary importance for the field-student. Indeed it is probably not too much to say that, as a general rule, if the careful field observer after due study fails to discover characters which enable him to recognize the herbarium botanist's species as a definite and distinct group of individuals in nature, it is so much the worse for the herbarium species which thus becomes of no practical forest value.

([1]) See *Indian Forester*, XXX, page 108 (1904).
([2]) See *Forest Bulletin* No. 23, pub. Calcutta, 1914.

The primary task of the authors of Descriptive Lists, therefore, is to translate the work of the systematic herbarium botanist into such terms as shall be readily intelligible to the average Forest Officer and thus to enable the latter to reap the full practical advantages of the labours of the systematist. The discovery and selection of the field-characters required for the keys, therefore, will necessitate much hard work in the field and a real knowledge of each species as it appears in the forest. Hardly less care and labour will be required for the selection of really useful and reliable vernacular names. Such labour, however, will be well repaid by the cordial appreciation of those Forest Officers who try to use the completed Lists and who will be the ultimate judges of their practical utility. From what has been said above it will be seen that, although the co-operation of the systematic botanist is essential, inasmuch as he supplies the foundation of identifications on which the present work must be based, the actual preparation of the Lists can be quite well done by the average trained Forest Officer. Indeed it is possible that the very important keys will be more satisfactorily prepared by the latter than by the expert systematist, inasmuch as the latter will be more inclined than the former to utilise and depend on minute technical characters." (1)

The chief features of this scheme were :—

(1) that each list should deal with a small area and therefore a restricted number of species,
(2) that the descriptions of species should be very brief and that the characters used in these and in the keys should as far as possible be forest characters,
(3) that sylvicultural and œcological notes, likely to be useful in the locality, should be included but stated as briefly as possible, *e.g.*, in the form of sylvicultural lists,
(4) that each list should be sufficiently small to serve as a pocket companion for use in the forest,
(5) that specimens of all species dealt with in the lists should be placed in the Dehra Dun herbarium for permanent record.

It was realised that, in many cases, in order to avoid undesirable delay, it would be necessary to publish the lists in a more or less incomplete form and that they would be subsequently improved and gradually perfected. Descriptive lists of this kind provided with useful keys are really very efficient local forest floras and although it was obvious that the preparation of such books would facilitate the subsequent preparation of more elaborate floras, generally dealing with a larger area (in each case usually not less than that of an entire Province) and a greater number of species, it was recognized that such large floras are primarily books of reference not pocket companions for the field and that the latter will, therefore, always possess a distinct and

(1) 1 c. pp. 4, 5.

permanent value of their own. The first descriptive lists issued under this scheme were those for the three Forest Circles of the Central Provinces which were published at Allahabad in 1916. (1) A striking testimony to the value of these lists is afforded by the fact that although the Bombay Presidency is provided with two excellent regional floras (2) yet a Divisional Forest Officer serving in a Bombay district adjoining the Central Provinces recently informed the writer that he found the list dealing with the adjacent area of the Central Provinces more generally useful to him in his work than the Bombay floras. Similar lists but in a preliminary form will shortly be published for the United Provinces by Mr. A. E. Osmaston and Mr. P. C. Kanjilal. The latter, it will be seen, is thus following in the footsteps of his father Rai Bahadur Upendranath Kanjilal (also a former forest student of Dehra Dun) who is really the pioneer in India in this matter of local forest floras, he having published the admirable *Forest Flora of the School Circle, N. W. P.* in 1901, of which a revised edition was issued in 1911. The value of this indispensable book (which owed its origin in the first place to the suggestion and support of Mr. J. S. Gamble) to our students and to those forest officers whose work brings them to Dehra Dun is a remarkable illustration of the fact that the value of a flora to the Forest Department is by no means necessarily proportionate to its bulk nor to the extent of the area with which it deals. Sir Dietrich Brandis referring to this book in 1906 remarks that it is "full of original observations, made by him during his many years' work in the forests attached to the Imperial Forest School. Following the example set by him, I trust that the local Forest Floras of the future will be based mainly upon the study of the trees and shrubs as they grow in the forest." (3).

The present publication dealing with the forest flora of the Andaman Islands has also been written by a former forest student of Dehra Dun and it is confidently believed that it will also prove to be indispensable to the Forest Department and of great value to forest officers in the Andamans, a region which has recently been

(1) *Descriptive List of Trees, Shrubs and Economic Herbs of the Southern Circle, Central Provinces*, by H. H. Haines.

Descriptive List of Trees, Shrubs, Climbers and Economic Herbs of the Northern and Berar Forest Circles, Central Provinces, by D. O. Witt.

(2) *The Flora of the Presidency of Bombay* by T. Cooke, Volumes I and II, London, 1903-1908.

Forest Flora of the Bombay Presidency and Sind by W. A. Talbot, Volumes I and II, Poona, 1909-1911.

(3) Indian Trees, London, 1906, page VII.

described as "literally a gold mine of timber wealth." Mr. Parkinson has carefully studied his plants in the forest and his work has materially increased our knowledge regarding the species of the Islands. Four new species have been discovered and more than 130 of the indigenous species described in this book either have not been mentioned at all, or have not been reported as occurring in the Andamans, in Brandis's *Indian Trees*. Mr. Parkinson's work has also indicated that several species which have been previously recorded for the Andamans probably do not occur in the Islands and that the well-known Andaman Marble-wood is not yielded by *Diospyros Kurzii*, Hiern, as has been hitherto thought to be the case.

Mr. Parkinson, in his Preface, has emphasized the great assistance that he has received in his work from the expert staff and splendid collections at the Sibpur herbarium, Royal Botanic Gardens, Calcutta, for which we are indebted to the generous assistance of Colonel Gage, Director of the Botanical Survey of India.

In conclusion, attention should be drawn to the great debt of gratitude which India and her forest department owe to Sir David Prain and the expert staff at Kew. They have fully recognized that a study of our plants in the forest is not only necessary for practical forestry but is also of real scientific value. With reference to this branch of our work Dr. Stapf, the Curator of the Herbarium at Kew in 1909, wrote that "field work on the lines laid down is of great importance as a supplement and corrective for herbarium work which is apt to suffer through becoming too narrow and detached from the actual conditions of plant life." while Sir David Prain, Director of the Royal Botanic Gardens, when forwarding this note wrote "with Dr. Stapf's remarks I entirely concur. We shall be glad to do whatever is in our power to assist you." In all our efforts to advance the study of forest botany in India we have invariably received the most generous and cordial assistance from the authorities at Kew who, in the case of the present book, for instance, have named a considerable number of specimens for us which could not be dealt with satisfactorily in India.

R. S. HOLE,
Forest Botanist.

DEHRA DUN :
April 10th, 1922.

PREFACE.

1. In 1913, at Dehra Dun, the Board of Forestry passed a resolution in favour of a general scheme for the preparation of Descriptive Lists and Simple Forest Floras, and this resolution subsequently received the approval of the Government of India. The object of this scheme was, on the one hand, to provide Forest Officers in India and Burma, as quickly as possible, with simple books which would help them to identify the more important species occurring in the forests, and, on the other hand, to initiate a systematic study of the forest vegetation with the collection of the information and material which eventually will make it possible to prepare complete, detailed, fully illustrated, reference Floras (see *Forest Bulletin* No. 23 of 1913). The present hand-book has been prepared in accordance with this general scheme, and it is hoped that it will, at least to some extent, make it easier for the Forester in the Andamans to get to know the trees and plants in his forests than has been possible in the past.

2. There is no existing work which deals only with the flowering plants of the islands, and the Forester who wishes to know the names of the less known plants would have to consult the *Flora of British India*, Kurz's *Forest Flora of British Burma*, or Brandis's *Indian Trees*. The ordinary Forest Officer, however, experiences considerable difficulty in utilizing these books, partly on account of their technical nature, and also because they include a large number of species which do not occur in the Andamans.

3. The present work lays no claim to absolute originality, and in its preparation various standard works of reference have been freely utilized. At the same time I have used my discretion in adopting the general arrangement, and in selecting the descriptive characters which seem most likely to be helpful to those for whose use the book is intended. Of the 650 plants or so described or mentioned in this book, I have seen about 530. Many of these I collected, and in doing so wrote descriptions of them which have been included in this book. In the case of those plants which I have not personally seen, the descriptions have been taken, often verbatim, from other works. In some cases I have modified these, I trust with good judgment, in order to secure some degree of general uniformity throughout the work. I have tried, as far as possible, to avoid the use of technical terms, and the explanations of those simple botanical terms which I have been obliged to use will be found in the glossary which has been included.

4. The study of the forest vegetation of the Andamans undertaken in connection with this work, has resulted in the discovery of four species new to science, *viz.*:—

Milinsa tectona, *Hutchinson.*

Polyalthia Parkinsonii, *Hutchinson.*

Linociera Parkinsonii, *Hutchinson.*

Linostoma andamanica, *Hutchinson.*

5. The reader who desires, with the aid of this book, to find out the name of a plant that he does not know, has three courses open to him, and each of these he may follow separately, so as to fix the name of the plant with more certainty. The first method, by far the simplest, but not always practicable, is to find out the vernacular name of a plant, if it has any, and by referring to the index the corresponding botanical name may be determined. In this connection it is necessary to say a few words. The present Penal Settlement at Port Blair was established in the year 1858, *i.e.*, little more than 60 years ago. With the exception therefore, of the original inhabitants of the islands, the Andamanese, the present permanent residents of the Settlement, have either themselves or their forefathers, recently come from various parts of India and Burma where the forests are often very different from those of these islands. They have moreover, as a rule, not been resident long enough in the islands to know the native plants really well, and consequently there are no well-established vernacular names for them. In the case of a few of the better-known plants reliable vernacular names may be obtained from the old residents of the islands, especially from those who have been employed for any length of time by the Forest Department in exploiting the well-known Andaman timbers, or those who have had uses for certain plants and to which they have accordingly given vernacular names which are now well established. All vernacular names, especially those of the less-known plants, should always be accepted with caution, and should be used only as a means for determining, by comparison with the descriptions given in the text, the correct botanical name of a plant. To accept a vernacular name without such comparison is the surest way of falling into error. The flora of the Andamans and that of Tenasserim and certain other parts of Burma have many plants in common, and on this account correct Burmese names are often available. The Burman, however, uses many names with great latitude, and often gives to Andaman plants the names of other Burmese plants if they bear any resemblance to each other. Thus the Burmese name *Chinyok* of *Garuga pinnata*, a plant which is found in these

islands. is given to *Dracontomelum mangiferum*, which somewhat resembles the former, but which, apparently, is not found in Burma. In this connection I would also mention that many Hindustani names are likewise given to plants in these islands which bear different names in India, such as the name *Jhingan*, which in India belongs to *Odina Wodier*, but which is here given to *Pajanelia Rheedii*. Thus many names are of purely local value, and until they become well-established in the islands are of little use and are often misleading. As regards Andamanese names, I have not given any, for they are, I think, of little practical use to us. The Andamanese are rapidly decreasing in numbers, their tribes have become mixed and in some cases have already disappeared, while those of them who have come in contact with civilization are losing to a great extent their jungle habits, and are forgetting their original dialects, consequently they often seem unable now to give the names which no doubt they were once able to "with accuracy and certainty of determination." The second method of determining the name of an unknown plant, is by means of the General Artificial Key at the beginning of the book. An artificial key of this kind should, perhaps, be complete for the locality dealt with, but the fact that this one is not quite exhaustive will, I trust, not detract from its value. All the native plants, with the exception of a few of the unimportant ones, have been included, as well as those of the introduced ones which are not well-known, and which it has been thought necessary to include. The other well-known cultivated plants have reliable vernacular and popular names, and their inclusion would only tend to crowd the key and to make it more complex. It will, perhaps, be well to remind the unscientific reader. that in dealing with the forms of plants mathematical accuracy is not to be expected, and on this account when using the key, it may sometimes be found difficult to decide to which of two or three groups a plant belongs, or ultimately, which of two or three species a plant is; this difficulty is, I think, unavoidable, owing to the variability of the forms of plants, especially of such characters as have been used in this artificial key, and I have endeavoured to include the plant in those groups to which it seems possible for it to be referred. By comparing the descriptions given in the text in turn, it can finally be decided to which of two or three description a plant best answers, and to do this only an elementary knowledge of Botany is required. The General Key is to be used only as a means to an end, and no plant should be named by its means alone. This should only be done after reference has been made to the text and it has been found that the description given there agrees with the characters of the plant to be named. The third way of determining the name of an unknown plant is open only to those who possess sufficient knowledge of

Systematic Botany to be able, by examining a plant and determining its chief characters, to refer it to its Family, thence to its Genus, and finally to its species. A conspectus of the families, giving their chief characteristics and the number of Andaman species, is given at the beginning of this book.

6. A reference has been made in the text after the name of each plant to the volume and page of the *Flora of British India*, or the page in Brandis's *Indian Trees* where its description is to be found. An asterisk placed before the name of a plant means that I have not seen it in the Andamans.

7. In concluding this preface, I beg permission to give thanks, and to render acknowledgments, to those concerned in the production of this book. That the work should have been entrusted to me, is due to Mr. R. S. Hole, the Forest Botanist at Dehra Dun, under whose guidance it has been carried out, and I desire here to express my deep gratitude to him for this and for all the kind help and encouragement he has given me in its production and for the patience with which he has watched its slow progress. To Messrs. J. L. Baker and J. W. A. Grieve, under whom I worked in the Andamans while this work was in the course of preparation, I also tender my heartfelt thanks for the encouragement and facilities which they gave me in my undertaking. To Mr. H. H Haines, who corrected some of my first work and gave me valuable advice thereon, and by whose work I have always been guided, I desire to express my thankfulness. I am also deeply indebted to the authorities of the Royal Botanic Garden, Calcutta, for all the help that I was given while I was permitted to work in the Herbarium, especially to Messrs. H. G. Carter and P. M. Debbarman of the Botanical Survey of India, and to Mr. C. C. Calder, the Curator of the Herbarium. To the authorities at Kew who permitted me to visit and to have access to the collections in that famous Herbarium, I also desire to express my thanks. To those Officers in the Andamans who have long felt the want of a hand-book of this nature, and who have patiently awaited its publication, I owe, for the great delay, an apology, but this delay has, perhaps, brought me a slightly better knowledge and experience of Botany, which I hope will increase the utility of the book. am indebted to Mr. C. E. Cox of the Indian Forest Service, for permission to reproduce the very fine photograph which forms the frontispiece of this book.

8. I have mentioned above the names of some botanical works of which I have taken the liberty to make full use, and to these I add the following; Kurz's *Report on the Vegetation of the Andaman Islands*,

1870; *King's Materials for a Flora of the Malayan Peninsula*, 1899-1908, published in the Journal of the Asiatic Society of Bengal; Prain's leaflets, *The Non-Indigenous Species of the Andaman Flora*, and *A Botanical visit to the Little Andaman and Nicobars*, published by the Asiatic Society of Bengal in 1891: Gamble's *List of Andaman Plants* published in the Andamans in 1903; *The Flowering Plants of Western India* by Nairne, 1894; *A Forest Flora of Chota Nagpur* by H. H. Haines, 1910; *a Glossary of Botanical Terms* by R. L. Heinig, and *A Manual of Botany* by R. S. Hole, 1909. The last mentioned is the text-book in use at the Forest College, Dehra Dun, and the terms and definitions given in this book have been used in general accordance with those of that Manual.

9. Finally, I am keenly aware of the fact that numerous errors and deficiencies will no doubt be discovered in the present work, and I shall be very grateful to all those who may use this book, if they will kindly communicate them to me from time to time.

DEHRA DUN; C. E. PARKINSON,

7th May 1921. *Extra Assistant Conservator of Forests.*

INTRODUCTION.

GENERAL SITUATION AND DESCRIPTION OF THE ISLANDS.

The Andaman Islands are situated in the Bay of Bengal, and lie between the latitudes of 13° 41' and 10° 30' North, and the longitudes of 92° 11' and 93° 7' East. They are separated by a sea-space of some 700 miles from the Coromandel coast in the west, and to the east, across the Andaman Sea, the Tenasserim coast is about 320 miles distant. The most northerly point of the islands, Landfall Island, is about 180 miles from Cape Negrais in Burma.

The entire length of the Andaman Group, from the northernmost point of Landfall Island to the southernmost point of the Little Andaman, is about 219 miles, and from the west coast of the Great Andaman to East Island in Ritchie's Archipelago, the extreme width is about 32 miles.

The islands, large and small, are said to number 204, and they generally form a chain lying in a northerly and southerly direction. The land area of the whole group is approximately 2,500 square miles.

The Great Andaman, which forms the main part of the group, and which roughly comprises the area covered by this work, is about 156 miles long. It varies from an extreme width of 19 miles, in the Middle Andaman, to narrow necks of land on both sides of which lie arms of the sea. This group consists of the North Andaman, Interview Island, the Middle Andaman, the largest of all the islands, Baratang Island, Ritchie's Archipelago, and the South Andaman, with the Labyrinth Islands and Rutland Island, together with numerous smaller adjacent islands and outliers. These are, in some instances, separated from each other by more or less wide sea passages, such as Diligent Strait and Macpherson Strait, and in others they lie close up against each other, being separated by narrow, but deep, mangrove-fringed creeks through which sweep fast tidal currents to and from the Andaman Sea and the Bay of Bengal.

Little Andaman, an island of about 300 square miles in area, lies to the south of the Great Andaman, and is separated from it by Duncan Passage.

The North and South Sentinel Islands are outliers, the former lying about 17 miles west of Tarmugli Island, and the latter about 34 miles south of it and 15 miles from the north-west shores of the Little Andaman.

Two remarkable islands of volcanic origin, Narcondam and Barren Island, are set in the Andaman Sea. The former, which lies about 60 miles east of Port Cornwallis in the North Andaman, is a cone-like island of impressive appearance attaining a height of 2333 feet above sea-level. The latter, which still shows signs of activity, is nearly 80 miles from Port Blair, and attaining a height of 1158 feet above sea-level, it is said to be visible on a clear day from the hill tops in the east of the Middle Andaman.

Physical and Geographical Features.

The coast line of the islands is everywhere irregular and is broken by numerous small and large indentations; some of these form spacious, deep and well-sheltered natural harbours, which are spoken of as being among the finest in the world, and which afford to shipping protection from the violent storms by which these islands are visited, and which blow from all directions.

The surface of the islands is irregular and more or less hilly. The hills, following the general direction of the islands, lie nearly north and south, and from them numerous spurs and ridges branch out in all directions. Stretches of undulating ground broken by knolls and ridges and intersected by ravines occur irregularly, and here and there along the sea-coast and in the valleys strips of flat ground are found.

The principal ranges of hills lie closer to the east than to the west. The highest point is reached in the North Andaman on Saddle Peak which is 2402 feet above sea-level. The other more important heights are, in the Middle Andaman, Mt. Diavolo, 1678 feet, and Mt. Angelica, 1527 feet; in the South Andamans Mt. Koyob, 1510 feet, the highest point of the Mt. Harriet Range, Mt. Hext, 1410 feet, and Mt. Harriet, 1193 feet, immediately north of and overlooking the harbour of Port Blair. Mt. Ford on Rutland Island attains 1420 feet. These hills are steeper in the east than in west, and the submarine formation immediately around the islands being continuous with these slopes, the bed of the ocean in their vicinity is deeper in the east than in the west.

Some ranges of importance occur near the west coast, where, in the Middle Andaman, Mt. Oldham attains 1016 feet, and in the South Andaman, Mt. Cadell and Mt. Cholunga attain 1063 and 1075 feet, respectively.

Tidal creeks penetrate the islands often far inland, and these form outlets to the numerous boulder-strewn fresh-water streams that flow from the interior. By the precipitation of silt brought down these creeks, muddy flats sometimes of great extent, are formed and on these mangroves love to grow.

The geological formation of the islands is, according to geologists, similar to that of several parts of the coast of Burma. Upon the nature of the underlying soil depends chiefly the type of forest found growing in any locality, and the different formations of soil present may be enumerated as follows:—

1. Saline low-lying land, the sub-soil of which is usually of alluvial formation. This is inundated at regular intervals by the rise and fall of the tides and is usually occupied by mangroves.

2. Alluvial land out of the reach of the sea lying along the sea-coast and in the valleys and consisting generally of deep fertile clayey or sandy loam. This is usually occupied by luxuriant tall evergreen forest.

3. Low undulating ground of a somewhat poor and hard rubble or sandstone formation, where the forests are usually of a leaf-shedding character and where many of the most valuable Andaman timber-trees grow. This formation has been described fully by Mr. C. G. Rogers in his *Exploration Report of the Forests of the South Andaman*, and is called by him the Baratang beds.

4. Hills consisting of a yellow-brown and rather stiff clayey soil of a micaceous sandstone formation usually covered by tall evergreen forests.

5. High and steep hills such as Saddle Peak and Mt. Ford, with a hard red-brown infertile soil and an underlying rock often of an intrusive serpentine, usually found clothed with dense scrub-growth, bamboos and small hard-wooded trees.

Sandstone is the commonest rock in the islands. Limestone occurs on Havelock Island near Yoto, on the east coast of the Middle Andaman and in a few other places. Quartz, indurated clays and calcareous sandstones are also found.

A knowledge of the different kinds of soil, together with the type of forest which generally favours them, will be found of great help to the Forester in getting to know the plants found growing in them, although the plants present in each type are not always strictly limited to that type.

CLIMATE.

The year may be divided into a hot season and a rainy season, with a perceptible touch of cold during the months of December and January, when, in the mornings, a mist often hangs low over the forest and causes a heavy drip from the trees.

The hot season, or dry season, comprises the months of January to April during which little, if any, rain falls. In the months of February and March the weather is often sultry, very little wind blows, and a glassy calmness prevails over the sea.

The rainy season occupies the rest of the year, and during this period rain generally falls to a greater or less extent. Two monsoons blow with regularity. The south-west monsoon commences in May, and is accompanied by high winds, and with it come heavy downpours of rain, most of which falls during the months of July to September. The north-east monsoon commences in November and brings with it heavy rain in its earlier part. Cyclones often occur at the changes of the monsoon, and are particularly likely during the months of May and June or November and December, although it has been said that these have been known to occur in every month, except the month of February.

The rainfall averages from 110 to 170 inches per year, and varies in different parts of the islands, the northern islands seeming to have less rain and to be comparatively drier than the southern. The mean temperature varies from 70 to 90 degrees Fahrenheit.

FOREST GROWTH.

With this we are most concerned. The vegetation divides itself into different types or classes, each having certain characteristic aspects according to the nature of the soil present, and upon the five classes already enumerated generally depends the kind of forest found growing and its distribution. Elevation and aspect are factors which can hardly influence the distribution of vegetation in islands of such low latitude, and altitude, hence climatically the islands may be considered to be more or less uniform throughout.

The types or classes of forest met with, though visibly distinct, usually intermingle with, or overlap, one another. In some cases the change in passing from one type to another is so very gradual as to be hardly noticeable, and in others it is more abrupt, specially as we pass from tidal forests to those uninfluenced by the sea, although along the large creeks, the freshwater flowing down-stream mixes with the sea water and, diminishing its saltiness and that of the soil as we ascend, a gradual change from mangrove to evergreen forest is effected.

The vegetation may be differentiated into five distinct types of forest growth and these may be described as follows :—

1. Mangrove forest, which confines itself to sea-washed soil, and which according to the formation of the seashores, forms belts varying from a few yards to a mile or more in width.

2. Littoral forest influenced by, but out of the reach of the sea, occupying flat strips of land along the coast varying from a few yards to several chains in width.

3. Evergreen forest found growing on the low alluvial damp strips of land in the valleys or on the moist loamy fertile hills.

4. Forests of a more or less deciduous or leaf-shedding character usually found growing on undulating land of a somewhat poor-looking and comparatively dry soil.

5. The type of forest found growing on the parched and shallow-soiled slopes of high hills such as Saddle Peak in the North Andaman, Sound Peak, the Claudius Range and Mt. Farrington in the Middle Andaman, and Mt. Ford on Rutland Island.

Looking at the islands from the sea, we observe that from the water's edge to the tops of the highest hills, they are nearly everywhere densely wooded. Around the Settlement of Port Blair in the South Andaman extensive clearings have been made, and these are either occupied by coconut, or other, plantations, or are covered by a long coarse grass. In some places, such as on the steep eastern slopes of Mt. Ford, on the Cinque Islands, and at Chiriatapu, there is often a dense matted growth of grass, shrubs, and creepers, which, during the hot season has a brown parched appearance, but in the early part of the rainy season changes to a bright green colour and, in contrast with the dark-coloured outcrop of precipitous rocks frequent in these localities, makes lovely scenery. Among the dark green forest growth, the tall white pillar-like stems of *Dipterocarps* and other trees stand out conspicuously.

The coast line of these storm-swept islands is of varied formation. In some places it is rock-bound, in others we have bluff limestone cliffs, and here and there strips of shingle are met with, but most conspicuous of all are the white sandy beaches, dazzling in the bright sunshine, and lined along the top at high-water mark with luxuriant vegetation. In the more protected places the mangrove has carried itself right into the sea, so that there is no foreshore, and, at high-water, the stems are submerged and the vegetation has the appearance of growing out of the sea.

The luxuriance of growth, and the variety of trees, shrubs and climbers with which the beaches are fringed is remarkable. Lining the top of the beach and often reached by the waves we find *Scævola Koenigii*, with fleshy leaves and fan-shaped one-sided flowers, and which, on account of its light green foilage is easily distinguished even from a long distance out at sea; or we may have a fringe of the well-known *Hibiscus tiliaceus*, with branches stretching towards the sea and with it the shrubs most common to this locality, namely, *Colubrina asiatica*, *Smythea calpicarpa*, *Crinum asiaticum*, with long fleshy leaves and white lily-like flowers on long stalks, *Caesalpinia Bonducella*, fearfully armed with sharp pickles, *Desmodium umbellatum*, *Mucuna gigantea*, with hanging pods, the modest *Clerodendron inerme*, and less frequently *Dalbergia tamarindifolia*, and others; or again we may find an impenetrable thicket of the fragrant Screw-pine, *Pandanus tectorius*, not easily passed by unnoticed when in flower. Strewn on the ground above the beaches we often find a twining growth of *Ipomœa biloba*, the Goat's foot creeper, with lobed leaves and large purple flowers, *Vigna retusa*, with yellow flowers like those of the pea, and the delicate *Clitoria Ternatea*, with spoon-shaped deep-blue and white flowers. Almost confined to the west coast and belonging to this zone are *Tournefortia argentea*, *Pemphis acidula*, and *Sophora tomentosa*, three plants well worth seeing.

Immediately behind the fringe of shrub-growth, and breaking through here and there, we see such small and large trees as *Thespesia populnea*, with its Hibiscus-like yellow flowers, *Pongamia glabra*, *Guettarda speciosa*, with white long-tubed flowers that bloom at night, *Ixora brunnescens*, with stalkless leaves, *Cycas Rumphii*, often used to adorn our gardens, *Ochrosia borbonica*, with handsome whorled leaves, *Hernandia peltata*, with inflated fruits open at the top and a dark-coloured seed inside, *Barringtonia speciosa*, with ample glossy leaves and large delicate pale pink flowers that look like powder-puffs, the prickly *Erythrina indica*, with bunches of large scarlet flowers on the leafless branchlets, the well-known *Heritiera littoralis*, *Cordia subcordata*, which has bright orange-coloured flowers, and others, and lastly towering above these we have the giants of the seashores, *Mimusops littoralis*, with its deeply-cracked stem and dense shady crown, *Calophyllum Inophyllum*, with beautifully veined leaves and delightfully fragrant flowers, *Gyrocarpus americanus*, *Terminalia Catappa*, and others. These and other species comprise the littoral type of forest which confines itself to the zone immediately bordering the sea.

Among the tell-tale drift with which these shores are strewn we are sure to find, besides shells of varied shapes and hues, sea-borne fruits and seeds of littoral plants. Commonest of all are the radicles of the mangroves, *Rhizophora mucronata* and *conjugata*, *Bruguiera gymnorhiza* and *Ceriops Candolleana*; these in some places are washed up by the sea in hundreds, and with them we may often find the fibrous fruits of *Cerbera Odollam*, or similar but smaller, those of *Ochrosia borbonica*, the angled fruits of *Barringtonia speciosa*, those of *Nipa fruticans*, *Calophyllum Inophyllum*, *Gyrocarpus americanus* with two erect wings, and the smooth large dark-brown seeds of *Entada scandens* and others.

On the strips of flat ground immediately above the beaches where sea-sand and lumps of old coral are plentiful and where hermit crabs frequently wander, *Mimusops littoralis* is often a common tree and forms a pleasant type of forest known as Mohwa forest. This type is seen at its best along the west coast of the islands and in the south of Rutland Island, where the contorted appearance of the crowns and the massive branches of these gigantic trees, together with the rifts formed in the dense canopy, give some idea of the force with which the winds of the south-west monsoon strike these islands.

On land washed by the sea, where their grasping roots can gain any foothold we have the mangroves. These are especially common along tidal creeks. By far the most frequent trees of this zone are the *Rhizophoras*, closely set and impenetrable and fringing the banks of the creeks. The other trees common here are *Bruguiera gymnorhiza*, the largest of the mangroves, *Bruguiera parviflora*, *Ceriops Candolleana* and *Sonneratia acida*, less frequent are *Sonneratia alba*, *Avicennia officinalis*, *Excoecaria Agallocha*, full of acrid milky juice, *Carapa obovata*, *Carapa moluccensis* and *Aegiceras majus*, while *Heritiera littoralis*, on which may be seen the swollen tuber-like stems of *Hydnophytum formicarum*, in which ants make their nests, is often found on the borders. Clumps of *Phoenix paludosa* and *Nipa fruticans* are often seen with these.

On passing into the interior away from the influence of the sea, and almost as soon as we get out of earshot of the splash of the waves, there is a change from the littoral to one or other of the dry or evergreen types of forest found in the interior, and often, in the course of a few miles, one passes through them again and again. To the new-comer or the occasional visitor the effect of the luxuriant and varied foliage is bewildering, and it is only after some time has been spent in the forests that one is able to recognise the different types met with.

The leaf-shedding or deciduous forest, which we have already said is usually found on undulating ground, is the type usually favoured by the *Padauk*. This well-known tree, often with large buttresses and stout spreading branches, forms, with the crowns of the other giants of these forests, the roof or upper canopy, which in these islands averages about 140 feet in height. Here we find *Canarium euphyllum*, *Albizzia Lebbek*, *Artocarpus Chaplasha*, *Dipterocarpus incanus*, a magnificent tree, *Terminalia procera*, with a flat umbrella-shaped crown, *Pajanelia Rheedii*, with long pinnate leaves, *Tetrameles nudiflora*, with buttresses often large enough to form the walls of a house, *Bombax insigne*, *Lagerstroemia hypoleuca*, conspicuous when in blossom, *Terminalia Manii*, with its very smooth stem, *Terminalia bialata*, *Bassia butyracea*, *Sterculia campanulata*, with unique follicles shaped like a lady's shoe, *Chukrasia tabularis*, *Parishia insignis*, the fruits of which have four weak reddish wings, and others. Under these dominating stems we have a second storey of moderate-sized trees the principal ones of which are, *Sterculia villosa*, *Sageraea elliptica*, the handsome *Chai*, *Miliusa tectona*, *Garuga pinnata*, *Cratoxylon formosum*, which when young looks very much like a young *Padauk* tree, *Semecarpus Kurzii* and the much smaller *Semecarpus Prainii*, *Diospyros pyrrhocarpa*, *Zanthoxylum Budrunga*, *Pterospermum aceroides*, and several others; and again below these, *Ochna Wallichii*, *Atalantia monophylla*, the leaves of which are lemon-scented when bruised, *Diospyros Kurzii* and *Diospyros pilosula*, *Limonia alata*, the useful *Licuala peltata*, and others. Of the shrubs which make up the undergrowth, the chief are *Alsodica bengalensis*, which is extremely common, and *Alsodeia Roxburghii*, *Phyllochlamys spinosa*, *Canthium gracilipes*, *Unona Dasymaschala*, *Harrisonia Brownii* with pretty trifoliolate leaves, *Linociera Parkinsonii* and *Ixora grandifolia*. Of climbers the principal ones are *Calamus andamanicus*, with its stems often forming large loops on the ground, *Delima sarmentosa*, with very rough leaves, *Acacia pennata*, *Plecospermum andamanicum*, with strong sharp spines, *Ventilago madraspatana*, *Sphenodesme unguiculata*, and others. Scattered about in this type of forest small bamboos often occur which I take to be *Bambusa lineata* and *Bambusa schizostachyoides*.

Of the different types of forests found in the islands the grandest perhaps, is the evergreen forest that clothes the high hills, where the vegetation has the ample growth and healthy colour of luxuriance, denoting the fertility of these localities. Some of the most handsome and interesting trees are to be found here; these are however not characterised by conspicuous or gaily-coloured blossoms, and usually the only way that one becomes aware of their flowering is by finding, scattered on the ground below the tree, their fallen corollas; such flowers as they do have are usually lost to sight from below amongst the plentifulness of their foliage, and are high up in the ethereal blue. The botanical collector in these islands often experiences no small difficulty in obtaining good and complete specimens of these large trees; their smooth branchless stems, often a hundred feet long or more, are as impossible to scale as a wall. The principal trees to be found in this class of forest are *Dipterocarpus Griffithii*, which has the largest fruits of all the Gurjans, and *Dipterocarpus turbinatus*, *Prunus martabanica*, *Planchonia andamanica*, *Sideroxylon longepetiolatum*, *Hopea odorata*, *Endospermum malaccense* and others. The second storey is made up of *Garcinia Xanthochymus*, *andamanica and speciosa*, *Buchanania*, *platyneura*, *Drimycarpus*, *Xanthophyllum andamanicum*, *Baccaurea sapida*, *Myristica glaucescens* and *andamanica*, occasionally *Podocarpus neriifolia* and others, as well as some small palms such as *Caryota mitis* and *Pinanga Kuhlii*. There is often a marked absence of small trees and shrubs, although of the latter *Anaxagorea luzoniensis* is common. Of climbers the following are frequent, *Ancistrocladus extensus*, with tufts of long handsome leaves, *Gnetum scadens*, *Sarcostigma Wallichii*, *Calamus palustris*, and the climbing bamboo *Dinochloa andamanica*.

In the moist valleys on the alluvial tracts along the large fresh water streams, many of the plants found growing on the evergreen hills also occur and in addition we find *Anthocephalus Cadamba*, with balls of small yellow flowers, *Dipterocarpus incanus*, *Sterculia alata*, a tall tree which I do not remember having seen quite leafless, *Pometia pinnata*, *Myristica Irya*, *Calophyllum spectabile*, *Elaeocarpus aristatus*, *Pisonia excelsa*, the stems of which around old forest camps we find ruthlessly hacked for elephant fodder, *Duabanga sonneratioides* and *Litsaea Panamonja*. Of smaller trees we find *Talauma andamanica*, with its large handsome flowers, *Mitrephora Prainii*, *Fagraea morindaefolia*, which seems to blossom most when it rains heaviest, *Garcinia andamanica*, *Cliedion javanicum*, *Macaranga Tanarius*, *Pandanus andamanensium* and others. Glades of the common bamboo *Oxytenanthera nigrociliata* occur, but this does not confine itself to evergreen forests. Shrubs such as *Saprosma ternatum* which is quite frequent

Clerodendron infortunatum, *Clinogyne grandis*, with smooth dark green polished stems and *Leea sambucina* and *acuminata*, together with some canes form impenetrable thickets where often, although armed with a *dah*, one is obliged to go, not where one would, but where one can. Of climbers the purple-flowered Convolvulus-like *Thunbergia laurifolia*, with several species of *Ipomoea* and *Illigera appendiculata*, with fruits resembling those of the White Chuglam, are often found, and also some canes such as *Calamus longisetus* and *Daemonorops Kurzianus* and *Manii*. Lower down in the open, along the streams, strips of *Saccharum arundinaceum* and *Phragmites Karka* occur, these with their erect silky panicles being very picturesque about the month of April.

The most uncommon and least-known type of forest belongs to the high hills of the Middle Andaman, Mt. Ford on Rutland Island, and Saddle Peak in the North Andaman. The trees here are smaller than those found in the other classes of forest, but they are more numerous and grow more closely together. The principal trees are *Dipterocarpus costatus*, which is not found in any of the other classes of forest already mentioned, *Mesua ferrea*, *Canarium Manii*, which has a resin with a strong smell like that of a mango, *Harpullia cupanioides*, *Hopea andamanica*, *Cratoxylon formosum*, *Euphorbia trigona* and *epiphylloides*. Among shrubs, *Memecylon caeruleum* and *Cryptocarya Ferrarsi*, with some small bamboos, are not uncommon. On the Cinque Islands and on the eastern slopes of Mt. Ford on Rutland Island, above Portman Bay, a species of *Phoenix* is frequent.

Botanical History and a Note on the Flora of the Islands.

In the year 1789, Lieutenant Blair, by orders of the Honourable East India Company, founded, under the name of Port Cornwallis, a settlement in the South Andaman on the site known to-day as Port Blair. In 1791 Colonel Kyd visited the islands and introduced to the Royal Botanic Gardens, Calcutta, some Andaman plants which were afterwards described in Roxburgh's Flora of India. In 1792, for strategical reasons, the settlement was removed to the North Andaman and it carried along with it its name, Port Cornwallis, to the port which still bears that name; the first place of settlement in the South Andaman, which is the present Port Blair, was then for a time known as 'Old Harbour.' In 1796 the whole settlement was removed from Port Cornwallis in the North Andaman to Penang.

In 1839 Dr. Helfer, a Russian scientist and geologist, visited the islands with a view to ascertaining their mineral possibilities, but unfortunately he was murdered by the aborigines on the North Andaman.

He made extensive botanical collections in the islands, but these, after his death, were unfortunately mixed up with his Tenasserim plants and all being together labelled 'Tenasserim and Andamans,' a great deal of confusion has resulted, many of his Tenasserim plants having been ascribed to the Andaman flora.

After a period of nearly 62 years had elapsed, the penal settlement was, in the year 1858, once more brought to the Andamans, and was started on the South Andaman under the name of Port Blair, and this settlement still continues to exist.

In the year 1866, during the months of April to July, Sulpiz Kurz, a German botanist and then Curator of the Herbarium of the Royal Botanic Gardens, Calcutta, was sent by the Government of India to collect material for a Flora of the Andaman Islands, to identify botanically the timber trees and to ascertain their proportion to the rest of the Andaman Flora. He made extensive collections during his short visit, which apparently was confined to the South Andaman as far north as the Middle Straits, and in 1870 published a report on the vegetation of the islands, notes on the Andaman flora also being included in his Flora of British Burma.

In the year 1863 the Reverend C. Parish, from Moulmein, visited the islands and made some collections.

Mr. H. E. Man, during his incumbency as Deputy Superintendent in the islands, assisted in making collections, and to him several new and interesting plants have been dedicated by Sir George King.

Sir David Prain visited the islands in November 1899 and made collections, an interesting note on the non-indigenous species of the Andaman flora being subsequently published by him in the Journal of the Asiatic Society of Bengal. In 1890 Sir George King also visited the islands and made collections, his notes being embodied in Sir David Prain's note.

Extensive collections were also made by Messrs. R. L. Heinig and C. G. Rogers of the Indian Forest Service, during the period of their incumbency in the islands, and in 1903 a preliminary list of the plants of the islands was drawn up for Mr. Rogers by Mr. Gamble, this being published and printed in the local press.

The present writer has collected extensively over the greater part of the islands, especially in the Middle Andaman, and many of these collections have been sent to the Dehra Dun, Kew, and Calcutta Herbariums.

The plants dealt with in this work number nearly 650. Of these about 540 are indigenous to the islands and about 110 have been introduced. Kurz, in his Andaman Report, writes that the number of really indigenous phanerogamic plants may range between 1,500 and 1,800 species, but Prain, in his note on the non-indigenous species of the Andaman flora, writes that, 'In all probability the second estimate is too high, and perhaps a number nearer 1,000 will be actually found to express the actual total of indigenous phanerogams.' This figure includes herbaceous plants which are not dealt with in this work. Of the 540 native species included in this book, about 310 have been classed as trees, nearly 90 as shrubs and the remainder as climbers. These belong to 85 families of which 22 are represented only by a single native species each, 9 are each represented only by 2 native species, and the remainder by more than 2. *Leguminosae* is represented by the greatest number of native species, then comes *Euphorbiaceae*, and after that *Rubiaceae*, *Moraceae*, *Anonaceæ* *Palmae* and *Meliaceae*. Of the native plants nearly 80 confine themselves naturally to littoral tracts, and about 20 of these have the habit of mangroves.

In the case of some species doubts still exist as to whether or not they are natives of these islands, and in some cases plants classed as natives by some writers and said by them to be frequent, have not been found or observed by subsequent and more extensive collectors and writers.

In conclusion, I think it is part of my duty to voice once more the opinion of an eminent botanist, Sulpiz Kurz, on the subject of the Andaman flora. "I cannot conclude," he writes, "without directing full attention to the great importance of exploring the Andaman Islands scientifically. These islands are the only masses of land at present known in India, which, owing to the low scale of their inhabitants, and their living isolated from all communication with the surrounding countries, have never been influenced by the agency of men, and, therefore, the type of its natural productions is still a most peculiar one. We do not possess information about a really unmixed or original flora or fauna of any part of British India, the fauna and flora of every district being mixed by foreign immigrations and importations, owing to the frequent communications which the inhabitants have possessed for many ages with various other countries. The knowledge of the flora of the Andamans is therefore, as important as has been shown to be that of the Galapogos Archipelago, St. Helena and other isolated islands. By the present rapid extension of the Penal Settlements around Port Blair and Port Mouat, the real type of vegetation of these islands will be lost in the course of a few years, or made unintelligible by the many importations of weeds and other plants which even now are rapidly spreading over the land by means of cultivation, birds, winds, etc." This was written fifty years ago and since then the Settlement has much increased in size, the workings of the Forest Department have extended over the greater part of the islands, and many foreign plants have probably been imported, and are constantly being imported. As doubts already exist as to whether or not some plants are natives of the Andamans, the task of ascertaining exactly the original unmixed flora of the islands is becoming more and more difficult every year. If such difficulty is experienced with trees which take many years to attain maturity and to reproduce themselves, there can be little doubt that, in the case of short-lived plants which rapidly and extensively reproduce themselves, it will, in a few years, be impossible to determine whether or not these belong to the original Andaman flora.

LIST OF LITERATURE DEALING WITH THE VEGETATION OF THE ANDAMAN ISLANDS.

Report on the Vegetation of the Andaman Islands. *S. Kurz. Superintendent of Government Printing. Calcutta. 1870.*

Flora of British India. *Sir J. D. Hooker. Vols. 1-7. Reeve. London 1875-1907.*

Contributions towards a Knowledge of the Burmese Flora. *S. Kurz Vol. 1. Calcutta. 1876-77.*

Forest Flora of British Burma. *S. Kurz. Vols. 1-2. Superintendent of Government Printing. Calcutta. 1877.*

The Non-indigenous Species of the Andaman Flora. *D. Prain. Journal of the Asiatic Society of Bengal. Vol. IX, Part II, No. 3. Calcutta. 1890.*

On a Botanical visit to the Little Andaman and Nicobars. *D. Prain. Proceedings, Asiatic Society of Bengal, December 1891.*

The Vegetation of the Coco Group. *D. Prain. Journal of the Asiatic Society of Bengal. Vol. LX, Part II, No. 4. Calcutta. 1891.*

On the Flora of Narcondam and Barren Island. *D. Prain. Journal of the Asiatic Society of Bengal. Vol. LXII, Part II, No. 2. Calcutta. 1893.*

Materials for a Flora of the Malayan Peninsula. *Sir George King. Journal of the Asiatic Society of Bengal. 1899-1908.*

Report on the Indian Species of Pterocarpus. *D. Prain. Superintendent of Government Printing. Calcutta. 1900.*

A Preliminary List of the Plants of the Andaman Islands. *C. G. Rogers. Port Blair. 1903.*

Report on the Exploration of the Forests of the South Andaman. *C. G. Rogers. Superintendent of Government Printing. Calcutta. 1906.*

Indian Trees. *Sir Dietrich Brandis. Constable. London. 1907.*

Some Andaman plants are also dealt with in the Annals of the Botanic Garden, Calcutta. *Bengal Secretariat Press.*

A SYNOPSIS OF THE FAMILIES.

1. Dicotyledons.

The stem consisting of pith, wood, bast and bark which form concentric cylinders, the wood and bast being separated in the growing stem by a continuous layer of long soft cells (the cambium), which forms new wood on the inside, and new bast on the outside of the cylinder. Leaves net-veined. Parts of the flower usually in fours or fives. Embryo with two cotyledons which, when the seed germinates, are as a rule raised above the ground.

A. Polypetalæ.

Flowers in the majority of species bisexual, as a rule with both calyx and corolla, the corolla consisting of distinct petals.

1. Thalamifloræ.

Sepals usually distinct. Petals and stamens inserted beneath the free ovary. Disk frequently present.

B. Gamopetalae.

Flowers usually bisexual, as a rule with both calyx and corolla; corolla gamopetalous.

PAGE.

48. MYRSINACEAE.—Leaves simple, alternate, gland-dotted. Flowers white or pink, 5-merous; stamens opposite the corolla lobes. Species 5, all native 194

49. SAPOTACEAE.—*The Mohwa Family.*—Juice milky. Leaves simple, alternate, entire. Flowers large or small; petals and stamens often numerous. Species 5 native, 1 introduced 195

50. EBENACEAE.—*The Ebony* and *Marble-wood Family.*—Leaves simple, alternate, entire. Flowers axillary, white or yellow; calyx persistent; corolla 3-6 lobed; stamens various. Species 7, all native 198

51. STYRACEAE.—Tree. Leaves simple, alternate, drying yellow. Flowers yellow; petals free; stamens many. Species 1 201

52. OLEACEAE.—*The Jasmine Family.*—Leaves simple or trifoliolate, opposite. Flowers usually white; corolla usually 4-5 lobed; stamens 2. Species [illegible], all native ... 201

53. APOCYNACEAE.—*The Oleander Family.*—Juice milky. Leaves simple, mostly opposite. Flowers usually showy; corolla lobes 5, twisted; stamens 5 often conniving. Fruit often in pairs. Seeds with tufts of hairs. Species 12 native, 6 introduced 205

54. ASCLEPIADACEAE.—Juice milky. Leaves simple, opposite. Flowers often umbellate, 5-merous; stamens connate and appendaged, with the pollen in masses. Fruit in pairs; seeds with tufts of hairs. Species 3 native, 1 introduced 208

55. LOGANIACEAE.—*The Strychnine Family.*—Leaves simple, opposite. Flowers 5-merous; stamens on the corolla tube. Species 2, both native 209

56. BORAGINACEAE.—Leaves simple, alternate. Flowers large or small, 5-merous; stamens 5, on the corolla tube; style often twice forked. Species 6, all native 210

57. CONVOLVULACEAE.—*The Convolvulus Family.*—Climbers. Leaves simple, alternate. Flowers large or small, 5-merous; corolla often folded. Species 8 native 2 introduced 212

58. SOLANACEAE.—*The Tobacco Family.*—Leaves simple, alternate, often lobed. Flowers often showy, pentamerous. Fruit a berry. Species 7, all introduced ... 213

Gymnosperms.

Flowers unisexual with an incomplete or no perianth. Seeds naked.

PAGE.

78. CYCADACEAE.—Littoral palm-like tree. Leaves at the top of the stem with many pinnately-arranged leaflets. Flowers in scaly cones. Fruit woody. Species 1, native 257

2. Monocotyledons.

Stem fibrous with no distinct pith, wood or bark, no continuous cambium, and no regular increase in thickness by the formation of concentric layers of wood and bark. Leaves on sheaths and usually with numerous fine parallel nerves. Flowers usually with parts in threes or multiples of threes. Embryo with one cotyledon remaining enclosed in the germinating seed.

79. AMARYLLIDACEAE.—*The Aloe Family.*—Leaves linear, fleshy, tufted from near the ground. Flowers borne on erect stalks; stamens 6. Species 1 native, 4 introduced 258

80. SCITAMINACEAE.—*The Banana Family.*—Stem usually herbaceous. Leaves with fine veins pinnately arranged from a strong midrib. Flowers irregular, small or large, with petaloid bracts; stamen 1, with petaloid staminodes. Species 2 native, 2 introduced 258

81. FLAGELLARIACEAE.—A cane-like climber. Leaves simple, petioles sheathing, the apex of the leaf ending in a fine curl. Flowers white. Species 1 native 259

82. PANDANACEAE.—*The Screw-pine Family.*—Leaves linear, spinulous in three spiral rows. Flowers on a spadix with a leafy spathe. Fruit a fleshy mass. Species 3, all native 260

83. LILIACEAE.—*The Lily Family.*—Leaves simple, various. Flowers with a petaloid perianth in two series of 3 segments each; stamens 6. Species 5, all native ... 261

84. PALMAE.—*The Palm* and *Cane Family.*—Stems unbranched. Leaves pinnate or fan-shaped with sheathing petioles. Flowers small, enclosed in a spathe; perianth in 2 series of 3 segments each; stamens 3 or 6. Fruit often with a fibrous covering. Species 19 native, 5 introduced 262

85. GRAMINEAE.—*The Grass* and *Bamboo Family.*—Stems hollow, interrupted by nodes. Leaves with sheaths below, veins numerous, fine and parallel. Flowers in variously arranged spikelets. Species 8 native, 5 introduced 269

NOTE ON USING THE ARTIFICIAL KEYS.

The Native plants treated of in this work—excepting a few of the unimportant ones—together with some of the less-known imported ones, have been included in the following General Key, and these have been numbered serially throughout the text. The Plants have primarily been classed under the following heads :—

Trees, (Large, Middle-sized and Small).

Shrubs.

Climbers.

Palms and Canes.

Grasses and Bamboos.

In using the key the reader should endeavour to obtain an average specimen of the plant to be determined, and, owing to the variability of the forms of plants, too great accuracy should not be expected or looked for in such characters as the dimensions of trees, shrubs, leaves, petioles, etc.

The proper way of arriving at the name of a plant with the Key is by a gradual process of elimination, that is to say, by first deciding to which group of characters, or to which alternative character, a plant does not belong, and then proceeding with the other. It is therefore important that all the characters under the same number should be read, before deciding upon which one is to be followed.

The reader should begin with the General Key and having followed the characters there, he will be brought to either, a species number, in which case he will refer direct to the species bearing that number on the page given and compare his specimen with the description, or he will arrive at a group number, which he should refer to on the page given, and continue the process in that group until the species number has been obtained, and this again he will refer to on the page given as in the former case.

To examine a plant for such characters as the gland dots on the leaves, it will be necessary to have a pocket magnifying lens.

The following abbreviations have been used in the key and in the text :—

L. = leaves. Lat. = lateral. Lfts. = leaflets. Pet. = Petiole. Fl. = Flower. Fr. = Fruit. In. = Inch. Ft. = Foot. Diam. = Diameter. Burm. = Burmese. Hind. = Hindustani. Vern. = Vernacular. H. S. = Hot Season. C. S. = Cold Season. R. S. = Rainy Season. H. v. 19 =

Hooker's Flora of British India, Volume 5, page 19. Br. 13 = Brandis' Indian Trees, page 13. Kz. ii. 136 = Kurz's Forest Flora of British Burma, Volume 2, page 136. J. A. S. B. = Journal of the Asiatic Society of Bengal.

In the description of trees in the text, the figures in brackets represent the average dimensions attained by the tree, for example the figures (60–120 × 7–9) would mean the tree averaged from 60 to 120 feet in height, and from 7 to 9 feet in girth at breast height. In the keys or analysis of the Families or Genera, the statement "Leaves up to 6 in. long" would mean that the maximum length attained by the leaves would be about 6 in., and that although their length might be less, it would ordinarily not exceed this. By the 'Cut' is meant a downward blaze or thin slice taken off the bark so as to expose the fibres underneath as far as the sapwood, thus "cut brownish, then white" would mean that, when cut, the upper, or outer, layers of the bark would be brownish, and the lower, or inner, would be white.

An asterisk placed before the name of a plant means that I have not seen it in the Andamans.

All the drawings in this book are one-third natural size. By using the scales provided with the plates actual measurements may be obtained.

GENERAL KEY.

Trees, with a distinct woody stem and branches, usually attaining 15 feet or more in height, (not including *Bamboos*, page 32, and *Palms*, page 31). For *Shrubs* see page 23, and *Climbers* page 27.

Key for trees.	Species No.	Group No.	Page No.
Large Trees, *i.e.*, those usually attaining 100 feet or more in height. (For *Middle-sized Trees* see page 14, and *Small Trees* page 19).			
α.– Leaves minute. Branches needle-like and scaly ...	477		256
β.—Trees with normal foliage leaves.			
I.– Leaves simple.			
A.– Leaves opposite or very nearly so, or whorled, with entire margins.			
(1) Juice milky.			
Leaves in whorls of 5 to 10, 6—12 in. long, lateral nerves many, joined by an intramarginal vein. Fl. white	387		204
(2) Juice not milky		1	33
B.—Leaves alternate.			
(1) Margins of leaves entire or very nearly so.			
(*a*) Leaves penninerved, (weakly basal-nerved in some species of *Ficus*).			
1. Juice milky.			
(*a*) Leaves with large stipules, (*Moraceæ*)		2	33
(*b*) Stipules none (*Sapotaceæ*)		3	34
2. Juice reddish (*Myristica*) ...		4	34
3. Juice neither milky nor reddish		5	34
(*b*) Leaves palminerved.			
1. Juice milky. Leaves with large stipules. Fruit a fig ...		6	35
2. Juice not milky... ...		7	35
(2) Margins of leaves not entire, *i.e.*, crenate or serrate		8	36

Key for trees.	Species No.	Group No.	Page No.
II.—Leaves trifoliolate.			
Lfts. digitately disposed, crenate. Fl. small, yellowish, in panicles. Fr. globose. Juice reddish...	442		244
Lfts. pinnately disposed, glandular stipulate. Fl. large, scarlet. Fr. linear-curved. Branchlets prickly	208		152
III.—Leaves digitately 5—10 foliolate.			
Largely butressed tree. Branchlets prickly. Fl. large, scarlet. Capsule full of cotton ...	69		98
IV.—Leaves pinnate.			
A.—Leaves opposite, imparipinnate.			
L. 3—4 feet long; lfts. 10—16 pairs. Fl. large, in erect panicles. Capsule 1—2 feet long, flat	364		215
B.—Leaves alternate.			
(1) Margins of leaflets entire.			
(*a*) Leaflets glabrous or nearly so ...		9	36
(*b*) Leaflets softly tomentose or puberulous beneath ...		10	37
(2) Margins of leaflets not entire, *i.e.*, crenate or serrate.			
Lfts. about 16, up to 9 in. long, serrulate, oblong-lanceolate to ovate. Fl. ½ in. diam. Drupe bluish-black	109		115
Lfts. 15—25, 3—6 in. long, coarsely crenate-serrate, oblong-lanceolate. Fl. creamy-yellow. Fr. ¾ in. diam.	108		115
V.—Leaves bipinnate, (all *Mimosæ* except *Peltophorum*).			
A.—Leaflets on the pinnæ opposite ...		11	37
B.—Leaflets on the pinnæ alternate.			
Pinnæ 4—6 pairs. Lfts. 1 in. long. Fl. yellow, in cylindrical racemes. Pod twisted. Seeds bright red ..	227		159
Middle-sized Trees, *i.e.*, those usually attaining a height of 30 feet or more, but rarely more than 70 feet.			
I.—Leaves simple.			

Key for trees.	Species No.	Group No.	Page No.
A.—Leaves opposite or sometimes in whorls, with entire margins.			
(1) Leaves penninerved.			
(a) Littoral trees having the habit of mangroves		12	38
(b) Trees not having the habit of mangroves.			
1. Leaves with interpetiolar stipules		13	38
2. Leaves with inconspicuous or no stipules.			
(a) Juice yellowish-red with a strong smell like mango.			
L. 3–4 in. long. Fl. white. Capsule torpedo-shaped ...	40		85
(b) Juice milky or yellow. Evergreen trees.			
X.—Leaves with many distinct lateral nerves joined by an intra-marginal vein.			
Littoral tree with whorled leaves. Fr. spongy-fibrous ...	336		204
XX.—Leaves with many, fine, distinct and evenly parallel lateral nerves. Fr. a berry (*Calophyllum*)		14	38
XXX.—Leaves coriaceous, with many, but not distinct or evenly parallel, lateral nerves. Fl. in axillary clusters or cymes (*Garcinia*)...		15	39

Key for trees.	Species No.	Group No.	Page No.
(c) Juice neither milky, nor yellowish, nor reddish.			
X.—Leaves dotted with fine translucent glands. Lateral nerves joined by an intramarginal vein (*Eugenia*) ...		16	39
XX.—Leaves not dotted with translucent glands		17	40
(2) Leaves palminerved		18	40
B.—Leaves alternate.			
(1) Margins of leaves entire (undulate in species 175).			
(a) Leaves penninerved.			
1. Juice milky (see also species 170) ...		19	40
2. Juice reddish (*Myristica*) ..		20	41
3. Juice black and acrid. L. more or less oblanceolate, pale beneath ...		21	41
4. Trees without milky, reddish or black juice.			
(a) Leaves distinctly pubescent or tomentose beneath		22	41
(b) Mature leaves glabrous, or very nearly so.			
X.—Leaves pale, glaucous, silvery or coppery beneath ...		23	42
XX.—Leaves not distinctly pale, etc., beneath.			
O.—Leaves not more than 5 in. long ...		24	42
OO.—Leaves more than 5 in., but not more than 8 in. long.		25	43

Key for trees.	Species No.	Group No.	Page No.
000. Leaves more than 8 in. long		26	44
(*b*) Leaves with palminerved venation.			
1. Juice milky. Stipules large. Fr. a fig.			
L. 4—7 in. long, ovate, acuminate, petiole 1—2¼ in. long; lateral nerves forming loops. Figs clustered on the stem ...	462		249
L. 4—8 in. long, elliptic or obovate; petiole ¾—1¼ in. long. Figs from the leaf axils or scars ...	463		252
2. Juice not milky.			
(*a*) Leaves peltate.			
L. 4—9 in. long. Fr. inside a globular receptacle open at the top. Littoral ...	396		228
L. up to 12 in. across. Capsule ¼ in. diam.	423		238
(*b*) Leaves not peltate ...		27	44
(2) Margins of leaves not entire, *i.e.*, variously crenate, serrate or lobed.			
(*a*) Leaves penninerved ...		28	45
(*b*) Leaves palminerved.			
1. Juice milky.			
L. 4—8 in. long, broadly ovate. Fl. in drooping spikes 2—4 in. long ...	471		255
2. Juice not milky ...		29	45
II.—Leaves trifoliolate (species 377 and 378 sometimes have 5 leaflets).			
A.—Leaves opposite. Leaflets digitately disposed.			
(1) Leaves dotted with translucent glands. Lfts. 4—10 in. long, obovate or obovate-elliptic. Fl. in dense corymbose cymes	93		109

Key for trees.	Species No.	Group No.	Page No.
(2) Leaves not gland-dotted. Branchlets 4-angled. Fl. bluish or purplish.			
Lfts. 3–5, with entire margins and hair tufts in the nerve axils beneath. Fl. in axillary lax cymes ...	377		221
Lfts. 3–5, with coarsely crenate-serrate margins. Fl. in dense panicles	378		221
B.—Leaves alternate.			
L. pinnately trifoliolate. Lfts. puberulous beneath. Fl. in panicles. Fr. globose ...	113		117
III.—Leaves digitately 5–9 foliolate.			
Tree with conical prickles. Lfts. 3–4 in. long, glaucescent beneath. Fl. 1½ in. long, silky, dirty white. Capsule cottony, 3–5 in. long	68		97
IV.—Leaves pinnate (sometimes bipinnate in species 284).			
A.—Leaves opposite, imparipinnate, with opposite entire leaflets		30	46
B.—Leaves alternate.			
(1) Leaves paripinnate (sometimes also paripinnate in species 181).			
(a) Margins of leaflets entire ...		31	46
(b) Margins of leaflets irregularly serrate.			
Lfts. 8—20, orbicular to oblong-lanceolate. Fl. in large panicles. Fr. purple, splitting irregularly ...	163		136
(2) Leaves usually imparipinnate (sometimes imparipinnate in species 118, 164, and 169 in group 31).			
(a) Margins of leaflets entire.			
1. Leaflets opposite ...		32	47
2. Leaflets sub-opposite (sometimes alternate in species 181).			
Lfts. 11—17, oblong to lanceolate, 4–7 in. long. Fl. in rusty panicles. Fr. coppery-brown ...	122		121

Key for trees.	Species No.	Group No.	Page No.
Lfts. 12—20, ovate-oblong, largest 7—8 in. long, with hair tufts in the nerve axils beneath. Fr. depressed-globose ...	181		142
3. Leaflets alternate ...		33	48
b) Margins of leaflets not entire, *i.e.*, crenate or serrate.			
Lfts. 11—19, sub-opposite, falcate-lanceolate, 1—3 in. long, serrate. Drupe yellow. Planted tree	131		123
Lfts. 10—20, ovate-oblong, 3—6 in. long, glandular crenate, aromatic when bruised. Fl. in panicles	96		110
V.—Leaves bipinnate or tripinnate.			
A.—Leaves opposite.			
L. 3—5 feet long. Lfts. ovate, 3—5 in. long. Fl. large, at the end of erect peduncles. Fr. 2—4 ft. long, sword-shaped	365		216
B.—Leaves alternate.			
L 2—4 feet long. Lfts. ovate, 3—6 in. long. Fl. in dense panicles. Juice yellowish-red	283		182
Pinnae 12—14 pairs. Lfts. 10—22 pairs on each pinna, [illegible]—[illegible] in. long. Fl. bright-yellow, in terminal panicles. Pod 2—4 in. long, flat	221		157
Small Trees, *i.e.*, usually attaining a height of 15 feet or more, but rarely more than 30 feet.			
a.—Soft-wooded and abounding in milky juice, with angled or flattened branches and fleshy leaves (*Euphorbia*).			
Branches 3—5 angled	405		233
Branches flat	406		233

Key for trees.	Species No.	Group No.	Page No.
β.—Trees with normal branches and leaves.			
I.—Leaves simple or unifoliolate.			
A.—Leaves opposite (sub-opposite in species 90, and tufted in species 488 and 489).			
(1) Margins of leaves entire.			
(a) Juice milky or pale-yellowish (species 177 sometimes has milky juice)		34	48
(b) Juice not milky.			
1. Stipules interpetiolar or convolute.			
(a) Trees having the habit of mangroves (*Rhizophoraceæ*)		35	48
(b) Trees not having the habit of mangroves (*Rubiaceæ*)... ...		36	49
2. Stipules minute or none.			
(a) Leaves dotted with translucent glands ...		37	50
(b) Leaves not dotted with translucent glands.			
X.—Leaves petiolate...		38	50
XX.—Leaves sessile, with cordate bases.			
L. 2½—5 in. long, oblong to ovate, lateral nerves many, indistinct. Fl. blue, from the leaf axils or scars ...	269		176
(2) Margins of leaves not entire, *i.e.*, serrate or dentate.			
(a) Leaves palminerved.			
Juice milky and branchlets hollow. L. 6–10 in. long, irregularly dentate. Figs in clusters from the stem ...	448		248

Key for trees.	Species No.	Group No.	Page No.
(*b*) Leaves penninerved.			
L. 2—5 in. long, broadly ovate or elliptic, crenate-serrate. Fl. small, in corymbs. Littoral.	368		218
L. 4—8 in. long, oblanceolate, distantly toothed. Fl. white, in racemes ..	234		163
B.—Leaves alternate, (tufted in species 488 and 489).			
(1) Margins of leaves entire, (also see species 246, 247 and 449).			
(*a*) Leaves with penninerved venation, (longitudinally veined in species 488 and 489).			
1. Juice milky.			
L. 2½–4 in. long, elliptic to elliptic-oblong, lateral nerves 12—16 pairs. Figs from the leaf axils or scars	455		250
L. 3—5 in. long, somewhat rhomboid, rough beneath, lateral nerves 4-6 pairs. Figs axillary, yellow ...	456		250
2. Juice not milky.			
(*a*) Leaves distinctly dotted with translucent glands...		39	50
(*b*) Leaves without distinct translucent glands.			
X.—Leaves glabrous or very nearly so.			
O.—Leaves up to 6 in. long, rarely longer ...		40	51
OO.—Leaves attaining more than 6 in. in length ...		41	52
XX.—Leaves more or less pubescent on one or both surfaces ..		42	53

Key for trees.	Species No.	Group No.	Page No.
(*b*) Leaves with palminerved venation.			
1. Leaves peltate.			
L. more than a foot across, orbicular, petioles 1 foot long. Capsules with soft prickles. Soft-wooded tree	434		238
2. Leaves not peltate ...		43	54
(2) Margins of leaves not entire, *i.e.*, crenate or serrate, (lobed in species 282).			
(*a*) Leaves penninerved.			
1. Juice milky.		44	54
2. Juice not milky.			
(*a*) Petioles rather short ...		45	54
(*b*) Petioles longish, *i.e.*, more than 1½ in. long ...		46	55
(*b*) Leaves palminerved.			
1. Leaves glabrous or nearly so		47	55
2. Leaves pubescent beneath		48	55
II.—Leaves composed of 2 leaflets only (species 114, 115, 1[illegible] and 211 sometimes have only one pair of leaflets).			
III.—Leaves trifoliolate.			
A.—Leaves opposite.			
Branchlets 4-angled. Petiole 1½ in. long. Lfts. 2—5 in. long, ovate to elliptic. Fl. in terminal panicles	376		221
B.—Leaves alternate		49	56
IV.—Leaves pinnate.			
A.—Leaves paripinnate		50	56
B.—Leaves imparipinnate.			
(1) Leaflets opposite, (sub-opposite in species 119 and 122, and sometimes opposite in species 165)		51	56
(2) Leaflets alternate		52	57
V.—Leaves bipinnate or tripinnate.			
Soft-wooded tree with angular branchlets. Lfts. 1—6 in. long, ovate or rhomboid. Fl. yellowish-white, in large terminal panicles. Pods twisted. Seeds bluish-black ...	231		161
Introduced soft-wooded tree with ovate leaflets pale beneath. Fl. white. Pod linear, ribbed.	182		142

Shrubs, *i.e.*, plants usually not exceeding 15 feet in height, generally having a distinct woody stem or stems, and branching near the ground, (not including *Bamboos*, page 32, *Grasses*, page 32, and *Palms*, page 31). For *Climbers* see page 27, and *Canes*, page 31.

Key for Shrubs.	Species No.	Group No.	Page No.
α.—Littoral herbaceous shrub with smooth fleshy leaves 3 to 5 feet long. Fl. white, on long stalks	481		258
β.—Shrub with straight, cylindrical, dark green, polished stems. Leaves ovate, up to 12 in. long, pale beneath, and with fine parallel veins. Fl. white ...	483		259
γ.—Delicate shrub with feathery, needle-like, light-green branchlets. Fl. small, white. Fr. red ...	491		262
δ.—Parasitic shrubs found growing on the stems or branches of other trees		53	57
ε. Shrubs not having the above characters, nor parasitic on the stems or branches of other trees.			
1.—Leaves simple or unifoliolate.			
A.—Leaves opposite (whorled in species 305).			
(1) Margins of leaves entire.			
(a) Leaves with penninerved venation.			
1. Juice milky.			
Shrub armed with long, sharp, often forked spines. L. 1—2¼ in. long, ovate to ovate-rotund, lateral nerves indistinct. Fl. white ...	342		206
Introduced shrub. L. 4—8 in. long, ovate-cordate, stem-clasping, underside with soft down. Fl. 1 in. long, white or purple ...	350		209
2. Juice not milky.			
(a) Leaves with convolute or interpetiolar stipules.			
X.—Shrubs having the habit of mangroves.			
L. 1½—3 in. long, obovate, glossy,			

Key for Shrubs.	Species No.	Group No.	Page No.
lateral nerves indistinct. Fl. white, axillary. Drupe ¼ in. long, grooved	300		180
L. 2–5 in. long, oblong or elliptic. Fl. white. Fr. with a long radicle ...	239		105
XX.—Shrubs not having the habit of mangroves ...		54	58
(*b*) Leaves with minute or no stipules.			
X.—Spinous or thorny shrubs.			
Littoral and spinulous. Branches stiff. L. 4–10 in. long, elliptic to elongate-oblong. Fl. white or blue	366 367		217 217
Littoral, with straggling branches and recurved thorns. L. 1–3 in. long. Fr. club-shaped, with sticky prickles ...	379		222
XX.—Unarmed shrubs.		55	58
(*b*) Leaves with palminerved venation.			
All parts bristly or hairy. L. 2–6 in. long, elliptic or ovate-lanceolate, often reddish when young. Fl. large, rose-coloured or purple with yellow filaments	268		176

Key for Shrubs.	Species No.	Group No.	Page No.
(2) Margins of leaves not entire, *i.e.*, crenate or serrate.			
L. 4—12 in. long, obovate, wavy serrate, glabrous, with numerous golden glistening glands on the undersurface, petiole short. Fl. greenish. Capsule prickly ...	438		241
L. 5—9 in. long, ovate, rounded or cordate, dentate-serrate, hairy beneath with numerous black dots, petiole 2—6 in. long. Fl. white. Drupe bluish-black in a red calyx.	372		219
B.—Leaves alternate.			
(1) Margins of leaves entire.			
(*a*) Leaves with penninerved venation.			
1. Leaves not exceeding 1½ in. in length ...		56	59
2. Leaves exceeding 1½ in., but not exceeding 6 in., in length		57	59
3. Leaves attaining a length of more than 6 in.			
(*a*) Littoral shrubs ...		58	60
(*b*) Inland shrubs ...		59	60
(*b*) Leaves with palminerved venation (see also species 85 which is weakly palminerved).		60	61
(2) Margins of leaves not entire, *i.e.*, crenate or serrate (lobed in species 65 and 435).			
(*a*) Leaves penninerved.			
1. Armed shrubs.			
Crooked shrub with sharp spines. L. 1—3 in. long, rhomboid-elliptic to obovate, irregularly serrate. Sepals enlarged in fruit ...	473		255
2. Unarmed shrubs ...		61	61

Key for Shrubs.	Species No.	Group No.	Page No.
(*b*) Leaves palminerved.			
1. Leaves glabrous or nearly so		62	61
2. Leaves with soft or stiff hairs.			
Shrub with rusty stellate hairs and scales. L. 4–8 in. long, glandular at the insertion of the long petiole. Fl. in racemes	430		240
Shrub with stiff harsh hairs. L. 8 in. across, orbicular, 5-lobed, petioles long. Fl. large, yellow with a purple centre ...	65		96
II.—Leaves trifoliolate.			
A.—Leaves opposite.			
Lfts. 1–3 in. long, elliptic or obovate, white tomentose beneath, petiole, 1½ in. long. Fl. pale bluish, in panicles ...	375		220
B.—Leaves alternate.			
(1) Margins of leaflets entire (sometimes crenulate in species [illegible]5)		63	62
(2) Margins of leaflets not entire, *i.e.*, crenate or serrate.			
Prickly shrub with dark brown branches. Lfts. 1½–2½ in. long, ovate to rhomboid, irregularly serrate. Fl. white ..	102		112
Lfts. 2—10 in. long, coarsely serrate with hair tufts in the nerve axils beneath. Fl. white, in narrow racemes	162		136
III.—Leaves pinnate.			
A.—Margins of leaflets entire.			
Branchlets dark-brown. Lfts. 17—31, opposite or nearly so, 1–3 in. long, softly pubescent beneath. Fl. yellowish	185		143

Key for Shrubs.	Species No.	Group No.	Page No.
Lfts. 2 to 4, elliptic or oblong, 4–6 in. long. Fl. ¼ in. diam., petals with fringed margins. Fr. usually in pairs.	160		135
B.—Margins of leaflets not entire, *i.e.*, serrate. Straggling and prickly. Lfts. 7–13, ovate-rhomboid, 1–1½ in. long, coarsely crenate-serrate. Fl. pinkish-white ...	103		113
Branchlets grooved. Lfts. 3–5, oblong to sub-orbicular, 9–12 in. long, serrate, with strong lateral nerves. Fl. in umbellate cymes	155		132
IV.—Leaves bipinnate (sometimes tripinnate in species 156, 157 and 158)		64	62

Climbers, (including climbing shrubs, but not including *Canes*, p. 31; see also species 51[illegible] which is a climbing bamboo).

Key for Climbers.	Species No.	Group No.	Page No.
α.—Cane-like climber with greenish, hollow stems. L. 6–10 in. long, lanceolate, ending in a fine tendril, petioles sheathing. Fl. white	484		259
β.—Stems whitish, marked with ring-like scars. L. in spiral tufts, 1–3 feet long, spinulose-serrate. Fr. 2½ in. long	487		260
γ.—Climbers not having the above characters.			
I.—Leaves simple.			
A.—Leaves opposite or whorled.			
(1) Margins of leaves entire.			
(a) Leaves with penninerved venation.			
1. Juice milky		65	63
2. Juice not milky.			
(a) Leaves with interpetiolar stipules (*Rubiaceæ*).		6[illegible]	63

Key for Climbers.	Species No.	Group No.	Page No.
(*b*) Leaves with minute or no stipules.			
X.—Leaves not more than 6 in. long ...		67	63
XX.—Leaves attaining more than 6 in. in length		68	64
(*b*) Leaves with palminerved venation. Stems irregular and twisted. L. 4–6 in. long, ovate, acuminate, strongly 3-nerved. Fl. white. Berry about 1 in. diam...	351		209
(2) Margins of leaves not entire, *i.e.*, serrate or crenate ..		69	64
B.—Leaves alternate (close together and tuft-like in species 62 and 63).			
(1) Margins of leaves entire.			
(*a*) Leaves with penninerved venation.			
1. Stems armed with sharp, stipular, recurved prickles. Scandent shrubs with white or rose-coloured flowers and long slender stamens. Fr. on a jointed stalk ...		70	65
2. Stems armed with long, sharp spines		71	65
3. Stems with woody recurved hooked branchlets.			
Leaves collected in tufts, obovate or oblanceolate, up to 12 in. or more in length. Fl. white or pink, in lax panicles. Fr. with 5 unequal wings	62 63		95 95
Leaves oblong or oblong-lanceolate, 6–8 in. long. Fl. 1–1¼ in. long, yellow, on the hooked branchlets.	21		78
4. Stems without prickles, spines or hooked branchlets.			

Key for Climbers.	Species No.	Group No.	Page No.
(a) Leaves wholly glabrous.		72	65
(b) Leaves more or less pubescent or tomentose beneath		73	66
(b) Leaves with palminerved venation (see also species 474 which is weakly palminerved).			
1. Juice milky. Fruit figs.			
L. 2—5 in. long, ovate to elliptic-ovate, petiole 1 in. long. Figs solitary or in pairs from the leaf axils or scars	457		250
L. 3—8 in. long, ovate to ovate-elliptic, petiole 1½ in. long. Figs axillary or clustered below the leaves, orange-red	462		252
2. Juice not milky... ...		74	66
(2) Margins of leaves not entire, *i.e.*, crenate or serrate or lobed (also see species 487 which has spinulose-serrate leaves).			
(a) Leaves with penninerved venation.		75	67
(b) Leaves with palminerved venation.			
1. Leaves not more than 3 in. broad, crenate or serrate ...		76	67
2. Leaves more than 3 in. broad, lobed.			
L. about 6 in. across, orbicular cordate, lobes shallow, pubescent. Fl. yellow with a purple centre	66		96
Branchlets fluted or ribbed. L. 3—7 in. across, cordate-ovate, 3—5 lobed. Fl. in axillary cymes. Fr. with bristles	77		102

Key for Climbers.	Species No.	Group No.	Page No.
II.—Leaves trifoliolate.			
A.—Leaves opposite. Lfts. pinnately disposed.			
Lfts. 2—4 in. long, acuminate, petiole 1 in. long, swollen at base. Fl. white, fragrant, in axillary cymes ...	331		202
Lfts. 1—3 in. long, apiculate. Fl. white, in terminal corymbose cymes ...	332		202
B.—Leaves alternate.			
(1) Leaflets digitately disposed.			
Lfts. 3—4 in. long, elliptic, cordate, apiculate, rough and pale beneath. Fl. in lax panicles. Fr. butterfly-shaped	254		170
Branchlets dark brown, prickly. Lfts. $1\frac{1}{2}$—$2\frac{1}{4}$ in. long, ovate to rhomboid, irregularly serrate. Fl. white. Bark bitter	102		112
(2) Leaflets pinnately disposed and stipellate (*Papilionaceæ*)		77	67
III.—Leaves digitately 5—7 foliolate.			
Climber clinging to supports by rootlets. Lfts. 3—8 in. long, elliptic to lanceolate, petiole stem-clasping. Fl. greenish-yellow, umbellate, in panicled racemes	285		183
IV.—Leaves pinnate.			
A.—Leaflets opposite or sub-opposite.			
(1) Leaflets more than 13 in each leaf.			
(a) Margins of leaflets entire ...		78	68
(b) Margins of leaflets coarsely crenate-serrate.			
Prickly. Lfts. 7—13, ovate-rhomboid, 1—$1\frac{1}{4}$ in. long. Fl. pinkish-white. Fr. depressed globular. Bark bitter ...	103		113
(2) Leaflets more than 13 in each leaf.			
L. paripinnate. Lfts. 10—20 pairs, $\frac{1}{4}$—$\frac{3}{4}$ in. long. Fl. pink or lilac, in racemes. Pod turgid. Seeds red with a black dot	202		150

Key for Climbers.	Species No.	Group No.	Page No.
Young parts pubescent. L. imparipinnate. Lfts. 17—31, oblong, 1—3 in long, softly pubescent beneath. Fl. fasciculate, from the leaf scars. Follicle falcate-curved ...	185		143
B.—Leaflets alternate.			
L. imparipinnate. Fl. papilionaceous, white, yellow or blue. Pod flat, longer than broad		79	68
V.—Leaves bipinnate.			
A.—Unarmed climbers.			
Stems twisted and angled. Lfts. 1—3 in. long, common petiole ending in a branched tendril. Fl. yellow, in narrow cylindrical spikes. Pod 1—4 feet long, jointed	222		158
B.—Climbers armed with sharp prickles ...		80	69

Palms and Canes, (including *Pandanus,* and also see species 487, and species 484 which is like a cane).

Key for Palms and Canes.	Species No.	Group No.	Page No.
Erect Palms, including *Pandanus,* with variously shaped leaves.			
I.—Leaves linear sword-shaped, arranged in whorls, spinulose along the margins and at the back of the midrib. Fl. small, enclosed in a leafy spathe. Fr. a mass of fleshy united drupes	485 486		260 260
II.—Leaves pinnate, with numerous linear sword-shaped leaflets		81	69
III. Leaves bipinnate.			
Leaves 8—10 feet long. Leaflets rhomboid or wedge shaped, 4 8 in. long. Fl. in pendulous spikes from the stem. Fr. fibrous ...	505		268
IV.—Leaves fan-shaped, the petioles armed with recurved spines. Fr. fibrous		82	69

Key for Palms and Canes.	Species No.	Group No.	Page No.
Scandent Palms or Canes.			
I.—Leaves pinnate, often ending in a slender whip-like appendage. Leaflets many, sword-shaped or lanceolate. Fruit scaly...		88	70
II.—Leaves pinnate, ending in a spinous tendril. Leaves 2—4 ft. long. Leaflets 4 - 8 in. long, ovate or cuneate-rhomboid, pale below, irregularly toothed. Fruit ½ in. long ...	504		267

GRASSES AND BAMBOOS.

Key for Grasses and Bamboos.	Species No.	Group No.	Page No.
Grasses. usually not attaining a height of more than 15 feet. Stems not woody.			
Native. Attains 10 -12 ft. Leaves up to 20 in. long. Panicles about a foot long	509		270
Native. Attains 12—15 feet. Leaves 4—5 feet long. Panicles 1—2 feet long	510		270
Introduced. Attains 8—12 feet. Leaves 1—2 feet long. Panicles 1—2 feet long	511		270
Bamboos, with woody stems attaining a height of more than 15 feet.			
Attains 30—50 feet with stems 2—4 in. diam. Leaves 8—18 in. long. Fl. in panicles	512		271
Internodes 16—24 in. Stems ½—1 in. diam. Leaves 10—15 in. long. Fl. in panicles	513		271
Attains 20—30 feet with stems 3—4 in. diam. Leaves 4—7 in. long. Fl. in clustered spikes	514		271
Attains 30 feet, with stems ¾ in. diam. Leaves 7—9 in. long. Fl. in long terminal spikes	515		272
Scandent Bamboo.			
Attains 300 feet in length. Branches zig-zag, up to 1 in. diam. Leaves 9—12 in. long. Fl. in panicles ...	516		272

SUBSIDIARY KEY FOR GROUPS UNDER GENERAL KEY.

The first number denotes the serial number of the species, and the second (in italics) the page on which it will be found.

GROUP 1.

JUICE NOT MILKY.

Stipules interpetiolar. Fl. small, in globose heads.

Stipules linear. L. 6—10 in. long, petioles 1—2 in. long. Fl. heads 2 in diam. ... ... 288—*185*

Stipules obovate. L. 6—12 in. long, petioles ½—¾ in. long. Fl. heads 1½ in. diam. ... ... 289—*186*

Stipules none. Fl. large and showy.

L. 5—8 in. long. Fl. lilac, in terminal panicles ... 277—*179*

L. 7—15 in. long. Fl. white, in corymbs at the ends of the long branches ... ... 278—*179*

GROUP 2.

LEAVES WITH LARGE STIPULES (*Moraceæ*).

Leaves not more than 4 in. long.

Lateral nerves many and fine, joined along the margin. Figs ⅓—½ in. diam., sessile ... ... 453—*249*

Lateral nerves many, with finer intermediate ones. Figs about ¼ in. diam. ... ... 454—*249*

Leaves more than 4 in., but less than 9 in. long.

L. 3—6 in. long, elliptic, petiole 1—2 in. long, flattened. Figs ¾—1 in. long, sessile, paired ... ... 459—*251*

L. 4—7 in. long, oblong or elliptic, petiole 1—4 in. long, slender. Figs ½ in. diam., almost sessile ... ... 460—*251*

L. 4—7 in. long, broadly ovate-elliptic. petiole 1—2 in. long, thick and channelled. Figs ¾—1 in. long ... ... 461—*251*

L. 5—7 in. long, oblong-lanceolate, petiole up to 2 in. long, slender and channelled. Figs ⅓ in. diam., sessile ... 466—*253*

L. 5—8 in. long, oblong to obovate-lanceolate, petiole ½—1½ in. long. Figs stalked, ¾ in. diam. ... ... 465—*252*

L. 4—9 in. long, oblong, petiole short. Fl. on mushroom-shaped receptacles ½ in. across ... ... 470—*254*

Leaves attaining a foot in length.

Branchlets marked with ring-like scars. Leaves and branchlets with minute stiff hairs. *Fr.* a fleshy receptacle .. 469–*254*

Branchlets glabrous. Leaves glabrous, but rough to the touch. Figs ¾ in. diam., stalked 464–*252*

GROUP 3.

Stipules none (*Sapotaceæ*).

Lateral nerves fine and parallel, joined by an intramarginal vein. Fr. a berry.

Littoral tree. L. 5–8 in. long, obovate. Fl. 1 in. diam. ... 318–*196*

Inland tree. L. 3–5 in. long, elliptic. Fl. ½ in. diam. ... 319–*196*

Lateral nerves prominent and strong.

L. 4–8 in. long (longer in young plants), petioles up to 2½ in. long. Fl. small. Fr. with one compressed seed ... 321–*197*

L. 5–9 in. long, petioles up to 1½ in. long. Fl. in clusters. Berry rusty puberulous 320–*196*

GROUP 4.

Juice reddish (*Myristica*).

Leaves 6–12 in. long, broadly elliptic-oblong. Fruit 1½ in. long, ovoid 384–*221*

Leaves 6–15 in. long, lanceolate. Fruit 1 in. long, globose 383–*221*

GROUP 5.

Juice neither milky nor reddish.

Resinous trees with large stem-clasping stipules. Fl. large, funnel-shaped. Fr. with two wings 55–59

Stipules inconspicuous or none. Fl. small. *92–93*

Petioles very short and thick. Leaves obovate, crowded at the ends of the branchlets.

L. 5–10 in. long, tapering at the base. Drupe 1½ in. long, ellipsoid ... 2–*167*

L. 8—12 in. long, small cordate or auricled at the base. Drupe 1—2 in. long, compressed and keeled all round . 243—*167*

Petioles up to an inch long, seldom more.

L. 3—6 in. long, elliptic to ovate-oblong, pale with black dots beneath. Fr. pointed. Bark with a smell like essence of almond ... ... 232—*162*

L. 4—6 in. long. Fl. in one sided racemes. Fr. small, with two finely-veined wings 1½ in. long ... ... 60—*94*

L. 4—8 in. long, petioles glandular near the insertion of the blade. Drupe ridged. ... ... 245—*168*

Petioles more than 1 in. long, often more than 2 in. long.

L. 3—7 in. long, ovate to ovate-lanceolate, petioles 1—3 in. long, slender. Bark deeply cracked ... ... 428—*240*

L. 6—9 in. long, obovate or oblanceolate, crowded, petioles 2—3 in. long. Fr. butterfly-shaped, about 4 in. across ... 244—*167*

L. 5—10 in. long, lanceolate to oblong-lanceolate, petioles 1—3 in. long, thickened at base. Drupe compressed 171—*139*

GROUP 6.

JUICE MILKY. LEAVES WITH LARGE STIPULES. FRUIT A FIG.

L. 3—6 in. long, broadly ovate, base truncate, white dotted on the upper surface. Figs sessile, in pairs from the leaf axils or the leaf scars ... ... 450—*248*

L. 6—9 in. long, broadly ovate, base cordate. Figs in clusters from the stem ... ... 451—*249*

GROUP 7.

JUICE NOT MILKY.

Leaves cordate at base.

L. 4—6 in. long, orbicular. Fl. bell-shaped, yellowish-green. Fr. a membranous follicle with one seed ... 71—*100*

L. 4—8 in. long, ovate. Fl. in large fragrant panicles. Fr. with radiating veined wings ... . 81—*104*

L. 5—10 in. long, broadly ovate. Fl. bell-shaped, brownish-green, rusty tomentose. Fr. a woody follicle packed with numerous winged seeds ... ... 70—*99*

Leaves rounded or truncate at base.

L. 3—6 in. long, broadly ovate, finely acuminate. Fl. small, in large terminal panicles ... ... 354—*211*

L. 5—8 in. long, broadly ovate-rotund. Fl. small, in large many-flowered cymes. Fr. with two erect obovate wings. Littoral tree ... ... 248—*169*

L. 5—12 in. across, peltate and with two swollen glands at the insertion of the petiole. Fl. small, yellow ... 425—*238*

GROUP 8.

Margins of leaves not entire, *i.e.*, crenate or serrate.

Leaves penninerved, with tapering bases, turning red before falling

L. 4—8 in. long, obovate to broadly elliptic, petioles flattened. Fl. large, like powder-puffs ... ... 266—*174*

L. 6—9 in. long, obovate, petiole slender, thickened at the top. Fl. small, with fringed petals ... ... 86—*105*

Leaves palminerved, with cordate bases.

Tree with large buttresses. L. 5—7 in. long, irregularly serrate, petiole 2—5 in. long. Fl. minute, in pendulous racemes ... ... 281—*181*

GROUP 9.

Leaflets glabrous or nearly so.

Leaflets opposite (sometimes alternate in species 129).

Leaflets 7—11, ovate, acuminate, 3—6 in. long. Fl. small. Drupe ¾ in. long, kidney-shaped ... ... 179—*141*

Leaflets 7—13, elliptic-oblong, with a distinct intramarginal vein, aromatic when bruised. Fl. in panicles. Drupe 1—1½ in. long ... ... 178—*141*

Leaflets 9—13, oblong to ovate-oblong, 4—8 in. long. Fl. in axillary panicles. Fr. 2½ in. long, tawny tomentose 129—*123*

Leaflets 12—20, ovate-oblong, with tufts of hairs in the nerve axils beneath. Fl. ½ in. diam. Drupe 1 in. diam., depressed globose ... ... 181—*142*

Leaflets alternate.

Tree with blood-red juice. Leaflets about 8. Fl. yellow, in panicles. Pod flat, orbicular, 2—2½ in. diam. ... 210—*152*

GROUP 10.

Leaflets softly tomentose or puberulous beneath.

Leaflets 13—19, opposite, 4—8 in. long, ovate-oblong, oblique, Fl. in pubescent panicles. Fr. with 4 linear reddish wings ... ... 180—*142*

Leaflets 10—20, falcate-lanceolate, 4½—7 in. long, pale beneath. Fl. small. Fr. 1½—2 in. long, pinkish, thin, oblong and blunt at the ends ... ... 105—*113*

Leaflets 20—30, ovate to oblong, 2—6 in. long, velvety beneath. Fl. yellow or pinkish-white. Capsule ovoid, brown, 3-valved ... ... 117—*119*

GROUP 11.

Leaflets on the pinnae opposite.

Pinnae 2—3 pairs. Leaflets 5—9 pairs, elliptic-oblong, 1—1½ in. long. Pod straw-coloured, 4—12 in. long ... 229—*160*

Pinnae 2—6 pairs. Leaflets 6—12 pairs, ovate to ovate-oblong, 1—1½ in. long. Pod bright reddish-brown, 4—8 in. long ... ... 230—*161*

Pinnae 6—20 pairs. Leaflets 25—45 pairs, about ½ in. long. Pod pale brown, dull, 5—6 in. long ... ... 228—*160*

Pinnae 12—14 pairs. Leaflets 10—22 pairs, ½—¾ in. long. Fl. large, bright yellow, in panicles. Pod flat, brownish, 2—4 in. long ... ... 221—*157*

GROUP 12.

LITTORAL TREES HAVING THE HABIT OF MANGROVES.

Stipules convolute, dropping off and leaving ring-like scars on the branchlets. Leaves more or less elliptic or lanceolate, 4—7 in. long (*Rhizophoraceae*).

- **Tree** developing stilt-like curved roots. Fl. 4-merous, in axillary cymes. Radicle 1—3 ft. long, smooth ... 235—*164*
- **Like** the former, but flowers usually in twos and sessile ... 236—*164*
- **Tree** sending up woody knees through the soft mud. Fl. 8—14-merous. Radicle 8 in. long, faintly ribbed ... 237-*164*

Stipules none. Leaves more or less broadly ovate to obovate, 2—4½ in. long. Fruit not developing a long radicle on the tree like the former.

- **L.** broadly obovate, petiole short. Fl. 1—1½ in. diam., with numerous thread-like stamens. Root branches woody, conical, pointed ... ... 275—*178*
- **Like** the former, but with leaves broadly ovate to orbicular. Fl. in threes ... ... 276—*179*
- **L.** obovate to elliptic, silvery white beneath. Fl. small, yellow. Root branches slender, flexible ... ... 370—*218*

GROUP 13.

LEAVES WITH INTERPETIOLAR STIPULES.

- **Leaves** 2—6 in. long, elliptic to elliptic-oblong, with black dots beneath. Fl. small, in axillary cymes .. 241—*165*
- **L.** 3—6½ in. long, elliptic to elliptic-lanceolate, with glands in the nerve axils beneath. Fl. large. Fr. 2 in. diam. ... 302—*192*
- **L.** 3—10 in. long, broadly ovate from a cordate base. Fl. small, in globose heads ... ... 287—*185*
- **Buds** resinous. L. 4—10 in. long, obovate, with hair tufts in the nerve axils beneath. Fl. large, white turning yellow ... ... 310—*192*

GROUP 14.

LEAVES WITH MANY, FINE, DISTINCT AND EVENLY PARALLEL LATERAL NERVES.

- **L.** 2—4 in. long, elliptic to lanceolate. Fl. white. Branchlets, petioles and inflorescence rusty pubescent ... 43—*87*

L. 5–9 in. long, elliptic to ovate or obovate. Fl. handsome, in racemes. Littoral tree with a crooked stem ... 41—87

L. 7–12 in. long, oblong. Fl. in axillary racemes. Fr. ovoid. Straight-stemmed tree ... ... 42—87

GROUP 15.

Leaves coriaceous, with many, but not distinct or evenly parallel, lateral nerves.

Leaves not more than 6 in. long. Sepals and petals 4.

L. 3–5 in. long, lanceolate, fine acuminate. Fr. globular, depressed, yellow ... ... 52—90

L. 3½–5½ in. long, elliptic to elliptic-oblong. Branchlets rounded ... ... 53—90

L. 4–6 in. long, broadly lanceolate. Branchlets angled. Fr. yellow, depressed-globular ... ... 49—89

L. 4–6 in. long, ovate to lanceolate. Branchlets angled. Fr. bright red when ripe ... ... 50—90

Leaves more than 6 in. long. Sepals and petals 5.

L. 8–16 in. long, oblong to oblong-lanceolate. Fr. 2–2½ in. diam., dark yellow when ripe . ... 47—89

L. 8–14 in. long, elongate-ovate, base broad. Fr. 1–1½ in. diam., bright yellow when ripe ... ... 48—89

GROUP 16.

Leaves dotted with fine translucent glands.

Lateral nerves not more than 12 pairs.

L. 3–5 in. long, elliptic, acuminate, with black dots on the under surface. Fl. ½ in. diam. .. ... 256—172

L. 4–6 in. long, ovate to elliptic. Fl. ¾ in. diam. .. 257—172

L. 6–10 in. long, ovate to oblong-lanceolate, base rounded to almost cordate. Fl. 1¼ in. diam. ... ... 255—171

Lateral nerves numerous, *i.e.*, 20 or more pairs.

L. 2½–4 in. long, lanceolate to oblong-lanceolate, acuminate. Fr. depressed-globular ... ... 258—172

L. 3—6 in. long, oblong to elliptic. Fr. ovoid-oblong, purplish-black ... ... 260—*173*

L. 4—8 in. long, elliptic-lanceolate, acuminate. Fr. ¾ in. long, white turning scarlet ... ... 259—*172*

GROUP 17.

Leaves not dotted with translucent glands.

L. 3—6 in. long, lanceolate, pale beneath, with many inconspicuous lateral nerves. Fl. white with bright yellow stamens ... . 44—*88*

L. 3—6 in. long, elliptic. Deciduous tree with angled branchlets and small yellowish-green flowers in cylindrical panicled racemes ... ... 279—*180*

L. 6—10 in. long, oblong or elliptic-oblong, dark green and glossy, pale beneath. Fl. funnel-shaped, in racemes ... 352—*210*

Soft-wooded tree. L. 9—12 in. long. Fr. 1½—2 in. long, covered with a tenacious matter ... ... 380—*222*

GROUP 18.

Leaves palminerved.

L. 4—9 in. long, broadly ovate, petiole glandular at the top. Fl. large, yellowish-brown. ... ... 371—*219*

All parts aromatic. L. 6—10 in. long, rigidly coriaceous. Fl. greenish-white, in terminal panicles. ... ... 386—*225*

L. 6—9 in. long, obovate to elliptic, petioles jointed and thickened at the top. Fl. small, in racemes ... ... 434—*242*

GROUP 19.

Juice milky.

Leaves with large stipules.

L. 4—8 in. long, elongate-elliptic or obovate. Figs ½ in. diam., sessile, from the leaf axils or leaf scars ... 458—*250*

L. 7—10 in. long, ovate or ovate-oblong, broad. Fr. fleshy, 2 in, long ... ... 467—*258*

L. 8—12 in. long, broadly ovate or oblong, soft velvety grey or rusty pubescent beneath. Fr. 2—4 in. diam., velvety. 468—*253*

Leaves with minute or no stipules.

Littoral tree. L. 5—10 in. long, oblanceolate, with many lateral nerves joined intramarginally. Fl. large, white. Fr. spongy-fibrous ... ... 341—*206*

L. 3—6 in. long, obovate or oblong-lanceolate, branchlets and young leaves ferruginous pubescent. Fl. small ... 322—*197*

GROUP 20.

JUICE REDDISH (*Myristica*).

L. 4—8 in. long, oblong-lanceolate. Fl. yellowish, in small panicles. Fr. $\frac{3}{4}$—$1\frac{1}{4}$ in. long, ovoid or ellipsoid ... 385—*224*

L. 6—12 in. long, lanceolate, glaucous beneath. Fl. pinkish, in axillary clusters. Fr. 1 in. long, ellipsoid, brown ... 381—*223*

L. 8—15 in. long, oblong to elliptic-lanceolate, silvery or coppery beneath. Fl. whitish, few in the leaf axils. Fr. about 2 in. long, ovoid, pointed ... ... 382—*223*

GROUP 21.

JUICE BLACK AND ACRID.

L. 4—9 in. long, with conspicuously undulate margins, lateral nerves 14—16 pairs. Fl. in panicles from the leaf axils or scars. Fr. broader than long ... ... 175—*140*

L. 5—12 in. long, lateral nerves 18—24 pairs. Fl. in terminal panicles. Fr. seated on a fleshy receptacle ... 173—*140*

L. 12—24 in. long, lateral nerves 20—26 pairs. Fl. and Fr. like the former ... ... 174—*140*

GROUP 22.

LEAVES DISTINCTLY PUBESCENT OR TOMENTOSE BENEATH.

L. 2—5 in. long, ovate-oblong, rounded or cordate at base.

Fl. $\frac{1}{4}$ in. diam., white turning yellow. Berry glossy ... 328—*200*

L. 5—9 in. long, elliptic, brown velvety-tomentose beneath, aromatic when bruised. Fl. small, collected in heads ... 390—*226*

L. up to 12 in. long, white stellate-pubescent beneath, strongly nerved. Fl. large. Capsule angled. Seeds winged... 79—*102*

GROUP 23.

Leaves pale, glaucous, silvery or coppery beneath.

L. 3—4½ in. long, elliptic, ovate or lanceolate, glaucous, with distinct net venation beneath, margins recurved. Fl. in panicles ... ... 39—*85*

L. 4—7 in. long, elliptic to elliptic-lanceolate, coppery beneath. Fl. in clusters from the leaf axils ... ... 420—*237*

L. 5—7 in. long, oblong or ovate-lanceolate, silvery-white beneath. Fl. in one-sided axillary panicled racemes. Fr. with two wings ... ... 61—*94*

L. 4—8 in. long, more or less oblong, glaucous beneath with obscure net venation. Fl. from the branchlets below the leaves ... ... 11—*76*

L. 5—10 in. long, elliptic or oblong, silvery-white beneath. Fr. woody and boldly keeled. Littoral tree ... 78—*102*

L. 6—10 in. long, oblong-lanceolate, glaucous beneath and aromatic when crushed. Fl. heads in axillary racemes... 389—*226*

GROUP 24.

Leaves not more than 5 in. long.

L. 2½—3 in. long, distichous, drying black, lateral nerves fine. Fl. small, white. Berry black, glossy ... ... 323—*198*

L. 3—4½ in. long, ovate to elliptic-oblong. Fl. rather large, reddish, on leafless branchlets. Fr. small ... ... 9—*75*

L. 3—4½ in. long, ovate or elliptic, turning dark-coloured in drying. Fl. yellowish-white. Fr. globose, scarlet ... 324—*199*

L. 3—5 in. long, obovate to elliptic or oblanceolate, lateral nerves 10—12 pairs, petiole channelled. Fl. small, in panicles ... ... 170—*139*

GROUP 25.

LEAVES MORE THAN 5 IN., BUT NOT MORE THAN 8 IN. LONG.

L. 3½—8 in. long, obovate to oblanceolate, margins recurved. Fl. 1 in. across, waxy, white withering to brown. Fr. globose, orange-coloured ... ... 54—*91*

L. 4—8 in. long, obovate to obovate-oblong, drying black, petioles 1½—2 in. long. Fl. in heads, umbellate from above the leaf scars ... ... 388—*226*

L. 5—6 in. long, obovate to elliptic-oblong, turning yellow or reddish in drying. Fl. small, in leaf-opposed clusters ... 419—*236*

L. 4—6½ in. long, elliptic to elliptic-oblong. Fl. white, in racemes. Fr. slightly compressed, pointed ... ... 233—*162*

L. 3—7 in. long, ovate to elliptic-oblong, petioles channelled. Fl. small, in cymes. Drupe red turning black ... 358—*212*

L. 3—7 in. long, oblong or oblong-lanceolate. Fl. greenish-yellow, in leaf-opposed fascicles. Fr. 3-lobed ... 418—*236*

L. 3—7 in. long, ovate to ovate-lanceolate, lateral nerves few. Fr. ellipsoidal, orange-red when ripe, from the stem and branches ... ... 404—*231*

L. 3—8 in. long, oblong-lanceolate, lateral nerves 6—12 pairs. Fl. in panicles. Fr. ellipsoidal, pointed ... 394—*227*

L. 4—8 in. long, elliptic-oblong, with fine distinct venation beneath. Fl. creamy white. Fr. 1½ in. diam., yellow ... 325—*199*

L. 4—8 in. long, elliptic to obovate-lanceolate, petiole 1—3 in. long, bent and thickened at the top. Fr. in pendulous clusters ... ... 427—*239*

L. 4—8 in. long, elliptic to elliptic-oblong, rough beneath. Fr. ½ in. long, ellipsoid-compressed, hispid. Stipules convolute ... ... 446—*246*

L. 5—8 in. long, ovate to elliptic-lanceolate, fine acuminate. Drupe ½ in. long, ovoid. Stipules convolute ... 447—*246*

L. 6—8 in. long, oblong or elliptic-oblong, venation fine and elegant. Capsule ellipsoid, with two vertical grooves ... 147—*129*

GROUP 26.

Leaves more than 8 in. long.

L. 4—10 in. long, linear, narrow, almost sessile, with obscure venation. Fl. in catkins. Fr. globose ... .. 479—257

L. 5—11 in. long, ovate to oblong-lanceolate, lateral nerves 12—16 pairs. Fl. in fascicles from the axils or the scars of the leaves. Fr. ovoid-ellipsoid ... ... 12—76

L. 6—12 in. long, oblong to oblanceolate, one-sided at base. Fl. greenish, in fascicles from the leaf scars. Fr. velvety ... ... 38—84

L. 8—12 in. long, narrowly oblong. Fl. yellowish, globose. Fr. ½ in. diam. Bark peeling in large strips ... 15—77

L. up to a foot long, lanceolate, lateral nerves 11—15 pairs. Fl. in panicles. Drupe ½ in. diam., purplish-black ... 172—159

L. 8—16 in. long, obovate, fleshy coriaceous. Fl. large, like powder-puffs. Fr. angled. Littoral tree ... 264—174

GROUP 27.

Leaves not peltate.

Petioles not more than an inch long.

L. 4—7 in. long, elliptic or ovate, strongly 3-nerved. Fl. ½ in. long, with a pungent smell. Fr. fibrous-fleshy ... 82—101

L. 4—9 in. long, elliptic to elliptic-oblong, strongly 3-nerved, rigidly chartaceous Fl. small. Drupe scarlet ... 443—245

L. up to 12 in. long, white stellate-pubescent beneath, basal nerves weak. Capsule angled. Seeds winged ... 79—102

Petioles more than an inch long, often up to 3 or 4 in. long.

L. 3—6 in long, cordate, acuminate. Fl. large, yellow with a purple centre. Capsule with yellow juice ... 67—97

L. 3—6 in. long, broadly ovate, acuminate to a fine point. Fl. small, in panicles. Fr ¼ in. diam. ... ... 354—211

L 5—8 in. long, oblong or elliptic, petioles thickened at the top. Fl. yellowish-brown, in panicles. Follicles coriaceous, scarlet ... . 72—100

L. 6—12 in. long, elliptic to ovate or obovate, petioles thickened at the top. Fl. reddish-brown, in rufous-tomentose panicles. Follicles 2 in. long, scarlet ... 73—*100*

GROUP 28.

Leaves penninerved.

L. 3—3½ in. long, ovate-oblong, faintly serrate, lateral nerves fine, petiole short. Fl. small, in clusters from the leaf axils or leaf scars ... ... 437—*242*

L. 4—7 in. long, ovate, crenate-serrate, petiole thickened at the top. Fl. ½ in. diam., white, with fringed petals ... 87—*106*

L. 6—9 in. long, obovate, crenate-serrate, petiole thickened at the top. Fl. 1 in. diam., with fringed petals ... 86—*105*

L. 4—10 in. long, oblanceolate, serrate in the upper portion. Fl. small, in slender rusty-tomentose racemes ... 397—*228*

L. 6—12 in. long, oblong to oblong-lanceolate, faintly serrulate. Fl. small, in clusters from the leaf axils or scars 280—*181*

L. up to a foot long or more, obovate or oblanceolate, strongly nerved, crenate-dentate, petioles channelled and sheathing. Fl. large, yellow ... ... 1-3—*71-72*

GROUP 29.

Juice not milky.

Leaves crenate or serrate, not lobed.

L. 3½—4½ in. long, oblong-ovate, oblique, crenate-serrate, strongly 3-nerved. Wood with a bad smell ... 444—*245*

L. 2—5 in. long, ovate or ovate-oblong, glandular at the insertion of the petiole, margin glandular-crenate. Fl. white ... ... 36—*84*

L. 4—6 in. long, ovate-acuminate, deeply cordate, serrulate, softly whitish-grey tomentose beneath. Fl. small ... 445—*245*

L. 4—8 in. long, papery, elliptic or oblong to obovate, faintly crenate-serrate. Fl. yellowish-white, in terminal panicles ... ... 84—*105*

Leaves of mature plants lobed; petioles more than 4 in. long.

L. 5—12 in. across, lobes shallow, pointed. Fl. coral-red. Follicles boat-shaped with two seeds at the top ... 75—*101*

L. 1—2 feet across, deeply lobed. Fl. creamy-yellow with a red centre. Follicles coriaceous, scarlet ... ... 74—*101*

GROUP 30.

Leaves opposite, imparipinnate, with opposite entire leaflets.

Leaflets petiolulate, glabrous. Fl. trumpet-shaped, white. Capsule, linear, cylindrical-curved, pointed. Littoral... 361—*215*

Leaflets sessile, brown pubescent beneath. Fl. 2½ in. long, yellowish-brown. Capsule cylindric, 1—3 feet long ... 362—*215*

Leaflets sessile, pubescent beneath. Fl. about 3 in. long, claret-coloured. Fr. hanging, gourd-like. Introduced tree ... ... 363—*215*

GROUP 31.

Margins of leaflets entire.

Leaflets always opposite.

Leaflets usually 2 pairs, sometimes 1 or 3 pairs. Littoral trees.

Leaflets 3—4 in. long. Fr. leathery, 7—10 in. diam. 115—*118*

Leaflets 3½—6 in. long. Tree sending up sharp pointed knees through the soft mud ... 116—*118*

Leaflets 2—4 in. long, oblong. Fl. with one white petal turning pink. Stamens reddish. Pod woody, flat ... ... 212—*154*

Leaflets 6—12 pairs, 2—3 in. long. Fl. 1½ in. across, pale yellow or rose-coloured. Pod cylindrical, 12—20 in. long ... ... 213—*154*

Leaflets sub-opposite (sometimes alternate in species 118).

Leaflets 4—6, elliptic or lanceolate, 2½—6 in. long, net venation fine. Fl. small. Capsule sharply 3-angled ... ... 166—*137*

Leaflets 4—8, oblong, 4—6 in. long, pale glaucous beneath. Fl. white, numerous, in terminal panicles ... ... 169—[illegible]

Leaflets 6—12, oblong to elliptic-lanceolate. Fl. greenish-white. Capsule 2-lobed, brilliant orange ... ... 164—[illegible]

Leaflets 8—13, oblong to lanceolate, 6—8 in. long. Fl. in tawny-tomentose panicles ... ... 118—[illegible]

GROUP 32.

Leaflets opposite.

Leaflets usually not more than 6 in. long.

Leaflets always 5, 2—4 in. long, lanceolate, pale beneath. Fl. white, in corymbose panicles. Fr. ¾ in. long, puberulous ... ... 126—[illegible]

Leaflets always 5, 3—5 in. long, ovate, pale beneath. Fl. in dense panicles. Fr. ellipsoid or globose ... ... 128—[illegible]

Leaflets 5—7, 3—4½ in. long, ovate to rotund, aromatic when crushed. Fl. in pubescent panicles. Fr. 1½ in. long ... 111—[illegible]

Leaflets 5—9, ovate, 2—6 in. long. Fl. in racemes, white with a pink or violet flush. Pod 2 in. long, woody, flat, pointed ... ... 209—[illegible]

Leaflets 7—11, ovate, 3—6 in. long. Fl. small, from the leafless branchlets. Fr. ½ in. long, kidney-shaped ... 179—[illegible]

Leaflets 7—13, 3—6 in. long, elliptic-oblong, with a distinct intramarginal vein, aromatic when bruised. Fr. 1—1½ in. long ... ... 178—[illegible]

Leaflets 15—17, obliquely ovate, 3—4 in. long, rachis thickened at the petiolules. Fl. umbellately clustered ... 284—[illegible]

Leaflets usually attaining more than 6 in. in length.

Leaflets always 5, elliptic-oblong, 5—7 in. long, pale beneath. Fl. white, in panicles. Fr. velvety ... ... 127—[illegible]

Leaflets 5—9, up to 8 in. long, ovate to oblong, aromatic when bruised. Fl. in velvety panicles ... ... 110—[illegible]

Leaflets 9—15, oblong, 3—9 in. long. Capsule 1½ in. diam., globose, yellow, 3-valved ... ... 130—[illegible]

GROUP 33.

Leaflets alternate.

Lfts. 5—7, ovate to oblong-elliptic, 4—6 in. long, scales on the branchlets, petioles, inflorescence and fruit. Fl. small, in panicles. Fr. $1\frac{1}{2}$ in. long, narrowly ellipsoidal 125—*121*

Lfts. 6—9, ovate to ovate-oblong, 4—8 in. long. Fl. white with a purplish-pink flush. Fr. obovoid ... ... 120—*120*

Lfts. 15—21, ovate to oblong-lanceolate, $2\frac{1}{2}$—5 in. long. Fl. small, in panicles. Fr. ellipsoid, pointed ... 112—*116*

GROUP 34.

Juice milky or pale yellowish.

L. 3—4 in. long, oblong or oblong-lanceolate, with many lateral nerves joined intramarginally. Fl. white. Fr. orange-red ... ... 338—*205*

L. 3—4 in. long, elliptic or lanceolate, lateral nerves many, indistinct. Fr. globular-depressed, red. Branchlets angled ... ... 51—*90*

L. 3—5 in. long, distichous, elliptic to obovate, softly tomentose. Fl. $\frac{3}{4}$ in. diam. Fr. linear, in pairs ... ... 340—*205*

L. $3\frac{1}{2}$—$5\frac{1}{2}$ in. long, elliptic to oblong, lateral nerves 10—12 pairs. Fl. in dense axillary fascicles ... ... 53—*90*

L. 3—7 in. long, oblong to obovate-lanceolate, petioles stem-clasping at base. Fl. white, 1 in. diam. Fr. in pairs ... 339—*205*

GROUP 35.

Trees having the habit of mangroves.

Leaves more or less elliptic, or lanceolate, acute or tapering at both ends.

L. 4—7 in. long, petioles 1—2 in. long. Fl. 4-merous. Radicle smooth, 1—3 feet long ... 235—236—*164*

L. 3—$4\frac{1}{2}$ in. long, petioles 1—$1\frac{1}{2}$ in. long. Fl. greenish-white, 8—14-merous. Radicle faintly ribbed, 3—4 in. long ... ... 238—*165*

Leaves more or less obovate.

L. 2—4 in. long, obtuse or rounded at the apex. **Sepals and petals 5.** Radicle ribbed, about a foot long ... **240**—***165***

GROUP 36.

Trees not having the habit of mangroves.

Leaves not more than 6 in. long.

L. 4—6 in. long, elliptic to oblong or lanceolate. Fl. white, in axillary cymes. Branchlets 4-angled ... ... **301**—***190***

L. 2½—4 in. long, lanceolate or elliptic-lanceolate, margins recurved. Fr. small, ribbed. Branchlets almost rounded **309**—***193***

Leaves attaining more than 6 in. in length.

Leaves nearly sessile.

Littoral tree with obovate or oblanceolate almost cordate leaves. Fl. white, in cymes .. **295**—***188***

Leaves with petioles up to ¾ in. long.

L. 4—7 in. long, elliptic-lanceolate, drying black, hair tufts in the nerve axils beneath. Fl. white **294**—***187***

L. 5—7 in. long, elliptic or oblong, lateral nerves 8—10 pairs, looping far from the edge. Fl. white, fragrant. Fr. ellipsoid. ... ... **296**—***188***

L. 5—8 in. long, elliptic or ovate-elliptic. Fl. small, in cymes. Fr. angled. Branchlets slender, 4-angular ... ... **306**—***191***

L. 4½—8½ in. long, elliptic or oblong-lanceolate. Fl. in heads 1½ in. diam. Stipules obovate ... **290**—***186***

L. 6—10 in. long, elliptic to elliptic-lanceolate. Fl. white, in heads. Fr. succulent-fleshy. Littoral tree with yellow wood ... ... **291**—***186***

Leaves with petioles attaining a length of 1½—2 in.

L. 3—7 in. long, elliptic. Fl. orange-red, with a conspicuous white calyx lobe. Soft-wooded tree ... ... **293**—***187***

L. 6—10 in. long, broadly ovate to orbicular, puberulous beneath. Fl. white, long-tubed. Littoral ... ... **299**—***189***

GROUP 37.

LEAVES DOTTED WITH TRANSLUCENT GLANDS.

L. 1½—3 in. long, broadly elliptic or ovate, lateral nerves many. Fl. white, in terminal or axillary cymes ... 261—*175*

L. 2—3½ in. long, ovate to lanceolate, glaucous-opaque beneath. Fl. sessile, in axillary or terminal panicles ... 262—*173*

L. 2—4 in. long, elliptic-lanceolate, acuminate, lateral nerves many, with a fine intramarginal vein. Fl. in panicles .. 263—*173*

L. 3—5 in. long, oblong, elliptic or obovate, lateral nerves forming double loops, aromatic when crushed. Fl. white 90—*108*

GROUP 38.

LEAVES PETIOLATE.

Lateral nerves not more than a dozen pairs.

L. 2—2½ in. long, almost orbicular, margins revolute. Fl. in umbellate cymes. Fr. oblong-clavate ... ... 141—*127*

L. 2—4½ in. long, elliptic or ovate, lateral nerves 5—8 pairs, indistinct. Fl. blue, from the leaf axils or scars ... 270—*177*

L. 3—5 in. long, elliptic, obovate to lanceolate, lateral nerves obscure. Petals joined in pairs. Drupe bluish-black ... 335—*203*

L. 4—6 in. long, oblong to lanceolate, lateral nerves 5—6 pairs. Fl. greenish-white, in cymes. Fr. globose ... 140—*127*

Lateral nerves more than a dozen pairs.

L. 4—5 in. long, narrowly oblong, lateral nerves about 15 pairs. Fl. in fasciculate racemes ... ... 45—*88*

L. 8—12 in. long, more or less lanceolate, lateral nerves 16—20 pairs with intermediate ones. Drupe yellow, ellipsoid ... ... 177—*141*

GROUP 39.

LEAVES DISTINCTLY DOTTED WITH TRANSLUCENT GLANDS.

L. unfolioilate, 1½—3 in. long, elliptic to ovate, notched, lemon-scented when bruised. Fl. white. Berry 1 in. diam. ... ... 91—*108*

L. 3—6 in. long, obovate to oblong. Fl. waxy, pink, in umbellate racemes. Littoral ... ... 313—*194*

L. 3—7 in. long, lanceolate. Fl. waxy, pink, in lax panicles 314—*194*

GROUP 40.

LEAVES UP TO 6 IN. LONG, RARELY LONGER.

L. 1—1¼ in. long, ovate, blunt with a mucro. Fl. white, bearded. Littoral tree armed with straight spines ... 133—*124*

L. 1½—3½ in. long, obovate, margins recurved. Fl. white, twisted, in umbels. Fr. cylindric-curved. Habit of a mangrove ... ... 315—*194*

L. 2½—3 in. long, elliptic, distichous, drying black, lateral nerves many, fine. Fl. white, axillary. Berry black, glossy ... ... 323—*198*

L. 2—4 in. long, elliptic to elliptic-lanceolate, lateral nerves very many, joining intramarginally. Fl. pinkish-yellow ... ... 107—*114*

L. 3—4 in. long, broadly elliptic, lateral nerves 5—7 pairs. Fl. small, yellow, in clusters. Fr. puberulous ... 413—*235*

L. 2½—4½ in. long, elliptic, lateral nerves fine, 6—8 pairs, looping far from the margin. Fl. yellowish-green. Fr. globular, glossy ... ... 8—*75*

L. 3—5 in. long, elliptic to obovate, lateral nerves 4—6 pairs, looping far from the margin. Fl. small, white. Fr. 2-lobed, grooved ... ... 132—*124*

L. 3—6 in. long, elliptic to elongate-elliptic, lateral nerves 8—12 pairs, weak. Fl. greenish, clustered. Fr. scarlet, velvety, furrowed ... ... 415—*235*

L. 3½—6 in. long, elliptic or oblong. Fl. in umbellate cymes. Fr. ellipsoid, grooved ... ... 137—*126*

L. 4—6 in. long, elliptic to elliptic-oblong, lateral nerves weak. Fl. tawny-velvety, from the branches. Fr. yellow or red, grooved ... ... 416—*236*

L. 4—6 in. long, ovate to elliptic or lanceolate, lateral nerves 7—9 pairs. Fl. greenish-white. Fr. nearly sessile, pointed ... ... 7—*74*

GROUP 41.

LEAVES ATTAINING MORE THAN 6 IN. IN LENGTH.

Petioles somewhat short, *i.e.*, seldom exceeding ¾ in. (stem-clasping in species 488 and 489).

- L. 4—7 in. long, ovate or ovate-oblong, acuminate with a mucro, somewhat oblique. Fl. small. Capsule purple ... ... 412—*235*
- L. 3—8 in. long, ovate, acuminate, lateral nerves 5—10 pairs. Fl. small, in axillary racemes ... ... 317—*195*
- L. 4—8 in. long, oblong to ovate or elliptic, lateral nerves few. Fl. creamy-yellow. Fr. with a cup-shaped calyx. Cut turning yellow ... ... 326—*199*
- L. 5—8 in. long, more or less ovate, pale below, lateral nerves 6—10 pairs. Fl. in panicles, white ... 393—*227*
- L. 5—9 in. long, oblong to elliptic-lanceolate, petiole channelled. Fl. in cymes from the leaf axils or scars. Fr. white, grooved ... ... 138—*126*
- L. 6—9 in. long, elliptic to oblong or obovate, lateral nerves 12 pairs, prominent and parallel. Fl. creamy-orange. Fr. pubescent ... ... 14—*76*
- L. 6—10 in. long, oblong-elliptic, lateral nerves about 8 pairs, petiole thickened at the top. Fl. in catkins. Fr. pointed, hairy ... ... 421—*237*
- L. 6—10 in. long, oblong-elliptic to lanceolate, lateral nerves weak. Fl. greenish, up to 5 in. long. Fr. clustered, whitish ... ... 13—*76*
- L. 7—10 in. long, oblong to elliptic-oblong, net venation lax. Fl. in umbels, yellow. Fr. pear-shaped, keeled ... ... 100—*112*
- L. 1—2 feet long, linear-lanceolate, veined lengthwise, petioles stem-clasping. Fl. in panicles. Soft-wooded ... ... 488—489—*261*

Petioles somewhat long, *i.e.*, 1 in. or more in length.

- L. 4—7 in. long, elliptic to ovate or lanceolate, lateral nerves arching, net venation fine. Fl. small. Fr. velvety ... ... 186—*144*
- L. 5—7 in. long, obovate. Fr. orange or crimson with a kidney-shaped nut on it. Introduced tree ... 176—*140*

L. up to 8 in. long, broadly ovate, almost cordate, petioles 1—3 in. long. Fl. orange-coloured. Littoral ... 353—*211*

L. 5—9 in. long, obovate, collected at the ends of the branchlets, glaucous beneath. Fl. small, in panicles. Fr. on a reddish swollen pedicel ... ... 395—*228*

L. 6—9 in. long, more or less lanceolate, lateral nerves 11—14 pairs, interarching. Fl. pinkish. Fr. 4 in. long, 4-angled ... ... 267—*175*

L. 5—10 in. long, ovate or elliptic-lanceolate, almost glaucous beneath, petioles 1—2 in. long. Fl. white, in heads ... 387—*226*

L. 8—12 in. long, elliptic to elliptic-oblong, glaucous beneath, petiole 2 in. long, thickened at the top. Fl. small, in slender racemes ... ... 37—*84*

L. 7—15 in. long, oblong-lanceolate, stipules stem-clasping, large. Fl. 2½ in. diam. Fr. a woody cone ... 5—*75*

GROUP 42.

Leaves more or less pubescent on one or both surfaces.

Leaves not exceeding 3 in. in length, petioles short.

L. 1—2 in. long, oblong to elliptic, glaucous and pubescent beneath. yellowish. Fr. 3-valved ... ... 407—*233*

L. 1—2½ in. long, elliptic to elliptic-lanceolate, pubescent beneath, Fl. yellowish. Fr. globular ... ... 327—*200*

L. 1—3 in. long, elliptic to lanceolate, glaucous and pubescent beneath, lateral nerves 7—12 pairs. Fl. in axillary clusters ... ... 410—*234*

Leaves exceeding 3 in. in length.

L. 5—7 in. long, elliptic-oblong, branchlets, petioles and leaves softly tomentose. Fl. yellow, in axillary clusters 414—*235*

L. 3—8 in. long, crowded at the ends of thick branchlets, obovate, silky tomentose. Fl. small, in one-sided rows. Littoral tree ... ... 356—*211*

L. 3—9 in. long, elliptic or oblong, rusty pubescent beneath. Fl. in panicles. Fr. 1 in. long ... ... 391—*227*

L. 5—9 in. long, elliptic, velvety brown tomentose beneath, aromatic when bruised. Fl. in heads from the leaf scars 390—*226*

GROUP 43.

Leaves not peltate.

L. 2—4 in. long, oblong-lanceolate, oblique, petiole ½ in. long. Fl. white, in axillary fascicles ... ... 80—*193*

L. 3—6 in. long, cordate, acuminate, petioles 1—4 in. long. Fl. large, yellow with a purple centre. Fr. with yellow juice ... ... 67—*97*

L. 4—8 in. long, ovate to elliptic-lanceolate, pale beneath, glandular near the long petiole. Fl. in racemes ... 429—*240*

L. 4—9 in. long, ovate-lanceolate, pale beneath with minute red glands. Fr. covered with a red powder ... 432—*241*

GROUP 44.

Juice milky.

L. 2—4 in. long, glossy, elliptic, crenate. Fl. greenish-yellow, in catkin-like spikes. Tree growing with mangroves ... ... 436—*242*

L. 2—4 in. long, elliptic to obovate, finely pointed, irregularly serrate, rough. Fl. in clusters ... ... 472—*255*

L. 4—12 in. long, shortly cuspidate, denticulate in the upper portion, rough. Figs solitary ... ... 449—*248*

GROUP 45.

Petioles rather short.

Trees with the habit of mangroves. L. thick, veinless, faintly crenate. Fl. white or scarlet ... 246—247—*168*

L. 3—6 in. long, obovate to lanceolate, serrulate, drying yellow. Fl. in villous-tomentose racemes ... 330—*201*

L. 4—7 in. long, obovate to elliptic-lanceolate, coarsely wavy serrate. Fl. whitish, in spikes. Fr. 3-lobed ... 439—*243*

L. 4—8 in. long, elliptic-lanceolate. Fl. bright yellow. Fr. seated on the enlarged reddish calyx ... ... 106—*114*

L. 6—12 in. long, obovate to oblanceolate, crenulate. Fl. pink, handsome, in pendulous racemes ... ... 265—*174*

GROUP 46.

PETIOLES LONGISH, *i.e.*, MORE THAN 1½ IN. LONG.

L. up to 7 in. long, oblong to elliptic-oblong, distantly wavy dentate, almost cordate, with black dots on the under surface. Fl. enclosed in bracts ... ... 422—*238*

L. 5—8 in. long, elliptic to lanceolate or oblong, blunt with a mucro. Fl. white, in racemes ... ... 438—*243*

L. 6–10 in. long, somewhat lanceolate, repand toothed. Fl. in racemes. Branchlets hollow ... ... 441—*244*

GROUP 47.

LEAVES GLABROUS OR NEARLY SO.

L. 4—6 in. long, elliptic to lanceolate, serrulate. Fl. umbellate, from the leaf axils ... ... 83—*104*

L. 4–8 in. long, elliptic to oblong or obovate, papery, crenate-serrate. Fl. in terminal panicles ... ... 84—*105*

L. 4—8 in. long, ovate to elliptic-lanceolate, pale with silvery or coppery scales beneath, glandular at the petiole. Fl. in spikes ... ... 429—*240*

L. 2–2½ feet across, palmately lobed, petioles long, stems pithy inside. Fl. umbellate, in large panicles ... 282—*182*

GROUP 48.

LEAVES PUBESCENT BENEATH.

L. 4—6 in. long, ovate, acuminate, cordate, softly whitish-grey tomentose beneath, serrulate. Fl. small ... 445—*245*

L. 4—8 in. long, ovate, cordate, crenate-serrate, silvery-grey pubescent beneath. Fl. in axillary spikes. Littoral ... 475—*256*

L. 3—8 in. diam., nearly orbicular, cordate, crenulate. Fl. large, yellow with a crimson centre. Littoral tree ... 64—*96*

GROUP 49.

Leaves alternate.

Lfts. 1—4 in. long, sessile, obovate, gland-dotted, petiole winged. Fl. in cymes. Berry 1 in. diam. ... ... 94—*109*

L. pinnately-trifoliolate. Lfts. 2—3½ in. long, broadly elliptic, pale beneath. Fl. white. Pod jointed. Littoral ... 206—*151*

L. pinnately-trifoliolate. Lfts. 4—8 in. long, puberulous beneath. Fr. 3 in. diam., globose, velvety ... 113—*117*

GROUP 50.

Leaves paripinnate.

Lfts. usually 4, obliquely obovate, ¾—2 in. long, sessile. Fl. pink. Pod wrinkled. Littoral tree ... ... 211—*153*

Lfts. usually 4, obovate, 3—4 in. long. Fr. large, leathery. Tree with the habit of a mangrove ... ... 115—*118*

Lfts. usually 4, ovate or broadly so, 2—4 in. long. Fr. the size of an orange. Littoral tree ... ... 114—*118*

Lfts. usually 2—4, elliptic to oblanceolate, 4—7 in. long. Fl. in compound panicles. Fr. with 3 vertical ridges ... 168—*137*

Lfts. 4—6, elliptic to oblong-lanceolate, 4—6 in. long, tufts of hairs in the nerve axils beneath. Capsule 2-lobed ... ... 167—*137*

GROUP 51.

Leaflets opposite.

Lfts. usually 5, oblong or elliptic-oblong, 3—5 in. long. Fl. white, in axillary panicles. Fr. white, supported by the calyx ... ... 104—*115*

Lfts. 4—6, elliptic-obovate, 2¼—5 in. long. Fl. in lax short panicles. Fr. globose with shallow grooves ... 119—*120*

Lfts. 5—9, ovate-lanceolate, 3—5 in. long. Fl. trumpet-shaped, white. Fr. linear-curved. Littoral ... 361—*215*

Lfts. 11—17, oblong or oblong-lanceolate, 4—7 in. long. Fl. in rusty panicles. Fr. almost 2-lobed, brown ... 122—*121*

Lfts. 11—17, elliptic to oval, ¾—1¼ in. long, grey tomentose beneath. Fl. yellow. Fr. linear, constricted between the seeds. Littoral tree ... ... 207—*151*

Lfts. 15—17, obliquely-ovate, 3—4 in. long. Fl. umbellately clustered. Fr. ovoid-oblong. Stems pithy inside 284—*182*

GROUP 52.

Leaflets alternate.

Lfts. 3—5, oblong to elliptic-lanceolate, 4—6 in. long, pungent when bruised. Fl. white. Fr. globose ... 99—*111*

Lfts. 5—7, oblong-lanceolate to ovate-oblong, lateral nerves 7—9 pairs. Fl. orange-yellow, small, in panicles 123—*121*

Lfts. 5—7, oblong to ovate-lanceolate, lateral nerves 7—9 pairs. Fl. small, in panicles ... ... 124—*121*

Lfts. 5—9, 1—3 in. long, elliptic to rhomboid, glossy. Fl. 1 in. long, bell-shaped. Fr. red, ovoid ... ... 98—*110*

Lfts. 5—13, oblong-lanceolate, 3—7 in. long, softly pubescent beneath. Fl. in long racemes. Fr. ¼—¾ in. long ... 165—*137*

Lfts. 7—15, oblong to ovate-lanceolate, 5—7 in. long. Fl. in terminal flat panicles, strongly scented. Fr. orange-red ... ... 97—*110*

GROUP 53.

Parasitic shrubs found growing on the stems or branches of other trees (see also *Hydnophytum*, p. 185).

Leaves usually opposite.

Leaves penninerved.

L. 2—3½ in. long, ovate-lanceolate. Fl. yellow, ¾ in. long. Fr. globular. Usually on *Papita* ... 402—*250*

L. 3—5 in. long, broadly ovate. Fl. scarlet, 1—1½ in. long. Fr. oblong ... ... 401—*230*

Leaves palminerved.

L. 2—3 in. long, ovate-oblong. Fl. clustered ... 400—230

Leaves usually alternate.

L. 3—5 in. long, broadly ovate. Fl. rusty tomentose, in simple axillary racemes. Fr. bottle-shaped ... 400—230

GROUP 54.

Shrubs not having the habit of Mangroves.

L. 1—3 in. long, ovate to elliptic or lanceolate, pale below with few silky hairs. Fl. greenish-white. Low deciduous shrub ... ... 307—191

L. 3—6 in. long, elliptic or ovate, hair tufts in the nerve axils beneath. Fl. in clusters. Armed rambling shrub 306—190

L. usually in whorls of threes, 4—8 in. long, elliptic-lanceolate. Fl. small, white, in axillary fascicled cymes ... 305—191

L. 5—8 in. long, oblong to ovate, upper ones cordate and nearly sessile. Fl. white ... ... 298—188

L. 4—10 in. long, very variable. Fl. crowded, white or rose-coloured, with long slender tubes ... ... 297—188

GROUP 55.

Unarmed Shrubs.

Litoral tree with fine branchlets. L. ½—1¼ in. long, elliptic or oblong, nearly sessile, silky pubescent. Fl. solitary, white or pink ... ... 274—178

Branchlets stiff. L. distichous, 1—2 in. long, elliptic or elliptic-rhomboid. Fl. axillary. Fr. globular ... 272—177

L. 2—3 in. long, oblong-lanceolate, lateral nerves 10—12 pairs, interarching. Fl. blue, umbellate ... ... 271—177

Littoral straggling shrub with branchlets at right angles to the stem. L. 1—3 in. long, ovate to obovate, with a strong smell when bruised. Fl. white, with purple stamens ... ... 373—219

Branchlets slender, whitish. L. 2—4 in. long, elliptic to obovate. Fl. small, in axillary clusters ... 334—205

Branchlets angled or winged. L. 3½—5½ in. long, oblong to elliptic. Fl. blue, in lax cymes. Fr. globular ... 273—*177*

GROUP 56.

Leaves not exceeding 1½ in. in length.

Riverine shrub with stiff branchlets. L. ½—1 in. long, spoon-shaped. Fl. pink or red. Fr. orange-red ... 357—*212*

Littoral shrub. Branchlets velvety pubescent. L. 1 in. long, linear-spathulate, silky velvety. Fl. yellow, in axillary racemes ... ... 101—*112*

L. distichous, 1—1½ in. long, elliptic to ovate, glaucescent beneath. Fl. in axillary clusters. Berry ¼ in. diam... 409—*234*

GROUP 57.

Leaves exceeding 1½, but not exceeding 6 in. in length.

Littoral shrub. L. 2—3 in. diam., orbicular, with petioles 2—3 in. long, winged and stem-clasping. Fr. linear curved ... ... 312—*193*

Straggling shrub. L. 2—4 in. long, ovate, acuminate. Fl. whitish, small, in axillary racemes. Fr. yellow when ripe . ... 316—*195*

L. 2½—4 in. long, oblong to lanceolate or obovate, lateral nerves 12 pairs, forming double loops. Fl. yellow ... 17—*77*

Littoral shrub with angled branchlets. L. 2—4½ in. long, obovate to oblanceolate. Fl. yellowish-green. Fr. winged 161—*135*

Straggling and spinescent. L. 3—5 in. long, elliptic, underside silvery or coppery scaly. Fr. succulent, red when ripe ... ... 399—*22[illegible]*

L. 3—5 in. long, elliptic to obovate, lateral nerves 4—6 pairs, interarching. Fl. small. Fr. 2-lobed, with a groove on either side ... . 132—*12[illegible]*

L. 3½—5½ in. long, ovate-elliptic or ovate-lanceolate Fl. in axillary cymes. Fr. ovoid .. .. 135—*125*

L. 3—6 in. long, elliptic to obovate-oblong. Fl. small, in umbel- or corymb-like racemes. Capsule 3—coccous, rough ... ... 417—*236*

L. 3½—6 in. long, oblong to elliptic-oblong. Fl. in umbellate cymes. Fr. 1 in. long, grooved ... ... 137—*126*

GROUP 58.

Littoral Shrubs.

L. 5—8 in. long, lanceolate, acuminate, silvery grey beneath with few weak nerves. Fl. white. Fr. brownish, scaly... 85—*105*

Stems pithy. L. fleshy, 4—10 in. long, obovate, petioles short. Fl. white, split on one side. Drupe ribbed ... 311—*193*

L. crowded, 6—12 in. long, elliptic to lanceolate or obovate, petioles short. Fl. white or pink. Fr. often in pairs... 159—*135*

GROUP 59.

Inland Shrubs.

Branchlets triangular. L. unifoliolate, 2—8 in. long, ovate to oblong-lanceolate. Fl. purple. Pods 1—3 in. long 205—*151*

L. 5—7 in. long, oblong or elliptic-oblong, depressed along the nerves. Fl. white, solitary. Fr. club-shaped ... 20—*78*

L. 3—8 in. long, elliptic-oblong to obovate, pale beneath, petioles up to 2 in., thickened at the top. Fr. 3-lobed 426—*239*

All parts densely woolly. L. 4—8 in. long. Fl. white or pale blue. Fr. ½ in. diam. Introduced ... ... 360—*214*

Branchlets yellow, hirsute tomentose. L. 4—8 in. long, elliptic to ovate-oblong, tawny hairy beneath. Fr. pointed ... ... 329—*200*

L. 4—8 in. long, elliptic to lanceolate, lateral nerves forming double loops. Fl. solitary. Fr. ½ in. diam. ... 19—*78*

L. 6—9 in. long, narrowly linear-oblong, sub-glaucous and finely rusty-pubescent beneath. Fl. in panicles ... 392—*227*

L. 5–9 in. long, elliptic to oblong or oblanceolate, pale glaucous beneath. Fl. yellow, 1½–3 in. long. Fr. radiating and constricted 16–*77*

L. 6–9 in. long, elliptic to oblong or obovate, lateral nerves 9–10 pairs, ascending. Fl. ½ in. diam. 18–*78*

GROUP 60.

Leaves with palminerved venation.

L. 2–4 in. long, oblong-lanceolate, glabrous or thinly stellate hairy. Fl. in axillary fascicles. Capsule rugose. 80–*103*

Branchlets and petioles silky pubescent. L. 3–6 in. long, ovate, petiole thickened at the top. Fl. greenish-white. Pod oblong 203–*150*

Introduced. L. 4–8 in. long, ovate, petioles 2–3 in. long. Fl. 2 in. diam., white or pink. Capsule prickly ... 35–*83*

GROUP 61.

Unarmed shrubs.

L. distichous, 1–1½ in. long, elliptic to rhomboid, crenate-serrate, pale and glandular in the nerve axils beneath. Fl. white 33–*83*

L. 2–5 in. long, lanceolate or broadly so. Fl. white, in axillary fascicles. Capsule ½ in. diam. 34–*83*

Branchlets zigzag. L. 3–5 in. long, oblong to lanceolate, crenate-serrate with hair tufts in the nerve axils beneath. Fl. greenish 149–*130*

Riverine shrub. L. 3–8 in. long, linear or linear-lanceolate, pale scaly beneath. Fl. in axillary spikes. 440–*243*

GROUP 62.

Leaves glabrous or nearly so.

Prickly shrub. L. 1½–2½ in. long, obliquely ovate to lanceolate, denticulate. Fl. small, in cymes 150–*130*

Introduced. Juice milky-watery. L. 6 in. across, 3—5 lobed, petiole 3—6 in. long. Fl. yellowish-green. Capsule 1—1¼ in. long ... ... 435—*242*

L. 3—8 in. long, ovate-oblong, peltate low down, petioles long, pale beneath. Fl. in terminal racemes. Fr. bristly ... ... 431—*241*

GROUP 63.

Margins of leaflets entire.

Littoral. Leaflets 2—3½ in. long, broadly elliptic, pale beneath. Fl. white. Pods jointed, up to 2 in. long ... 206—*151*

Sometimes armed. Leaflets 2—5 in. long, crenulate, dotted with fine translucent glands. Fl. white ... ... 95—*109*

Leaflets 3—6 in. long, ovate, brownish-silky hairs on the nerves beneath, petiole long, angled. Fl. purplish ... 204—*150*

GROUP 64.

Leaves bipinnate.

Introduced thorny shrub. L. with 4—8 pairs of pinnae, and small leaflets. Fl. golden-yellow, in round heads. Pod cylindric, pointed at the ends .. .. 225—*159*

Unarmed introduced shrub. L. with 5—7 pairs of pinnae, each with 12—14 pairs of leaflets. Fl. white, in round heads. Pods brown, 6 in. long ... ... 226—*159*

Native forest shrubs with angled or grooved branchlets, petioles with sheathing bases. Leaflets serrate with prominent lateral nerves. Fl. in corymbose cymes ... 156—158
132—*133*

GROUP 65.

Juice milky.

L. 1—3 in. long, elliptic-lanceolate or oblong, thick, with obscure nerves. Fl. yellow, in axillary cymes. Follicles in pairs ... ... 349—*209*

L. 2—4 in. long, oblong or elliptic. Fl. yellow with brown streaks, the corolla lobes ending in long tails ... 344—*207*

L. 3—4 in. long, oblong or elliptic-oblong, lateral nerves joined intramarginally. Fl. white. Follicles paired, 6—18 in. long ... ... 345—*207*

L. 3—5 in. long, with hair tufts in the nerve axils beneath. Fl. white, fragrant. Follicles necklace-shaped, 6—12 in. 343—*207*

L. 3—5 in. long, oblong or elliptic. Fl. small, yellowish, in lax panicles. Follicles 5—6 in. long, woody ... 346—*207*

L. 4—5 in. long, elliptic-ovate, cuspidate. Fl. yellow, in small cymes ... ... 348—*209*

Branchlets softly pubescent. L. about a foot long, ovate to orbicular, pubescent beneath. Fl. 2—3 in. diam. Follicles 12—18 in. long, boldly 3-angled ... ... 347—*208*

GROUP 66.

Leaves with interpeticlar stipules.

Branchlets bearing stout recurved hooks, young parts rusty pubescent. L. 4—6 in. long, elliptic, rusty pubescent beneath, petioles twisted. Fl. in globose heads ... 292—*186*

L. 4—6 in. long, elliptic or elliptic-oblong. Fl. in axillary compact cymes or heads. Fr. ¼ in. diam. ... ... 308—*191*

L. 4—7 in. long, elliptic to ovate. Fl. an inch long, in cymes from the scars of the fallen leaves ... 304—*190*

GROUP 67.

Leaves not more than 6 in. long.

Stems hooked. L. 2—3 in. long, ovate, elliptic or lanceolate, lateral nerves many. Fl. small. Fr. with 2 concave membranous wings ... ... 398—*229*

Branches drooping. L. 2½—4 in. long, ovate, minutely tomentose. Fl. yellowish-green, in panicles. Fr. angled 249—*169*

L. 2—4½ in. long, ovate, acuminate. Fl. white, in axillary or terminal cymes. Fr. often in pairs ... ... 333—*203*

Luxuriant garden creeper with long-tubed white or pink flowers. L. 2—5 in. long ... ... 253—*170*

L. about 5 in. long, elliptic to obovate, with minute scales and dots. Fl. in solitary spikes. Fr. $1\frac{1}{2}$ in. long, with 4 lateral wings ... ... 252—*170*

Plant with pale-edged scales. L. 3—$5\frac{1}{2}$ in. long, broadly elliptic. Fl. in cylindrical spikes. Fr. with 4 lateral wings ... ... 251—*170*

L. 4—$5\frac{1}{2}$ in. long, oblong to elliptic. Fl. small, in panicles. Capsule flat, containing brown-winged seeds ... 145—*128*

L. 3—6 in. long, elliptic to orbicular-ovate. Fl. small, in umbellate panicles. Fr. in threes, ovate, membranous-reticulate, 2 in. long ... ... 89—*107*

L. 4—6 in. long, elliptic-lanceolate. Fl. white dashed with yellow. Fr. with 3 wings 1—2 in. long and 2 shorter ones ... ... 88—*106*

GROUP 68.

LEAVES ATTAINING MORE THAN 6 IN. IN LENGTH.

Stems twisted. L. 4—7 in. long, ovate to lanceolate. Fl. very fragrant, in panicled clusters. Fr. with a spoon-shaped bract ... ... 374—*220*

Stems flattened and twisted. L. 3—9 in. long, elliptic to ovate-oblong, drying black. Fl. green, cylindrical ... 478—*257*

L. 4—10 in. long, elliptic to ovate, petiole 1—$1\frac{1}{2}$ in. long. Fl. yellowish-red, in cylindrical racemes. Fr. with 4 lateral wings ... ... 250—*169*

GROUP 69.

MARGINS OF LEAVES NOT ENTIRE, *i.e.*, SERRATE OR CRENATE.

Branchlets angular. L. 2—$3\frac{1}{2}$ in. long, lanceolate, crenate-serrate. Fl. greenish-yellow. Stamens 3. Fr. $\frac{1}{2}$ in. diam. 142—*127*

L. 3—5 in. long, ovate or elliptic, puberulous beneath. Fl. small, white, in dense corymbs. Fr. $\frac{1}{4}$ in. long, smooth... 369—*218*

L. 3—6 in. long, rotund-lanceolate, Fl. greenish-yellow, $\frac{1}{4}$ in. diam. Stamens 3. Fr. nearly 1 in. diam. ... ... 143—*128*

L. 4—5 in. long, elliptic to rotund-elliptic. Fl. white or pale yellow. Capsule flat with brown-winged seeds ... 144—*128*

GROUP 70.

SCANDENT SHRUBS WITH WHITE OR ROSE-COLOURED FLOWERS, ETC.

L. 2—4 in. long, elliptic to elliptic-ovate or lanceolate. Fl. white, in axillary umbels. Fr. globose ... ... 27—*81*

L. 2—4 in. long elliptic. Fl. white, 2—4 in a line above the leaf axil. Fr. like a pea ... ... 30—*82*

L. 3—5 in. long, ovate. Fl. 1 in. long, white or rose-coloured, 2—3 in a line above the leaf axil. Fr. like a prune, red. Younger parts rusty-reddish ... ... 31—*82*

L. 4—5 in. long, elliptic to obovate or lanceolate. Fl. white, umbellate in terminal panicles. Fr. pointed 29—*81*

L. 4—8 in. long, oblong-ovate. Fl. showy, white dashed with maroon. Fr. ovoid ... ... 32—*82*

GROUP 71.

STEMS ARMED WITH LONG, SHARP SPINES.

L. 2½—5 in. long, ovate to oblong-lanceolate, lateral nerves 3—5 pairs. Fl. small, in axillary tomentose spikes ... 134—*125*

Spines 2 in. long. L. unifoliolate, 4—9 in. long, elliptic to oblong, gland-dotted, petiole thickened above. Fl. white 92—*108*

Juice milky. L. 3—6 in. long, elliptic to obovate. Fl. in heads, yellowish-white, ¼ in. diam. ... ... 474—*255*

GROUP 72.

LEAVES WHOLLY GLABROUS.

Branchlets slender, drooping. L. 2—4 in. long, elliptic-oblong, lateral nerves 5—7 pairs. Fl. small, in axillary clusters ... ... 411—*234*

L. 3—4 in. long, elliptic to oblong, light green, lateral nerves obscure. Fl. white, in axillary panicles. Fr. globose, 1 in. diam. ... ... 28—*81*

Young parts reddish-brown tomentose. L. 3—5 in. long, elliptic, pale beneath. Fl. white, in panicles. Fr. black 358—*212*

L. 3½—5½ in. long, ovate, to oblong or lanceolate. Fl. white, in axillary racemes. Fr. enveloped by the accrescent calyx ... ... 136—*125*

L. 4–6 in. long, ovate-lanceolate, lateral nerves indistinct, petiole thickened and bent above. Fl. small. Fr. scarlet 26—*80*

L. 4–6 in. long, ovate to obovate or oblong. Fl. ½ in. diam., pale-green, reddish inside. Fr. 1½ in. diam.... ... 6—*73*

L. 4–7 in. long, oblong, net venation prominent. Fl. small, in velvety tomentose slender spikes. Fr. velvety, pulpy 139—*126*

GROUP 73.

Leaves more or less pubescent or tomentose beneath.

Branchlets drooping. L. 1–2 in. long, oblong or elliptic, glaucescent and puberulous beneath. Fl. usually clustered. Fr. purple ... ... 408—*234*

Young branchlets ferruginous pubescent. L. 1½—3½ in. long, oblong-ovate, pubescent. Fl. in slender spikes, often with tendrils. ... 153—*131*

L. 4–5 in. long, elliptic or obovate, grey silky beneath. Fl. funnel-shaped, 1½ in. long, rose-purple ... ... 359—*213*

Young parts coppery pubescent. L. 4—8 in. long, oblong to lanceolate, glaucous and pubescent beneath. Fl. large, solitary ... ... 22—*79*

L. 4—8 in. long, elliptic, softly stellate tomentose beneath. Fl. 1½ in. diam., red. Fr. scarlet ... ... 23—*79*

L. 5½–9 in. long, oblong-lanceolate, stellate rufous pubescent on the nerves beneath. Fl. small, in cymes. Fr. rusty tomentose ... ... 24—*79*

GROUP 74.

Juice not milky.

L. 2—4 in. long, broadly cordate, petiole long and slender. Fl. yellow. Fr. red, glossy ... ... 25—*80*

L. 3–6 in. long, elliptic to obovate with hair tufts in the nerve axils beneath. Fl. white, fragrant. Drupe black 286—*183*

Stems armed with sharp prickles. L. 4—8 in. long, ovate or oblong, petioles stem-clasping. Fl. greenish, small ... 490—*262*

L. 5—8 in. long, cordate-oblong, puberulous beneath, petiole long. Fl. umbellate, in cymes. Capsule prickly ... 76—*102*

Large climber. L. almost orbicular or ovate, the young leaves with a border of silky hairs along the margin, petiole long. Fl. small, reddish, in heads ... ... 476—*256*

GROUP 75.

Leaves with penninerved venation.

Stems rough, reddish-brown. L. 3—6 in. long, sinuate-crenate, harsh, lateral nerves strong. Fl. white, in panicles ... ... 4—*72*

Stems cracked. L. 3—4 in. long, ovate or elliptic. Fl. crowded in large panicles. Fr. with a linear wing ... 148—*129*

L. 2½—5 in. long, ovate or obovate, crenate-serrulate. Fl. yellowish, in raceme-like panicles. Capsule 3-valved ... 146—*128*

Branchlets zig-zag. L. 3—5 in. long, oblong to lanceolate, crenate-serrate, hair tufts in the nerve axils beneath. Fl. greenish, in axillary fascicles ... ... 149—*130*

GROUP 76.

Leaves not more than 3 in. broad, crenate or serrate.

Clothed with ferruginous hairs. L. 1½—2½ in. long, ovate to lanceolate, denticulate. Fl. in axillary cymes. Prickly ... ... 150—*130*

L. 1½-2½ in. long, ovate, crenate-serrate. Fl. small. Fr. on the persistent calyx. Littoral ... ... 152—*131*

Often with spiral tendrils. L. 1½—3½ in. long, ovate, crenate-serrate. Fl. white in long slender racemes ... 154—*131*

L. 2½—4½ in. long, ovate or ovate-oblong, crenate-serrulate. Fl. greenish-white, in axillary cymes. Prickly ... 151—*130*

GROUP 77.

Leaflets pinnately disposed and stipellate.

Lfts. 5—7 in. long. Fl. purple, or white with purple spots, calyx with brown hairs. Pods with folds and irritating hairs. Seeds 2-3 ... ... 168—*146*

Lfts. 3—4 in. long. Fl. purple, calyx with bristles. Pods with folds and irritating hairs. Seed one ... ... 189—*146*

Lfts. 4—5 in. long. Fl. greenish, calyx with silky hairs. Pod with a double wing along the edges and with irritating hairs ... ... 187—*145*

Lfts. 4—6 in. long. Fl. pink and white, in ample panicles. Pod a membranous, silky pubescent wing with a seed at the end ... ... 190—*146*

Lfts. 4 in. long. Fl. bright or orange-red, beaked, in pendulous racemes. Pod oblong, inflated ... ... 191—*147*

Lfts. 5 in. long. Fl. pale pink, in dense racemes. Pod 3—4 in. long, inflated ... ... 192—*147*

GROUP 78.

MARGINS OF LEAFLETS ENTIRE.

Fl. white or pink, papilionaceous, usually in racemes. Pod thin and flat, with a narrow wing along one or both edges ... ... 193—197—*147—148*

Branchlets rusty puberulous. Lfts. 3—5. Fl. white, in rusty pubescent panicles. Fr. ovoid-oblong, compressed and pointed ... ... 183—*143*

Lfts. 5—9, 3—8 in. long. Fl. white, in racemes collected into panicles. Fr. ovoid-oblong, pointed ... ... 184—*143*

GROUP 79.

LEAVES IMPARIPINNATE. FL. PAPILIONACEOUS, ETC.

Branchlets twining and twisted spirally. Lfts. usually 5, 1—1½ in. long, obovate. Fl. white, in unilateral racemes. Pod falcate ... ... 198—*149*

Branchlets often twisted. Lfts. 9—13, 1—2 in. long, obovate to obovate-oblong. Fl. in panicles. Fr. narrow ... 199—*149*

Lfts. 11—15, about 1 in. long, oblong to obovate-oblong. Fl. yellow or white, in panicles. Pod 2—3 in. long ... 200—*149*

Lfts. 25—41, ½—¾ in. long, obliquely-oblong. Fl. white, in corymbiform panicles. Pod 1½—3 in. long ... 201—*149*

GROUP 80.

Climbers armed with sharp prickles.

Prickles small. Lfts. ¼ in. long. Fl. white, in lax panicled racemes. Pod 2½ in. long, a seed with a membranous scarlet wing ... ... 214—*155*

Prickles on corky tubercles. Fl. yellow, in panicled racemes, the lower petal like a hood. Pods flat, dark-brown, with a papery wing along one edge ... ... 215—218—*156*

Lfts. ½—2 in. long. Fl. yellow dashed with red, in racemes. Pod armed with sharp prickles ... ... 219—*157*

Lfts. 1—2 in. long. Fl. yellow dashed with red, in racemes. Pod flat, falcate-elliptic, pointed, 2 in. long ... 220—*157*

L. with numerous minute leaflets. Fl. white or yellow, in heads arranged in panicles. Pod flat, linear ... 223—224—*159*

GROUP 81.

Leaves pinnate, with numerous linear sword-shaped leaflets.

L. 4—6 ft. long. Lfts. 1—2 ft. long, folded inwards lengthwise, pale beneath. Fl. yellow. Fr. orange-red turning black. Littoral palm. ... ... 492—*263*

Littoral with underground stem. L. 15—30 ft. long. Lfts. 4—5 ft. long, glaucous beneath. Fr. 4—6 in. long, angular... 493—*263*

Slender palm. L. 4—6 ft. long. Lfts. 1½—3 ft. long, falcate-lanceolate. Fr ¾ in. long, orange turning scarlet 494—*264*

Slender palm. L. 15—20 ft. long. Lfts. 2—3 ft. long, the sheaths 4 ft. long. Fr. ½ in. long ... ... 495—*264*

Slender palm. L. 3—4 ft. long. Lfts. 1—2 ft. long, falcate to linear-lanceolate. Fr. ½ in. long ... ... 496—*264*

GROUP 82.

Leaves fan-shaped, etc.

Small palms with rough stems and leaves divided to the base into numerous wedge-shaped segments. Fl. in drooping spikes.

L. 2—4 ft. across, petioles 2—4 ft. long ... ... 508—*269*

L. 3—6 ft. across, petioles 4—12 ft. long. ... ... 507—*269*

Large palm, stems 30—60 ft. high and 1—2 ft. diam. L. 8—16 ft. across, petiole 18—25 ft. long ... ... 506—*268*

GROUP 83.

Leaves pinnate, etc.

Leaflets arranged equidistantly along the rachis.

Rachis prolonged into an armed whip-like appendage.

L. 6—10 ft. long. Lfts. 2—3 ft. long ... ... 497—*265*

L. 6—12 ft. long. Lfts. 1—2 ft. long ... ... 502—*267*

L. 4½—6 ft. long. Lfts. 8—12 in. long ... ... 503—*267*

Rachis not prolonged into a whip-like appendage.

L. 3½—4 ft. long. Lfts. about 28 pairs, up to a foot long 498—*265*

Leaflets not arranged equidistantly along the rachis, *i.e.*, two or more together or fascicled.

Rachis prolonged into a whip-like appendage. L. about 8 ft. long. Lfts. 1—1½ ft. long ... ... 499—*266*

Rachis not prolonged into a whip-like appendage.

L. 10—14 ft. long. Lfts. 1½—2 ft. long ... ... 500—*266*

L. 3—5 ft. long. Lfts. up to a foot long ... ... 501—*266*

FOREST FLORA
OF THE
ANDAMAN ISLANDS

For explanation of abbreviations used in the text, see pages 10 and 11.

Fam. 1. DILLENIACEÆ.

THE DILLENIA FAMILY.

Deciduous trees or climbers with strongly parallel-nerved, often rough, alternate, serrate leaves; petioles sheathing. Flowers yellow or white, often large and showy and appearing when the tree is leafless; sepals 5, imbricate and persistent; petals 5, deciduous; stamens many. Fruit dry or succulent.

Trees with large oblanceolate leaves. Fl. large, solitary and fasciculate ... . 1. Dillenia.
A climber with rough stems and leaves. Fl. rather small, in panicles ... . 2. Delima.

1. DILLENIA.

Deciduous trees with large, crenate-dentate, strongly parallel-nerved leaves; petioles sheathing and channelled. Flowers large, yellow, solitary or fascicled.

Leaves attaining a foot or so in length.
Flowers solitary ... ... D. pilosa.
Flowers fasciculate .. .. D. scabrella.
Leaves attaining 3 ft. or more in length ... ... D. pentagyna.

• 1. **D. pilosa,** *Kurz*; H. i. 38; Br. 4. Vern. *Zinbyun*, Burm.

A moderate-sized tree (40—60×4—6), of irregular growth, with a rough, brownish-grey bark, peeling in flakes. Leaves up to a foot or so in length, obovate to oblong-lanceolate, narrowed to the base, pubescent when young but soon becoming glabrous, lateral nerves 20—30 pairs. Flowers about 2 in. diam., solitary, or exceptionally in a pair, on stalks 1—1½ in. long, from the scars on the leafless branchlets; petals bright yellow.

Very common in the deciduous forests of the islands in all localities. Leafless in the H. S., the flowers appearing in April. Fr. during the R. S. Kurz in his Andaman Report writes of a tree at Tarmugli Island 10 ft. 3 in. in girth, and also gives the height attained by this as 80—100 ft.

2. *D. scabrella, *Roxb.*; H. i. 38; Br. 4.

A tree (40—50×3—4) with grey, rather smooth bark. Leaves up to a foot long, oblong to obovate-oblong, acute at both ends, rough above, densely roughish pubescent beneath; lateral nerves 30—40 pairs; petiole 1-1½ in. long. Flowers large, about 1½ in. across, usually in fascicles of 3—4, pedicels slender, 1—2 in. long. Fruit globular, orange-coloured.

According to Brandis this is a native of the Andamans. I have looked for it in the forests and examined many *Dillenias*, and with rare exceptions found the flowers to be solitary. I have seen no Andaman specimens, but the collection of these is a matter of some difficulty owing to the leaves and flowers appearing at different seasons. This includes *D. parviflora, Griff. H. i.* 38.

3. D. pentagyna, *Roxb.*; H. i. 38; Br. 4.

A moderate-sized tree (30—40×2—4). Leaves very large, up to 3 feet long, or longer in small trees, and about 16 in. broad, obovate, blunt, narrowed to the petiole, glabrous or slightly pubescent on the nerves beneath; lateral nerves 30—40 pairs, often branching near the margin and excurrent into the fine teeth. Flowers 1 in. across, yellow, in fascicles of 5—10, on slender stalks 1—3 in. long.

Middle Andaman, in the interior forests at the head of the Betapur and Bomlungta streams. Flowers in the H. S. or at the beginning of the R. S. Conspicuous in the forests and easily distinguished from the two preceding ones by its large leaves. It is uncommon, and I have seen it only in the localities mentioned above.

2. DELIMA.

4. D. sarmentosa, *Linn.*; H. i. 31; Br. 5.

A large woody evergreen climber with strong, rough, reddish-brown stems. Leaves 3—6 in. long, elliptic, ovate or oblong, acute or blunt, sinuate-crenate especially in the upper portion, very harsh; lateral nerves 12—14 pairs, ascending; petioles channelled. Flowers rather small, white, in lax axillary panicles. Fruit a pointed, dehiscent follicle, supported by the calyx.

Very common in all localities. Fl. R. S. Fr. August. The rough leaves are used in India for polishing wood and ivory.

Fam. 2. MAGNOLIACEÆ.

A tree and a climber with alternate leaves; stipules stem-clasping or none. Flowers unisexual or bisexual, the sepals and petals arranged in threes; stamens many. Fruit composed of many carpels arranged in a cone or head.

A tree with large stem-clasping stipules and long leaves. Fl. large Fr. like a cone ... ... 1. Talauma.
A climber. Leaves without stipules. Fl. ½ inch diam. Fr. globose ... ... 2. Kadsura.

1. TALAUMA.

* 5. **T. andamanica,** *King*; Br. 8 ; J.A.S.B. No. 4. 1889, p. 372.

A small tree (15—30 × 2—4) usually branching low, bark discoloured, cut mealy, dirty cream-coloured; stipules large, leaving annular scars. Leaves 7—15 in. long, 2½—5 in. broad, oblong-lanceolate, acuminate, narrowed into the petiole, entire, dark green, glabrous and glossy; lateral nerves 10-15 pairs. Flower buds sub-globose, purplish; flowers solitary and terminal, handsome and fragrant; about 2½ in. diam.; sepals concave, pinkish-purple; petals 6, white. Fruit like a woody cone, up to 2 in. long.

Uncommon but not rare; usually found in evergreen forests in damp places along streams. Middle Andaman, Mt Wimberley, Bomlungta; Baratang; South Andaman, Ali Masjid Reserve. Fl. April-May. Fr. Nov.-Dec. The young leaves, which are yellowish-pink and conspicuous, come out in the month of February. The flowers are well worth seeing.

2. KADSURA.

6. ***K. Roxburghiana,** *Arnott*; H. i. 45 ; Br. 9.

A stout glabrous woody climber with a rough bark. Leaves 4—6 in. long, 1¾—2½ in. broad, ovate to obovate or oblong, acute or shortly acuminate, narrowed to the petiole, entire, membranous, dark green and glossy; lateral nerves 7—8 pairs. Flowers ½ in. diam., pale green, and reddish inside, axillary and solitary, on pedicels ½ in. or more in length; sepals and petals rotund. Fruit 1½ in. diam., carpels beaked.

Mt. Harriet. Evidently rare. Collected only by Dr. King's Collectors.

Fam. 3. ANONACEÆ.

THE CUSTARD APPLE FAMILY.

Trees, shrubs or climbers. Leaves simple, alternate, entire, shortly petioled and without stipules. Flowers white, or more or less yellowish or greenish, solitary or in few-flowered cymes; sepals 3; petals 6, in 2 series, variously elongated or hooded; stamens many. Fruit of numerous, often stalked and distinct, carpels, resulting from one flower. Seeds usually black and glossy.

A tropical Family, well represented in these islands, but of the members given here few are of any importance to the Forester. Its members are often difficult to identify "even for experts in Systematic Botany", but the Family as a whole may well be recognised by the flowers with parts in whorls of threes, by the fruits which usually separate on distinct stalks, and often by the fibrous matted appearance of the sliced bark. Its leaves often resemble those of some of the plants of the Families *Ebenaceæ, Lauraceæ,* and some *Euphorbiaceæ.*

Trees.

Leaves up to 6 in. long.

Flowers axillary, small, greenish-white or greenish-yellow ... 1. Orophea.

Flowers on leafless branchlets, rather large, reddish ... 2. Miliusa.

Leaves attaining 8 in. or more in length.

Leaves glaucous beneath with indistinct lateral nerves. Fl. on the branches below the leaves. Fr. globular ... 3. Polyalthia.

Leaves not glaucous beneath, glabrous.

Fl. long, greenish, on the branches below the leaves. Fr. oblong, white, clustered ... ... 4. Melodorum.

Fl. axillary, greenish-yellow to purple. Fr. orange-red or bluish-black, ovoid ... ... 3. Polyalthia.

Fl. axillary, creamy-orange, petals clawed and hooded, tomentose. Fr. pubescent ... ... 5. Mitrephora.

Fl. axillary or in fascicles on the branches below the leaves, yellow, globose. Fr. globose ... ... 6. Sageræa.

Shrubs. Flowers mostly solitary.

Leaves glaucous beneath. Fl. long pointed, pale yellow. Carpels constricted between the seeds ... ... 7. Unona.

Leaves not glaucous beneath.

Leaves 2½—4 in. long Fl. yellow, ¾ in. diam ... ... 8 Popowia.

Leaves 4–7½ in. long Fl. campanulate, ½-¾ in diam. ... 9. Phaeanthus.

Leaves 5—7 in. long, glossy. Fl. ¼ in diam., white, solitary 10. Anaxagorea.

Leaves 6–9 in. long. Fl. silky, ½ in. diam. ... 8. Popowia.

Leaves 6–9 in long. Fl. greenish, ¼ in. diam., solitary or a few together ... ... 3. Polyalthia.

Scandent shrubs and Climbers.

Leaves 6–8 in long, glabrous, branchlets with recurved woody hooks on which flowers are borne ... ... 11. Artabotrys.

Leaves more or less pubescent beneath.

Leaves 4–8 in. long, glaucous beneath. Fl. large, yellowish, solitary ... . 12. Oxymitra.

Leaves 4–8 in. long, soft stellate-pubescent beneath. Fl. yellowish ... ... 13. Uvaria.

1. OROPHEA.

Flowers axillary, small; sepals valvate; inner petals clawed, vaulted, (cohering in *O. hexandra*). Stamens 6—12.

Leaves 4—6 in. long. Petals cohering ... ... O. hexandra

Leaves 2¼—4½ in. long. Petals with their apices curved outwards ... ... O. polycarpa.

- 7. **O. hoxandra**, *Blume*; Br. 18; Kz. 1. 49.

A small tree (15—25 × 1—2) with blackish branchlets. Leaves 4—6 in. long, 1—2¼ in. broad, ovate to elliptic or oblong-lanceolate, acuminate, base rounded, glabrous and glossy above, with hairs on the midrib and nerves beneath; lateral nerves 7—9 pairs. Flowers about ¼ in. long, greenish-white, outer petals ovate-cordate, inner trapezoid with a long claw, vaulted and cohering; stamens 6. Ripe carpels 1—1¾ in. long, oblong and pointed, nearly sessile.

Fairly frequent. Middle and South Andaman; Havelock Island. Often found growing in evergreen forest near streams, and usually having moss and lichens on its branchlets. Fl. and Fr. Jan.-April.

8. **O. polycarpa,** *A. DC.*; H. 1. 91; Br. 18.

A small tree (15—20 × 1—2). Leaves 2½—4½ in. long and about half as broad, broad elliptic, shortly acuminate, well rounded at the base, glabrous, lateral nerves 6—8 pairs, fine and looping rather far from the margin. Flowers small, nearly ½ in. long, yellowish-green; inner petals twice as long as the outer, thick, their apices curved outwards; stamens 6 or 7. Ripe carpels about ½ in. diam., globular, glabrous and glossy.

Middle and South Andaman. Fairly common; often found growing with the last one and somewhat resembling it. Fl. March-April.

2. MILIUSA.

9. **M. tectona,** *Hutchinson.* Vern. *Jungli Saguan,* Hind.

A straight-stemmed moderate-sized tree (40—80 × 2—4), with a dark brown, thinly fissured, rather smooth bark; cut yellowish-brown with fine white streaks. Leaves 3—4½ in. long, ovate to ellipt c-oblong, acuminate, base rounded to almost cordate, glabrous, lateral nerves fine. Flowers fairly large, from the scars of fallen leaves on the leafless branchlets; inner petals concave, ovate, reddish, about an inch long. Fruit ½ in. diam.

A frequent tree in deciduous forests in all localities. Leafless at the end of the H. S. Fl. at the beginning of the R. S. Apparently called *Jungle Teak* on account of the slight resemblance of its bark and stem to those of the Teak tree, but otherwise very unlike it.

3. POLYALTHIA.

Flowers solitary or fascicled; sepals valvate; petals valvate, spreading.

Shrub. Leaves 6—9 in. long, with bold interarching nerves. Fl. ½ in diam. ... ... P. andamanica.
Trees. Flowers small.
Leaves glaucous beneath with indistinct venation. Fl. slender, fasciculate from nodules on the branches ... . P. Parkinsonii.
Leaves nearly glabrous beneath. Fl. fasciculate from the leaf axils or scars ... ... P. simiarum.

10. **P. andamanica,** *Kurz*; Br. 14.

A shrub. Leaves 6—9 in. long, 1½—3 in. broad, oblong-elliptic to oblong-lanceolate, shortly acuminate, base acute, coriaceous, glabrous, dark green and glossy above; lateral nerves rather fine and interarching rather far from the edge; petioles ¼ in. long. Fl. ½ in. diam., solitary or a few together, axillary or from the leaf scars, stalks ¾ in. long; sepals and petals thick, incurved. Ripe carpels 6-8 together, cylindric, ¾ in. long.

Evergreen forests. Middle Andaman; Havelock Island; Chiriatapu. Fl. and Fr. Dec.-Febr.

11. **P. Parkinsonii,** *Hutchinson* ; Kew. Bull, 1917, p. 25.

An elegant tree (20×45×1½—3) with a greyish bark, cut light-brown, mealy-fibrous. Leaves 4—8 in. long, 1½—2½ in. broad, oblong to oblong-elliptic or oblong-lanceolate, base rounded or obtuse, glabrous, dark green above, glaucous beneath ; petiole about ⅛ in. long, lateral nerves hardly visible. Flowers ½ in. long, on slender reddish pedicels 1 in. long, from nodules on the branchlets below the leaves. Ripe carpels ¾ in. diam., almost globular, 3-7 from a flower.

Uncommon but not rare. Middle Andaman ; Baratang Island ; Havelock Island ; South Andaman. Fl. Dec. Fr. Febr-March. Easily recognised by its glaucous and almost veinless leaves. Wood rather soft, light yellowish when freshly cut.

12. ***P. simiarum,** *Benth and Hook. fil.* ; H. i. 63 ; Br. 15.

A tree 50—80 feet high. Leaves 5—11 in. long, 2—4½ in. broad, ovate-oblong to oblong-lanceolate, acute or shortly acuminate, glabrous above, dull and sometimes puberulous on the nerves beneath ; petiole ½ in. ; lateral nerves 12—16 pairs. Flowers in fascicles from the leaf axils or the leaf scars ; sepals small ; petals linear, greenish-yellow to purplish ; pedicels 1—1½ in. long. Ripe carpels 1—1½ in. long, stalked, ovoid-ellipsoid, orange-red to bluish-black when ripe.

Andaman Islands_*Brandis.* I have seen no Andaman specimens.

. MELODORUM.

13. **M. macranthum,** *Kurz.* ; Br. 20 ; Kz. i. 42.

A straight-stemmed tree (25—30×1½—3), with a greyish-brown discoloured bark, cut brownish, stringy, faintly streaked. Leaves 6—10 in. long, 2 - 4 in. broad, oblong-elliptic to oblong-lanceolate, shortly acuminate, glabrous, lateral nerves weak ; petioles strong, ½—¼ in. long. Flowers greenish, in fascicles of 1-3 on the branchlets below the leaves ; outer petals linear-lanceolate, up to 5 in. long, the inner 1—1½ in. long. Fruit 1—1½ in. long, oblong, whitish.

Occasionally found in evergreen forests. Middle Andaman, Long Island, and the South Andaman. Fl. June-July. Fr. Dec.-March.

5. MITREPHORA.

14. **M. Prainii,** *King* ; Br. 19 ; J.A.S.B. No. 1. 1892, p. 88.

A straight-stemmed tree (20—30×1—2), with slender straight branches ; bark dark greenish, fairly smooth. Leaves 6—9 in. long, 2¼—3 in. broad, elliptic to oblong or obovate, acuminate, glabrous, lateral nerves about 12 pairs, rather prominent : petioles short. Flowers ¾ in. long, creamy-orange, on slender stalks from the scars of fallen leaves ; inner petals densely tomentose, clawed and vaulting over the stamens and forming a cap. Ripe carpels ¾ diam., softly pubescent.

Fairly common and seen in nearly all localities. Usually found growing in evergreen forest and favouring damp places. Fl. Nov.-May. Fr. Dec.-July.

6. SAGERÆA.

15. **S. elliptica.** *Hook. fil. and Thoms.* H. i. 92; Br. 13. *The Andamanese Bow-wood tree.* Vern. *Chai.*

A moderate-sized but tall tree (50—80×3—5), with a straight stem and smooth dark brown or greenish bark, often with conspicuous white patches and peeling in long strips. Leaves 8—12 in. long, and 2—3 in. broad, narrowly oblong, acute or obtuse at the base or apex, glabrous and glossy, lateral nerves 14—16 pairs. Flowers globose, yellowish, petals thick, ovate-orbicular, concave. Ripe carpels globose, about ½ in. diam.

A frequent tree in the deciduous and semi-deciduous forests of the Islands. Fl. March. Fr. R. S. Wood yellowish-white, heavy, straight grained and elastic, used by the Andamanese, from whom we get the vernacular name, for making their bows. It is also used locally for boat-building.

Alphonsea ventricosa, *Hook. fil. and Thoms*; Br. 18; by which name the *Chai* has been erroneously known, is a tree of which I have seen no Andaman specimens, and, I believe, is not found in these islands.

7. UNONA.

16. **U. Dasymaschala,** *Blume*; H. i. 61; Br. 16.

A shrub. Leaves 5—9 in. long, 1½—3 in. broad, elliptic to oblong or oblanceolate, shortly acuminate or acute, base unequally rounded, glabrous, dark green above, glaucous beneath; lateral nerves 8—9 pairs, petiole short. Flowers 1½—3 in. long, pale yellow, on stalks 1—2 in. long; petals fleshy, lanceolate. Carpels many, radiating from the base, linear and constricted between the seeds.

Very common in all localities. Fl. May-June. Fr. R. S. Easily known by its leaves, flowers, or fruits.

8. POPOWIA.

Shrubs. Flowers and fruits rather small; petals valvate.

Leaves not more than 4 in. long ... ... P. nitida.
Leaves more than 6 in. long ... ... P. Kurzii.

17. **P. nitida,** *King*; Br. 13; J.A.S.B. No. 1. 1892, p. 92.

A shrub with softly pubescent young branchlets. Leaves 2½—4 in. long, ½—1½ in. broad, oblong to oblong-lanceolate or obovate, bluntly acuminate, base rounded, glabrous and glossy, lateral nerves about 12 pairs, rather thin and forming double loops; petiole very short. Flowers ½ in. diam., yellow, petals ovate-orbicular. Ripe carpels ¾ in. long, ovoid-pointed, glabrous.

Middle and South Andaman. Fl. April.

18. **P. Kurzii**, *King*; Br. 13.

A shrub 5—8 feet high. Leaves 6—9 in. long, 1¾—2¼ in. broad, elliptic to oblong or obovate, bluntly acuminate, glabrous or nearly so, dark green and glossy above; lateral nerves 9—10 pairs, ascending; petioles stout, ½ in. long. Flowers ½ in. diam., axillary; petals with silky hairs. Fruit unknown.

Middle and South Andaman, in evergreen low forests, associated with and resembling *Saprosma ternatum*. Not common. Fl. April-June. This is *Polyalthia macrophylla*, *H. f. and Th.*

9. PHÆANTHUS.

19. ***P. andamanicus**, *King*; Br. 12; J.A.S.B. No. 1, p. 122.

A small glabrous shrub. Leaves 4—8 in. long, 2—3 in. broad, elliptic or elliptic-lanceolate, acute, slightly narrowed to the rounded base, lateral nerves faint and slender, forming double loops near the margin; petiole ¾ in. long. Flowers ½—¾ in. diam., campanulate, usually solitary and extra-axillary; inner petals oblong-ovate, united at the base. Ripe carpels sub-globular, ⅓ in. diam., 2-seeded.

South Andaman.

10. ANAXAGOREA.

• 20. **A. luzoniensis**, *A. Gray*; H. i. 68; Br. 21.

A common little shrub. Leaves dark green and glossy, 5—7 in. long, oblong to elliptic-oblong, shortly acuminate, depressed on the upper surface along the 6 to 8 pairs of nerves and the reticulations; petiole about ¾ in. long. Fl. ½ in. diam., white, solitary, petals elliptic. Fruit club-shaped, narrowed into a long stalk, with one or two shining black seeds.

Very common everywhere in evergreen forests. Fl. and Fr. H. S. and R. S.

11. ARTABOTRYS.

21. **A. speciosus**, *Kurz*; H. i. 55; Br. 21.

A woody climber with dark-coloured finely-furrowed stems, and bearing woody recurved hooked branchlets on which the flowers are borne. Leaves 6—8 in. long, 2—2½ in. broad, oblong or oblong-lanceolate, shortly and bluntly acuminate, base acute, dark green and glossy above; lateral nerves 6—10 pairs, interarching at some distance from the edge; petioles somewhat thickened. Flowers 1—1½ in. long, yellow; petals linear, blunt.

Uncommon but not rare. Middle and South Andaman; Havelock Island and the Labyrinth Islands. Easily known by its hooked branchlets and its often somewhat bluish and glossy leaves. Fl. April. *Ancistrocladus* and *Uncaria* are also climbers with hooked branchlets.

12. OXYMITRA.

22. **O. fornicata,** *Hook. fil. and Thoms.*; H. i. 71; Br. 19.

A large scandent shrub, the younger parts coppery pubescent. Leaves 4—8 in. long, oblong to lanceolate, acuminate, narrowed towards the rounded base, glabrous above, glaucous and grey pubescent beneath; petioles short. Flowers solitary, on long stalks, opposite the leaves or extra-axillary, rusty pubescent, yellowish; outer petals 2 in. long. Ripe carpels nearly sessile, cylindrical, elongate-oblong.

South and Middle Andaman. Fl. May. It resembles *Unona Dasymaschala.*

13. UVARIA.

Scandent and stellate-pubescent. Flowers yellow, purple, or brown; petals spreading, imbricate in bud.

Lateral nerves 12-14 pairs. Fl. large ... ... U. Hamiltoni.
Lateral nerves 18-22 pairs. Fl. small ... ... U. andamanica.

23. ***U. Hamiltoni.** *Hook. fil. and Thoms.*, var. Kurzii, *King*; H. i. 48; Br. 17.

A powerful climber. Leaves 4—8 in. long, 2—3½ in. broad, elliptic to elliptic-oblong, acuminate, with a somewhat broad and often minutely cordate base, almost glabrous above, softly stellate-tomentose beneath; lateral nerves 12—14 pairs; petioles short. Flowers 1¼ in. diam., brick-red, solitary or 2 or 3 together on pedicels 1—1½ in. long, sepals broadly triangular; petals ovate-oblong. Ripe carpels 1½ in. long, ovoid, tomentose, scarlet, on slender stalks.

South Andaman, *King's collectors.*

24. ***U. andamanica,** *King*; J.A.S.B. No. 1. 1892, p. 21.

Scandent. Young branches scurfy stellate-tomentose. Leaves 5½—9 in. long, oblong-lanceolate, shortly acuminate, base rounded or cordate, glabrous above, stellate rufous pubescent on the midrib and 18—22 pairs of lateral nerves beneath. Flowers small, in terminal or axillary cymes; sepals orbicular; rusty stellate tomentose outside; petals orbicular. Ripe carpels blunt at each end, densely covered with rusty stellate tomentum.

South Andaman, *King's collectors*. Brandis does not mention this but gives *U. micrantha, Hook. fil. and Thoms.*, a climber with glabrous leaves 3—5 in. long, and white flowers about ½ in. diam., the leaves closely resembling those of *Popowia nitida*.

The following cultivated plants which have been introduced belong to this Family :—

Anona squamosa, *Linn. The Custard Apple. The Sweet Sop* or *Sugar Apple of the West Indies*. Vern. *Awza*, Burm.; *Sitaphal*, Hind. A small tree. Leaves 2—4 in. long, oblong-lanceolate, glaucous and pubescent beneath, pellucid-punctate. Flowers solitary, greenish. Fruit 2—4 in. diam.

Anona reticulata, *Linn. The Bullock's Heart* or *True Custard Apple of the West Indies*. A small tree. Leaves 4 - 8 in. long, glabrous, lateral nerves 15—18 pairs. Flowers yellowish-green. Fruit like the last but more smooth. Vern. *Awza*, Burm.; *Ramphal*, Hind. A native of the Antilles.

Fam. 4. MENISPERMACEÆ.

Climbers with alternate, exstipulate, entire leaves. Flowers minute; sepals 6 or 8; petals 6 (2 in *Antitaxis*); stamens 4-8. Fruit with a curved or horse-shoe-shaped seed.

An unimportant Family and of little or no interest to the Forester. It is sometimes called the *Moon-seed Family* on account of the curved shape of its seeds.

Leaves cordate and palminerved .. .. 1. Tinospora.
Leaves ovate-lanceolate, penninerved ... ... 2. Antitaxis.

1. TINOSPORA.

25. **T. cordifolia**, *Miers.*; H. i. 97; Br. 24.

A glabrous climber with a corky warted bark. Leaves 2—4 in. long, broadly cordate, acute or shortly acuminate, with 5-7 basal nerves, membranous; petioles about as long as the leaves, slender. Flowers yellow, appearing when the plant is leafless; sepals, petals and stamens 6, the first in two series and larger than the petals. Drupe the size of a pea, glossy and succulent.

Not uncommon. Middle Andaman; Long Island; South Andaman and Dundas. Fl. Febr.-April.

2. ANTITAXIS.

26. ***A. calocarpa**, *Kurz*; Br. 27; Kz. i. 57.

An evergreen woody climber. Leaves 4—6 in. long, 1½—2 in. broad, ovate-lanceolate, acuminate, glabrous, penninerved, the nerves not more conspicuous than the finely reticulate venation; petioles about ½ in. long, slender, bent and thickened at the top. Flowers small, on slender pedicels; sepals and stamens 8; petals 2. Drupe ¾ in. long, scarlet.

South Andaman, Brookesabad; also at Narcondam. Fl. April. A plant of uninteresting appearance.

Fam. 5. CAPPARIDACEÆ.

THE CAPER FAMILY.

Scandent shrubs often armed with stipular prickles. Leaves simple, alternate. Flowers usually white and showy, on slender pedicels, with many, long, exserted, slender stamens; sepals and petals 4. Ovary on a slender stalk at the base of which is inserted the stamens. Fruit a fleshy berry.

1. CAPPARIS.

Characters the same as those of the Family. All prickly except *C. floribunda.*

Flowers in terminal or axillary umbels ... ... C. sepiaria.
Flowers in terminal or axillary panicles.
  Fl. in axillary panicles; stamens 8. Fr. globular ... C. floribunda.
  Fl. umbellate, in terminal panicles; stamens about 30. Fr. ellipsoid-pointed ... ... C. ambigua.
Flowers in an axillary or supra-axillary row.
  L. 2—4 in. long. Fl. about ¾ in. diam. ... ... C. tenera.
  L. 3—5 in. long. Fl. about 1 in. long ... ... C. horrida.
  L. 4—8 in. long. Fl. 1 in. across ... ... C. micracantha.

27. C. sepiaria, *Linn.*; H. i. 177; Br. 34, 700.

A scandent shrub, armed with sharp black prickles, and with light-green foliage. Leaves 2—4 in. long, ¾—1½ in. broad, elliptic to elliptic-ovate or lanceolate, blunt, base rounded, glabrous, lateral nerves 4—5 pairs, looping rather far from the margin; petiole strong, ¼ in. long. Flowers 4—8 in an axillary umbel, white, nearly ¾ in. long, on slender pedicels up to an inch long. Fruit globose, ½ in. diam., black when ripe.

Often found along the seashores, in the interior deciduous forests, and along streams. North, Middle and South Andaman, in several localities. Fl. H. S.

28. C. floribunda, *Wight*; Br. 35, 700.

Scandent and unarmed. Leaves light green, 3—4 in. long, 1—2 in. broad, narrowly elliptic to oblong, acute, base rounded, glabrous, with rather obscure lateral nerves; petioles ¼—¾ in. long. Flowers white, very fragrant, on slender pedicels collected near the tops of axillary panicles; stamens 8, with slender white filaments. Fruit about 1 in. diam., globose and slightly narrowed at the base.

Along the seashores. Havelock Island; South Andaman; North Cinque Island. Fls. Febr.-April. This is *C. andamanica, King.*

29. C. ambigua, *Kurz*; Br. 35; Kz. i. 65.

Scandent, armed with short, sharp, recurved prickles. Leaves 4—5 in. long, 1¾—2½ in. broad, elliptic to ovate or lanceolate, shortly acuminate with a short bristle, base rounded, glabrous, with indistinct lateral nerves but with a strong midrib; petiole ¼ in. long. Flowers, white, umbellate, in terminal panicles; sepals 4, concave; petals 4, smaller than the sepals; stamens about 30. Fruit ¾ in. long, ellipsoid, pointed at both ends.

Middle Andaman, Mt. Baker; Kyd Island; South Andaman, Port Blair and Port Mouat. Fl. R. S. Fr. Jan.

30. **C. tenera,** *Dalz.*; H. i. 179; Br. 36.

Scandent, armed with short prickles. Leaves 2—4 in. long, ¾—2 in. broad, elliptic, shortly acuminate, rounded at the base, glabrous, glossy and thin; petiole ¼ in. long. Flowers about ¼ in. diam., white, on slender pedicels by 2 or 4 in a line above the leaf axils; petals ¼ in., creamy-white, tomentose outside. Fruit like a pea, small, with few seeds.

Middle Andaman, Betapur and Bomlungta forests; South Andaman; Rutland Island. Fl. H. S. and R. S. Fr. R. S.

31. **C. horrida,** *Linn.*; H. i. 178; Br. 35. Vern. ***Namisithanlyet***, Burm.

A scandent shrub armed with strong sharp, recurved prickles; branches and younger parts all covered with rusty-reddish tomentum. Leaves 3—5 in. long, ¾—2½ in. broad, ovate, acute, glabrous when mature; petiole ¼ in. long. Flowers about an inch long, white or rose-coloured, arising by 2 or 3 in a line above the leaf axils. Berries the size of a prune, on long stalks, red when ripe.

Middle Andaman; Havelock Island. Along the seashores. Fl. Mar.-April.

32. **C. micracantha,** *DC.*; H. i. 179; Br. 36. Vern. ***Namasithanlyet***, Burm.

Elegant, scandent and armed with few prickles; stems dark green. Leaves 4—8 in. long, 1½—3½ in. broad, oblong-ovate, acute, base rounded, glossy and glabrous above, pale and dull beneath, with firm distinct reticulate venation; petiole ½ in. long. Flowers showy, white, axillary or supra-axillary, 1 in. across; petals white, the upper ones dashed with maroon, filaments about an inch long. Fruit 2—3 in. long, smooth, ovoid.

Porlob Island and Baratang. Fl. in the H. S., very pretty.

Fam. 6. VIOLACEÆ.

Shrubs with alternate, serrate or crenate leaves with stipules. Flowers small, in axillary clusters or fascicles; sepals and petals 5;

stamens 5, with an appendaged connective. Fruit a 3-valved, few-seeded capsule.

1. ALSODEIA.

Common and plain-looking shrubs. Characters as above.

Leaves 1–1½ in. long, elliptic or rhomboid, crenate-serrate ... A. Roxburghii.
Leaves 2–5 in. long, lanceolate, serrulate ... ... A. bengalensis.

33. **A. Roxburghii,** *Wall.*; H. i. 186; Br. 38.

A small shrub 2–4 feet high, with alternate or fasciculate distichous leaves 1–1½ in. long, ½–¾ in. broad, elliptic to rhomboid, base narrowed, apex blunt or acute and ending in a small bristle, pale beneath with glands in the axils of the nerves; petiole very short. Flowers small, white, in nearly sessile axillary clusters. Fruit somewhat 3-sided, with round white seeds.

Extremely common in the deciduous and semi-deciduous forests of the islands. Fl. and Fr. almost all the year round.

* 34. **A. bengalensis,** *Wall.*; H. i. 186; Br. 37. Vern. *Taung-letpet*, Burm.

A shrub 5–12 feet high. Leaves 2–5 in. long, 1–3 in. broad, lanceolate or broadly so, acuminate, base acute or rounded, serrulate, glabrous, lateral nerves curved, with smaller intermediate ones; petiole ¼ in. long. Flowers small, white, on slender pedicels in axillary fascicles, globular, the apices of the petals recurved. Capsule ¼ in. diam.

Abundant. One of the commonest shrubs in the leaf-shedding forests of the islands and found in all localities. Fl. and Fr. Nov.-April. The leaves, which somewhat resemble those of the tea plant, are said to be used to adulterate tea.

Fam. 7. BIXACEÆ.

The Arnotto Family.

Trees or shrubs with simple alternate, exstipulate leaves. Flowers often unisexual; sepals 4, 5 or 6, imbricate; petals small, 4 or 5, sometimes absent: stamens usually many; disc often with glands. Fruit fleshy or dry, indehiscent or opening by valves.

* 35. **Bixa orellana,** *Linn.*; *The Arnotto.* Vern. *Thidin*, Burm.

A small handsome evergreen tree. Leaves 4–8 in. long, 2½–5 in. broad, ovate, with a broad or almost cordate base, acute or acuminate; petiole 2–3 in. long. Flowers 2 in. diam., white or pink. Capsule clothed with long stiff prickles.

A native of America, widely cultivated in India and introduced to the Settlement. Fl. Aug.-Sept. The pulp which surrounds the seeds gives the well-known dye, used for dyeing silk and for colouring cheese, butter, or other edibles. Its leaves resemble those of *Hibiscus*, and it has the fruit of a *Buettneria*.

The following are native :—

Leaves palminerved, usually crenate; stamens numerous ... 1. Scolopia.
Leaves penninerved, entire.
Petioles long, thickened at the apex; filaments united; anthers 5 ... 2. Ryparosa.
Petioles short, base of leaves one-sided; stamens 15, free; petals scaled ... ... 3. Hydnocarpus.

1. SCOLOPIA.

36. **S. crenata**, *Clos.*; H. i. 190; Br. 39.

A moderate-sized tree, sometimes attaining a height of 70 feet and a girth of 5 feet, thorny while young: bark grey, cut dark red. Leaves 2—5 in. long, 1—2½ in. broad, ovate or ovate-oblong, acute, more or less rounded at the base, with 3—5 basal nerves and glands at the insertion of the petiole, glabrous, glandular-crenate to almost entire, venation lax and fine; petiole ⅛—⅜ in. long. Flowers white, in axillary or terminal racemes, ¼ in. diam.; stamens numerous, with yellow glands outside them. Fr. globose, ⅜ in. diam.

Not common. Middle Andaman, Mt. Baker, Rongat Bay, Bomlungta; South Andaman, Wimberleygunj; Rutland Island; South Cinque Island. Fl. H. S. A very variable plant.

2. RYPAROSA.

37. **R. Kurzii**, *King*; Br. 41; J.A.S.B. No. 2. 1890, p. 125.

A small tree (15—25×1—2) with a brownish-grey bark, cut mealy, with fine dark-brown streaks. Leaves 8—12 in. long, 4—6 in. broad, broadly elliptic to elliptic-oblong, shortly and bluntly acuminate, entire, dark green above, glaucous beneath, with 6—8 pairs of lateral nerves; petioles up to 2 in. long, thickened at the insertion of the blade. Flowers small, yellowish, in slender racemes 8—12 in. long, from the axils of the leaves or the scars of the fallen ones. Fruit globose.

Uncommon. Yeratilajig, Bomlungta, South Andaman; usually along streams in evergreen forests. A rare and interesting plant found only in the Andamans and Nicobars. Fl. Febr.-April. Fr. April.

3. HYDNOCARPUS.

38. **H. castanea**, *Hook. fil.*; H. i. 197; Br. 42.

A moderate-sized tree (25—40×2—4) with a grey, discoloured bark, cut pale yellowish. Leaves standing out at right angles to the branchlets, on stout petioles, 6—12 in. long, 2—4 in. broad, oblong to oblanceolate, shortly and bluntly acuminate, the base very one-sided, glabrous and coriaceous, with few irregular ascending lateral nerves. Flowers nearly

½ in. diam., greenish-white, fragrant, in fascicles from the scars of the fallen leaves. Fruit ovoid, ½ in. long, covered with a yellow velvety tomentum.

Frequent in the Islands and seen in nearly every locality in evergreen forests. Fl. Nov.-Jan. Fr. Febr.-April. It has the commonplace appearance that many of the plants of the *Euphorbiaceæ* have.

Fam. 8. POLYGALACEÆ.

Leaves simple, alternate, without stipules. Flowers irregular; petals 5; stamens 8.

1. XANTHOPHYLLUM.

* 39. **X. andamanicum**, *King*; Br. 44; J.A.S.B. No. 2. 1890, p. 135. Vern. *Letpyaw.*

A moderate sized tree (40—70 × 3—9) with a dense crown; bark pale grey, smooth, cut mealy, yellowish-brown; branchlets black. Leaves 3—4½ in. long, 1—1½ in. broad, elliptic to ovate or lanceolate, glabrous, dark green above, glaucous beneath, lateral nerves irregular, not much more prominent than the reticulate venation, margins entire and recurved. Flowers nearly ½ in. long, in lax small panicles; petals 5, white with a rose flush, 2 reflexed and dashed with yellow, 2 spreading and the lower keeled and to which 2 of the 8 stamens are attached. Fruit ½ in. diam.

A very common evergreen tree met with in evergreen forest in all localities. Fl. Febr.-March. Fr. April-May.

The leaves are not very unlike those of the *Gangaw*, but they are alternately disposed. The flowers have the superficial appearance of those of the Pea Family.

Fam. 9. HYPERICACEÆ.

Decidious trees with yellowish juice, and opposite gland-dotted leaves without stipules. Flowers with 5 imbricate sepals, and 5 twisted, clawed petals; stamens many, in 3 groups, with a bright red shining gland between each group. Fruit a capsule with small winged seeds.

1. CRATOXYLON.

* 40. **C. formosum**, *Benth. and Hook. fil.* H. i. 258; Br. 48.

A moderate-sized, straight-stemmed tree (50—80 × 2½—3), with a thin, yellowish-brown bark, peeling in small, thin, irregular flakes cut reddish, with a clear yellow juice and a strong pleasant smell like that of the mango. Leaves 3—4 in. long, broadly elliptic to oblong, glabrous, lateral nerves interarching, petiole ⅓—½ in. long. Flowers from the leafless branchlets, ¾ in. long, pretty; calyx reddish; petals pure white, fringed. Capsule torpedo-shaped, ¾ in. long.

Frequent in deciduous forests in all localities and very common on the high dry hills of the Middle Andaman and Rutland Island. Deciduous in the H. S., and flowering when the tree is leafless at the end of the H. S. Fr. ripe, Aug.-Nov. When leafless it is poor-looking and much resembles a young *Padouk* tree, but when in full blossom it is a splendid sight, its numerous white blossoms making it conspicuous, even from a long distance.

* **C. polyanthum**, *Korth.*, is said to be a native of the Andamans but, I believe, is not found here. The only specimens are of Helfer's collections, and these are very probably from Tenasserim, where it is rather frequent.

Fam. 10. GUTTIFERÆ.

THE MANGOSTEEN FAMILY.

Evergreen trees with yellowish juice, and simple, opposite, glabrous, exstipulate leaves. Flowers white or yellowish, unisexual or bisexual; sepals and petals usually 4 or 5, (the latter absent in *Calophyllum spectabile* and *amœnum*); stamens many, closely packed. Fruit a berry.

A family of some importance to the Forester, and to which belong some of the most beautiful trees of the Andaman forests, a few of them yielding fine timber.

Lateral nerves of leaves numerous fine, close, distinct and evenly parallel ... ... 1. Calophyllum.
Lateral nerves of leaves numerous and fine but indistinct. Leaves glaucous beneath ... ... 2. Mesua.
Lateral nerves few or many, but indistinct, uneven, and often distant
  Flowers bisexual ... ... 3. Kayea.
  Flowers polygamous ... ... 4. Garcinia.

1. CALOPHYLLUM.

Leaves glossy and coriaceous, finely veined, the lateral nerves numerous, closely and evenly parallel. Flowers white, in panicles; sepals and petals imbricated, the former often petaloid, and the latter sometimes wanting. Fruit a berry with a hard rind.

Leaves 5—12 in. long.
  Littoral. Petals 4 ... ... C. Inophyllum.
  Inland. Petals none ... ... C. spectabile.
Leaves 2—4 in. long ... ... C. amoenum.

*41. **C. Inophyllum,** *Linn.*; H. i. 273; Br. 53. *The Alexandrian Laurel.* Vern. *Pónyet*, Burm.

A shady littoral tree (50—60 × 6—14), with dark green shining foliage and usually with stout, low, crooked branches leaning towards the sea; bark dark coloured, rough with deep furrows; cut dark reddish, then pink, finely streaked. Leaves 5—9 in. long, elliptic to ovate or obovate, acute at the base, apex more or less rounded; petiole ¾ in. long. Flowers very handsome and delightfully fragrant, 1 in. diam., on slender pedicels. Fruit globular, smooth and greenish, about an inch in diam.

Very common. Found growing at the water's edge along the seashores; never found inland. Fl. profusely during the R. S., and to a smaller extent at other times of the year. Fr. June-Aug. The berries are as perfectly spherical as one can imagine. There are two small trees on Ross Island near the road along the sea-wall, below the Catholic Chapel.

The wood, which is known as *Borneo Mahogany*, is said to be used for masts and spars, but, I think, it grows too crooked for this purpose; that of the next one would be more suitable. Kurz in his Andaman Report writes: "One tree measured at South Corbyn's Cove of 50 feet clear stem, by a girth of 22 feet 2 inches." The seeds yield oil.

*42. **C. spectabile,** *Willd.*; H. i. 271; Br. 55. *The Nicobar Canoe Tree.* Vern. *Lalchini*, Hind.

A straight-stemmed tree (60—80 × 4—7), bark yellowish, usually with fine longitudinal fissures, cut pink, turning brown. Leaves 7—12 in. long, 1½—3 in. broad, narrowly to broadly oblong, seldom elliptic, pale below with beautiful venation; petiole ½—¾ in. long. Flowers rather small, on slender pedicels in axillary umbelliform racemes; sepals white; stamens bright yellow. Fruit greenish, ovoid, ¾ in. diam.

Frequent, especially in low, damp, evergreen forest and on the high evergreen hills; also along the sea in brackish places with *Barringtonia racemosa* and *Myristica Irya.* In all localities. Fl. May. Fr. Jan.

Wood reddish, suitable for planking and for masts and spars. The vernacular name given above is not very reliable; neither is the one, *Tharapee*, sometimes used by Burmans.

43. **C. amœnum,** *Wall*; Br. 55; Kz. i. 95.

A straight-stemmed tree (40—60 × 3—4), with smooth yellowish bark, cut brownish, young branchlets, petioles, inflorescence and petals rusty pubescent. Leaves 2—4 in. long, ¾—1¼ in. broad, elliptic to oblong-lanceolate, acute, tapering at the base. Flowers ¾ in. diam., in few-flowered racemes. Berry ½ in. long, ovoid-globose.

Rather uncommon. In evergreen forests on hills. Middle Andaman, on the high hills along the east coast; South Andaman. Fr. Dec. It has the general appearance of the preceding one, but is smaller in all its parts. New leaves pinkish-yellow, appearing in December.

2. MESUA.

44. M. ferrea, *Linn.*; H. i. 277; Br. 55. Vern. *Gangaw*, Burm.

A moderate-sized or large tree (50—60 × 6—7), with a thin greyish-brown bark, often with white patches and peeling in flakes; cut pinkish-brown. Leaves 3—6 in. long, oblong to linear-lanceolate, dark green and glossy above, the undersurface covered with a whitish powder, rigidly coriaceous, lateral nerves numerous but indistinct; petioles up to ⅓ in. long. Flowers large, solitary or in pairs, silvery-white with bright yellow anthers.

Evergreen forests, especially on hills. Frequent on Mt. Baker and the other high hills of the Middle Andaman, but not growing to a very large size; also on Baratang and the South Andaman and on Rutland Island. Fl. Jan.-Mar. Fr. May-June. New leaves pink and crimson. There are several trees on Ross Island along the road leading from the Library to the British Infantry barracks below Government House.

The wood is dark reddish-brown, very hard, heavy and strong. It is called by some writers the *Ironwood*, but the *True Ironwood* is a *Sideroxylon*, and the *Ironwood of Malabar* is *Hopea parviflora*. The wood is extensively used in Assam for railway sleepers.

3. KAYEA.

45. *K. Manii, *King*; Br. 56.

A glabrous tree, the young branches slender and polished. Leaves 4—5 in. long, 1—1½ in. broad, narrowly oblong and tapering to each end, acuminate, lateral nerves about 15 pairs, slightly prominent and curved; petiole short. Flowers nearly ½ in. diam. on slender ½ in. pedicels, in fasciculate racemes; petals 4 concave; stamens many, longer than the petals. Fruit (unripe) compressed and enveloped in the accrescent sepals.

Evidently rare. Collected only at North Bay. Fl. Jan.

4. GARCINIA.

Medium-sized, straight-stemmed trees with dark green foliage. Leaves coriaceous with indistinct venation. Flowers usually yellowish or greenish-white; sepals and petals 4 to 5, with numerous stamens collected in a central mass. Fruit a berry with many seeds.

46. **G. Mangostana,** *Linn.*, *The Mangosteen.* Vern. *Mingut*, Burm., is cultivated in the Haddo gardens. It is a handsome tree with foliage resembling that of *G. speciosa*, and with a globose dark purple fruit with snow-white delicious edible pulp. It is extensively grown in the Malay Peninsula and in Tenasserim, and its original home is said to be unknown.

The rest given here are native:—

Leaves 8 in. or more in length. Sepals and petals 5.
L. narrowly oblong to oblong-lanceolate Fr. 2—2½ in. diam. ... ... G. Xanthochymus.

L. elongate-ovate from a broad base. Fr. 1—1½ in. diam. ... ... G. andamanica.
Leaves not more than 6 in. long. Sepals and petals 4.
Branchlets 4 angular.
L. 4-6 in long. Fl. ½ in. diam. in few-fld. cymes. Fr. yellow, the size of a lime, shallowly grooved ... G. Cowa.
L. 4-6 in. long. Fl. ¾—1 in. diam., 4-5 fasciculate. Fr. 2 in. diam., red ... ... G. speciosa.
L. 3-4 in. long. Fl. reddish, ½ in. diam., Fr. 1-1½ in. diam., reddish ... ... G. microstigma.
Branchlets more or less rounded.
L. lanceolate Fl. ½ in. diam., in umbels. Fr. with 6-8 grooves .. .. G. Kydia.
L. elliptic to elliptic-oblong. Fl. ½ in. diam. ... G. Cadelliana.

• 47. **G. Xanthochymus**, *Hook. fil.*; H. i. 269; Br. 49. Vern. *Madaw*, Burm.

A handsome tree (30—50 × 3—5) with greenish, angled, branchlets; bark dark coloured, cut yellowish. Leaves 8—16 in. long, 1¾—4 in. broad, narrowly oblong to oblong-lanceolate, acute or rounded at the base and apex, thick; petioles ¾—1 in. long, strong. Flowers ½—¾ in. diam., greenish-white, in axillary fascicles or from the scars of the fallen leaves. Fruit globose, 2—2½ in. diam., dark yellow when ripe.

Fairly frequent in evergreen forests and found in nearly all localities. Fl. Febr.-March. Fr. Nov.-Jan. The young leaves are greenish-white or almost white and come out in the month of February. The acid fruit is eaten.

• 48. **G. andamanica**, *King*; Br. 49; Vern. *Madaw*, Burm.

A tree (20—40 × 2—4), much resembling the last, bark yellowish-green, cut mealy. Leaves 8—14 in. long, 4—7 in. broad, elongate-ovate from a broad base, petiole ½—1½ in. long. Flowers greenish-white, ¼—½ in. diam., in fascicles from the leaf axils or from the scars of the fallen ones. Fruit 1½ in. diam., globular, bright yellow.

As frequent as the preceding one and also found in evergreen forests especially in damp places or near streams. Middle and South Andaman; Baratang; Long and Havelock Islands; Rutland Island. Fl. Jan.-March. Best distinguished from the last one by the shape of its leaves.

• 49. **G. Cowa**, *Roxb.*; H. i. 262; Br. 52. *The Cowa Fruit* or *The Cowa Mangosteen*. Vern. *Taungthalè*, Burm.; *Kataphal*, Hind.

A slender tall tree (40—70 × 3—5), with a thin, slightly rough, blackish bark; cut red, turning brown. Leaves 4—6 in. long, 1½—2½ in. broad, broadly lanceolate, shortly acuminate, acute at the base, glabrous and glossy above, lateral nerves numerous but indistinct, petiole ¼ in. long. Flowers yellow, waxy and polished, ½ in. diam., in few-flowered axillary cymes; petals thick, rounded, erect and slightly inflexed. Fruit depressed globular with shallow grooves, the size of a lime, smooth and yellow when ripe.

Rather frequent in evergreen and semi-evergreen forests; found in all localities. Fl. Jan.-Febr. Fr. May-June. The acid fruit is eaten and is pleasant to the taste, but is full of a yellow juice which sticks to the teeth and gives one an uncomfortable feeling in the mouth. The young leaves are cooked and eaten as a vegetable by Burmans.

* 50. **G. speciosa**, *Wall.*; H. i. 260; Br. 50. Vern. *Parawa*, Burm.

A pretty tree (30—50 × 3—5) with a dark greenish bark peeling in flakes which leave small yellowish-brown patches, cut dark reddish. Leaves 4—6 in. long, 1¼—2½ broad, ovate to elliptic or lanceolate, blunt acuminate, lateral nerves many but faint; petiole ¾—1 in. long. Flowers ¾—1 in. diam., yellow, usually 4—5 fasciculate, axillary or between the terminal pair of leaves. Fruit 2 in. diam., bright red when ripe.

Frequent in evergreen and semi-evergreen forests and dispersed throughout the islands. Fl. profusely Jan.-March. Fr. R. S.

Under this is included *G. Kurzii*, *Pierre* and *G. Kingii*, *Pierre*, both nearly allied. (Br. 50).

51. **G. microstigma**, *Kurz*; Br. 52.

A small tree (15—25 × 1—2) with a dark-coloured bark, cut reddish-brown. Leaves 3—4 in. long, 1½—2 in. broad, elliptic to obovate or lanceolate, acute, glossy, with many indistinct lateral nerves. Flowers ½ in. diam., reddish, axillary and single. Fruit globular, slightly depressed, 1—1½ in. diam., glossy and dark-red when ripe.

Rather uncommon. Middle Andaman, Betapur, Bomlungta, and north of Bongat Bay near Mt. Farrington, also on the South Andaman. The fruit is edible, and the young leaves are cooked and eaten as a vegetable by Burmans, who sometimes give it the name of *Taung-thale-ome*.

52. ***G. Kydia**, *Roxb.*; Kz. i. 90.

A slender tree 25—40 feet high with dark-coloured young branchlets. Leaves 3—5 in. long, ¾—1½ in. broad, lanceolate, acuminate to a fine point, acute at the base, glossy on both surfaces with rather few lateral nerves; petiole up to ½ in. long. Flowers ¾ in. diam., the males shortly stalked and in umbels, the females sessile and solitary. Fruit globular—depressed with 6—8 grooves near the apex and a small protuberance, yellow and glossy when ripe.

Uncommon. South Andaman, Wimberleygunj and Mt. Harriet. Fl. Jan.

53. ***G. Cadelliana**, *King*; J. A. S. B. No. 2. 1890, p. 154.

A tree about 30 feet high; young branchlets polished and brownish-yellow when dry. Leaves 3½—5½ in. long, 1½—2½ in. broad, elliptic to elliptic oblong with a cuneate base, thinly coriaceous and shining, with 10—12 pairs of lateral nerves interarching near the margin. Flowers ½ in. diam., in dense axillary fascicles. Female flowers and fruit unknown.

South Andaman. Evidently rare.

Fam. 11. TERNSTRŒMIACEÆ.

THE TEA FAMILY.

Evergreen. Leaves simple, alternate, turning dark-brown in drying, and without stipules. Flowers white, showy; sepals and petals 5, the latter joined at the base; stamens numerous. Fruit a berry.

To this Family belongs *Camellia Thea, Link. The Tea Plant,* Vern. *Letpet*, Burm.; *Chae.* Hind. Introduced and cultivated in Port Blair.

1. TERNSTRŒMIA.

• 54. **T. penangiana,** *Choisy*; H. i. 281; Br. 57.

A small or moderate-sized shady tree (30—50 × 2—4) with a dark-coloured bark; cut mealy, reddish-brown. Leaves 3½—6 in. long, 1½—2½ in. broad, obovate to oblanceolate, tapering at the base, margin entire and slightly recurved, dark green, drying brown; lateral nerves few and rather obscure. Flowers solitary, about 1 in. diam., creamy-white turning dark-brown in withering; petals waxy with denticulate margins. Berries globose, smooth, 1—1½ in. diam., bright orange-coloured with a thickened wrinkled calyx.

Not uncommon. Usually in evergreen forests. Middle and South Andaman, Long Island. Fl. Dec.-Febr. Fr. Jan.-May. The fruits resemble large apricots.

Fam. 12. DIPTEROCARPACEÆ.

Large resiniferous trees with simple, alternate, penninerved leaves, often bearing large stipules. Flowers usually showy; calyx with 5 lobes, 2 of them lengthening in fruit into linear veined wings; petals 5, twisted and overlapping to the left; stamens many, prolonged at the top into a fine bristle. Nut enclosed in the calyx.

In the Andamans this is an important family to the Forester, all the members here mentioned being timber-yielding trees, some of them being among the largest in the islands. They also yield useful resins.

Stipules large, stem-elasping and enclosing the terminal bud and leaving a large scar when falling. Fl. large, showy	1. Dipterocarpus.
Stipules minute. Petioles rather slender. Fl. rather small	2. Hopea.

1. DIPTEROCARPUS.

Leaf-shedding trees. Stipules large, dropping off early. Leaves coriaceous with conspicuously undulate margins and bold, rather straight lateral nerves. Flowers large, white and pink; corolla funnel-shaped; fruiting calyx enclosing the nut, smooth or with lateral wings, 2 of the lobes enlarging into linear reticulately-veined wings.

The vernacular names *Gurjan* and *Kanyin* are indiscriminately applied to the *Dipterocarps* in the Andamans, and those corresponding to the large-leaf and small-leaf gurjans are very unreliable and must be accepted with caution when used to determine the species. Illustrations, which are all one-third natural size, of the five Andaman *Dipterocarps* here described, will be found near the end of this book.

The leaves of seedlings or of young plants are often very different to those of older or mature plants, the former usually being narrower and longer and more hairy. In the analysis of the species given in this book, the leaves of mature plants only have been used.

- Leaves perfectly glabrous.
  - Fruiting calyx with 5 lateral wings or ribs ... D. Griffithii.
  - Fruiting calyx smooth and globular, without lateral wings or ribs.
    - Leaves 5—10 in. long ... ... D. turbinatus.
    - Leaves 3—6 in. long ... ... D. Kerrii.
- Leaves stellate-pubescent on the under-surface. Calyx with 5 lateral wings or ribs.
  - L. 5—9 in. long. Fr. 1 in. long, with terminal wings 6 in. long ... ... D. incanus.
  - L. 2½—5 in. long. Fr. ¾ in. long, with terminal wings 3 in. long ... ... D. costatus.

• 55. **D. Griffithii,** *Miq.*; H. i. 290: Br. 701. *The Large leaf Gurjan.*

A large tree (90—140 × 9—15) with a grey bark peeling in flakes. Leaf buds ovoid, pointed, covered with tawny shining hairs. Leaves 5—11 in. long, 3—5½ in. broad, broadly ovate, rounded at the base and small cordate at the insertion of the petiole, acute, margins undulate, thickly coriaceous, lateral nerves 12—18 pairs forming an angle of about 50—60 degrees with the midrib; petiole 3—4 in. long, stout and shallowly grooved. Flowers 2—2½ in. diam., handsome, petals 2 in. long, white with dark crimson down the centre. Fruit 2—2½ in. long, with oblanceolate wings about 8 in. long and 1½ in. broad, 3-nerved nearly the whole length.

Frequent in evergreen forest especially on evergreen hills and seen in all localities. It sheds its leaves in Dec.-Jan. and is leafless for a short while just before the new leaves and flowers come out. Fl. Jan.-Febr. Fr. April-June. It is unmistakable for it has the largest stipules, leaves, flowers and fruits of all the Andaman species of this genus. The timber is often used.

• 56. **D. turbinatus,** *Gærtn. f.* var. **andamanica,** *King*; Br. 65.

A large tree (80—120 × 6—12) with a grey bark. Leaves 5—10 in. long, 3—5 in. broad, broadly elliptic to ovate, acute or shortly acuminate, rounded at the base, entire or slightly undulate, thinly coriaceous, lateral nerves 12—18 pairs making an angle of 35—40 degrees with the midrib; petiole smooth, 1—2 in. long. Flowers very handsome, 1½—2 in. diam., calyx obconic, ¾ in. long; petals 1½ in. long, white and scarlet in the upper portion. Fruit globular, the nut barely ¾ in. diam., the wings linear-oblong, 4—6 in. long and ¾ in. broad.

Common in evergreen forests both in the valleys and on the hills, and usually found associated with all the others of this genus except *D. costatus*. It is leafless for a short while in December and the new leaves and flowers come out in Jan.-March. Fr. May-July. Under this is included *D. laevis, Ham.*

57. **D. Kerrii,** *King* ; J. A. S. B. No. 2. 1893, p. 93.

A large tree (80—120 × 6—12) with a dark grey bark which peels in flakes; branchlets dark-coloured, thin and smooth. Leaves 3—6 in. long, 1½ - 3 in. broad, elliptic to elliptic or ovate-lanceolate, blunt to shortly acuminate, base obtuse or rounded, margins undulate, thinly coriaceous, lateral nerves 12 - 16 pairs, forming an angle of 35—40 degrees with the midrib; petiole 1—1½ in long. Flowers resembling, but smaller than, those of the preceding one. Fruit globular, 1—1½ in. diam., the wings 4—6 in. long and 1½ in. broad, oblong-lanceolate, 3-nerved nearly the whole length.

South Andaman. Seen only in the Goplakabaung valley, where a sample plot of it has been made. It will probably also be found further in the interior on the Cholunga Range. It resembles the preceding one but has much smaller leaves and its fruiting nut is much larger. The wood is said to be harder than that of the other *Gurjans* and it is also said to yield more oil. It flowers later than the others.

58. **D. incanus,** *Roxb.*; H. i. 298; Br. 66.

A very large and magnificent tree (110—140 × 8—18), with a straight cylindrical bole and a large crown with stout, fantastically curving branches. Leaves 5—9 in. long, 2¾—5 in. broad, ovate or broadly so, acute or blunt, with a rounded base, margins slightly undulate, coriaceous, lateral nerves 10—15 pairs making an angle of about 45 degrees with the midrib, both surfaces, or only the lower, softly stellate-pubescent. Flowers nearly 1 in. diam., petals 1 in. long, white or yellowish-white, with a light crimson streak down the centre. Fruit about 1 in. long, with broad lateral ribs, the terminal wings 6 in. long and 1 in. broad.

This noble tree is perhaps the largest of all the trees of these magnificent forests. It is found in deciduous forests and in evergreen along the large streams where it may be seen growing at its best, and where it attains its greatest girth and height. Leafless for a short time in November or December. Fl. Jan.-March. It is sometimes confused with *D. Griffithii*, and is the only kind of *Gurjan* I have seen growing on Long Island.

59. **D. costatus,** Gærtn. fil.; H. i. 298; Br. 66.

A large tree (80—100 × 6—10) with a rather rough dark grey bark; buds silky pubescent. Leaves 2½—5 in. long, 1¾—3½ in. broad, ovate to elliptic, and often broadly so, acute to shortly acuminate, base rounded, entire or slightly sinuate, lateral nerves 10—14 pairs making an angle of about 45 degrees with the midrib, softly stellate-pubescent beneath especially on the nerves and reticulations. Flowers ¾ in. diam., much like, but smaller than, those of the former. Fruit about ½ in. long, the terminal wings 3 in. long and ½ in. wide.

Not very common. Middle Andaman on the high hills in the east, and on Mt. Ford. The best trees were seen on the western slopes of Mt. Ford near Woodmason Bay; those on the hills of the Middle Andaman are not of a very large size. Fl. Febr.-April. Fr. R. S.

Some other species of this Genus, such as *D. obtusifolius*, *alatus* and *pilosus*, have been said to be found in the Andamans, but of these I have seen no Andaman specimens, and I am of the opinion that they are not found in the islands.

2. HOPEA.

Stipules inconspicuous. Flowers rather small, in one-sided racemes.

A large tree. Leaves 4—6 in. long, green on the under-surface ... ... H. odorata.
A moderate-sized tree. Leaves 5—7 in. long, silvery-white on the under-surface ... ... H. sp.

▲ 60. **H. odorata**, *Roxb.*; H. i. 308; Br. 67. *The White Thingan.* Vern. *Thingan*, *Safed Thingan*, Burm. and Hind.

A large evergreen tree (100—130 × 7—14) with a dark-coloured bark cracked lengthwise; cut pale yellowish-white; branchlets slender, polished. Leaves 4—6 in. long, 1½—2 in. broad, ovate-oblong to oblong-lanceolate, bluntish-acuminate, base obtuse and unequal, margins entire and wavy folded, lateral nerves 9-12 pairs, distinct but not very prominent; petiole ⅜ in., slender. Flowers rather small, fragrant, yellowish-white, in one-sided racemes. Fruit small, wings oblanceolate, rounded, 1½ in. long, finely veined lengthwise.

Not very common, but dispersed in nearly all localities. Fl. Febr.-March. Fr. at the beginning of the R. S.

Wood yellowish or yellowish-brown, fairly hard, with a close even grain. It is used for planking and for house-posts and is said to be immune from attack by white ants. In Burma it is much used for making dug-out canoes. It yields the *Rock Dammar of Commerce*.

61. **H. sp.**

A moderate-sized tree attaining about 40 feet. Leaves 5—7 in. long, 1¼—2 in. broad, oblong or ovate-lanceolate, acute or blunt and more or less rounded at the base, glabrous, silvery-white beneath, lateral nerves 14—18 pairs; petiole ½—¾ in. long. Flowers small, in unilateral axillary panicled racemes; stamens 15, in 3 rows. Fruit the size of a pea, the wings veined, oblanceolate, 1⅓—2 in. long.

Rare. Flowering specimens were collected by King's collectors in 1884 and 1892, and some of these in the Calcutta Herbarium bear, in Sir George King's handwriting, I think, the name *Hopea andamanica*. In 1916 fruiting specimens were obtained on the high hills north of Rongat Bay.

Fam. 13. ANCISTROCLADACEÆ.

Evergreen woody climbers with strong hooked branchlets. Leaves elegant, nearly sessile, collected in tufts, penninerved. Flowers white or pink, in lax panicles; petals twisted; stamens 5-10. Fruit with 5 unequal wings.

1. ANCISTROCLADUS.

Characters as above.

Leaves not more than 12 in. long	A. extensus.
Leaves 12 in. or more in length	A. attenuatus.

62. **A. extensus**, *Wall.*; H. i. 299; Br. 73.

A climber with twisted dark-coloured stems and often with circinately hooked branchlets. Leaves tufted, 5—12 in. long, 1½—3 in. broad, obovate to oblanceolate, apex rounded, base attenuate, glabrous, dark green, lateral veins joined intramarginally, reticulate venation fine and distinct. Flowers barely ¼ in. diam., pink and white; lobes of fruiting calyx three 1½—1¾ in. long, and two shorter.

A very common climber in evergreen forests and easily recognised by its handsome, dark green, tufted leaves. Fl. Jan.-March. Fr. March-May. The wood of the stems is hard and is used by the Andamanese for making pig arrows. The fruits are easily confused with those of *Hiptage Madablota*.

63. **A. attenuatus**, *Dyer*; H. i. 300; Br. 74.

A climber much like the preceding one, but with larger and narrower leaves 12—15 in. long, 1½—1¾ in. broad, oblanceolate. Lobes of fruiting calyx unequal, 2 enlarged about ⅝ in. long, and the rest about half as long.

In the same localities as the preceding one.

Fam. 14. MALVACEÆ.

THE HIBISCUS AND COTTON TREE FAMILY.

Trees, shrubs, or climbers, usually with soft wood and a fibrous bark, the younger parts clothed with stellate hairs. Leaves alternate, stipulate, simple or digitately compound, often lobed. Flowers large and showy, white, yellow or red, the petals twisted; stamens usually many, joined in a tube through which passes the style. Fruit a dehiscent capsule.

A family of some importance to the Forester. *Bombax insigne* is one of the largest timber trees of the islands and the others are also of interest. All may be recognised by their conspicuous flowers.

Leaves simple.
- L. lobed, serrate or crenate. Fl. with an involucre of bracteoles; styles 5. Capsule opening by valves ... 1. Hibiscus.
- L. entire. Fl. without bracteoles; style entire. Capsule hardly opening ... ... 2. Thespesia.

Leaves digitately compound.
Flowers creamy-white; stamens 5 ... ... 2. Eriodendron.
Flowers reddish; stamens many ... ... 3. Bombax.

Durio zibethinus, *Linn.*, *The Doorian* or *Civet-cat Fruit*; Vern. *Duyin*, Burm.; has been introduced to Port Blair. It is a native of the Malay Archipelago. The fruit is said to be the most delicious in the world, but it has an odour "which the unsophisticated European arriving in the country, would ascribe to the unsanitary condition of the drains."

1. HIBISCUS.

Leaves palminerved, more or less serrate or lobed. Flowers large and showy, white, yellow or reddish; calyx supported by a whorl of persistent bracteoles; staminal tube slender and long; styles 5. Capsule 5-valved.

A littoral tree. Leaves orbicular, crenulate ... ... H. tiliaceus.
A shrub with stiff harsh hairs. Leaves orbicular, 5-lobed ... H. Abelmoschus.
A climber. Leaves orbicular, shallowly lobed .. ... H. scandens.

• 64. **H. tiliaceus**, *Linn.*; H. i. 343; Br. 75. *The Coast Cotton Tree*, or *Yellow Mallow tree*. Vern. *Thinban*, Burm.; *Safed Chilka*, Hind.

A small much-branched tree (15—30 × 1—3), with a thin grey fibrous bark. Leaves 3—8 in. diam., nearly orbicular, deeply cordate, acute or shortly acuminate, margin usually crenulate, almost smooth above, pale and pubescent beneath; petiole 1—5 in. long, slender. Flowers 2—3 in. diam., bell-shaped, yellow with a crimson or purple centre. Capsule $\frac{3}{4}$ in. long.

A purely littoral tree exceedingly common along the seashores, characteristic of the vegetation along the sandy beaches and often fringing them at high-water mark. Fl. and Fr. all the year round. The flowers towards evening, or when withering, turn brick-red. It yields a strong, white, useful fibre, used for making ropes and elephant gear for dragging timber.

65. **H. Abelmoschus**, *Linn.*; H. i. 384. *The Musk Mallow.*

A shrub 6—8 feet high, the branchlets, leaves and other parts covered with stiff hairs. Leaves about 5 in. long and 8 in. broad, orbicular, about 5 lobed, the margins coarsely serrate, base cordate, petioles 2—6 in. long. Flowers 3—4 in. diam., light yellow with a dark purple centre. Capsule 2 in. long.

Middle and South Andaman; Long Island and Baratang. Usually along tidal streams where the fresh and sea-water meet. Fl. and Fr. Nov.-Dec.

66. **H. scandens** *Roxb.*; H. i. 377. *The Climbing Hibiscus.*

Scandent. Leaves about 6 in. across, orbicular with shallow lobes, deeply cordate, pubescent; petioles 2—4 in. long. Flowers $\frac{3}{4}$—1 in.

across, handsome, in terminal panicles, yellow with a large deep purple centre.

Middle and South Andaman; Havelock and Rutland Islands. Fairly frequent and often found among vegetation along streams. Fl. Febr.-April.

The following have been introduced and are grown as garden plants for the beauty of their flowers or for culinary purposes:—

H. Rosa sinensis, *Linn.* *The Shoe Flower* or *Chinese Shoe Plant*, so called because the flowers were at one time used to black shoes. Corolla large, scarlet or crimson. Native country unknown, believed to be China or Japan.

H. schizopetalus, *Hook fil.* A shrub resembling the former. Flowers dark pink or pale scarlet, drooping, on slender stalks, with a long style and reflexed fringed petals. It is a native of Zanzibar, and is, I think, more common in Port Blair than the preceding one.

H. mutabilis, *Linn.* *The Changeable Rose.* Corolla 3—4 in. across, white or pink in the morning and turning reddish before night. Not so common as the two preceding.

H esculentus, *Linn.* *The Lady's Finger* or the *Vegetable Bhendi*. Cultivated for the unripe fruits which possess valuable demulcent properties.

H. Sabdariffa, *Linn.* *The Roselle*, or *Indian Sorrel*; *The Red Sorrel* of the West Indies. Stem and branches purple. Flowers yellow or purple, with a dark centre. A jelly is made from the red succulent calyces.

The next, a native of the Islands, also deserves mention.

Urena lobata, *Linn.* Vern. *Katshiwin* Burm. A lowly herbaceous shrub, with variably lobed leaves but delicate pink funnel-shaped flowers about 1 in. diam. It may be seen thriving in waste places in Port Blair, and is also found in the forests in open places among shrubbery.

2. THESPESIA.

* 67. **T. populnea**, *Correa.*; H. i. 345; Br. 75. *The Indian Tulip* or *Portia Tree.*

A small or moderate-sized tree (20—40 × 2—4) with a furrowed bark. Leaves 3—6 in. long, cordate, almost triangular with the lower corners rounded off, acuminate, entire, glabrous and with minute round scales; petiole 1—4 in. long, slender. Flowers large and handsome; calyx cup-shaped, truncate; corolla yellow with a purple centre. Capsule 1—1½ in. diam., depressed, with 4 blunt ridges above, full of a pale yellow juice when green.

Very common along the seashores and never naturally found growing inland. The flowers resemble those of *Hibiscus tiliaceus*, and like them turn purplish or brick-coloured when withering, but the styles are entire in this one and 5 branched in the other. The wood, which is known as the *Seychelles Rosewood*, unlike that of other trees of this Family, is hard, dark reddish-brown and beautifully streaked. It is sometimes called the *Umbrella Tree.*

68. **Eriodendron anfractuosum**, *DC.*; Br. 76. *The Kapok Floss* or *White Cotton Tree.* Vern. *Thinbaw-letpan*, Burm.

A small or moderate-sized tree with a pale grey bark, armed with conical prickles. Leaves digitate: leaflets 5—9, 3—4 in. long, lanceolate and glaucescent beneath. Flowers 1—1½ in. long, dirty-white; petals silky tomentose externally; stamens 5. Pod. 3—5 in. long.

This, according to Brandis, is indigenous on the Andamans, and Kurz writes, "a single tree observed wild in the forests of Macpherson Strait." The locality referred to is probably Chiriatapu, where it may have been planted in old forest camps. It may be seen in Port Blair but not in the forests beyond. I am of the opinion, as Burmans who have worked for many years in these forests also are, that it is not a native of the islands.

3. BOMBAX.

• 69. **B. insigne**, *Wall.*; H. i. 349; Br. 77. *The Silk Cotton Tree.* Vern. *Didu*, Burm.; *Simal*, Hind.

A large deciduous tree (60—120 × 5—16) with huge butresses and a thick dark grey furrowed bark, the branchlets armed with conical prickles. Leaves digitately 5—9 foliolate, on common petioles up to a foot long; leaflets 5—8 in. long, obovate to oblanceolate, glaucous beneath. Flowers 4—6 in. long, solitary; calyx 1½ in. long, silky inside; petals deep red; stamens very many, the filaments united into 4 or 5 groups. Capsule up to 10 in. long and 2 in. diam.

There are two varieties :—

Var. andamanica, *Prain*. *The Short Pod Didu*, which has flowers about 6 in. long and pods 6—8 in. long.

Var. Wightii, *Prain*. *The Long Pod Didu*, which has flowers about 4 in. long and pods up to 10 in. long.

The latter is, I believe, confined to the seashores and does not grow to such a large size as the former, which is usually found in the interior forests and sometimes also near the seashores. This is one of the largest trees of the islands, and owing to its flowers, fruits, and leaves appearing at different times of the year, complete and good specimens are very difficult to obtain. Leafless in the H. S. Fl. in Jan. Fr. opening just before the R. S. The wood is used for making tea boxes.

B. malabaricum, *DC. The Cotton Tree.* Vern. *Letpan*, Burm.; *Simal*, Hind.; has been introduced. It has 5—7 leaflets, 4—6 in. long. Flowers 3 in. long with about 70 united stamens. Capsule 4—6 in. long. Planted in several localities in Port Blair. Leafless in the H. S. Fl. Febr.-March. Fr. April.

Fam. 15. STERCULIACEÆ.

THE COCOA FAMILY.

Trees, shrubs, or climbers with simple, often lobed and palminerved leaves, with stipules; hairs frequently stellate. Flowers bisexual or unisexual, sometimes small; sepals 5, valvate; petals 5 or none; stamens few or many, generally united. Fruit a capsule or a follicle.

Many members of this Family are important forest trees. The bark of some yield strong fibres, and the timber of others, though soft, is useful.

Leaves long petioled and boldly palminerved; margins of leaves lobed, serrate or entire.
- Deciduous trees. Petals none. Follicles woody, leathery or membranous ... . . 1. Sterculia.
- Climbers. Petals 5, clawed and appendaged. Capsules covered with bristles ... ... 2. Buettneria.

Leaves more or less shortly petioled, penninerved or with weak basal nerves, entire.
- Littoral tree. L. silvery-white beneath. Fl. small. Fr. woody, indehiscent ... . 3. Heritiera.
- Inland tree. L pale stellate-pubescent beneath. Fl. large. Capsule angled .. .. 4. Pterospermum.
- Shrub. L. almost glabrous. Capsule coriaceous ... 5. Leptonychia.

Theobroma Cacao, *Linn. The Cocoa Bean*, has been introduced to Port Blair and cultivated but has not done well. It is a native of the West Indies. The seeds give us the valuable cocoa from which chocolates are made.

1. STERCULIA.

Deciduous trees with entire or lobed palminerved leaves. Calyx usually with 5 segments, often coloured, the lobes valvate and sometimes cohering by their tips; petals none; anthers united into a column. Follicle membranous, coriaceous or woody, with few or many seeds.

Leaves entire.
- Leaves cordate at base. Fl. bell-shaped.
  - L. 5—10 in. long. Fl. rusty tomentose. Fr. woody, globular, with winged seeds ... ... S. alata.
  - L. 4—6 in. long. Fl. yellowish-green. Fr. membranous, boat-shaped, with 1 seed ... S. campanulata.
- Leaves with rounded bases. Fl. rather small, calyx segments conniving at the tips. Follicles coriaceous, scarlet.
  - L. 5—8 in. long. Calyx globular ... ... S. parviflora.
  - L. 6—12 in. long. Calyx widely campanulate ... S. rubiginosa.

Leaves palmately lobed.
- L. 1—2 ft. across, deeply 5—7 lobed. Fl. yellowish-pink. Fr. scarlet, coriaceous ... . S. villosa.
- L. 5—12 in. across, shallowly 3—5 lobed. Fl. bright coral-red. Fr. membranous, boat-shaped .. S. colorata.

* 70. **S. alata**, *Roxb.*; H. i. 360; Br. 83. *The Buddha's Coconut Tree.* Vern. *Letkôk*, Burm.

A tall tree (100—150 × 5—9) with thin buttresses and a slender straight stem, bark smooth, greyish with lighter and darker patches, cut creamy streaked. Leaves 5—10 in. long, 3—7 in. broad, broadly ovate, cordate and 5 nerved at the base, glabrous; petioles slender, 2—5 in. long. Flowers bell-shaped, ¾ in. long, deeply divided into 5 or 6 thick segments, brownish-green and rusty tomentose outside, crimson and veined inside. Follicles woody, almost globular, the size of the fist; seeds numerous, each terminated by a spongy, obovate, light-brown wing. 2—2½ in. long.

Abundant. Found in all localities and most common along large streams where it attains its greatest height. It is one of the tallest trees in the islands but is of comparatively small girth. Almost leafless in the H. S. Fl. Febr.-March. Its conspicuous fruits shed their seed about the month of December, but remain hanging on the tree for months.

Wood cream-coloured, fairly hard. It is a good avenue tree but easily gets broken by windstorms owing to its height and slenderness. Seed was sent from the Andamans for the avenues at Delhi.

• 71. **S. campanulata**, *Wall.*; H. i. 362; Br. 85. Vern. *Papita*, Hind.

A large and tall tree (100—130 × 7—11) with a smooth cylindrical bole, not buttressed, but with strong spreading roots at the base; bark greyish, patchy, cut strongly but irregularly dark-red and white streaked. Leaves 4—6 in. long, 3—5 in. broad, broadly ovate-cordate and 3—5 nerved at the base, pubescent beneath; petiole slender, 2—5 in. long. Flowers yellowish-green, in terminal panicles, bell-shaped, with triangular segments. Follicles 3—6 from a flower, on slender hooked stalks, membranous, veined, boat-shaped, with a narrow keel in the middle; seed 1, at the top.

Very common; found almost everywhere in deciduous forests. Fl. Febr.-March when the tree is leafless. Fr. soon after. In young trees the branches are in whorls. Its delicate and singularly shaped follicles are very attractive. About the month of March the bunches of reddish fruits hanging on the leafless trees make them conspicuous in the jungles. Wood white, light, soft and perishable, used for floating heavy timber in rafts.

• 72. **S. parviflora**, *Roxb.*; H. i. 359; Br. 84.

A tall tree (40—70 × 3—5) with a light-coloured bark resembling that of the *Dhup*, cut reddish-brown. Leaves 5—8 in. long, 2—4 in. broad, oblong to elliptic, blunt, base rounded and 3-nerved, glabrous, with about 10 pairs of lateral nerves; petiole about 1½ in. long, thickened at the top. Flowers rather small, yellowish-brown, in panicles from just below the leaves; calyx globular, the segments joined by their tips. Follicles coriaceous, scarlet when ripe.

Middle Andaman, in the interior, Betapur and Bomlungta; Baratang and the South Andaman. Fl. Jan.-Febr.

• 73. **S. rubiginosa**, *Ventenat*, var. glabrescens, *King*; H. i. 358; Br. 84, 701.

A tree 20—50 feet high with a pale grey bark. Leaves 6—12 in. long, 2—4 in. broad, elliptic to ovate or obovate, acuminate, somewhat narrowed to the rounded 3-nerved base, glabrous above, pale pubescent or glabrescent beneath; lateral nerves 6—10 pairs; petiole 1—2 in. long, thickened at the top. Flowers reddish-brown in rufous-tomentose lax panicles; calyx widely campanulate, the lobes lanceolate and cohering by their tips. Follicles 2 in. long, coriaceous, yellow when unripe, turning scarlet in ripening, pubescent outside, glabrous within.

Fairly frequent along the coasts of the islands. Middle and South Andaman, Baratang, Havelock Island, Rutland and the Cinque Islands. Fl. Dec.-Feb. Fr. March-May. Both this and the preceding one are often called *Shaw* by Burmans.

• 74. **S. villosa**, *Roxb.*: H. i. 355; Br. 80. Vern. *Shawni*, Burm.; *Chilka*, *Lal Chilka*, Hind.

A moderate-sized or large tree (60—80 × 4—8) with a smooth, glossy, grey bark, with numerous corky warts and often with a wavy appearance, cut reddish-brown. Leaves large, 1—2 feet across, reniform, palmately and deeply 5—7 lobed, base cordate, 5—7 nerved, upper surface ultimately glabrous, the lower pale and softly pubescent. Flowers handsome, nearly ½ in. diam., creamy-yellow with a reddish centre, on slender pedicels in drooping many-flowered panicles at the ends of the leafless branchlets. Follicles 1½—3 in. long, coriaceous, scarlet, clothed with stiff stellate hairs; seeds many.

A common tree in deciduous forests. Leafless in the H. S. Fl. Jan.-Febr. Fr. March-April. The fibre, which is coarse, but strong, is used for making ropes and elephant gear for dragging timber. The wood is reddish, soft and perishable.

• 75. **S. colorata**, *Roxb.*; H. i. 359; Br. 84. Vern. *Wetshaw*, Burm.

A moderate-sized tree (30—50 × 3—5) with light-green foliage, bark grey, smooth, cut whitish with creamy streaks. Leaves 4—9 in. long, 5—12 in. across, reniform, with 3—5 shallow, pointed lobes, base cordate, 5—7 nerved, glabrous; petiole slender 4—8 in. long. Flowers handsome and conspicuous, bright coral-red, in scurfy-tomentose panicles; calyx funnel shaped, ¾ in. long, with triangular segments. Follicles yellowish, membranous veined, 2—3 in. long, boat-shaped, with 2 oval seeds attached to the edge near the stalk.

Fairly frequent, especially in deciduous forests. Middle Andaman, dispersed; Long Island; South Andaman and Rutland Island. Leafless in the H. S. Fl. Febr.-April. Fr. at the beginning of the R. S. The wood is practically useless and the fibre is inferior.

2. BUETTNERIA.

Woody climbers with long-petioled palminerved leaves. Flowers rather small, in axillary cymes, bisexual, yellow or pink; petals clawed and appendaged; staminal tube with 5 teeth between which are the 5 anthers. Capsule clothed with stiff sharp black prickles.

Leaves entire	B. aspera.
Leaves shallowly 3—5 lobed	B. andamanensis.

76. **B. aspera**, *Colebr.*; H. i. 377; Br. 89.

A powerful climber with a thick trunk often 2—3 feet in girth. Leaves 5—8 in. long, cordate-oblong, 7-nerved at the base, minute stellate puberulous or altogether glabrous; petiole 2—5 in. long. Flowers yellowish-pink, on slender pedicels, collected into little umbels and forming axillary cymes; petals conniving with their two-cleft tips, the claw incurved and purple. Capsule 1—1½ in. diam., armed with many, short, stiff, sharp prickles.

South Andaman, common, especially in the interior, *Kurz*. Fl. April-May. Often given the same vernacular name as the next one.

77. **B. andamanensis**, *Kurz*; H. i. 377; Br. 90. Vern. *Tayaw*, Burm.

Scandent with fluted or ribbed branchlets. Leaves 3—7 in. across, cordate-ovate, shallowly 3—5 lobed, the lobes acuminate, coarsely serrate, base 5—7 nerved, cordate, glabrous or nearly so and somewhat rough to the touch. Flowers yellowish, rather small, in axillary cymes, pedicels slender. Capsule smaller than the last, covered with stiff, straight, black, bristles.

Not uncommon; often found near the coast and along creeks. Middle and South Andaman; Baratang and Havelock Islands. Fl. May-Aug. Fr. Oct. The bark yields a mucilage which is used for making a hair-wash.

3. HERITIERA.

• 78. **H. littoralis**, *Dryander*; H. i. 363; Br. 85. *The Red Mangrove of Queensland*. Vern. *Pinle-kanazo*, Burm.; *Sundri*, Hind.

Moderate-sized (20—40 × 4—6) of irregular growth, with thin, often curving, buttresses, bark grey or discoloured, cracked lengthwise. Leaves 5—10 long, 2½—5 in. broad, elliptic or oblong, acute or more or less rounded at the base, dark green above, silvery-white beneath, lateral nerves 7—9 pairs. Flowers small, creamy-pink. Fruit 1½—3 in. long, woody, compressed, ovoid and boldly keeled.

Very common along all seashores and in mangrove swamps. Fl. and Fr. in the R. S. Unmistakable on account of the silvery whiteness of the under-surface of its leaves which gives to it the name of *Looking Glass Plant*. The wood is dark reddish-brown, fairly hard and heavy.

4. PTEROSPERMUM.

• 79. **P. aceroides**, *Wall.*; H. i. 368; Br. 91. Vern. *Taung-petwun*, Burm.

A medium-sized evergreen tree (40—80 × 3—4) with a dark brown bark, cut dark reddish. Leaves *of young plants* palmately lobed.

peltate, and with long petioles; *of mature plants*, up to a foot long, oblong, apiculate, base cordate and somewhat unequal, dark green and smooth above, whitish stellate-pubescent beneath, lateral nerves 11—14 pairs, strong, the lowest from the base; petiole $\frac{3}{4}$ in. long, stout. Flowers 2—3 in. long, white; sepals thick, covered outside with brown tomentum. Capsule 5—6 in. long, blackish, sharply 5-angled; seeds with a brown wing.

A common tree dispersed throughout the islands in all localities. Fl. Nov.-Jan. Fr. Febr.-June. A graceful tree whose large leaves, pale on the undersurface, enable it to be easily picked out amongst the great variety of the foliage of these forests. Wood pinkish-red, rather soft.

5. LEPTONYCHIA.

80. ***L. glabra,** *Turcz.*; H. i. 379; Br. 92.

An evergreen shrubby tree. Leaves 2—4 in. long, oblong-lanceolate, acuminate, base somewhat oblique and 3—5 nerved, entire, glabrous or thinly stellate hairy, membranous; petiole $\frac{1}{8}$ in. long. Flowers in axillary fascicles, small, whitish; sepals 5, valvate; petals 5, 2-lobed; stamens 10, between 2 series of staminodes. Capsule $\frac{1}{3}$ in. long, coriaceous, rugose, with one black seed.

South Andaman, in tropical forests, *Kurz*. I have seen no Andaman specimens. The leaves are like those on *Grewia calophylla*.

Fam. 16. TILIACEÆ.

Trees or shrubs. Leaves simple, alternate, often with basal nerves. Flowers white or yellow, usually bisexual; sepals 5, valvate; petals 5; stamens many, usually raised with the ovary on a short stalk. Fruit dry or fleshy.

Leaves palminerved.	
Large deciduous tree. L. entire, more or less cordate at the base; petioles long. Fr. with radiating wings	1. Berrya.
Medium-sized or small trees. L. often serrate or crenate; petioles short. Fr. a drupe	2. Grewia.
Littoral shrub with scaly lanceolate leaves. Fr. leathery	3. Brownlowia.
Leaves penninerved, margins crenate-serrate; petioles thickened at the top. Petals fringed	4. Elaeocarpus.

1. BERRYA.

* 81. **B. Ammonilla,** *Roxb.* H. i. 383; Br. 94. *The Trincomali Wood.* Vern. *Petwun*, Burm.

A large deciduous tree (60—90 × 6—8) with a brownish-grey, smooth, thin bark, fissured lengthwise, cut fibrous, pink turning brown. Leaves 4—8 in. long, 3—5 in. broad, ovate, acuminate, the base narrowed and rounded, cordate with 5—7 basal nerves, membranous, almost glabrous; petiole 4—5 in. long, slender. Flowers nearly ½ in. diam., on slender pedicels, in large fragrant panicles. Fruit with radiating, membranous, veined wings.

Middle Andaman; Long Island and Havelock Island; South Andaman and Rutland Island; not common, often found in beach forests. Leafless in the H. S., the leaves turning bright yellow before falling. Fl. July-Aug. Fr. Dec.-March. The fruits resemble a ship's propellor but the blades are turned both ways.

Wood dark red, close grained and tough, hard and flexible. It is used in India for making carts and in Madras for making Masula boats.

2. GREWIA.

Leaves strongly 3-nerved at the base, margins more or less crenate or serrate (except in *G. calophylla*). Flowers in cymes or terminal panicles; petals with a scale at the base, usually smaller than the sepals. Fruit a drupe, often lobed.

Leaves entire. Drupe fleshy fibrous ... ... G. calophylla.
Leaves crenulate or serrulate. Drupe hard, lobed or not.
L. 4—6 in. long, serrulate. Fl. in axillary umbels ... G. laevigata.
L. 4—8 in. long, faintly crenato-serrate. Fl. in terminal panicles ... ... G. Microcos.

• 82. **G. calophylla**, *Kurz*; H. i. 392; Br. 99.

A moderate-sized tree (20—40 × 2—4) with dense dark green foliage; bark dark grey, thin, cut dark reddish-brown with fine white streaks. Leaves 4—7 in. long, 2—3 in. broad, elliptic or ovate and slightly one-sided, acuminate, base more or less rounded, glossy, petiole ¼ in. long. Flowers ¾ in. long, cream-coloured, with a pungent smell, usually in 3's, enveloped by a bract and arranged in terminal few-flowered panicles; stamens deep-yellow. Drupe 1 in. long, obovoid, fleshy fibrous, orange-yellow when ripe.

Frequent in mostly all localities, especially in semi-deciduous and in coast forests in moist places. Fl. May-July. Fr. Dec.-March.

• 83. **G. laevigata**, *Vahl.*; H. i. 389; Br. 96. Vern. *Tayaw, Kyet-tayaw*, Burm.

A small tree (15—30 × 1—2), bark light grey, cut fibrous, white with creamy streaks. Leaves 4—6 in. long, 1½—2 in. broad, elliptic to elliptic-lanceolate, acuminate, base acute, serrulate, nearly glabrous; petiole ¼ in. long. Flowers ¾—1 in. long, yellow, 2—5 umbellate in the leaf axils. Drupe hard and shining, 1—4 lobed, the lobes the size of a pea.

Common, especially in open places and often along seashores. Fl. and Fr. Oct.-March. It resembles and is sometimes confused with *Trema amboinensis*.

* 84. **G. Microcos,** *Linn.*; H. i. 392; Br. 99. Vern. *Myatya*, Burm.

A small or moderate-sized tree (30—50 × 2—4) often with a crooked or fluted stem, bark brown, thin and smooth, cut dark reddish-brown. Leaves papery, 4—8 in. long and about half as broad, elliptic to oblong or obovate, acuminate, base more or less rounded, glossy and almost glabrous, faintly crenate-serrate; petiole ⅛ in. long. Flowers yellowish-white, rather small, in terminal panicles. Drupe blackish, the size of a pea.

Not common. Middle Andaman, in several localities; South Andaman. Leafless early in the H. S. Fl. and Fr. March-July. The best covering leaf for Burma cigars, *Brandis*.

There occurs on Mt. Baker in the Middle Andaman, and probably in similar localities, another *Grewia* with leaves 1—1½ in. long, elliptic, crenate-serrate and flowers in the leaf axils. Fl. H. S. Very uncommon.

3. BROWNLOWIA.

85. **B. lanceolata,** *Benth.*; H. i. 381; Br. 93.

A littoral shrub, the branchlets slender, scaly, and greyish like the under-surface of the leaves. Leaves 5—8 in. long, 1—2 in. broad, lanceolate, acuminate, base rounded with weak basal nerves, dark green and glossy above, silvery-grey beneath, entire, lateral nerves few and weak; petioles ½ in. long. Flowers small, whitish, in narrow axillary panicles; petals 5; stamens many, with 5 staminodes opposite the petals. Fruit ½ in. diam., brownish, scaly.

Along salt-water creeks, high up stream beyond the mangrove, forming dense thickets along the banks and almost submerged during the high tides. Seen along all the large creeks of the Middle Andaman; Dhani Khari creek. Fl. May-June. Fr. Aug.-Sept.

4. ELÆOCARPUS.

Evergreen trees with penninerved crenate-serrate leaves, collected at the ends of the branchlets and turning red before falling; petioles thickened at the top. Flowers white; petals with laciniated or fringed margins; stamens many, the anthers terminated by a fine point or hair.

Leaves 6—9 in long, obovate. Flowers 1 in. diam.	...	E. aristatus.
Leaves 4—7 in. long, ovate. Flowers ½ in. diam.	...	E. robustus.

* 86. **E. aristatus,** *Roxb.*; H. i. 405; Br. 104.

A fairly large tree (60—90 × 4—8) with a smooth grey bark, cut dirty brown, mealy and watery near the sapwood. Leaves 6—9 in. long, 2½—4 in. broad, obovate, shortly apiculate, tapering at the base, distantly crenate-serrate, almost glabrous, lateral nerves about 8 pairs; petioles ½—¾ in. long, thickened at the top. Flowers 1 in. diam., yellowish-white, in axillary racemes; petals silky. Fruit 1–1½ in. long, ellipsoid-ovoid, smooth and greenish; stone 2-ridged.

Middle Andaman; Long Island; South Andaman; Baratang. Usually along streams and in damp places and often with thin large buttresses; also in evergreen forest. *Fl.* Nov.-Jan. *Fr.* Jan.-March.

The leaves before falling do not all turn red at the same time, like those of the Red Bombway, but only a few at a time in a tuft, so that bright red and green leaves may be seen together on the tree.

• 87. **E. robustus**, *Roxb.*; H. i. 402; Br. 103.

A moderate-sized tree (40—60 × 3—5). Leaves 4—7 in. long, 1½—2½ in. broad, ovate or ovate-oblong, acuminate, base rounded, crenate-serrate, glabrous, lateral nerves 8—12 pairs; petioles ¾—1½ in. long, thickened and bent at the top. Flowers pure white, ¼ in. diam., the leaf axils or from the scars just below the leaves. Fruit 1—1¼ in. long, ovoid; stone slightly 3-grooved.

Middle Andaman, Cuthbert Bay, Rongat Bay, Bomlungta; South Andaman. *Fl.* March-April. *Fr.* May-July. The leaves before falling turn red like the preceding one, and both are sometimes given the vernacular name *Panmaka* by Burmans.

Fam. 17. MALPIGHIACEÆ.

Climbing shrubs with simple, opposite, exstipulate leaves. Flowers white or yellowish, bisexual, pentamerous; stamens 10. Fruit of 1—3 winged samaras.

Flowers irregular; calyx glandular near the pedicel. Fr. with 3 wings ... . 1. Hiptage.
Flowers regular; petals sessile. Fr. orbicular, reticulate-membranous ... . 2. Aspidopterys.

1. HIPTAGE.

88. **H. Madablota**, *Gaertn.*; H. i. 418; Br. 108.

A large climbing shrub with a stout trunk. Leaves 4—6 in. long, elliptic-lanceolate, acuminate, glabrous, petiole ¼ in. long, stout. Flowers ¾ in. long, very fragrant, in axillary racemes collected at the ends of the branches; pedicels slender with a gland near the calyx; petals white, fimbriate, reflexed, the upper one dashed with yellow; stamens 10, one longer than the rest. Fruit with 3 wings 1—2 in. long, and 2 short lateral ones.

Fairly frequent. Middle Andaman; Porlob Island and Long Island; South Andaman, Mt. Harriet. *Fl.* March-April. *Fr.* April-May.

2. ASPIDOPTERYS.

89. **A. andamanica**, *Hutchinson* ; Kew Bull. 1917, p. 99.

A woody climber. Leaves 3—6 in. long, 2½—5 in. broad, elliptic to orbicular-ovate, apiculate, base rounded, glabrous with 4—5 pairs of lateral nerves. Flowers rather small, white or yellowish-white, in axillary umbellate panicles. Samaras in threes, 2 in. long, ovate, membranous and reticulate, brownish, depressed in the centre.

Yemtilajig and Bomlungta ; South Andaman. Fl. April. Fr. Nov.-Febr. A climber of little interest except for its attractive fruits, which, on account of their somewhat similar shape, call to mind those of the *Padauk*.

Geraniaceæ. To this family belongs **Averrhoa Carambola.**, *Linn.*, a small pretty tree with drooping branches and alternate imparipinnate leaves ; leaflets 7—9 pairs, ovate or ovate-lanceolate, accuminate, glabrous and glaucous beneath. Flowers small, variegated purplish and white. Fruit about the size of, and shaped like, a banana, but glossy and sharply 5-angled, acid, known as the *Karmal*, Hind. Vern. *Saungya*, Burm. Introduced and planted in the Settlement.

Fam. 18. RUTACEÆ.

THE LIME AND ORANGE FAMILY.

Trees or shrubs. Leaves usually strongly aromatic, dotted with translucent glands, alternate or opposite, simple or composed of a single or many leaflets. Flowers usually white, regular, with 4—5 sepals and petals and as many, or twice as many, stamens. Fruit a berry.

Leaves composed of one leaflet only.
  Shrubby tree. L. sub-opposite, 3—5 in. long. Fr. the size of a pea ... ... 1. Acronychia.
  Small tree. L. 1½—3 in. long, alternate. Fr. 1 in. diam. 2. Atalantia.
  Scandent ; armed. L. 4—9 in. long, alternate. Fr. ½ in. diam. ... ... 3. Paramignya.
Leaves composed of 3 leaflets.
  Leaves opposite.
    Leaflets 4—10 in. long ; petiole naked ... ... 4. Evodia.
  Leaves alternate
    Small unarmed tree. Lfts. 1—4 in. long ; petiole broadly winged ... ... 5. Limonia.
    Shrub ; often armed. Lfts. 2—5 in. long, crenulate petiole naked ... ... 6. Zanthoxylum.
Leaves imparipinnate, composed of more than three leaflets.
  Leaflets opposite, glandular crenate-serrate ... ... 6. Zanthoxylum, 96.
  Leaflets alternate, with entire margins.
    Lfts. 7—15. Fl. small, in panicles ... ... 7. Micromelum.
    Lfts. 5—9. Fl. bell-shaped, large ... ... 8. Murraya.
    Lfts. 3—5. Fl. small, in axillary panicles ... ... 9. Glycosmis.

1. ACRONYCHIA.

90. ***A. laurifolia**, *Blume* ; H. i. 498 ; Br. 116.

A small tree (10—25 × 1—2). Leaves unifoliolate, sub-opposite, collected at the ends of the branchlets. Leaflet 3—5 in. long, oblong, elliptic or obovate, blunt or acuminate, narrowed to the base, glabrous, lateral nerves 14—18 pairs forming a double series of loops within the edge ; petiole short Flowers white or pale-yellow, ¼ in. diam ; petals villous at the base inside ; stamens 8. Fruit the size of a large pea, obscurely 4-angled.

Not infrequent in the tropical coast forests of the islands, *Kurz*. Fl. June.

2. ATALANTIA.

* 91. **A. monophylla**, *Correa* ; H. i. 511 ; Br. 121. *The Wild Lime Tree*. Vern. *Tawthanbya thee*, Burm ; *Jungli Nimbu*, Hind.

A small evergreen tree (20—30 × 2—3) with a deeply fluted stem, the bark with white, grey, or dark-brown patches, cut creamy yellow. Leaves unifoliolate, elliptic to ovate, apex obtuse and notched, base rounded, dark green and glossy above, pale beneath, lemon scented when bruised, lateral nerves fine and many : petiole ¼—½ in long. Flowers white, slender pedicelled ; stamens 6—8. Berry ovoid at first, finally globose, 1 in. diam.

Common everywhere in deciduous forests and often associated with *Padauk* : also frequent along the coasts in open dry forests, not in swampy places. Fl. Nov.-Febr. Fr. Febr.-May. Easily known by its fluted stem. The vernacular names of this and of *Limonia alata* are often confused. This includes Kurz's *A. macrophylla*, which is only a more luxuriant form.

3. PARAMIGNYA.

* 92. **P. armata**, *Oliver*, var. andamanica, *King* ; H. i. 511 ; Br. 122.

Scandent. Stems greenish, armed with curved axillary spines about 2 in. long. Leaves unifoliolate, 4—9 in. long, 1¼—3½ in. broad, elliptic to elliptic-oblong, acute, base more or less rounded, glabrous and almost scentless when bruised, lateral nerves rather obscure, interarching rather far from the edge ; petiole 1 in. long, thickened in the upper part. Flowers white, ½ in. long, on slender 1—1½ in. pedicels ; filaments woolly. Fruit ¾ in. diam., globular or obscurely 2-lobed.

Fairly frequent. Middle Andaman, Rongat Bay, Boulangta ; Long Island ; Baratang ; Havelock and Neill Islands ; South Andaman. Fl. May. Fr. May.

4. EVODIA.

93. ***E. glabra**, *Blume* ; H. i. 489 ; Br. 112.

A tree 40—70 feet high. Leaves opposite, 3-foliolate; leaflets 4—10 in. long, 2—5 in. broad, the middle the largest with the longest petiolule, obovate or obovate-elliptic, shortly acuminate, tapering to the base, coriaceous and shining, lateral nerves 10—15 pairs. Flowers densely crowded in corymbose cymes; stamens 4—5, exserted. Fruit separating into 2—3 cocci, ¼ in. long; seeds black.

South Andaman, around Port Blair.

5. LIMONIA.

94. **L. alata**, *W. and A.* ; H. i. 508 ; Br. 119.

A small unarmed pretty tree (15—25 × 1—2), with a brownish-grey or discoloured bark, cut dirty yellowish-brown. Leaves trifoliolate; leaflets 1—4 in. long, the centre the largest, obovate, notched at the apex, glabrous, dark green and glossy above, light green beneath, sessile, pungent when bruised; common petiole ½—1 in. long, obovately winged. Flowers white, fragrant, in axillary or terminal cymes; petals 4—5, reflexed; stamens double the number of petals; filaments flattened. Berry globose, 1 in. diam.

Not quite common, but may often be seen in deciduous and semi-deciduous forests. Middle Andaman; Long Island; Baratang and Havelock Island. Fl. March. Fr. May-June. Sometimes called *Taw-shauk* and often given the same names as *Atalantia monophylla*.

6. ZANTHOXYLUM.

Shrubs or trees, sometimes armed. Leaves alternate, trifoliolate or imparipinnate, leaflets crenate. Flowers small, 4—5-merous; stamens as many as the petals. Fruit with shining blue or black seeds.

A shrub. Leaves 3-foliolate	Z. ovalifolium.
A tree. Leaves imparipinnate	Z. Budrunga.

95. **Z. ovalifolium**, *Wight* ; H. i. 492 ; Br. 118.

A straggling shrub, unarmed or with a few short straight prickles. Leaves trifoliolate; leaflets 2—5 in. long, the middle the largest, elliptic-oblong to obovate, apex obtuse and emarginate, narrowed at the base, margin crenulate, lateral nerves 10—14 pairs, rather fine; common petiole 1¼—2½ in. long. Flowers white, small. Fruit almost globular, nearly ⅓ in. diam.

Not uncommon. Middle Andaman; Baratang; South Andaman.

• 96. **Z. Budrunga,** *Wall*; H. i. 495; Br. 118. Vern. *Mayanin*, Burm.

A medium-sized deciduous tree (50—60 × 3—5), the base of the trunk and roots corky furrowed, cut yellow with faint brown streaks, turning dark-brown in a little while. Leaves imparipinnate, collected at the ends of the branchlets, rachis slender, up to 2½ feet long: leaflets 5—10 pairs, 3—6 in. long, broadly ovate-oblong, one-sided at the base, crenate-serrate with a large transparent gland in each sinus; pungent when bruised. Flowers small, greenish-white, in axillary panicles with opposite branches. Fruit the size of a pea.

Not uncommon; usually in deciduous forest and associated with *Padauk*. Middle and South Andaman; the Archipelago; Baratang; Long Island and Rutland Island. Leafless in the H. S. Fl. with the new leaves in May. *Fr.* in the R. S. The young leaves are cooked and eaten as a vegetable by Burmans.

Z. andamanicum, *Kurz*. The leaves of Kurz's type specimens in the Calcutta Herbarium closely resemble those of *Harrisonia Bennettii*, and the flowers and fruits are unknown.

7. MICROMELUM.

• 97. **M. pubescens,** *Blume*; H. i. 501; Br. 114. *The Sea Island Apple Berry.*

A small evergreen tree (20—30 × 1—3) with a light-coloured rough bark. Leaves large, imparipinnate, up to 2 feet long; leaflets 7—15, alternate, 5—7 in. long, 2—3 in. broad, oblong to ovate-lanceolate, acuminate, base oblique, glabrous or puberulous, margins wavy folded. Flowers ¼ in. diam., whitish, numerous, in terminal flat panicles, strongly but not sweetly scented; petals ¼ in. long; stamens 10. berry glabrous, orange-red when ripe.

Not very common; often found along streams. Middle Andaman; Havelock Island; South Andaman, often in the clearings around Port Blair. *Fl.* Nov.-Febr. *Fr.* April-June. Wood yellowish-white, hard and rather heavy.

8. MURRAYA.

• 98. **M. exotica,** *Linn.*; H. i. 502; Br. 113. *The Chinese Myrtle. The Burmese Boxwood* or *Andaman Satinwood*. Vern. *Malai lakri*, Hind.

A small evergreen tree (15—25 × 1—2) of irregular growth: bark thin, whitish, mealy, branchlets white. Leaves imparipinnate; leaflets 5—9, alternate, 1—3 in. long, elliptic to rhomboid, shortly and bluntly acuminate, base sometimes unequal, dark green and glossy. Flowers bell-shaped, nearly 1 in. long, fragrant, petals ⅓—¾ in. long; stamens 10. Berry ½ in. long, ovoid, shining red when ripe.

Common in deciduous forests in nearly all localities. Fl. at the beginning of the R. S. Fr. May-June. The wood, which resembles boxwood, is light yellow, hard and heavy, but is liable to split, and is obtainable only in small sizes. It is used in the local workshops for ornamental work and for making walking sticks. The *Indian Satinwood* is *Chloroxylon Swietenia*.

M. Kœnigii, *Spreng.*, is the *Curry Leaf Tree*, introduced and planted on account of its leaves which are used to flavour curries. Leaves imparipinnate with 10--25 leaflets, obliquely-ovate, 1 in. long, serrate, strongly smelling. Flowers white. Fruit 1-in. long, red.

9. GLYCOSMIS.

99. **G. pentaphylla,** *Correa*; H. i. 499; Br. 112. Vern. *Taw-shauk*, Burm.

A small evergreen tree (15—25 × 1—2½), with a crooked stem, often stunted and scraggy. Leaves imparipinnate; leaflets 3—5, alternate, 4—6 in. long, 1½—3 in. broad, oblong to elliptic-lanceolate, acuminate, lateral nerves looping far from the edge, glabrous and glossy above, dark green, with a disagreeable smell when bruised. Flowers white, in axillary panicles; stamens 10, filaments flat. Fruit nearly ½ in. diam., globose.

Middle Andaman; Long Island; South Andaman. Fl. and Fr. at various times during the year. A very variable plant, which is divided by some botanists into several species. The branchlets are used for tooth-sticks.

The following well-known trees have been introduced.

Citrus medica, *Linn.*, has several varieties, the *Citron*, *Lemon*, *Sweet*, and *Acid Lime*. Vern. *Nimba*, Hind., usually thorny; leaves unifoliolate, perfectly glabrous, the petioles more or less naked. Flowers white, often tinged with pink.

Citrus decumana, *Linn.* *The Shaddock* or *Pumelo*, also called *Forbidden Fruit* or *Paradise Apple*. A small tree about 25 feet high. Leaves pubescent beneath, petiole winged. Flowers white. Fruit as large as a man's head.

Aegle Marmelos, *Correa.* *The Bael Tree* or *Bengal Quince*. Vern. *Ókshit*, Burm.; *Bel*, Hind. A small tree armed with sharp straight spines. Leaves trifoliolate, leaflets crenate. Fruit woody, 4—6 in. diam., containing a sweet yellow pulp which is used for making sherbet and also as a specific for dysentery. Fl. H. S.

Fam. 19. SIMARUBACEÆ.

THE BITTER-BARK FAMILY.

Trees or shrubs with bitter propensities. Leaves simple, trifoliolate or pinnate. Flowers white, yellowish or pinkish; sepals and petals 3—6, with as many or twice as many stamens.

Leaves simple.
- L. 7—10 in. long, glossy and glabrous ... ... 1. Samadera.
- L. 1 in. long, silky-velvety. Littoral ... ... 2. Suriana.

Leaves 3-foliolate.
Prickly shrub. Lfts. irregularly-serrate ... ... 3. Harrisonia.
Leaves imparipinnate.
Prickly and scandent. Lfts. 7—13, crenate-serrate ... 3. Harrisonia, 102.
Unarmed small tree. Lfts. 5—7, entire and glabrous ... 4. Picrasma.
Unarmed tall tree. Lfts. 10—20 or more, falcate-lanceolate, puberulous beneath ... ... 5. Ailanthus.

1. SAMADERA.

100. *S. lucida, *Wall.*; H. i. 519; Br. 124.

A small evergreen tree, the bark transversely cracked. Leaves 7—10 in. long, oblong to elliptic-oblong, glossy and glabrous, coriaceous with lax net venation, entire, petioles short. Flowers bisexual, in short-stalked umbels; calyx glandular at the base; petals 4, 1 in. long, yellow, twisted in bud; stamens 8; filaments slender with a hairy scale at the base. Fruit pear-shaped with a narrow wing or keel, dark-brown, strongly reticulate.

Andamans, *Helfer*. I have seen no Andaman specimens and this, I believe, is not a native of the islands. The Kew and Calcutta specimens are of Helfer's collections.

2. SURIANA.

101. *S. maritima, *Linn.*; H. i. 522; Br. 124.

A littoral shrub, the branchlets covered with velvety pubescence. Leaves 1 in. long, linear spathulate, obtuse, entire, silky-velvety. Flowers nearly ½ in. across, yellow, in short axillary racemes; petals ¼ in. long.

A littoral species found along the sea-coast and said to be a native of these islands. I have seen no Andaman specimens, and from the description there ought to be no difficulty in recognising it.

3. HARRISONIA.

Prickly shrubs with long slender straggling branches. Leaves 3-foliolate or imparipinnate, with coarsely crenate-serrate leaflets. Flowers whitish or pinkish, 4—5-merous; stamens twice as many as the petals, each with a hairy scale at its base.

Leaves 3-foliolate; leaflets 1½—2½ in. long. Flowers small, white ... ... H. Brownii.
Leaves imparipinnate; leaflets 1—1½ in. long. Flowers rather large, pinkish ... ... H. Bennettii.

102. H. Brownii. *A. Juss*; Br. 125. Vern. *Soogyin*, Burm.

A straggling shrub with dark brown branches armed with pairs of short, sharp, dark prickles. Leaves digitately 3-foliolate; leaflets 1½—2½ in. long, the terminal the largest and narrowed to the base, ovate to rhomboid, acuminate, irregularly serrate; petioles slender, channelled. Flowers rather small, white, on slender pedicels from axillary tubercles; petals 4, reflexed. Fruit barely ¼ in. long, slightly depressed.

Fairly common in deciduous forests and often forming little thickets. Middle and South Andaman; Baratang; the Archipelago and Rutland Island. Leafless and unsightly during the H. S., the leaves all turning yellow before falling. The new leaves come out at the beginning of the R. S. and are very pretty. Fr. up to November.

103. **H. Bennettii**, *Hook. fil.*; H. i. 519; Br. 125. Vern. *Soogyin*, Burm.

A straggling scandent shrub, armed with slightly recurved prickles. Leaves 4—6 in. long, imparipinnate; leaflets 3—6 pairs with an odd one, 1—1½ in. long, ovate-rhomboid, blunt or bluntish acuminate, narrowed to the base, coarsely crenate-serrate. Flowers pinkish-white, rather large; petals usually 5. Fruit depressed globular.

Not as common as the preceding one. Middle Andaman; Havelock and Rutland Islands; South Andaman. Fl. April-May. Fr. Aug. This also grows into a small shrubby tree.

4. PICRASMA.

104. **P. javanica**, *Blume*; H. i. 520; Br. 127.

A small pretty tree (20—30 × 2—4) with a grey bark, cut whitish. Leaves imparipinnate; leaflets usually 5, sometimes 7, opposite, 3—5 in. long, oblong or elliptic-oblong, caudate-acuminate, glabrous and membranous, rachis slender. Flowers white, nearly ¼ in. diam., many crowded at the ends of long-peduncled panicles; petals and stamens 4—5. Fruit nearly ½ in. diam., white, 2—4 supported together by the persistent calyx.

Middle Andaman, along the streams of the east coast and at Bomlungta; South Andaman. Usually found along fresh-water streams. Fl. March. Fr. March-April. It is evergreen and its foliage resembles that of *Pongamia glabra*.

5. AILANTHUS.

• 105. **A. Kurzii**, *Prain*; Br. 703.

A lofty elegant deciduous tree (80—120 × 6—9) without buttresses, bark grey, rather smooth, cut mealy brown with pale spots. Leaves 1—2½ ft. long, pinnate, collected at the ends of the branches, rachis with a raised line above; leaflets 10—20 or more in young plants, 4½—7 in. long, 1½—2½ in. broad, falcate-lanceolate, acuminate, base oblique, pale and softly puberulous beneath. Flowers inconspicuous, greenish, in axillary panicles. Samaras 1½—2 in. long, thin, pinkish, oblong and blunt at the ends.

Not uncommon. Middle Andaman, dispersed; Baratang and Havelock Island; South Andaman; Rutland island. Leafless about January, the leaves turning red before falling. Fl. Jan.-Febr. with the new leaves. Fr. April. The samaras, which may easily be mistaken for fallen leaflets, are like the pods of some *Dalbergias*. Wood, white, soft and light, said to be useless.

Fam. 20. OCHNACEÆ.

Small trees with simple alternate stipulate leaves. Flowers showy, usually yellow; sepals 5, imbricate, persistent in fruit; stamens 10 or many, the filaments persistent. Drupes seated on the enlarged disc.

Leaves faintly crenate-serrate. Stamens many ... ... 1. Ochna.
Leaves entire. Stamens 10 ... ... 2. Gomphia.

1. OCHNA.

• 106. **O. Wallichii,** *Planchon*; H. i. 524; Br. 128. Vern. *Indaing seni, Yodaya*, Burm.

A small straight-stemmed tree (20—40 × 1½—3) with a smooth greyish patchy bark, cut reddish-brown, darkening, watery near the sapwood, the bark easily separating from it. Leaves 4—8 in. long, 1½—2 in. broad, elliptic-lanceolate to oblanceolate, faintly crenate-serrate, glabrous and glossy, membranous with irregular lateral nerves; petiole short. Flowers bright yellow, conspicuous, on slender stalks which lengthen in fruiting; petals clawed; stamens many, persistent; sepals enlarged, reddish. Drupes greenish, nearly ½ in. long.

Common in all localities in deciduous forest. Leafless during the H. S. Fl. at the beginning of the R. S., with or before the leaves. Fr. July. Unmistakable on account of its flowers and fruits. Wood reddish-brown, moderately hard and close-grained, used in the Andamans only as *bullis* for making huts, etc.

2. GOMPHIA.

107. **G. Hookerii,** *Planchon*; H. i. 525.

A small tree (15—25 × 1—2), bark brown, rather smooth and thin, cut reddish-brown. Leaves 2—4 in. long, ¾—1½ in. broad, elliptic to elliptic-lanceolate, base and apex acute, glabrous; lateral nerves fine and numerous, curving upwards and anastomosing intramarginally; petiole short. Flowers in crowded umbels on slender white pedicels; sepals 5, white, turning pinkish in fruiting; petals white or orange; stamens 10. Drupes ovoid, seated on the enlarged torus.

Uncommon. Middle Andaman, Mt. Baker, on the high hills along the east coast, and on a small steep hill north-west of the Bomlungta camp. Fl. H. S. Wood pinkish, hard and fine-grained.

Fam. 21. BURSERACEÆ.

THE MYRRH FAMILY.

Resiniferous trees with alternate imparipinnate leaves, the leaflets usually opposite. Flowers rather small, bisexual or polygamous; sepals and petals 3—5, with twice as many stamens. Fruit a drupe.

A family of some concern to the forester, some of its members, though not valuable timber trees, are most interesting and are well-known in these islands.

Leaflets opposite.
- Fl. in terminal panicles; sepals and petals 5. Fr. globose ... 1. Garuga.
- Fl. in axillary panicles; sepals and petals 3. Fr. trigonous ... 2. Canarium.

Leaflets alternate.
- Littoral tree. L. up to 2 ft. long with 15—21 leaflets. Fl. small ... ... 3. Ganophyllum.

1. GARUGA.

• 108. **G. pinnata,** *Roxb.*; H. i. 528; Br. 131.

A moderate-sized or often large tree (60—80 × 4—7) with a rather thick, whitish, thinly-fissured bark, cut reddish-brown, sometimes milky. Leaves nearly 2 feet long; leaflets 7—12 pairs, opposite, 3—6 in. long, 1—1½ in. broad, oblong-lanceolate, acuminate, base oblique, margin coarsely crenate-serrate, glabrous or pubescent, lateral nerves 12—16 pairs. Flowers creamy-yellow, on short slender pedicels in terminal panicles; petals 5; stamens 10, with hairy filaments. Fruit globose, fleshy, ¾ in. diam.

Dispersed in deciduous forests; not very common. Middle and South Andaman; Long and Havelock Islands. Leafless in the H. S. Fl. March-April, before the new leaves appear. Fr. May-June. In Burma this tree is called *Chinyôk*, a name which is here given to *Dracontomelum mangiferum*, a more common and attractive tree than this one, with a similar edible fruit.

2. CANARIUM.

Usually aromatic trees. Leaflets opposite. Flowers unattractive; calyx 3-cleft, persistent; petals 3; stamens 6. Drupe hard, more or less trigonous.

Leaflets serrulate; not aromatic ... ... C. euphyllum.

Leaflets entire; aromatic in all parts.
- Lfts. 3½ - 7½ in. long ... ... C. coccineo-bracteatum.
- Lfts. 3 - 4½ in. long ... ... C. Manii.

• 109. **C. euphyllum,** *Kurz*; H. i. 535; Br. 130. Vern. *Dhup*, Hind.

A large deciduous tree (80—100 × 8—14) with small buttresses and with massive branches, bark whitish-grey, smooth, with numerous small protuberances. Leaves up to 3 feet long, collected at the ends of the branches; leaflets about 8 pairs and an odd one, up to 8 or 9 in. long, ovate to oblong-lanceolate, acuminate, tapering, rounded or truncate at the base, glabrous, lateral nerves conspicuous. Flowers ¼ in. diam., in axillary panicles. Fruit 1¼—1¾ in. long, ovoid-ellipsoid, supported by the persistent woody calyx, bluish-black when ripe.

Frequent in deciduous forests throughout the islands. During the H. S., when it is leafless, the ripe fruits may be seen standing up erect at the ends of the thick branchlets. Unsightly when leafless, but at the beginning of the R. S. when it has just put on its new foliage it is one of the most handsome trees of these forests. Fl. May-June.

Wood light-coloured and perishable, with a smell like that of vinegar when freshly cut. The logs are sometimes used as floats for rafting timber. It yields a useful resin which is used by the Andamanese for burning and for making a composition for covering the binding of their arrows.

110.*C. coccineo-bracteatum, *Kurz.*; H. i. 536; Br. 131.

A moderate-sized tree (40—50 × 4—5) with a dark grey bark, cut reddish, strongly aromatic. Leaves 10—18 in. long; leaflets 2—4 pairs and an odd one, 3½—7½ in. long, 2—3 in. broad, broadly ovate to oblong, shortly acuminate, glabrous, aromatic when bruised, lateral nerves 10—12 pairs. Flowers in axillary velvety panicles. Drupe unknown.

A rare tree. South Andaman near Port Blair. I believe I had specimens of this collected on Rutland Island near Portman Bay, with the fruit which was ellipsoid and bluish-black, but these were unfortunately lost.

111. C. Manii, *King*; Br. 131.

A moderate-sized tree (25—40 × 3½—5) with stout branches and a light grey bark, cut light brown, strongly aromatic. Leaves 9—12 in. long; leaflets 2—3 pairs and an odd one, 3—4½ in. long, ovate to ovate-rotund, shortly acuminate, base broad, rounded to almost cordate, glossy, aromatic when crushed, lateral nerves about 10 pairs. Flowers ¼ in. diam., white, in pubescent panicles. Fruit ovoid-ellipsoid, 1¼ in. long.

Not uncommon on the high hills of the Middle Andaman and on Mt. Ford. Associated with *Dipterocarpus costatus*, *Gomphia Hookerii* and *Memecylon coeruleum*. Also probably occurs on Saddle Peak. Leafless in the H. S., new leaves Febr.-March, with the flowers. Fr. April-June. It has a pure white aromatic resin.

3. GANOPHYLLUM.

• 112. G. falcatum, *Blume*. Vern. *Jungli Neem*, Hind.

A large or moderate-sized littoral tree (40—70 × 5—8) with a rough reddish-brown bark, cut light-brown, then yellowish; branchlets ash-coloured. Leaves up to 2 feet long; leaflets alternate, 15—21, 2½—5 in. long, ovate to oblong-lanceolate, shortly acuminate, base one-sided, the largest about three-fourths up the rachis, the smallest at the bottom, glossy, lateral nerves fine and distinct, looping far from the margin. Flowers small, in axillary panicles. Fruit $\frac{1}{4}$–$\frac{1}{2}$ in. long, slightly pointed.

Fairly frequent along the seashores from north to south. Fl. and Fr. Dec.-March. It apparently gets its vernacular name on account of its slight resemblance to the well-known *Neem tree*.

Fam. 22. MELIACEÆ.

THE MAHOGANY FAMILY.

Trees with alternate, exstipulate, pinnate leaves (3-foliolate in *Sandoricum*). Flowers usually small and panicled, white, yellow or pink; sepals and petals 3—6; stamens twice as many as the petals, the filaments united to form a deep tube. Fruit a dehiscing capsule, or indehiscent.

Leaves trifoliolate.
  Leaflets 4–8 in. long, puberulous beneath. Fr. 3 in. diam., velvety ... ... 1. Sandoricum.
Leaves pinnate.
  Margins of leaflets entire.
    Leaves paripinnate
      Littoral trees with 1–3 pairs of opposite lfts. Sepals and petals 4 ... ... 2. Carapa.
      Inland tall tree. Lfts. 20–30. Capsule 3 valved with winged seeds ... 3. Chukrasia.
      Inland tree. Lfts. 8–13, pubescent beneath. Capsule 3 valved . ... 4. Chisocheton.
    Leaves imparipinnate.
      Lfts. 5–9, alternate.
        Lfts. glabrous. Staminal tube cylindrical ... 5. Dysoxylum.
        Lfts. glabrous or scaly. Staminal tube globose. Juice often milky ... ... 6. Aglaia.
      Lfts. opposite or sub-opposite
        Lfts. 5 in each leaf, pale glaucous beneath ... 7. Walsura.
        Lfts. 4–6. Fr $1\frac{1}{2}$ in. diam., shallow grooved ... 5. Dysoxylum, 118.
        Lfts. 9–17.
          Leaflets glabrous ... ... 8. Amoora.
          Leaflets with scaly blisters beneath ... ... 6. Aglaia.
  Margins of leaflets serrate
    Introduced tree. Lfts. falcate-lanceolate ... ... 9. Azadirachta.

1. SANDORICUM.

113. **S. indicum,** *Cav.*; H. i. 533; Br. 137. Vern. *Thitto,* Burm.

An evergreen tree 30—40 feet high with a rough, grey and minutely wrinkled bark. Leaves pinnately trifoliolate, common petiole softly pubescent, up to 8 in. long; leaflets 4—8 in. long, 2—5 in. broad, broadly ovate, shortly and abruptly acuminate, glabrous above puberulous beneath ; petiolules up to 3 in. long. Flowers nearly ½ in. long, yellow, in narrow axillary panicles ; staminal tube narrow. Fruit globose, 3 in. diam., yellow and velvety when ripe.

South Andaman, Haddo. This is the only locality in the Andamans where this has been found. It is very improbable that it is a native of the islands. Fl. Dec.-March. Fr. March-May. The leaves turn bright red before falling. New leaves Jan.-Febr.

2. CARAPA.

Littoral trees. Leaves paripinnate with 1—3 pairs of opposite leaflets. Flowers in lax axillary panicles ; sepals and petals 4 ; staminal tube globose. Fr. globose, leathery or woody.

Leaflets broad at the base, apex acute ... ... C. moluccensis.
Leaflets narrow at base, apex broad and blunt
Lfts. 3—4 in. long, obovate ... ... C. obovata.
Lfts. 3½—6 in. long, elliptic-oblong ... ... C. sp.

114. **C. moluccensis,** *Lamk.* ; H. i. 567 ; Br. 141.

A small tree (15—30 × 1½—3) often crooked and irregularly grown, bark grey with longitudinal fissures, cut stringy, pinkish-red. Leaves up to a foot long ; leaflets usually 4, rarely 2, more often 6, 2—4 in. long, ovate or broadly so, base broad, apex acute, dark green and glossy when new and with yellowish lateral nerves. Flowers pinkish-yellow, ¼—⅓ in. diam. Fruit the size of an orange.

Beach forests and rocky coasts of the islands, never in mangrove swamps. Prain writes, "*C. moluccensis* is common on the rocky coasts, while *C. obovata* is confined to muddy flats and mangrove swamps of the vegetation of which it forms an integral portion ... In the Andamans, *C. moluccensis* flowers in Nov.-Dec., *C. obovata* in March-April." I have also seen this one flower in Dec.-Jan. and *C. obovata* in Febr.-May and during the R. S. at various times. This is less common than the next one.

• 115. **C. obovata,** *Blume* ; H. i. 567 ; Br. 140. *The Puzzle Fruit Tree.* Vern. *Pinlè-ön*, Burm.

A small or moderate-sized tree (20—40 × 3—6), often of irregular growth, bark smooth, yellowish-grey, peeling in thin irregular flakes, cut stringy, reddish. Leaves about 8 in. long, rachis brownish ; leaflets usually 4, 3—4 in. long, obovate with a narrow base and broad blunt apex. Flowers cream-coloured. Fruit leathery, smooth, 7—10 in. diam.

Very common along seashores and along creeks, especially in mangrove forest. Fl. Febr.-May and also to a small extent at other times during the year. Fr. R. S. and C. S., conspicuous. The wood is hardly ever used in the Andamans.

116. Another species of *Carapa* occurs, I believe, in these islands. It is a moderate-sized elegant tree (40—60 × 4—7) with a dark coloured, rough and cracked bark peeling in oblong flakes, cut purplish-red, finely and beautifully wavy marked. Leaves usually with 2 pairs of

leaflets, rarely with 3, more often with 1 pair: leaflets 3½—6 in. long, 1¾—2½ in. broad, elliptic-oblong, base one-sided, apex rounded. Flowers like those of *C. obovata*. Mature fruit not seen.

In mangrove swamps. Betapur, Yeratil, Romlungta and Charalungta creeks. It resembles *C. obovata* in its leaves and flowers, but is otherwise very different. It sends up through the soft saline mud, sharp pointed 'knees', like those of *Bruguiera* and *Sonneratia*, and unlike the others of this genus given here it is deciduous in March, the leaves all turning bright orange-red or yellow before falling; the new leaves and flowers come out soon after. It has bark resembling that of *Chukrasia*.

3. CHUKRASIA.

• 117. **C. tabularis**, *Andr. Jussieu*; H. i. 568; Br. 144. *The Chittagong Wood.* Vern. ***Yinma bin***, Burm.

A tall handsome tree (50—90 × 4—8) with a brownish-black cracked bark, cut dark reddish. Leaves paripinnate, up to 2½ feet long, leaflets 20-30, sub-opposite or alternate, 2-6 in. long, ovate to oblong, unequal at the base, almost glabrous above, velvety pubescent beneath. Flowers in terminal panicles, yellowish or pinkish-white, 4—5-merous; petals erect, ½ in. long. Capsule the size and shape of a hen's egg, pointed, brown, splitting into 3 valves, with numerous winged seeds.

Not very common; usually in deciduous and semi-deciduous forests. Middle Andaman; Long Island; Baratang and Havelock Island. Leafless in the H. S. Fl. May-Aug. Fr. Nov.-Jan. Wood hard, varying from reddish to yellowish brown with a satin lustre. It is used in India for making furniture. I have followed Brandis in the spelling of *Chukrasia*.

4. CHISOCHETON.

118. ***C. grandiflorus**, *Kurz.*; H. i. 552; Br. 139.

An evergreen tree 40—50 feet high; bark rough with corky warts, cut rather dry, reddish. Leaves paripinnate, with the common petiole produced beyond the last pair of leaflets, or imparipinnate; leaflets 8—13, 6—8 in. long, oblong or oblong-lanceolate, softly pubescent beneath. Flowers ½ in. long, in dense racemes arranged in tawny-tomentose axillary panicles; petals ½ in. long, pubescent; staminal tube cylindric. Capsule loculicidally 3-valved.

I have seen no Andaman specimens of this. Brandis gives this as an Andaman plant, and although Kurz in his Andaman Report says "A high forest tree dispersed throughout the islands of the South Andaman," he does not, in his Flora of British Burma, ascribe this to these islands.

5. DYSOXYLUM.

Evergreen. Leaves pari- or imparipinnate with entire, more or less acuminate leaflets. Flowers 4—5-merous; staminal tube cylindric, crenulate at the mouth, with included anthers. Fruit leathery, globose or pear-shaped.

Leaflets 4—6, opposite or sub-opposite. Flowers 5-merous .. D. arborescens.
Leaflets 5—9, alternate. Flowers 4-merous.
  Moderate-sized tree. Fl. white and pink ... ... D. thyrsoideum.
  Small tree. Fl. cream-coloured ... ... D. andamanicum.

119. **D. arborescens**, *Miq.*; Br. 138.

A tree 20—30 feet high. Leaves 6—9 in. long, imparipinnate; leaflets 4—6, 2½—5 in. long, 1½—2½ in. broad, elliptic-obovate, shortly and abruptly acuminate, membranous, lateral nerves 6-8 pairs. Flowers 5-merous, ¼ in. long, in lax short panicles; petals linear, slightly thickened and narrowed towards the apex. Fruit 1¼ in. diam., globose or top-shaped with shallow grooves.

South Andaman, Dhani Khari, Port Mouat.

• 120. **D. thyrsoideum**, *Griff.*, var. andamanica, *King*; H. i. 547; Br. 138.

A tree (50—70 × 4—6), bark dark brownish-green, cut mealy, dirty brownish-yellow with an offensive smell. Leaves imparipinnate, 12-16 in. long; leaflets 6—9, 4—8 in. long, 1½—3 in. broad, ovate to ovate-oblong, shortly acuminate, oblique at the base. Flowers white, tinged with purplish pink, rather handsome but with an unpleasant smell, ¾ in. diam.; petals reflexed. Fruit obovoid, 2-3-lobed, about an inch long.

In evergreen forests. South Andaman, in several localities. Fl. Dec.-Febr.

121. **D. andamanicum**, *King*; J. A. S. B. No. 1. 1895, p. 49.

A small tree 15—25 feet high and about a foot in girth. Leaves about a foot long, imparipinnate; leaflets 5—9, 4—6 in. long, ovate to oblong or elliptic, suddenly acuminate, unequal at the base, lateral nerves 6—9 pairs. Flowers pale-yellow or cream-coloured, nearly ½ in. long, in short axillary spiciform racemes; petals ½ in., reflexed; stamens 8. Fruit depressed globular, 1¼ in. diam.

Long Island; Chiriatapu, Port Blair. Fl. January.

6. AGLAIA.

Small or moderate-sized trees, often with milky juice. Leaves imparipinnate with entire leaflets, often scaly or stellate-pubescent. Flowers small, polygamous, usually 5-merous; petals imbricate; staminal tube globose. Fruit indehiscent.

Leaflets 11-17, opposite or sub-opposite ... ... A. Ganggo.
Leaflets 5-7, alternate.
  Leaflets glabrous.
    Flowers 4—5-merous, orange-yellow ... ... A. glaucescens.
    Flowers 4-merous ... ... A. fusca.
  Leaflets with brownish scales beneath ... ... A. andamanica.

122. **A. Ganggo,** *Miq.*; Br. 143.

A small tree (25—40 × 2—4) with a greyish, fairly smooth bark, cut salmon coloured, faintly streaked, turning brown. Leaves up to 2 feet long, rachis slender; leaflets 11—17, 4—7 in. long, oblong or oblong-lanceolate, acute or shortly acuminate, base somewhat unequal. Flowers small, in rusty panicles; petals 5; staminal tube ovoid, with 5 anthers. Fruit ¾ in. across, compressed reniform, almost 2-lobed, coppery-brown.

Evergreen or semi-evergreen forests. Middle and South Andaman; Long Island and Havelock Island. Fl. R. S. Fr. Jan.-March. Wood light pinkish-brown, slightly fragrant.

123. **A. glaucescens,** *King.*; Br. 142.

A small tree (15—25 × 1—2) resembling a young *Letauk* tree. Leaves 8-12 in. long; leaflets 5—7, 2½—5 in. long, oblong-lanceolate to ovate-oblong, acute or shortly acuminate, lateral nerves 7—9 pairs, ascending. Flowers small, orange-yellowish, globular, in lax axillary panicles; petals 4-5; staminal tube globular with 4—5 anthers.

Not uncommon. Middle Andaman; Long Island and Guitar Island; South Andaman, around Port Blair. Fl. Dec.-Febr.

124. ***A. fusca,** *King.*; Br. 142.

A small tree. Leaves 6—10 in. long; leaflets 5—7, sometimes sub-opposite, 2½—4½ in. long, oblong to ovate-lanceolate, acute or shortly acuminate, lateral nerves 7—9 pairs, ascending. Flowers small, in axillary panicles; sepals and petals 4; staminal tube globular with 4 anthers. Fruit (not ripe) globular, nearly ½ in. diam.

South Andaman, Hobdaypur.

* 125. **A. andamanica,** *Hiern.*; H. i. 555; Br. 143. Vern. *Letauk*, Burm.

A moderate-sized tree (40—70 × 3—6) with a brownish-green bark peeling in flakes, cut pale-coloured; young branchlets, petioles, inflorescence and fruits covered with pale brown scales. Leaves up to 18 in. long; leaflets 5—7, 4—6 in. long, ovate to oblong-elliptic, base slightly oblique, lower surface with a few scattered scales. Flowers small, yellowish-white, in axillary panicles at the ends of the branchlets; petals 5; anthers 8—9. Fruit narrowly-ellipsoid, 1½ in. long.

Fairly frequent in deciduous and semi-deciduous forest, seen in nearly all localities. Fl. Nov.-Dec. Fr. April-July.

Wood pinkish-brown, moderately hard, used for making house posts, and said to be durable.

A. argentea, *Blume*; is a handsome tree found on the South Sentinel Island and in the Nicobar Islands. Leaves up to 2½ feet long; leaflets 7—11, 5-12 in. long, the upper ones the largest, silvery-white beneath; lateral nerves 12—24 pairs, bold beneath. Fl. H. S.

7. WALSURA.

Deciduous trees. Leaves imparipinnate with 5 leaflets, pale glaucous beneath. Flowers white; sepals and petals 5; stamens 10 or more with flat filaments, free or united at the base. Fruit a berry.

Leaves less than 1 foot long ... ... W. Candollei.
Leaves 1 foot long or longer.
Leaflets 5—7 in. long ... ... W. hypoleuca.
Leaflets 3—5 in. long ... ... W. robusta.

126. W. Candollei, *King*; Br. 136.

A moderate-sized tree with a fairy smooth light-brown thin bark. Leaves 4—7 in. long; leaflets 2—4 in. long, lanceolate, rounded at the base, acute, pale beneath with 7—11 pairs of spreading lateral nerves. Flowers white, small, at the ends of the branches of corymbose panicles; stamens yellow, filaments connate ½ of their length. Fruit ¾ in. long, ovoid-globose, densely and minutely rusty puberulous.

Porlob Island; South Andaman, Port Mouat, Dhani Khari. Fl. H. S. Fr. at the beginning of the R. S.

127. W. hypoleuca, *Kurz*; H. i. 564; Br. 136.

A tree (40—50 × 3—6) with a brownish-grey bark, cut pinkish-brown then light pink. Leaves 12—14 in. long; leaflets 5—7 in. long, 2—3 in. broad, elliptic-oblong, sub-acute, base narrowed, lateral nerves 7—8 pairs; petiolules ½ in. long. Flowers white, small, crowded at the ends of the branchlets in axillary panicles; stamens 10; the filaments united only at the base. Fruit (unripe) oblong, pointed, greyish-velvety.

In deciduous forests; not common. Middle Andaman near Bomlungta; Port Mouat. Fl. H. S.

128. W. robusta, *Roxb.*; H. i. 565; Br. 137. Vern. *Gyobo*, Burm.

A moderate-sized tree (40—60 × 2—4) with a dark-grey bark, cut dark reddish turning brown. Leaves about a foot long, rachis dark brown, lenticellate, thickened at the insertion of the petiolules; leaflets 3—5 in. long, ovate to ovate-oblong, bluntly acuminate lateral nerves 6—7 pairs, interarching. Flowers in dense panicles; stamens 10, filaments free. Fruit ½ in. diam., ellipsoid or globose.

Middle and South Andaman; Baratang and Rutland Island. Fl. Jan.-Febr.

8. AMOORA.

Leaves imparipinnate; leaflets usually opposite, oblique. Flowers small polygamous; sepals 3—5; petals usually 3; staminal tube globose with 6—10 anthers. Fruit coriaceous, splitting open when ripe.

Leaves up to 2 feet long. Fruit 2½ in. long, obovoid, tawny-tomentose ... . A. Wallichii.
Leaves up to 3 feet long. Fruit 1½ in. diam., globose, smooth ... ... A. Rohituka.

• 129. **A. Wallichii**, *King*; Br. 142. Vern. *Lalchini*, Hind.

A large tree (60—90 × 6—12) with spreading branches and a brownish-grey or brownish-yellow bark peeling in flakes, cut fibrous, reddish-pink with milky juice. Leaves up to 2 feet long; leaflets 9—13, 4—8 in. long, oblong to ovate-oblong, acute, base unequal, glabrous, petiolules ¼—½ in. long. Flowers yellowish, small, globular, in axillary panicles. Fruit 2½ in. long, obovoid, orange-yellow, tawny-tomentose.

In evergreen forest; frequently in damp places and on moist evergreen hills. Middle and South Andaman; Rutland Island. Fl. Aug.-Sept. Fr. Febr.-April. Wood reddish-brown, close-grained and fairly hard. It is often given the same vernacular name as that of *Callophyllum spectabile* and is sometimes called *Bara Lalchini*, but neither of these are well-known.

130. ***A. Rohituka**, *W. and A.*; H. i. 559; Br. 141.

An evergreen tree 50—60 feet high with a heavy crown, bark dark brown, rough, corky-cracked, cut reddish. Leaves up to 3 feet long: leaflets 9—15, 3—9 in. long, 1¼—4 in. broad, oblong to linear-oblong, bluntish-acuminate, base unequal, almost glabrous. Flowers greenish or pale yellow, about ¼ in. diam., almost sessile, the males in panicles, the females in solitary spikes; petals 3; staminal tube globose, with 6 anthers. Capsule 1½ in. diam., globose, yellow, 3-valved.

South Andaman and Narcondam.

***A. Manii**, *King*; Br. 142. South Andaman. Leaflets 11—15. Fertile flowers in long axillary panicles. I have seen no specimens.

9. AZADIRACHTA.

• 131. **A. indica**, *A. Juss.*; Br. 139. *The Neem* or *Margoza Tree*. Vern *Tamaka*, Burm.; *Neem*, Hind.

A moderate-sized evergreen tree with pinnate leaves 8—15 in. long, leaflets 11—19, sub opposite, 1—3 in. long, falcate-lanceolate, acuminate, serrate, base unequal, glabrous. Flowers white, fragrant. Drupe yellow.

Planted in Port Blair. Very common on Ross Island. Fl. H. S.

Swietenia Mahagoni, *Linn. The Mahogany Tree* has been introduced to the Andamans and is grown in Plantations in Wimberleyganj. It has seeds which very much resemble those of *Hippocratea*.

S. **macrophylla**, *King*, is a variety of the former of which Prain writes "Planted (in the Andamans) and thriving well, does much better than the true Mahogany."

Fam. 23. CHAILLETIACEÆ.

Leaves simple, alternate, entire. Flowers small, unisexual, 5-merous; petals bifid. Fruit 2-lobed.

1. CHAILLETIA.

132. **C. andamanica,** *King*; Br. 147.

A shrub or small tree with brownish lenticellate branchlets. Leaves 3—5 in. long, 1—2½ in. broad, elliptic to obovate, narrowed at the base, shortly and abruptly blunt acuminate, lateral nerves 4—6 pairs, interarching far from the margin. Flowers small, white, in axillary cymes; sepals and petals 5; stamens 5, with short filaments, sometimes adnate to the base of the petals. Fruit compressed, ½ in. broad, divided into 2 lobes, each with a groove on either side.

South Andaman, in several localities. Fl. May-July. Fr. Oct.-Dec.

Fam. 24. OLACACEÆ.

Trees or shrubs, sometimes climbing. Leaves simple, alternate, short petioled, entire and without stipules. Flowers usually small; petals 3—6; stamens as many as the petals and opposite them, or more. Fruit a drupe.

Littoral spiny tree Petals bearded; stamens 8—10 ... 1. Ximenia.
Shrubs, often scandent or straggling
Spinous. Flowers in axillary spikes; stamens 4—5 ... 2. Cansjera.
Unarmed. Flowers in axillary cymes; stamens 6 ... 3 Anacolosa.
Unarmed scandent. Flowers in small axillary racemes; stamens 3, with 5 staminodes ... ... 4. Olax.

1. XIMENIA.

133. **X. americana,** *Linn.*: H. i. 574; Br. 148. *The False Sandalwood.* Vern. *Pinlè-zi,* Burm.

A small shrubby and scraggy littoral tree, with straight, stiff, angled branchlets and armed with long, straight spines; foliage light-green. Leaves 1—1½ in. long, ovate to broadly elliptic, blunt with a small mucro, glabrous. Flowers yellowish-white, fragrant; nearly ½ in. diam., in short few-flowered axillary racemes; petals nearly ½ in. across, revolute, the upper-surface bearded with white hairs. Fruit the size of and resembling, a small lime, yellow when ripe.

Along all the seashores of the islands and growing near the beaches, but not common. Fl. Febr. The fruit is edible.

2. CANSJERA.

134. **C. Rheedii**, *Gmelin* ; H. i. 582 ; Br. 149.

A straggling half-scandent shrub armed with stout spines ; branchlets greenish. Leaves dark green and glossy above, 2½—5 in. long, 1—2 in. broad, ovate to oblong-lanceolate, acuminate, rounded at the base, glabrous, lateral nerves 3—5 pairs. Flowers small, greenish, in axillary tomentose spikes 1—2 in. long ; perianth with 4-5 recurved lobes and as many stamens opposite to them. Drupe ½ in. long, glabrous.

North Andaman, Mangrove Bay ; South Andaman, Macpherson Strait. Fl. January.

3. ANACOLOSA.

135. **A. puberula**, *Kurz*, var. andamanica, *King*; H. i. 581 ; Br. 149.

A large shrub with dark-coloured branchlets. Leaves 3½—5½ in. long, ovate-elliptic or ovate-lanceolate, glabrous, lateral nerves 4—6 pairs ; petiole about ¼ in. long. Flowers small, in axillary cymes ; petals 6, in pairs ; stamens as many as and opposite the petals. Fruit ovoid, about ½ in. long.

Common in the Andamans, *King*. Middle and South Andaman. Fl. and Fr. in April

4. OLAX.

136. **O. imbricata**, *Roxb.* ; H. i. 575 ; Br. 148.

A scandent unarmed shrub. Leaves 3½—5½ in. long, ovate-oblong to oblong-lanceolate, acute, base more or less rounded, glabrous, lateral nerves 8—9 pairs, faint. Flowers ½ in. long, white, crowded in small axillary racemes ; petals 6, united in pairs ; perfect stamens 3, with 5—6 bifid staminodes. Fruit ½ in. diam., almost globular, enveloped by the accrescent calyx.

South Andaman, in several localities. Fr. Febr.

Fam. 25. ICACINACEÆ.

Small trees or climbers with simple entire, alternate leaves without stipules. Flowers usually small, whitish ; stamens as many as the petals or perianth segments and alternating with them. Fruit a drupe.

Trees or shrubs. Flowers in axillary cymes. Fr. ellipsoid, smooth and grooved ... ... 1. Gomphandra.

A climber. Fl. very small, in velvety tomentose spikes. Fr. globular, velvety ... ... 2. Sarcostigma.

1. GOMPHANDRA.

Calyx cup-shaped with short teeth; corolla campanulate, with lanceolate, inflexed lobes, midrib prominent on the inside.

A shrub. Leaves 3½—6 in. long ... . G. comosa.
A small tree. Leaves 5—9 in. long ... ... G. andamanica.

137. ***G. comosa.** *King*; Br. 151.

A glabrous shrub, the young branchlets ash-grey. Leaves 3½—6 in. long, 1½—2 in. broad, oblong to elliptic-oblong, shortly acuminate, narrowed to the base, petioles about ½ in. long. Flowers in umbellate cymes; petals 4—5, broadly oblong with an inflexed point; stamens 4—5, filaments flattened with a large tuft of hairs near the apex. Fruit 1 in. long, narrowly ellipsoid, vertically grooved.

South Andaman, around Port Blair. Fl. June. Fr. October.

138. **G. andamanica,** *King*; H. i. 589; Br. 151.

A small tree (20—35 × 1½—2) with a thin greenish-grey bark, cut whitish, branchlets pubescent. Leaves 5—9 in. long, 1½—3 in. broad, oblong to elliptic-lanceolate, narrowed at the base, pale beneath, lateral nerves about 10 pairs, irregular Flowers white, in compact cymes, axillary or from the scars of the fallen leaves; petals 5, lanceolate; stamens glabrous. Fruit 1 in. long, white, compressed-ellipsoid, grooved on one side.

Not uncommon. Middle and South Andaman; Baratang and Long Island. Fl. Dec.-Febr. Fr. Febr.-May.

2. SARCOSTIGMA.

139. **S. Wallichii,** *Beillon*; H. i. 525; Br. 154.

A slender climber. Leaves 4—7 in. long, 1½—2½ in. broad, oblong to elliptic-oblong, shortly acuminate, base narrowed or rounded, glabrous, coriaceous, with 5—6 pairs of lateral nerves and distinct and prominent net venation. Flowers small, in axillary or extra-axillary velvety-tomentose spikes nearly as long as the leaves. Fruit ovoid or globular, 1 in. long, yellow and velvety, with sickly sweet pulp.

Common, especially on evergreen hills and among tangled undergrowth. Middle and South Andaman; Baratang and Havelock Islands. Fl. Dec. Fr. Jan.

Fam. 26. CELASTRACEÆ.

Trees or shrubs, often scandent, with opposite or alternate, simple leaves. Flowers small, white, greenish or yellowish calyx with 4—5 persistent imbricate segments; petals 4–5, or absent; disc conspicuous; stamens 3–5. Fruit dry or fleshy.

Leaves opposite or sub-opposite. Stamens 3, 4 or 5.
Small trees with entire leaves. Stamens 4 or 5.
Leaves 4–6 in. long. Fr. a globose capsule ... 1. Glyptopetalum.
Leaves 2–3 in. long. Fruit indehiscent ... ... 2. Elæodendron.
Scandent shrubs with entire or crenate leaves. Stamens 3.
Littoral. Fruit a globose berry .. 3. Salacia.
Inland. Fruit flat, dehiscent; seeds with a large membranous wing ... ... 4. Hippocratea.
Leaves alternate. Stamens 5.
A scandent shrub with crenate leaves. Flowers paniculate 5. Celastrus.
A moderate-sized tree. Flowers in slender fascicled racemes 6. Kurrimia.

1. GLYPTOPETALUM.

140. ***G. calocarpum,** *Prain*; H. i. 609; Br. 159.

A small tree with rounded branchlets. Leaves opposite, 4—6 in. long, oblong or oblong-lanceolate, shortly and bluntish acuminate, entire glabrous and coriaceous, with 5—6 pairs of lateral nerves. Flowers small, greenish-white, in axillary or extra-axillary cymes; petals and stamens 4. Capsule ½ in. diam., globose, with a red seed in each cell.

North and South Andaman; Narcondam. Along the seashores.

2. ELÆODENDRON.

141. ***E. subrotundum.** *King*; Br. 165.

A tree 20 feet high. Leaves opposite or sub-opposite, 2—2½ in. long, broadly sub-rotund to almost orbicular, entire with the edges slightly revolute, lateral nerves 6—7 pairs; petiole ⅓ in. long, slender. Flowers about ¼ in. diam., numerous, in axillary or terminal umbellate cymes, usually 4-merous; petals broadly oblong, blunt and spreading. Fruit oblong-clavate, dark coloured.

Evidently rare. Port Blair at Shaithan Khari, *King's collectors.*

3. SALACIA.

Scandent shrubs with opposite leaves. Flowers greenish yellow; stamens 3.

Leaves 2—3½ in. long. Flowers ⅕ in diam. Fr. ¼ in. diam. S. prinoides.
Leaves 3—6 in. long. Flowers ⅓ in. diam. Fr. nearly 1 in. diam. ... ... S. latifolia.

142. **S. prinoides,** *DC.*; H. i. 626; Br. 166.

A straggling half-scandent shrub with angular branchlets. Leaves opposite, 2–3½ in. long, lanceolate or oblong-lanceolate, shortly and bluntish acuminate, crenate-serrate, coriaceous, glabrous and glossy, petioles ¼—½ in. long, slender. Flowers ¼ in. diam., fragrant, greenish-yellow, in axillary panicles; petals often clawed at the base. Fruit globose, ½ in. diam., bright red and shining when ripe.

Littoral forest, bordering on mangrove and tidal creeks. Fairly frequent and in nearly all localities. Often on *Avicennia.* Fl Jan.-Febr.

143. **S. latifolia,** *Wall.*; H. i. 629; Br. 165.

A scandent glabrous shrub resembling and allied to the last one, but differing in being a larger climber, having larger and more rotund leaves 3—6 in. long, larger flowers nearly ½ in. diam., and larger fruit nearly 1 in. diam.

South Andaman; Jolly Boy's Island. Fl. and Fr. H. S.

4. HIPPOCRATEA.

Scandent shrubs with opposite leaves. Flowers greenish or yellowish-white; sepals and petals 5, the latter spreading; stamens 3, with flat recurved filaments. Fruit of 2 to 3 flattened capsules joined at the base, and packed with numerous winged seeds.

Leaves 4—7 in. long, shallowly crenate	H. macrantha.
Leaves 4—5½ in. long, entire	H. andamanica.

144. **H. macrantha,** *Korthals*; Br. 161.

Climbing. Leaves 4—7 in. long, elliptic to rotund-elliptic or obovate, shortly cuspidate, shallowly crenate, glabrous, with 5 or 6 pairs of lateral nerves; petioles ¼ in. long. Flowers pale-yellow or white, nearly ¼ in. diam., in axillary panicles. Carpels oblong to obovate, 2½—4 in. long, splitting down the centre and along the edges. Seeds with a thinly membranous brown wing 2—3 in. long.

South and Middle Andaman. It has attractive bright-brown winged seeds which may often be seen strewn about the jungles during Febr.-April; they resemble those of *Pterospermum acerroides* and of the *Mahogany*, and have the shape of those of *Sterculia alata.*

145. ***H. andamanica,** *King*; Br. 161.

A climber. Leaves 4—5½ in. long, 1¾—2¼ in. broad, oblong to elliptic, acute or obtusely cuspidate, base cuneate, entire, glabrous, with 5—7 pairs of ascending lateral nerves; petioles ⅓ in. long. Flowers rather small, in axillary and terminal panicles. Fruit not known.

South Andaman, Port Mouat.

5. CELASTRUS.

146. **C. paniculata,** *Willd.*; H. i. 617; Br. 162. *The Black Oil or Oleum Nigrum Plant.* Vern. *Myinkauknayaung*, Burm.

A large scandent straggling shrub. Leaves alternate, 2½—5 in. long, ovate or obovate, shortly blunt acuminate, crenate-serrulate, glabrous or puberulous beneath; petioles slender. Flowers yellowish, in long raceme-like panicles; disc concave; stamens 5. Capsule 3-valved with scarlet seeds.

Middle and South Andaman, not common. Fr. Jan. The seeds yield a black oil which is used as a diuretic.

6. KURRIMIA.

147. *K. pulcherrima, *Wall.*; H. i. 622; Br. 164.

A tree 40—70 feet high. Leaves 6—8 in. long, oblong to oblong-elliptic, acuminate, coriaceous and glabrous, with about 12 pairs of curved lateral nerves and fine elegant venation; petioles ¾—1 in. long. Flowers small, in slender, axillary, often fascicled, racemes, 5-merous, filaments flattened. Capsule 1—1½ in. long, ellipsoid with 2 vertical grooves. Seeds 2, yellow or orange.

South Andaman, Gopiakabang and Hopetown. Fl. July-Oct.

Fam. 27. RHAMNACEÆ.

THE JUJUBE FAMILY.

Trees or shrubs, often scandent and thorny. Leaves simple, alternate, serrate or denticulate, strongly nerved. Flowers small, greenish-yellow with a large disc; sepals valvate; petals 5, or none; stamens 5, opposite the petals and often enclosed by them. Fruit a drupe or a capsule.

Leaves penninerved.
- An extensive climber. Fruit with a flat narrow terminal wing ... 1. Ventilago.
- A straggling shrub. Capsule coriaceous, compressed, opening by 2 valves ... ... 2. Smythea.

Leaves palminerved
- Prickly. Leaves serrate, strongly 3-nerved ... .. 3. Zizyphus.
- Littoral straggling shrub. Fruit a berry ... ... 4. Colubrina.
- Inland. Climber with terminal spiral tendrils. Fruit 3-angled ... ... 5. Gouania.

1. VENTILAGO.

148. V. madraspatana, *Gaertn.*; H. i. 631; Br. 167.

A climber, with dark-coloured cracked stems, ascending the tallest trees. Leaves 3—4 in. long, ovate or elliptic, one-sided at the base, acuminate, glabrous, with strong ascending lateral nerves, entire or serrate, petiole rather short. Flowers with an offensive smell, numerous crowded in large terminal panicles. Fruit ½ in. diam., terminated by a long blunt one-nerved wing 1½—2½ in. long.

Common in the interior forests of the islands and also often along the seashore; in almost all localities. Fl. Dec.-Febr. Fr. Febr.-March.

2. SMYTHEA.

149. **S. calpicarpa**, *Kurz.*; H. i. 632; Br. 175.

A scandent or straggling shrub with zig-zag branchlets. Leaves 3—5 in. long, 1½—2 in. broad, oblong-lanceolate or lanceolate, acuminate, base obtuse or rounded, crenate-serrate, glabrous, with tufts of hairs beneath in the axils of the 5—6 pairs of lateral nerves; petiole short. Flowers small, greenish, in axillary fascicles. Fruit 3-celled, flat, dehiscent vertically in 2 valves, the lower part enclosed in the persistent calyx tube.

Not common. Havelock Island; South Andaman; along the beaches. Fl. Febr.

3. ZIZYPHUS.

Scandent shrubs (except the last one), armed with prickles. Leaves serrate, strongly 3-nerved. Flowers small, greenish-white.

Native scandent shrubs.
Underside of leaves clothed with ferruginous hairs ... Z. Oenoplia.
Leaves perfectly glabrous ... ... Z. glabra.
Introduced tree. Underside of leaves white or brown tomentose ... ... Z. Jujuba.

150. **Z. Oenoplia**, *Mill.*; H. i. 634; Br. 170.

A straggling, often climbing, shrub; prickles often solitary; branchlets, underside of leaves and inflorescence clothed with ferruginous hairs. Leaves 1½-2½ in. long, obliquely ovate to ovate-lanceolate, acute, minutely denticulate, with 3 bold vertical nerves and numerous connecting ascending ones; petioles ¼ in. long. Flowers in short axillary cymes. Drupe ¼ in. diam., turning from yellow to black.

South Andaman, Goplakabang, Port Mouat. Fl. Aug. Fr. March.

151. **Z. glabra**, *Roxb.*; Br. 171.

A scandent shrub with sharp recurved prickles. Leaves 2½—4½ in. long, 1—2 in. broad, ovate or ovate-oblong, bluntly acuminate, base one-sided, crenate-serrulate, perfectly glabrous and glossy, with 3 strong unbranched nerves. Flowers slender pedicelled, greenish-white, in axillary cymes. Fruit bluntly ellipsoid, ½—¾ in. long, yellow when ripe.

Fairly frequent. Middle and South Andaman; Havelock and Rutland Islands. Fl. Jan.-Febr. Fr. April.

[a] Z. Jujuba, *Lam.*; Br. 169. *The Baer*, or *Jujube* or *Chinese Date*. Vern *Ziben*, Burm.; *Ber*, Hind. A small or middle-sized tree, branchlets and under side of leaves covered with a white or brown tomentum. Drupe ⅔ in. long, glossy, orange or red when ripe, edible. Planted in Port Blair.

4. COLUBRINA.

152. **C. asiatica**, *Brongn.*; H. i. 642; Br. 174. *The Indian Snake-wood*. Vern. *Kanaywet*, Burm.

A straggling glabrous littoral shrub. Leaves 1⅓—2½ in. long, 1—2 in. broad, ovate, acuminate, base rounded or slightly one-sided, margin crenate-serrate with 3—5 basal nerves and 2—3 pairs of lateral nerves; petioles ½—¾ in. long. Flowers small, greenish or yellowish-white, nearly ¼ in. diam. Berry nearly ⅓ in. diam., seated on the persistent calyx.

Very common along all the seashores of the islands. Fl. and Fr. Dec.-March. It is also called the *West Indian Hoop-withe*.

5. GOUANIA.

Unarmed climbing shrubs, often with terminal spiral tendrils. Leaves entire or serrate. Flowers in slender terminal spikes or racemes. Fruit 3-angled.

Leaves penninerved with entire margins ... ... G. andamanica.
Leaves palminerved, with crenate-serrate margins ... ... G. leptostachya.

153. **G. andamanica**, *King*; Br. 175.

Young branches ferrugineous pubescent. Leaves 1⅓—3½ in. long ¾—2 in. broad, oblong-ovate, subacute, entire, narrowed to the base, both surfaces, especially the lower, adpressed pubescent, petioles ⅓ in. long. Flowers sessile, collected by 3—4 in slender spikes 3—9 in. long, which often have a cirrhus at the base. Fruit about ⅓ in. long, rusty tomentose, boldly angled.

Middle Andaman, common; South Andaman, Goplakabang and Port Mouat. Fl. December.

154. **G. leptostachya**, *DC.*; H. i. 643; Br. 175.

Scandent, often on the highest trees. Leaves 1¾—3½ in. long, broadly ovate, acute to acuminate, base rounded or slightly cordate and 3-nerved, with 4—5 pairs of lateral nerves, margins crenate-serrate, glabrous; petioles ¾—1 in. long. Flowers small, white, in slender racemes 6—18 in. long, usually with a cirrhus at the base. Fruit ⅓ in. diam.

Middle and South Andaman. Long Island. Fl. Oct.-Dec. Fr. H. S.

Fam. 28. AMPELIDEÆ.

THE VINE FAMILY.

Shrubs or climbers with alternate, simple or variously compound, often lobed leaves. Flowers usually many, in cymes opposite a leaf, 4—5 merous; petals with the stamens opposite them and outside the disc. Fruit a berry.

Shrubs or small trees. Leaves pinnate or bipinnate; petioles sheathing; leaflets serrate. Filaments united ... 1. Leea.
Climbers, usually with tendrils opposite the leaves. Filaments free ... ... 2. Vitis.

1. LEEA.

Stems and branches often angled or grooved. Leaves imparipinnate to tripinnate, with opposite serrate leaflets, lateral nerves of leaflets usually opposite at their junction with the midrib; petioles with leafy sheathing bases. Flowers many, in corymbose cymes. Berry often lobed.

Leaves simply pinnate; leaflets 3—5 ... ... L. latifolia.
Leaves 1—3-pinnate with many leaflets.
Leaflets glabrous on both surfaces
Stems greenish. Flowers greenish-white ... L. sambucina.
Stems and flowers purple-red or coral red ... ... L. acuminata.
Leaflets pubescent on the lower surface. Flowers white ... L. aquata.

155. ***L. latifolia**, *Wall.*; J.A.S.B. No. 3. 1896, p. 411.

A shrub with rusty puberulous young branchlets. Leaves imparipinnate; leaflets 3—5, 9—12 in. long, oblong to sub-orbicular, nearly acute, the base almost cordate, doubly serrate, glabrous above with few scattered hairs beneath, lateral and transverse nerves very distinct. Flowers in umbellate cymes.

Andamans, *King*. I have seen no Andaman specimens.

156. **L. sambucina**, *Willd.*; H. i. 664; Br. 179.

A shrub 4—10 feet high. Leaves 15—20 in. long, bipinnate, rarely tripinnate; leaflets 3—9 in. long, 1½—3 in. broad, oblong or elliptic, sharply acuminate, coarsely serrate, lateral nerves 7—12 pairs, prominent. Flowers greenish-white, in spreading cymes about 6 in. across; staminal tube yellowish-white with notched lobes. Fruit nearly ½ in. diam., bluish-black.

Very common in the islands in damp places along streams in all localities. Fl. R. S. Fr. Nov.-Febr. The young leaves are cooked and eaten as a vegetable by the Burmese who sometimes call it *Nagamauk*.

157. **L. acuminata**, *Wall.*; H. i. 664; Br. 179.

A small shrub 3—5 feet high, the stems, leaves, flowers and fruits coral red or purple red. Leaves about 8 in. long, usually bipinnate or with one of the lower pinnæ pinnulate; leaflets 2—6 in. long, elliptic to ovate-oblong, serrate, dark green and glossy above, reddish-purple below. Flowers coral red, in compact cymes about 2 in. across. Fruit depressed globular, about ½ in. across.

In the same localities, but not as common as the preceding one. Fl. at the beginning of the R S. Fr. C. S.

158. **L. æquata**, *Linn.*; Br. 179.

A shrub 8—10 feet high, the branchlets petioles and underside of leaves hirsute. Leaves bipinnate or tripinnate; leaflets 5—10 in. long, oblong-lanceolate, sharply acuminate, unequally serrate, the undersurface with numerous scattered scales, lateral nerves 8—12 pairs. Flowers white, in sessile cymes. Fruit ¼ in. diam., depressed globular, black when ripe.

Not as common as the two previous ones. Fl. R. S. Similar to this but without the scales on the under-surface is *L. robusta*, *Roxb.*, also found in the Andamans.

There is also another *Leea*. found in these islands. A small tree (15—30 x 1—2), the stems armed with rows of prickles. Leaves bipinnate; leaflets up to 9 in. long, oblong-ovate, acuminate, serrate-crenate; petiole winged. Fruit ½ in. diam., golden-brown. Middle Andaman, on the east coast, north of Betapur, and on Havelock Island. Fr. Febr.

2. VITIS.

Climbing shrubs, often with angled stems and with tendrils opposite the leaves. Leaves lobed or compound. Flowers small, 4—5-merous. Fruit a berry.

These are mostly climbers of little importance and they have not been included in the general key. They often have herbaceous stems and copious watery sap.

Leaves simple.
  Leaves glabrous. Flowers in umbellate cymes.
    L. 3—8 in long, bristly-serrate, cordate ... ... V. discolor.
    L. 2—4 in. long, wavy dentate, cordate ... ... V. repens.
    L. 2—4 in. long, bristly serrato-crenulate, saggitate-cordate ... . V. glaberrima.
  Leaves clothed with soft woolly hair. Flowers in tendril-bearing panicles ... ... V. barbata.
Leaves compound.
  Leaves 3—5 foliolate.
    Lfts. 4½—6 in. long, elliptic-oblong ... ... V. andamanica.
    Lfts. 4½—6 in. long, oblong to ovate or lanceolate ... V. lanceolaria.
    Lfts. 1½—4 in. long, ovate or oblanceolate ... ... V. japonica.
  Leaves 7—9 foliolate ... ... V. novemfolia.

*V. discolor, *Dalz.*; Br. 176. Stems woody at the base, red when young. L. 3—8 in. long, ovate-lanceolate, acuminate, base cordate, margins bristly serrate, the upper surface variegated with red and white, the lower purple, lateral nerves 5—7 pairs; petiole ½—3 in. long. Fl. small with purple calyx and yellow petals. Fr. ¼ in. diam., globular, red when ripe. South Andaman Tarmugli Island. Fl. Aug.-Dec.

* **V. repens**, *W. and A.*; Br. 177. A large climber. L. 2—4 in. long, ovate, shortly acuminate, distantly wavy dentate, base cordate, pale green, lateral nerves about 4 pairs; petioles 1—2½ in. long. Cymes half the length of the leaf. Fr. globose or ovoid. South Andaman. Fl. and Fr. June-Dec.

V. glaberrima, *Wall.* Stems weak, 4-angled and glaucous. L. 2—4 in. long, 1–2 in. broad, ovate lanceolate and tapering to the acute apex, margins minutely bristly serrate-crenulate, base saggitate-cordate, lateral nerves 4–5 pairs; petioles ¾—1½ in. long. Fl. umbellate, in small cymes. Fr. obovoid. Long Island and South Andaman. Fl. Dec. Fr. March-April.

* **V. barbata**, *Wall.*; Br. 177. A woody climber with rounded branchlets, the branchlets, petiole and inflorescence clothed with soft woolly hair and long thin brown bristles. L. 6—10 in. long, ovate, shortly acuminate, deeply cordate, the margins unequally wavy dentate, woolly pubescent beneath, lateral nerves 6—7 pairs; petiole 3–6 in. long. Cymes in large panicles bearing forked tendrils. Berries globular. South Andaman, fairly frequent. Fl. June-Aug. Fr. Sept.

* **V. andamanica**, *King*; Br. 706. Glabrous except the inflorescence. Lfts. 4½—6 in. long, elliptic-oblong, shortly cuspidate, the edges remotely serrate, lateral nerves 6–8 pairs. Cymes 1½ in. diam., many flowered and much-branched, puberulous. Fl. small, petals rusty puberulous outside. Fr. globular-ovoid, with a single seed. South Andaman. Fl. and Fr. Nov.-March.

* **V. lanceolaria**, *Wall.*; Br. 78. A large woody evergreen climber, the stems often corky tuberculate. L. 3–5-foliolate; lfts. 1¾–6 in. long, oblong to ovate or lanceolate, tapering at either end, remotely serrate, lateral nerves 6—10 pairs; petiole 2—5 in. long. Fl. pale-yellow, in axillary cymes with shortly forked tendrils. Fr. ½ in. diam., white when ripe. South Andaman.

* **V. japonica**, *Thunbg.*; Br. 704. Stems slender. L. 3—5 foliolate; lfts. 1½—4 in. long, ovate or oblanceolate, coarsely and unequally serrate in the upper part, lateral nerves 7—9 pairs; petiole 1½—2½ in. long. Fl. in spreading branched cymes, 2–3 in. across, puberulous, 4-merous. Fr. nearly ¾ in. diam., with 3 or 4 triangular seeds. South Andaman, common. Fl. and Fr. Nov.-March.

* **V. novemfolia**, *Wall.* Glabrous with slender stems. L. usually 7—9 foliolate; lfts. 2—3½ in. long, oblong-lanceolate, shortly acuminate, margin with a few teeth near the apex; common petiole 2½–3 in. long, petiolules long. Fl. in puberulous much-branched cymes 3—6 in. across, 4-merous. Fr. ovoid, with 2 seeds. Frequent around Port Blair. Fl. H. S Fr. Oct.-Dec.

Fam. 29. SAPINDACEÆ.

THE SOAP-NUT FAMILY.

Trees or shrubs with simple, alternate, trifoliolate or pinnate leaves. Flowers usually white or yellow, small, polygamous; calyx with 4—5 imbricate, often unequal, lobes; petals 4–5 or none; often with scales or tufts of hairs; stamens 5–10, generally 8, often with hairy filaments. Fruit dry or succulent, often angled or winged.

Leaves simple.
- A shrub. Leaves 6—12 in. long, crowded together. Fl. white or pink ... 1. Aphania. 150.
- Shrubby tree. Leaves 2—5 in. long, scattered. Fl. yellow ... ... 2. Dodonæa.

Leaves trifoliolate.
 Leaflets coarsely serrate. Fl. in narrow racemes ... 3. Allophylus.
Leaves pinnate; usually paripinnate.
 Leaflets 8-20, serrate.
  Leaves 2—3 ft. long. Fl. in large panicles ... 4. Pometia.
 Leaflets 5—13, entire.
  Lfts. more than 8 in each leaf.
   Lfts. glabrous. Capsule inflated, 2—lobed ... 5. Harpullia.
   Lfts. rusty tomentose. Drupe shining ... 6. Erioglossum.
  Lfts. not more than 8 in each leaf.
   Lfts. glabrous. Fr. sharply angled ... ... 7. Mischocarpus.
   Lfts. with hair tufts in the nerve axils beneath. Capsule 2—lobed ... ... 8. Arytera.
   Lfts. glabrous. Fr. globular with deep vertical ridges 9. Lepisanthes.
   A shrub. Lfts. 2-4. Fr. in pairs .. 1. Aphania, 160.
   Lfts. glaucous beneath. Fl. many, in terminal panicles ... ... Nephelium.

1. APHANIA.

Shrubs. Flowers in axillary panicles; sepals large and petaloid. Fruit fleshy, usually in pairs.

Littoral. Leaves simple, collected in tufts. Flowers small ... A. Danura.
A shrub with paripinnate leaves. Flowers ⅓ in. diam. ... A. montana.

159. **A. Danura,** *Radlk*; H. i. 684; Br. 191.

A littoral shrub. Leaves with short stout petioles, crowded together in tufts on the branchlets, simple, 6—12 in. long, elliptic to lanceolate or obovate, acute, narrowed to the sometimes small-cordate base, glossy. Flowers small, whitish or pinkish; petals with a hairy scale at the base; stamens 6—8, glabrous. Fruit ellipsoidal, ⅓—½ in. long, reddish, often in pairs.

Coast forests of the islands. North Andaman, west coast. Fl. and Fr. in April.

160. ***A. montana,** *Blume*; Br. 192.

A shrub with paripinnate leaves. Leaflets 1—2 pairs, 4—6 in. long, elliptic to oblong, sub-acute, the base tapering, glabrous, minutely reticulate. Flowers ⅓ in. diam., 4-merous, petals ovate, with fimbriate edges and a basal scale; stamens 8, with pubescent filaments. Fruit ellipsoidal, ½ in. long, generally in pairs.

Andamans and Nicobars, *Brandis*. The specimens in the Calcutta Herbarium are from the Nicobars.

2. DODONÆA.

* 161. **D. viscosa,** *Linn.* H. i. 697; Br. 186. *The Ake-Ake Tree of New Zealand.*

A small much-branched shrub with light green foliage; branchlets brownish, angled. Leaves 2—4½ in. long, ⅓—1¼ in. broad, obovate to oblanceolate, tapering to the short petiole, margins recurved, glabrous and rather rough to the touch, lateral nerves numerous and looping. Flowers yellowish-green, on slender pedicels; petals none; stamens 8 or less. Fruit compressed, $\frac{3}{4}$ in. across, heart-shaped with a wing all round.

Uncommon. A few trees were seen growing near the beaches in the Middle Andaman at the mouth of the Betapur, on Neill Island and on Jolly Boy's Island. Also on Barren Island and on Narcondam. It has the superficial appearance that many plants of the Euphorbiaceæ have. It is also called the *Clammy Hop-seed Bush*.

3. ALLOPHYLUS.

162. **A. Cobbe,** *Blume*; H. i. 673; Br. 185.

A shrub. Leaves digitately 3-foliolate, the common petioles 2—4 in. long; leaflets variable in size, 2—10 in. long, ovate or elliptic or lanceolate, acuminate, coarsely serrate, glabrous with tufts of hairs in the nerve axils beneath. Flowers whitish, in narrow tassel-like racemes; petals with a hairy scale above the claw; stamens 8, with hairy bases. Fruit $\frac{1}{4}$ in. diam., red when ripe.

Fairly common; often along seashores. Middle Andaman, in several localities; Porlob Island; Long Island; Baratang and South Andaman. Fl. April-July. Fr. Oct.

4. POMETIA.

163. **P. pinnata,** *Forst*; H. i. 691; Br. 185. Vern. *Thitkandu*.

A moderate-sized or large evergreen tree (50—80 × 5—10), usually branching low, with a dense shady crown, bark reddish-brown, peeling in flakes. Leaves paripinnate, 2—3 feet long; leaflets 8—20, increasing in size towards the top of the leaf, the lowest almost sessile and orbicular 1—2 in. diam., the topmost oblong-lanceolate, 9—12 in. long, irregularly serrate. Flowers small, yellowish, in large panicles. Fruit oblong, $\frac{1}{2}$—$1\frac{1}{2}$ in. long, splitting irregularly, purple when ripe.

A very common tree found everywhere in low moist places along streams. Fl. Dec.-Jan. Fr. April-May. New leaves in Nov.-Dec., pinkish. Wood reddish-brown, easily splitting, used for fuel.

5. HARPULLIA.

164. **H. cupanioides,** *Roxb.*; H. i. 692; Br. 187.

A moderate-sized tree (30—50 × 2—4) with somewhat discoloured greyish bark; cut mealy, dark cream-coloured; bark easily separating from, and watery near, the sapwood; branchlets whitish. Leaves pari- or imparipinnate; leaflets 3—6 pairs, opposite or sub-opposite, 3—8 in. long, oblong to elliptic-lanceolate, one-sided at the base. Flowers greenish-white; sepals petals and stamens 5. Capsule brilliant orange, 1¼ in. across, 2-lobed, splitting, reddish-brown inside.

Uncommon. Middle Andaman, near Mt. Farrington, Bomlungta; South Andaman, Port Mouat. Fl. beginning of the R. S. Fr. Oct.-Nov.

6. ERIOGLOSSUM

• 165. **E. rubiginosum,** *Blume*; H. i. 672; Br. 192.

A small tree (15–35 × 1–3) with slightly rough dark-coloured bark, cut light brown, branchlets young leaves and inflorescence covered with a rusty golden tomentum. Leaves usually imparipinnate, 10—14 in. long; leaflets 5—13, 3—7 in. long, oblong-lanceolate, slightly one-sided at base, softly pubescent beneath. Flowers white, in long racemes; petals small, with a woolly base. Drupes ½—¾ in. long, shining, yellow or reddish and turning dark purple when ripe, handsome.

Middle and South Andaman; Baratang and Havelock Island; Rutland and the South Cinque Islands. Often in clearings around Port Blair. Fl. Jan.-April. Fr. Mar.-June. Wood light-coloured, hard and heavy.

7. MISCHOCARPUS.

166. ***M. sundaicus,** *Blume*; H. i. 678; Br. 183.

An evergreen tree 25—50 feet high. Leaves usually paripinnate; leaflets 2—3 pairs, 2½—6 in. long, elliptic to ovate or lanceolate, acuminate, tapering at the base, glabrous, lateral nerves 12—14, looping, with weaker intermediate ones, net venation fine. Flowers minute, in panicled racemes; petals none; stamens 8, glabrous. Capsule pear-shaped, sharply 3-angled.

Uncommon. South Andaman, Dhani Khari. Fl. May-July. Fr. July-Oct.

8. ARYTERA.

167. **A. littoralis,** *Blume*; H. i. 677; Br. 188.

A small tree 15—30 feet high, young branchlets and rachis pale brown. Leaves paripinnate; leaflets 2—3 pairs, 4—6 in. long, 1—1¾ in. broad, elliptic to oblong-lanceolate, acuminate, glabrous with minute tufts of hairs in the nerve axils beneath, lateral nerves 8—10 pairs. Flowers small, yellowish, in branched racemes; petals with a notch, hairy above; stamens 8, hairy. Capsule 2-lobed, coriaceous, lobes compressed, one lobe much smaller than the other.

Uncommon. Middle Andaman, at Bomlungta below the camp; South Andaman, North Corbyn's Cove. Fl. April.

9. LEPISANTHES.

168. ***L. andamanica,** *King*; Br. 189.

A small tree. Leaves paripinnate, 7—12 in. long; leaflets 1—2 pairs, on stout petioles, 4—7 in. long, elliptic to oblanceolate, acute, much narrowed to the base, glabrous and minutely reticulate. Flowers ¼ in. diam., in compound panicles; sepals 5, unequal, obovate, tomentose outside; petals 5, scaled; stamens 8, with villous filaments. Fruit ¾ in. long, almost globular, with 3 deep vertical ridges.

South Andaman, Port Mouat. Evidently rare. Fl. Febr.-April. Fr. April.

? 169. **Nephelium sp.** A moderate-sized tree (30—60 × 2—4) with a brownish bark, cut reddish-brown. Leaves pari- or imparipinnate; leaflets 4 - 8, sub-opposite, 4—6 in. long, oblong, somewhat one-sided at the base, dark green above, pale glaucous beneath, main nerves 10—14 pairs. Flowers white, numerous, in terminal panicles. Fr. not seen.

Middle Andaman, Cuthbert and Rongat Bays and adjoining localities. Fl. March-April. Conspicuous when in blossom.

Nephelium Litchi, *Camb.* *The Chinese Litchi.* Cultivated in India for its delicious fruit. Has been introduced to the Andamans but has not done well.

Fam. 30. ANACARDIACEÆ.

The Mango Family.

Moderate or large-sized trees often with a milky or acid juice. Leaves simple or imparipinnate, without stipules, often collected at the ends of the branchlets. Flowers usually small, white or yellowish; sepals and petals 3—5; stamens usually as many, or up to double that number, sometimes imperfect. Fruit usually a drupe.

Leaves simple. Evergreen trees.
  Leaves alternate.
    Leaves dark green on the lower surface.
      Fruit a drupe.
        Only one stamen perfect. Drupe large ... ... 1. Mangifera.
        Stamens 10. Drupe small ... ... 2. Buchanania.
    Leaves pale-glaucous beneath. Juice black.
        Inflorescence terminal. Drupe seated on a fleshy receptacle ... ... 3. Semecarpus.
        Inflorescence axillary or from the leaf scars. Drupe broad ... ... 4. Drimycarpus.
        Introduced tree. Drupe seated on a fleshy receptacle 5. Anacardium.
  Leaves opposite.
    Flowers small. Fruit like a small mango ... ... 6. Bouea.
Leaves imparipinnate. Deciduous trees.
  Leaflets 7—13.
    Lfts. aromatic when bruised, marginal vein conspicuous. Drupe ovoid ... ... 7. Spondias.
    Lfts. not aromatic. Drupe kidney-shaped ... ... 8. Odina.

Leaflets 12—20.
Juice milky. Lfts. pubescent. Fruit with 4 linear wings ... ... 9. Parishia.
Lfts. with hair tufts in the nerve-axils beneath. Drupe globose ... ... 10. Dracontomelum.

1. MANGIFERA.

Sepals and petals 4—10; stamens 8—10, only one perfect. Drupe compressed.

Leaves 3—5 in. long ... ... M. andamanica.
Leaves 5—12 in. long ... ... M. sylvatica.

170. ***M. andamanica,** *King*; Br. 206.

A tree (30—40 × 5—6). Leaves 3—5 in. long, obovate to broadly oblanceolate or elliptic, lateral nerves 10—12 pairs, curving upwards; petioles ½—1 in. long, channelled. Flowers ¼ in. diam., 4-merous, in lax terminal panicles, petals twice as long as the lanceolate sepals. Drupe 1—1½ in. long, elliptic.

South Andaman, Mt. Harriet.

171. **M. sylvatica,** *Roxb.*; H. ii. 15; Br. 206. Vern. *Taw-thayet, Sinin-thayet,* Burm.; *Jungli Am,* Hind.

A large tree (50—100 × 2—4) with a greyish bark, cut streaked dark reddish, then brown, with little milky juice. Leaves 5—10 in. long, lanceolate to oblong-lanceolate, shortly acuminate, lateral nerves 16—24 pairs; petioles 1—3 in. long, slender and thickened at the base. Flowers white, in ample terminal panicles. Drupe nearly as large as a mango, much compressed, yellow when ripe.

Not common. Middle Andaman; Long Island; Baratang; South Andaman; Rutland Island. Fl. at the beginning of the R. S. Fr. in the R. S. It somewhat resembles an ordinary mango tree in appearance, but it grows to a much larger size. Sometimes called the *Wild Mango Tree.*

M. indica, *Linn.* *The Mango Tree.* Vern. *Thayet,* Burm.; *Am,* Hind. Has been introduced and planted in Port Blair.

2. BUCHANANIA.

172. **B. platyneura,** *Kurz.*; Br. 205.

A moderate-sized tree (50—80 × 3—4), bark greenish-grey, the outer layer thin and papery, cut dark reddish-brown, then lighter and streaked. Leaves up to a foot long and 2½ in. broad, lanceolate or oblong-lanceolate, acuminate, tapering downwards, glossy, lateral nerves 11—15 pairs; petiole strong, ¾—1 in. long. Flowers in axillary panicles crowded at the ends of the branchlets, sepals and petals 4; stamens 8. Drupe about ½ in. diam., purplish-black when ripe.

Middle and South Andaman; Rutland Island. Not uncommon and usually found in evergreen forests. Fl. Oct. Wood pinkish with a satin lustre, perishable.

3. SEMECARPUS.

Straight-stemmed trees with black acrid juice. Leaves coriaceous, strongly nerved and glaucous beneath. Flowers small, with 5—6 sepals, petals and stamens. Fruit an oblique drupe seated on a fleshy receptacle.

Leaves up to 1 foot long	...	...	...	... S. Prainii.
Leaves up to 2 feet long	...	...	...	... S. Kurzii.

?. 173. **S. Prainii**, *King*; Br. 209. Vern. *Chota Bhilawa*, Hind.

A tree somewhat resembling the next-mentioned but smaller in all its parts. Leaves 5—12 in. long, lanceolate to oblong or obovate, shortly and abruptly acuminate, the margins undulate, lateral nerves 18—24 pairs; petiole $\frac{1}{4}$—$\frac{3}{4}$ in. long. Flowers in terminal panicles. Fruit $\frac{1}{2}$ in. long, the receptacle a little shorter.

Associated with the next one, but not so common. Fl. R. S. Fr. Nov.-Febr.

174. **S. Kurzii**, *Engler*; Br. 209. Vern. *Bara Bhilawa*, Hind.

A handsome tree (40—70 × 3—5) with a light grey fairly smooth bark, cut brown. Leaves 12—24 in. long, 3—4 in. broad, oblong-lanceolate, shortly acuminate, tapering at the base, lateral nerves 20—26 pairs, interarching near the edge; petioles stout, about 1 in. long. Flowers pale-yellowish, in large terminal panicles. Fruit 1 in. long, orange-coloured when ripe.

Frequent and dispersed throughout the forests. Fl. R. S. Fr. Nov.-Febr. The acrid juice causes blisters on the skin. The leaves are used for elephant fodder and the fruits are eaten by Imperial pigeons.

4. DRIMYCARPUS.

?. 175. **D. racemosus**, *Hook. fil.*; Fl. ii. 36; Br. 204.

An evergreen tree (40—50 × 2—3) resembling *Semecarpus*; bark smooth, greyish-yellow, cut brownish. Leaves 4—9 in. long, lanceolate to oblong or oblanceolate, shortly acuminate, margin conspicnonsly undulate, pale glaucescent beneath, lateral nerves 14—16 pairs; petiole $\frac{1}{4}$—$\frac{3}{4}$ in. long. Flowers small, in short panicles, axillary or from the leaf scars. Fruit broader than long, 1 in. across, red when ripe.

Uncommon. Middle Andaman, on evergreen hills; South Andaman. Fl. Febr. Fr. May. It is easily mistaken for *Semec rpus*, but the fruits and inflorescence are different and the margins of the leaves more conspicuously undrlate.

5. ANACARDIUM.

* 176. **A. occidentale**, *Linn.*; Br. 204. *The Cashew Nut.* Vern. *Thihon Thayet* (*The Ceylon Mango*), Burm.; *Kaju*, Hind.

A small tree with spreading branches and glabrous, coriaceous, obovate leaves 5—7 in. long. Flowers yellow streaked with red; stamens 8—10. Fruit orange or crimson with a kidney-shaped nut seated on it.

Introduced. Common around Port Blair. Fl. H. S. "A native of Brazil, sometimes called the *Goa Almond*, its fruit is one of the curiosities of the Vegetable Kingdom, the shell of the nut contains a very acrid oil (from which anacardic acid is made), the fumes of which (Kingsley says) will blister the face if the cook bends over the fire." *Nairne.*

6. BOUEA.

177. **B. burmanica**, *Griff.*; H. ii. 21; Br. 204. *The Marian Tree,* Vern. *Mayan,* Burm.

A small tree (20—35 × 2—3) with a dark-coloured bark, cut brownish with a little yellowish juice. Leaves opposite, 8—12 in. long, 1½—2½ in. broad, lanceolate to oblong-lanceolate, bluntly acuminate, glabrous, lateral nerves 16—20 pairs with smaller intermediate ones; petiole ½—1¼ in. long. Flowers small, greenish-yellow, in axillary and terminal panicles. Fruit ellipsoid, 1¼ in. long, yellow when ripe.

In evergreen forests. Middle Andaman, in several localities; Baratang; Havelock Island; South Andaman. Fl. Jan.-Febr. Fr April-June. The fruit has a taste like that of the mango, but is rather more acid; it is used for pickling and is sometimes called *Jungli Am.*

7. SPONDIAS.

178. **S. mangifera**, *Willd.*; H. ii. 42; Br. 201. *The Hog Plum,* Vern. *Gwè,* Burm., *Ambāra,* Hind.

A fairly large deciduous tree (50—90 × 4—8) with a light grey, smooth, thick bark, cut streaked reddish-brown and white. Leaves imparipinnate, up to 2 feet long; leaflets opposite, 3—6 pairs, 3—6 in. long, elliptic-oblong, acuminate, slightly one-sided at the base, glabrous, with a distinct nerve running along the margin and connecting the fine lateral nerves, smelling like a mango when bruised. Flowers white or yellowish, in panicles. Drupe 1—1½ in. long, yellow when ripe.

Dispersed in deciduous forests in the Middle and South Andaman, Long Island, Ritchie's Archipelago and Rutland Island. Fl. March-April when the tree is leafless. Fr. Aug.-Nov. The wood is soft and perishable and it yields a gum resembling gum-arabic. The fruit is edible and the young leaves are cooked and eaten as a vegetable by Burmans.

8. ODINA.

179. **O. Wodier**, *Roxb.*; H. ii. 29; Br. 200. Vern. *Nabè,* Burm.

A deciduous tree (40—60 × 5—12) with a dark brownish-grey bark with longitudinal furrows, cut dark reddish. Leaves imparipinnate, 1—1½ feet long; leaflets opposite, 7—11, 3—6 in. long, ovate, acuminate with rounded bases, glabrous. Flowers small, greenish-yellow, in racemes at the ends of the thick leafless branchlets. Drupes ½ in. long, kidney-shaped, reddish when ripe.

Frequent and dispersed in leaf-shedding forests throughout the islands. Leafless in the H. S., the leaves all turning yellow before falling. Fl. Jan.-March Fr. Sept.-Oct. It attains a large girth but lacks the long, clean, straight stems which are characteristic of the trees of these islands. Wood reddish-brown, very useful and meriting more attention than it gets in the Andamans. The bark yields tannin, and the tree a gum. The vernacular name *Jhingan*, which belongs to this tree in India, is here given to *Pajanelia Rheedii*. Brandis writes, "A handsome tree when in full foliage, an eyesore when leafless."

9. PARISHIA.

180. **P. insignis**, *Hook, fil.*; H. ii. 30; Br. 200.

A large and tall deciduous tree (80—130 × 8—12) with a grey bark peeling in flakes, cut reddish with milky juice. Leaves imparipinnate, up to 2 feet long; leaflets 13—19, opposite, 4—8 in. long, 1—2½ in. broad, ovate-oblong, oblique, pubescent beneath. Flowers ¼ in. diam., yellowish, 4-merous, in large pubescent panicles. Fruit ½ in. diam., with 4 linear-oblong, reddish and pubescent wings 3—4 in. long.

Fairly common in many localities. Leafless in the H. S., the leaves all turning bright red about the months of Dec.-Jan. before falling. The wood is soft and light and can be used in the same way as that of the *Papita* for rafting purposes. Named after the Reverend Parish of Moulmein who once made a botanical visit to these islands. It is easily known by its winged fruits.

10. DRACONTOMELUM.

181. **D. mangiferum**, *Blume*; H. ii. 43; Br. 201. Vern. *Chinyôk*, Burm.

A tall handsome and conspicuous tree (50—100 × 5—10) with a brownish-grey bark, cut reddish. Leaves usually imparipinnate, 1—1½ ft. long; leaflets 12—20, alternate to sub-opposite, the lowest 1—3 in. long, the upper ones 7—8 in. long, ovate-oblong, acuminate, oblique, with tufts of hairs in the nerve axils beneath. Flowers greenish-white, ½ in. diam., in large axillary panicles; stamens 10. Drupe 1—1½ in. diam., depressed globose, yellow when ripe.

Frequent in all localities, especially in damp places along streams. Leafless Oct.-Nov. for a short while. Fl. in Febr. Fr. in the H. S. Along the open stream-beds where it is more frequent than in the high forests, it does not attain the large dimensions it grows to in the interior. The fruit is edible and looks like that of *Garuga pinnata* from which it borrows its vernacular name.

FAM. 31. MORINGACEÆ.

182. **Moringa pterygosperma**, *Gaertn.*; Br. 209. *The Indian Horse-radish Tree.* Vern. *Dandhalun*, Burm.; *Sanja*, Hind. A soft-wooded tree with corky bark and large tripinnate leaves; leaflets ovate, pale beneath. *Flowers* white, honey-scented. Pods

ribbed, 9-18 in long. Introduced and cultivated in Port Blair for its fruit known as *Drumsticks*. "The scraped roots furnish an excellent substitute for horse-radish." The seeds yield an oil known as *Ben Oil*, which is highly valued by watchmakers as a lubricant. The leaves, flowers and fruits are eaten.

FAM. 32. CONNARACEÆ.

Small trees or scandent shrubs with alternate unifoliolate or pinnate leaves; leaflets entire. Flowers small, 5-merous; stamens 10, alternately shorter, the filaments often united at the base.

A family of little interest to the *Forester*.

Scandent shrubs with imparipinnate leaves.
- Leaflets 3—5, 3—5 in. long ... ... 1. Connarus.
- Leaflets 5—9, 3—8 in. long ... ... 2. Rourea.
- Leaflets 17—31, 1—3 in. long ... ... 3. Cnestis.

Small tree with unifoliolate leaves 4—7 in. long ... ... 4. Ellipanthus.

1. CONNARUS.

183. **C. gibbosus**, *Wall.*; H. ii. 52; Br. 212.

A large scandent shrub, the young branchlets rusty puberulous. Leaves 6—9 in. long; leaflets 3—5, 3—5 in. long, 1¼—2½ in. broad, elliptic-oblong, shortly acuminate, base rounded, glabrous and thinly coriaceous. Flowers ¼ in. long, white, in rusty pubescent panicles; petals linear. Follicles 1—1½ in. long, ovoid-oblong, compressed and pointed, striate; seed glossy and black.

Porlob Island; South Andaman; Rutland Island. Fl. April-May. Fr. May-June.

2. ROUREA.

184. **R. commutata**, *Planch.*; H. ii. 47; Br. 210, 706.

A large scandent evergreen shrub. Leaves 8—12 in. long; leaflets 5—9, sub-opposite, 3—8 in. long, elliptic to elliptic-lanceolate, bluntish acuminate, base rounded, lateral nerves 2—5 pairs, glabrous and shining. Flowers small, white, in racemes collected in panicles; petals twice as long as the sepals. Follicles 1 in. long, obliquely ovoid-oblong, pointed, with a red seed.

Long Island; South Andaman, around Port Blair and Port Mouat. Fl. May. Fr. Dec.

3. CNESTIS.

185. **C. ramiflora**, *Griff.*; H. ii. 54; Br. 213. Vern. *Kyetmaukni*, *Twabyetmauk*, Burm.

A scandent shrub with dark brown branchlets, all softer parts pubescent. Leaves 8—12 in. long; leaflets 17—31, opposite or sub-opposite, 1—3 in. long, narrowly oblong, blunt or rounded at the base and apex, dark green and glossy above, softly pubescent beneath, nearly sessile. Flowers ½ in. diam., yellowish, fasciculate from the scars of fallen leaves; petals 5. Follicle falcate, curved, 1—3 together, bright-red.

Very common everywhere. Fl. Nov.-Jan. Fr. March.

4. ELLIPANTHUS.

186. ***E. calophyllus**, *Kurz*; Br. 213.

A small evergreen tree (15—25 × 2 – 3) with slender young branchlets. Leaflet single, on a petiole 1 in. long, 4—7 in. long, 2—2½ in. broad, elliptic to ovate or lanceolate, shortly acuminate, base rounded, glabrous, with elegant net venation, the lateral nerves reddish beneath and interarching. Flowers small, in axillary cymes; stamens 10, 5 without anthers. Fr. 1 in. long, ellipsoid, velvety tomentose.

South Andaman. Fl. March. Fr. June-July.

FAM. 33. LEGUMINOSÆ.

The Pea or the Pod Family.

Trees, shrubs or climbers. Leaves unifoliolate or compound with few or many leaflets, stipulate or stipellate. Flowers small or large; petals and sepals usually 5; stamens usually 10, often many. Fruit a pod of various shapes, splitting open or not.

A large tropical family, well represented in these islands, and one of some importance to the Forester. Its members may well be recognised by their leaves which are of multifarious forms, and by their variegated flowers which are often of surpassing beauty.

The Family is divided into three sub-families :—

Leaves unifoliolate, trifoliolate, or pinnate. Flowers (papilionaceous), with unequal and usually free petals; stamens about 10, usually joined in one or more groups ... 1. Papilionaceæ.

Leaves paripinnate or bipinnate. Petals unequal; stamens free ... ... 2. Caesalpinieæ.

Leaves all bipinnate. Flowers small, in tufts or heads; petals more or less equal and joined; stamens usually many ... ... 3. Mimoseæ.

Sub-fam. 1. PAPILIONACEÆ.

Leaves unifoliolate, trifoliolate or pinnate. Flowers consisting of a large upper petal (the *standard*), 2 lateral petals (the *wings*), and 2 lower petals (the *keel*) often joined and enclosing the stamens and pistil; stamens usually 10, variously united.

Climbers.
  Leaves trifoliolate.
    Fl. showy, purple or greenish-yellow. Pods covered with irritating hairs ... ... 1. Mucuna.
    Fl. small, pink and white. Pod flat and membranous ... 2. Spatholobus.
    Fl. scarlet, pointed. Pod turgid ... ... 3. Strongylodon.
    Fl. pink. Pod turgid ... ... 4. Dioclea.
  Leaves imparipinnate.
    Leaflets opposite. Fl. white or pink. Pod with a narrow wing on one or both edges ... ... 5. Derris.
    Leaflets alternate. Fl. white or yellow. Pod flat, linear and pointed ... ... 6. Dalbergia.
  Leaves paripinnate.
    Leaflets small; common petiole ending in a point. Seeds scarlet with a black eye ... ... 7. Abrus.

Shrubs or shrubby trees.
  Leaves unifoliolate.
    Leaflet strongly 3-nerved and gland-dotted beneath. Pod small, turgid ... ... 8. Flemingia, 203.
    Branchlets triangular. Petiole winged ... ... 9. Desmodium, 205.
  Leaves digitately trifoliolate.
    Leaflets strongly 3-nerved and gland-dotted beneath. Pod small, turgid ... ... 8. Flemingia, 204.
  Leaves pinnately trifoliolate.
    Littoral shrubby tree. Flowers white. Pod flat, jointed ... 9. Desmodium, 206.
  Leaves imparipinnate.
    Littoral. Flowers yellow. Pod linear, constricted between the seeds ... ... 10. Sophora.

Trees.
  Leaves trifoliolate.
    Littoral. Branchlets prickly. Flowers large, scarlet. Pod linear-curved ... ... 11. Erythrina.
  Leaves imparipinnate.
    Littoral. Leaflets opposite. Flowers pinkish. Pod flat and pointed ... ... 12. Pongamia.
    Inland. Leaflets alternate. Flowers yellow. Pod orbicular 13. Pterocarpus.

1. MUCUNA.

Climbers with pinnately trifoliolate leaves. Flowers purple or greenish-yellow; keel larger than the standard or wings; stamens 9 united and 1 free. Pods covered with irritating hairs or bristles. Seeds with a conspicuous scar around them.

  Flowers greenish or yellowish-white. Pod smooth with winged edges ... ... M. gigantea.
  Flowers purplish. Pods with folds on the faces.
    Flowers in lax racemes. Seeds 2 or 3 ... ... M. imbricata.
    Flowers in short corymbs. Seed 1 ... ... M. monosperma.

187. **M. gigantea,** *DC.*; H. ii. 186; Br. 226. *The Cowitch Bean.* Vern. *Myauk-gônyin*, Burm.

An extensive climber with thin stems. Leaves 5–9 in. long; common petiole about 5 in. long; leaflets 4–5 in. long, oblong-cuspidate, glabrous. Flowers greenish or yellowish-white, in pendulous clusters; calyx covered with silky yellow-brown hairs; corolla 1—1½ in. Pod 4—8 in. with smooth faces and double winged along both edges. Seeds 2—4.

Very common along seashores. The pods may often be seen hanging by the slender stems. Fl. Nov.-April. Fr. H. S. and R. S.

188. **M. imbricata,** *DC.*; H. ii. 185; Br. 225.

A large woody climber. Leaves 9—15 in. long; common petiole 4—8 in. long; leaflets 5—7 in. long, ovate-oblong, cuspidate, the lateral ones unequal sided. Flowers dull purple or white with purple spots, in lax racemes; calyx covered with brown hairs; corolla 2 in. long. Pod 4–6 in. long, with many oblique folds and plaits on the faces, and wings ½ in. wide along the edges. Seeds 2 or 3.

Common in the interior forests. Yeratil; South Andaman, Mt. Harriet, Dhani Khari. Fl. Aug.-Dec. Fr. H. S.

189. **M. monosperma,** *DC.*; H. ii. 185; Br. 225. *The Negro Bean.*

A woody climber. Leaves 6—9 in. long; common petiole 3—5 in.; leaflets 3—4 in. long, similar in shape to those of the last one. Flowers purple, in short corymbs; calyx ¼ in., densely covered with bristles; corolla 1½ in. long. Pod about 3 in. long, and about as broad, similar to the last one but with only one seed.

Middle and South Andaman, common. Fl. Dec. Fr. H. S.

M. pruriens, *DC.*, is a slender climber with dark purple flowers and a curved pod without folds on the faces, but densely covered with velvety stinging hairs. Often found in shrub-growth along creeks and streams. Fl. H. S.

2. SPATHOLOBUS.

190. **S. acuminatus,** *Benth.*; H. ii. 194; Br. 230.

A woody climber as thick as a man's arm and ascending the tallest trees. Leaves pinnately trifoliolate, 8—10 in. long, common petiole 2—4 in. long; leaflets 4—6 in. long, elliptic-oblong, acuminate, nearly glabrous. Flowers in ample axillary panicles; corolla ¼ in. long, pink and white, standard orbicular-emarginate. Pod 3—5 in. long, membranous, silky-pubescent, with a seed at its end.

Fairly frequent. Middle and South Andaman. Fl. March. The fruits may be found scattered about in the month of April.

3. STRONGYLODON.

191. **S. ruber**, *Vogel*; H. ii. 191.

A climber with thin hollow stems. Leaves trifoliolate; leaflets 4 in. long, shortly and bluntly cuspidate; common petiole 2½ in. long. Flowers conspicuous, bright or orange-red, in long pendulous racemes; standard reflexed, keel beaked; stamens 9 united and 1 free. Pod 3 in. long, oblong, inflated.

Fairly common everywhere both in the interior and in coast forests. Fl. and Fr. Sep.-Febr. Its unique and pretty flowers are not easily mistaken for those of any other.

4. DIOCLEA.

192. ***D. reflexa**, *Hook. fil.*; H. ii. 196; Br. 228.

A woody climber 20—30 feet long. Leaves trifoliolate, 9 in. long; common petiole 4 in. long, channelled above; leaflets 5 in. long, ovate, shortly acuminate, glabrous. Flowers pale-pink, in dense racemes 8—12 in. long; corolla ¾ in., standard orbicular emarginate; stamens in one group, alternately with empty and perfect anthers. Pod inflated, 3—4 in. long, with 1 or 2 seeds.

I have not seen it, but from its description I think it should resemble *Canavalia turgida*, *Grah.*, a more slender climber which is common along the seashores.

5. DERRIS.

Climbers with imparipinnate leaves, the leaflets opposite and often without stipels. Flowers white or pink; stamens usually monadelphous (vexillary free in *D. Wallichii*). Pod indehiscent, thin and flat with a narrow wing along one or both edges.

Leaflets usually 5. Pod with a wing along one edge only.
  Lfts. 1½—3 in. long. Pod almost orbicular ... ... D. uliginosa.
  Lfts. 3—8 in long. Pod rounded-oblong ... ... D elegans.
Leaflets 5—9 or more.
  Pod with a wing along one edge only. Lfts. 1—2 in. long ... D. scandens.
  Pod winged along both edges.
    Juice reddish. Pod 1½—4 in. long ... ... D. Wallichii.
    Littoral. Pod 3—4 in. long ... ... D. andamanica.

193. **D. uliginosa**, *Benth.*; H. ii. 241; Br. 241.

A spreading climber. Leaves 5-8 in. long; leaflets usually 5, 1½—5 in. long, ovate, acuminate or acute, with rounded bases, polished above. Flowers in short showy axillary racemes, 3—5 in. long; corolla about ½ in. long, rose-pink, fragrant, standard orbicular. Pod oval or almost orbicular, 1—1½ in. long, pale straw-coloured when ripe.

Littoral forests of the islands. Baratang; Havelock Island; South Andaman and North Cinque Island. Fl. Mar.-May. Fr. R. S. Its specific name refers to its habit of growing near swamps.

194. ***D. elegans.** *Benth.*; H. ii. 242; Br. 242.

A slender creeper with brown-pubescent branchlets. Leaves 8—12 in. long; leaflets stipellate, usually 5, rarely 3 or 7, 3—8 in. long, oblong to lanceolate with a rounded base, glabrous above, rusty pubescent beneath. Flowers in axillary solitary or fascicled racemes; calyx reddish; corolla pure white with pink tips. Pod rounded-oblong, oblique. 1½ in. long and 1 in. broad, covered with fine pubescence.

South Andaman, Manpur, Manglutan. Fl. March.

195. **D. scandens,** *Benth.*; H. ii. 240; Br. 241. *The Fish-poison Pod.* Vern. *Migyaung-nwe,* Burm.

An evergreen extensive climber with stems as thick as a man's wrist. Leaves 4—6 in. long; leaflets 7—13, stipellate, 1—2 in. long, elliptic-lanceolate, polished and dark green above, dull and pale below. Flowers handsome, in long cylindrical axillary racemes; corolla white or pale-rose. Pod 1—3 in. long, linear lanceolate, narrowed to both ends.

Extremely common everywhere, especially along the seashores and tidal creeks, and often covering trees with its luxuriant growth. Fl. R. S. Fr. C. S.

196. **D. Wallichii,** *Prain*; Br. 242.

A climber with a woody stem, exuding a reddish juice when cut. Leaves 8—12 in. long; leaflets 5—9, 3—5 in. long, oblong-lanceolate, acute, with rounded bases, glabrous, lateral nerves 8—9 pairs, prominent beneath. Flowers in ample panicles, calyx reddish, corolla white; standard reflexed with inflexed edges; vexillary stamen quite free. Pod broadly strap-shaped, 1½—4 in. long, finely veined.

Middle Andaman, rather common around Bomlungta; South Andaman. Usually in the interior forests and not so common as the preceding one. Fl. Aug.-Sept. Fr. Oct.-Dec.

197. **D. andamanica,** *Prain.*; Br. 243.

A strong climber with stems as thick as a man's arm; branchlets pale brown, silky. Leaves 10—16 in. long; leaflets usually 7, sometimes 5 or 9, glabrous, 4—6 in. long, elliptic, acute or blunt, base rounded, lateral nerves 8—10 pairs. Flowers in axillary or terminal racemiform panicles; calyx reddish-brown; corolla ½ in. long, white or yellowish-white. Pod 3—4 in. long, strap-shaped and silky.

In littoral forests. Middle Andaman, in several localities; South Andaman. Fl. Aug.-Febr. Fr. H. S.

6. DALBERGIA.

Scandent. Leaves imparipinnate with alternate exstipellate leaflets. Flowers rather small, calyx dentate, the lowest tooth generally the longest; wings of the corolla as long as, and the keel shorter than, the standard; stamens variously united. Pod flat, indehiscent, longer than broad, wingless on the edges.

Leaflets 5—9 in each leaf.
 Flowers white. Pod 1 in. long; seed one ... ... D. monosperma.
Leaflets 9—15 in each leaf.
 Flowers pale-blue: stamens in 2 groups of 5 in each ... D. volubilis.
 Flowers yellow or white; stamens 9 in one group ... D. confertiflora.
Leaflets 25 to 41 in each leaf. Flowers white ... ... D. tamarindifolia.

198. **D. monosperma,** *Dalz.*; H. ii. 237; Br. 238.

Branchlets twining, often twisted into spiral hooks. Leaves 3 in. long, leaflets usually 5, rarely 3 or 7, 1—1½ in. long, obovate, obtuse and emarginate, glabrous above, puberulous beneath. Flowers in unilateral racemes; corolla ¼ in. long, white; petals clawed; stamens 10, monadelphous. Pod 1 in. long, ½ in. broad, brown and glabrous, falcate. Seed one.

Common along the seashores and mangrove creeks. South Andaman, in several localities. Fl. March-June.

199. ***D. volubilis,** *Roxb.*; H. ii. 235; Br. 237. Vern. *Daukta-laung*, Burm.

A woody climber with branchlets often bent and twisted into spiral hooks. Leaves 4–5 in. long; leaflets 9—13, 1—2 in. long, obovate to ovate-oblong, apex often mucronate, glabrous and pale beneath. Flowers in compact crowded panicles; corolla pale-blue, standard reflexed; stamens 10, in 2 groups of 5 each. Fruit 2—3 in. long, narrowed.

Very common in the Andamans, *Prain.* South Andaman. Fl. Dec.-March.

200. **D. confertiflora,** *Benth.*; H. ii. 233; Br. 234.

An extensive climber with dark-coloured branches. Leaves 4—6 in. long; leaflets 11—15, about 1 in. long, oblong or obovate-oblong, apex retuse, usually pale and puberulous beneath. Flowers small, in ample panicles; corolla yellow or white, barely ¼ in. long; stamens 9, in one group. Pod 2—3 in. long, thin, glabrous, 1—3 seeded.

Very common; usually in open places. Middle and South Andaman. Fl. Dec.-March.

201. **D. tamarindifolia,** *Roxb.*; H. ii. 234; Br. 234.

A shrubby climber with stout, often twisted, branches. Leaves 3—6 in. long; leaflets 25—41, ⅓—½ in. long, obliquely-oblong, pubescent. Flowers in sessile compact corymbiform panicles; corolla white; stamens monadelphous, usually 9, seldom 10. Pod bright brown, shining, 1½—3 in. long and about ½ in. wide.

Not uncommon. Often found in open places and along the seashores. Middle Strait; Havelock Island; South Andaman; Labyrinth Islands and Rutland Island. Fl. Dec. Fr. April-June. Its leaves resemble those of the tamarind tree, whence its specific name.

7. ABRUS.

202. **A. precatorius**, *Linn.*; H. ii. 175; Br. 225. Vern. *Ywe-nge*, Burm.; *Gūnchi*, Hind.

A climber with woody stem and twining branchlets. Leaves paripinnate, 2—3 in. long, the common petiole ending in a short point; leaflets opposite, 10—20 pairs, ¼—¾ in. long, oblong, rounded with a fine mucro. Flowers ½ in. long, white, pink or lilac, in axillary racemes. Pod 2 in. long, oblong, turgid, splitting open and showing the 3—5 pretty seeds, which are bright red with black dots.

Common, especially along the coasts among shrubbery, from the north islands to the south. Fl. and Fr. Sept.-Nov. It is sometimes called the *Indian Liquorice*. The seeds resemble crab's eyes and contain an acrid poison.

A. pulchellus, *Wall.*; Br. 225; is similar in habit to the preceding one but with 12—16 pairs of leaflets, ¾—1¼ in. long. Flowers pink or pale blue. Pod linear-curved, flat, 2—2½ in. long, with 8–12 seeds. Port Blair, common, *Prain*. Port Mouat.

8. FLEMINGIA.

Shrubs with zig-zag branchlets and 1—3 foliolate leaves, gland-dotted, the lowest pair of nerves basal. Flowers inconspicuous, in dense terminal racemes; petals equal in length. Pod small, swollen, with one or two seeds.

Leaves unifoliolate.	Flowers greenish-white	... F. strobillifera.
Leaves trifoliolate.	Flowers pink and purple	... F. congesta.

• 203. **F. strobilifera**, *R. Br.*; H. ii. 227; Br. 231.

A shrub 5—10 feet high, the branchlets, petioles and nerves of young leaves silky pubescent. Leaves unifoliolate, leaflet 3—6 in. long, ovate, with a rounded base, sharply acute; petiole ¼—¾ in. long, thickened at the top. Flowers greenish-white, in terminal racemes, enclosed in round, greenish, veined bracts folded close together. Pod oblong, ½ in. long, 2 seeded.

Common in open places especially in stream beds in the Middle Andaman and South Andaman. Fl. Dec.-Jan.

204. **F. congesta**, *Roxb.*; H. ii. 228; Br. 232. Vern. *Pike-san-bin*, Burm.

A shrub 4—6 feet high. Leaves trifoliolate, 6–9 in. long; petiole 2½—4 in. long, angled and puberulous; leaflets 3—6 in. long, ovate, finely acute, the lateral one oblique, lateral nerves with brownish silkly hairs beneath. Flowers nearly ⅓ in. long; calyx brown, silky; corolla pink and purple streaked. Pod ⅓ in. long.

Middle and South Andaman; Baratang and the Archipelago. Common in stream beds. Fl. and Fr. March-May.

9. DESMODIUM.

Shrubby. Leaves unifoliolate or pinnately trifoliolate, stipellate. Flowers white or purple; stamens 10, diadelphous, or the tenth free at the base and adhering higher up to the sheath. Pods flat, consisting of several one-seeded joints.

Leaves unifoliolate. Flowers purple ... ... D. triquetrum.
Leaves trifoliolate. Flowers white ... ... D. umbellatum.

205. **D. triquetrum,** *DC.*; H. ii. 163; Br. 224. Vern. *Laukthe-yeet*, Burm.

A shrub with grooved triangular branchlets. Leaves distantly alternate; leaflets 2—8 in. long, 1—2½ in. broad, ovate to oblong-lanceolate, acuminate, base rounded; petiole 1—1½ in. long, obovately or oblanceolately winged. Flowers in narrow racemes, corolla purple. Pod 1—3 in. long, pointed.

Middle Andaman, the east coast, Bomlungta and Rongat streams; Long Island; Havelock Island; South Andaman; often in shrubbery along the seashores. Fl. and Fr. Dec.-Febr.

206. **D. umbellatum,** *DC.*; H. ii. 161; Br. 223.

A shrubby tree up to 15 feet high. Leaves trifoliolate, up to 7 in. long; leaflets 2—3½ in. long, broadly elliptic, the central the largest, pale beneath; petiole 1 in., channelled. Flowers white, ½ in. long, in short-stalked axillary umbels. Pod up to 2 in. long, silky-pubescent when young, glabrous when ripe.

Extremely common along all the coasts of the islands and found growing near the beaches. Fl. and Fr. at all times of the year and profusely during the R. S.

10. SOPHORA.

207. **S. tomentosa,** *Linn.*, H. ii. 249; Br. 244. *The Sea-coast Laburnum.* Vern. *Thinbaw-magyi*, Burm.

A much-branched evergreen shrubby tree 15—20 feet high, branchlets, leaves and inflorescence, softly grey tomentose. Leaves imparipinnate, 5—12 in. long; leaflets 11—17, opposite, ¾—1¼ in. long, broadly elliptic to oval, thick. Flowers sulphur-yellow, ¾ in. long, in terminal racemes; stamens almost free. Pod 4—8 in. long, like a necklace, constricted between the seeds.

A littoral plant frequent along the west coast of the islands from north to south. On the east coast only a couple of trees were seen on the sands near the mouth of the Betapur. Fl. and Fr. Jan.-April.

11. ERYTHRINA.

• 208. **E. indica,** *Lam.*; H. ii. 188; Br. 226. *The Indian Coral Tree.* Vern. *Kathit, Pinlè-kathit,* Burm.

A deciduous tree (50–80×5–9), bark yellowish-brown, usually with conspicuous white patches, cut bright green, then yellowish; branchlets armed with short, sharp, black prickles. Leaves trifoliolate, on long petioles; leaflets glandular stipellate, 5–8 in. long, broadly ovate and 3-nerved, lateral ones oblique at base. Flowers 2–2½ in. long, bright scarlet, in dense racemes at the ends of the leafless branchlets. Pod curved and beaked, constricted between the seeds, up to 1 foot long.

Extremely common along all seashores. Leafless in the H. S., the flowers appearing about the month of Febr. or March; new leaves in May. Fr. in the R. S., the old fruit remaining on the tree for a long while. The wood is white, soft and light, and is used in Southern India for making toys.

12. PONGAMIA.

• 209. **P. glabra,** *Vent.*; H. ii. 240; Br. 243. *The Ponga Oil Tree.* Vern. *Thinwin,* Burm.; *Karanj, Sukchan,* Hind.

A moderate-sized deciduous tree (30–50 × 3–6), the bark grey, with horizontal black or reddish markings. Leaves imparipinnate; leaflets 5–9, 2–6 in. long, ovate and shortly acuminate, smooth. Flowers ¼–½ in. long, with a pink or violet flush, handsome; stamens 10. Pod 1½–2 in. long, woody, indehiscent, obliquely elliptic and pointed; seed one.

Very common along the seashores and near creeks. Deciduous in the H. S.; the new leaves and flowers at the beginning of the R. S. Unsightly when leafless, but handsome when it has had its new foliage. I have never seen it growing naturally in the interior. A clear oil, which is used for burning, is extracted in India from the seeds.

13. PTEROCARPUS.

• 210. **P. dalbergioides,** *Roxb.*; H. ii. 238; Br. 239. *The Andaman Redwood.* Vern. *Padauk,* Burm.

A very large deciduous tree (80–120 × 8–14) with stout ascending and spreading branches, often with very large buttresses; juice blood-red. Leaves imparipinnate; leaflets about 8, alternate, 2–4 in. long, ovate-lanceolate, bluntly acuminate. Flowers golden-yellow, about ¾ in. long in ample terminal and axillary panicles. Pod flat, orbicular winged, 2–2½ in. diam.

Common in deciduous and semi-deciduous forests. Leafless in the H. S. Fl. R. S. Fr. Dec.-Jan. Its principal associates are *Terminalia procera, bialata,* and *Manii, Canarium euphyllum, Sterculia campanulata, villosa,* and *colorata, Dillenia pilosa, Garuga pinnata, Odina Wallichii, Atalantia monophylla,* the *Koko* and the *Pyinma,* together with which it forms what is known as *Padauk* forest.

It is the principal timber tree of the Andamans. The wood, which is used for innumerable purposes, varies in colour from a light-brown, known as "off-colour," to a deep reddish-brown, rich red, or a gorgeous crimson, known as "good colour."

P. indicus, *Willd.*, has been introduced from Burma and planted in Port Blair.

The following, which belong to this sub-family, deserve mention :—

Sesbania grandiflora, *Pers. The Large White-flowered Pea Tree.* Vern. *Pauk-pan-byu*, Burm. Introduced and planted in the Settlement for the leaves and fruits which are eaten. A slender tree with paripinnate leaves 8—10 in. long; leaflets 16 pairs, 1—1¼ in. long, linear oblong. Flowers large and beautiful, creamy-white, the standard flushed with pink. Pod slender, pointed, 10—20 in. long.

Canavalia turgida, *Grah.* Vern. *Pelalet-nwe*, Burm. A weak climber with trifoliolate leaves. Flowers delicate pink, standard orbicular-emarginate, 1 in. across. Pod inflated. Common along the seashores. Its handsome flowers may be seen all the year round.

Vigna retusa, *Walp. The Seashore Pea.* Vern. *Pinle-pè*, Burm. A twiner with trifoliolate leaves and yellow flowers. Very common on sandy beaches and found growing with the *Purple-flowered Convolvulus* and with the next one.

Clitoria Ternatea, *Linn.* A twiner with beautiful spoon-shaped deep-blue and white flowers. Found on the seashores and also to be seen in Port Blair scrambling over fences. It is sometimes called the *Mussel-shell Creeper*.

Sub-Fam. 2. CAESALPINIEÆ.

Leaves paripinnate or bipinnate. Flowers often zygomorphic, usually large and showy, the petals slightly unequal; stamens 10 or fewer, generally free; often unequal in size.

Leaves paripinnate; leaflets always opposite.
  Leaflets few, usually 4. Littoral trees.
    Lfts. small, obovate, the upper pair larger than the lower. Pod wrinkled ... ... 1. Cynometra.
    Lfts. broad, nearly equal in size. Fl. with one petal. Pod woody, flat ... ... 2. Afzelia.
  Leaflets many, usually more than 8. All introduced except *C. nodosa*. Pod linear ... ... 3. Cassia.
Leaves bipinnate. Prickly shrubs or climbers.
  Flowers white. Pod with a membranous terminal scarlet wing ... ... 4. Pterolobium.
  Flowers yellow. Pod with a papery wing along one edge 5. Mezoneurum.
  Flowers yellow dashed with red. Pod armed or not ... 6. Caesalpinia.
Leaves bipinnate. Littoral tree.
  Flowers yellow and red. Pod not winged ... ... 7. Peltophorum.

1. CYNOMETRA.

• 211. **C. ramiflora**, *Linn.*; H. ii. 267; Br. 255. Vern. *Myinkc*, Burm.

A small littoral tree with dark-coloured thin bark, cut pinkish-brown. Leaves paripinnate; leaflets usually 4, ¾—2 in. long, the upper pair larger than the lower pair, obliquely obovate-oblong, nearly sessile, dark green and glossy above. Flowers small, white or pink, many, in short racemes from the leaf-axils or leaf scars; stamens 10. Fruit fleshy-wrinkled, 1 in. long, brownish.

There are two varieties :—

Var. heterophylla, *Thw.*; leaflets acute, the terminal pair much larger than the lower.

Var. mimosoides, *Baker*; leaflets obtuse and emarginate, the terminal pair hardly larger than the lower.

Both varieties are littoral, the former said to be very rare, the latter very common everywhere especially behind mangrove and around brackish *jheels*. I could never satisfactorily determine the varieties of this species. A variety which has its upper leaflets rounded and emarginate and much larger than the lower is frequent; this I take to be the latter.

2. AFZELIA.

212. **A. bijuga**, *A. Gray*; H. ii. 274; Br. 251.

A tall littoral tree (50—70 × 3—5), with a grey bark, cut pinkish, mealy. Leaves peripinnate; leaflets 4, seldom 2, 2—4 in. long, 1½—2 in. broad, oblong, broad and emarginate, base rounded, oblique, papery. Flowers in terminal racemes; calyx ⅓ in. long; petal one, ⅓ in. long, orbicular, clawed, margins wavy, white turning pink in withering; stamens 1½ in., claret coloured, 3 perfect. Pod woody, linear, 6—8 in. long and about 2 in. wide.

Common along the seashores of all the islands from north to south, frequently near mangrove. Fl. R. S. Fr. H. S. It is sometimes called *Pinlè-pyinkado*. *A. retusa* is a variety of this.

* **A. palembanica**, *Baker*; Br. 251. *The Merabaw Tree of Malacca*; has been introduced from the Straits Settlements and Ceylon and was planted in the Brigade Creek valley in 1907. It is said to be 'the best known Malacca timber tree.'

3. CASSIA.

Trees or shrubs with paripinnate leaves. Flowers large, yellow or pink; stamens 7 or 10, some imperfect or absent. Pod linear, flat or cylindrical, with partitions between the seeds.

Native tree. Flowers yellow or rose-coloured. Pod 12—20 in. long ... ... C. nodosa.
Introduced. Flowers yellow.
  Leaflets 2—5 in. long. Pod 1—2 ft. long ... ... C. Fistula.
  Leaflets 1—2½ in. long. Pod 5—9 in. long .. ... C. siamea.
  Leaflets 2—6 in. long. Pod 4—8 in. long, winged. A shrub ... ... C. alata.

213. **C. nodosa**, *Hamilton*; H. ii. 261; Br. 253. Vern. *Gnu-thein*. Burm.

A moderate-sized tree (30—50 × 3—4), with a grey bark, finely fissured lengthwise, cut streaked reddish turning brown near the sapwood. Leaflets 6—12 pairs, opposite, 2—3 in. long, ovate or elliptic-oblong, smooth. Flowers on slender stalks from the scars of the fallen leaves, handsome, 1½ in. across; petals 1 in., white, pale yellow or rose coloured; stamens 10, 3 large and curved with a swelling in the centre Pod cylindrical, 12—20 in. long, ¾ in. diam.

Not common. Seen only in the Middle Andaman, in the forests of the Bomlungta; it had both flower and fruit in April. Port Mouat. Fl. H. S. Fr. Dec.-May

C. Fistula, *Linn. The Indian Laburnum* or *Monkey-stick Tree.* Bark whitish-grey. Leaflets 8—16, ovate, 2—5 in. long. Flowers large, bright-yellow, in long hanging racemes. Pod cylindrical, 1—2 feet long. Vern. *Ngu*, Burm., *Amaltás*, Hind. It is also sometimes called the *Pudding-pipe Tree.* Introduced.

C siamea, *Lam.* Vern. *Mezali*, Burm. A tree with dense dark green foliage. Leaves 6—12 in. long; leaflets 8—30, 1—1½ in. long, oblong obtuse, mucronate. Flowers golden-yellow, in erect terminal panicles. Pod flat, thin, 6—9 in. long, swollen opposite the seeds. Uncommon in Port Blair. Introduced.

C. alata, *Linn.* A shrub. Leaves 1—2 feet long; leaflets 16—28, 2—6 in long, increasing in size towards the top of the leaf. Flowers large, yellow. Pod 4- 8 in. long, with a crenulated wing along each valve. Common in waste places around villages in Port Blair. Brandis says it is possibly indigenous. *Thinbaw-mezali*, Burm.

The following introduced trees have paripinnate leaves :—

Tamarindus indica, *Linn. The Tamarind Tree.* Vern *Magyi*, Burm., *Imli*, Hind. Leaflets 20—30, up to an inch long. Flowers yellow, beautifully streaked with red. Pod thick, pulp dark-brown, acid; seeds shining. Introduced and planted in Port Blair. Also seen at the old abandoned settlement of Port Cornwallis.

Amherstia nobilis, *Wall.* Vern. *Thawka*, Burm. Evergreen, 30—40 feet high. Leaves 1—1½ ft long; leaflets 12—16, 3—5 in. long. Flowers large and showy; calyx crimson; petals 3, yellow. Pod 7 in. long, oblong, flat. Planted and thrives well in Port Blair, *Prain.* Haddo gardens. "A masterpiece of the Vegetable Kingdom" and "One of the most beautiful flowering trees in the world."

Saraca indica, *Linn. The Asoka Tree.* Leaflets 8—12, oblong-lanceolate, 6—9 in. long. Flowers beautiful, orange-coloured changing red. Pod 6—9 in long. Haddo gardens. "When this tree is in full blossom, I do not think the whole Vegetable Kingdom affords a more beautiful object," *Roxburgh.*

Brownea Ariza, *D. C.* A tree somewhat resembling the last two. Leaflets 8—14, oblanceolate, caudate-acuminate, 4—7 in long. Flowers very beautiful, collected in dense clusters, scarlet pink. Haddo gardens, uncommon. "Few things can excel the elegance or the richness of the colouring in the beautiful flowers of this plant," *Graham*; they are as beautiful as any I have seen and I think the above well-merited praise. Fl. April.

4. PTEROLOBIUM.

214. P. macropterum, *Kurz*; Br. 248; Kz. i. 410.

A large climber sparingly armed with small prickles. Leaves bipinnate; pinnae 7—10 pairs, 2—2½ in. long; leaflets 7—10 pairs, ½ in. long, elliptic-oblong. Flowers white, in lax panicled racemes; stamens 10, free. Pod 2½ in. long, a seed at base terminated by a membranous scarlet wing.

Not common. Middle Andaman, Cuthbert and Rongat Bays; South Andaman, Port Blair. Fl. May. Fr. June-July. Its fruits, which may be seen strewn about the jungles, are very pretty and attractive when newly fallen, but they soon lose their bright colour.

5. MEZONEURUM.

Climbers armed with strong recurved prickles seated on corky tubercles. Leaves bipinnate. Flowers yellow, in panicled racemes; calyx deeply cleft and imbricate, the lowest sepal covering the others like a hood in bud; stamens 10, free. Pod dark brown, thin, with a papery wing along one edge.

Leaflets opposite.
- Pinnæ 2—5 pairs. Leaflets 3—4 pairs ... ... M. cucullatum.
- Pinnæ 6—11 pairs. Leaflets 9—11 pairs ... ... M. enneaphyllum.

Leaflets alternate or sub-opposite.
- Pinnæ 4—10 pairs. Leaflets 8—10 pairs ... ... M. andamanicum.
- Pinnæ 1—5 pairs. Leaflets 10—14 pairs ... ... M. hymenocarpum.

215. **M. cucullatum,** *W. and A.*; H. ii. 258; Br. 247.

A large climber as thick as a man's arm. Leaves 1—1½ ft. long, with 2—5 pairs of opposite pinnæ 4—7 in. long; leaflets 3—4 pairs, ½—3 in. long, ovate, blunt with a small mucro. Flowers numerous and conspicuous, ⅓ in. long, greenish-yellow. Pods 3—4 in. long, 1-seeded.

Common in the islands. Middle Andaman, frequent along the stream beds on the east coast; Long Island; South Andaman, Wimberleygunj and Port Mouat. *Fl.* Sept.-Febr., mostly in Jan. *Fr.* March-April. Its flowers may be seen among the topmost branches of the tallest trees.

216. ***M. enneaphyllum,** *W. and A.*; H. ii. 258; Br. 248.

Pinnæ 6—11 pairs. Leaflets 9—11 pairs, ½ in. long, oblong-obtuse. Flowers like those of the last; stamens densely woolly at the base. Pod 4—8 in. long, reddish, with 4—6 seeds.

Andamans, *Brandis*. The specimens in the Calcutta Herbarium are from the Coco Islands. *Fl.* R. S.

217. ***M andamanicum,** *Prain*; Br. 248.

A large climber with few prickles. Leaves 1—1½ in. long; pinnæ 4—10 pairs; leaflets 8—10, alternate, ½—1½ in. long, obovate, retuse, base cuneate, glabrous. Flowers in long panicled racemes; petals yellow with the base and veins reddish; filaments pilose in the lower part. Pod 5 in. long, 3—5 seeded.

South Andaman, very common near Port Blair, *Prain*. *Fl.* Jan.-Febr.

218. ***M. hymenocarpum,** *W. and A.*; Br. 248.

Pinnæ 1—5 pairs, 3—4 in. long; leaflets alternate or sub-opposite, 10—14, ½—1 in. long, obovate, puberulous beneath; calyx densely puberulous. Pod 4 in. long, 5 seeded.

Andamans. "Very plentiful near Port Blair, resembles the last but is easily distinguished by its leaves and calyx being pubescent, by its slender shorter pedicels, its pods being smaller and not so distinctly reticulated." *Prain*.

6. CAESALPINIA.

Prickly shrubs, often climbing. Flowers usually bright-yellow and red; petals nearly equal, clawed; stamens free. Pod armed or not.

Pinnæ 6—8 pairs. Leaflets 6—10 pairs.
Pod armed with wiry prickles ... ... C. Bonducella.
Pinnæ 2—5 pairs. Leaflets 2—3 pairs.
Pod flat, unarmed, pointed ... ... C. Nuga.

219. **C. Bonducella,** *Fleming*; H. ii. 254; Br. 246. *The Fever Nut.* Vern. *Kalein*, Burm.; *Kanja, Kath Karanj*, Hind.

A large climbing shrub fearfully armed with sharp prickles. Pinnæ 6–8 pairs, 2—5 in. long; leaflets 6—10 pairs, opposite, ½—2 in. long, elliptic to oblong, slightly one-sided, mucronate, glabrous above, slightly puberulous beneath. Flowers ½ in. across, in many-flowered racemes, the fifth petal dashed with red. Pod 2—3 in. long, armed on the faces with sharp wiry prickles. Seeds 2, smooth, lead-coloured.

Frequent along seashores among shrubbery. Fl. R. S. Fr. Dec.-January.

220. **C. Nuga,** *Ait.*; H. ii. 255; Br. 246. *The Nuga Brasiletto.* Vern. *Sugauk, Sunletthè*, Burm.

An extensive climbing shrub armed with short, dark, hooked prickles. Leaves 6—12 in. long; pinnæ 2—5 pairs; leaflets 2—3 pairs, 1—2 in. long, ovate, glossy above, pale beneath. Flowers bright yellow dashed with red, ½ in. long, in axillary or terminal panicled racemes. Pod flat and woody, indehiscent, falcate-elliptic, pointed, 2 in. long. Seed 1, black.

Extremely common along the seashores and tidal creeks and forming with *Entada scandens* and *Derris scandens*, tangled masses of dense verdant growth. The flowers are conspicuous. Fl. mostly in the R. S. Fr. Dec.-March.

C. pulcherrima, *Sw.* *The Peacock Flower.* An introduced garden shrub armed with few prickles. Flowers orange, bright yellow or scarlet. Pod thin, strap-shaped. Fl. at all times of the year, especially during the R. S. Often seen in gardens in Port Blair. It is also called the *Barbadoes Pride*.

7. PELTOPHORUM.

221. **P. ferrugineum,** *Benth*; H. ii. 257; Br. 247. *The Rusty Braziletto Wood.*

An evergreen tree (50–70 × 4—6), bark dark brown, rough and cracked in old trees, cut reddish; branchlets, rachis, pinnæ and inflorescence ferrugineous pubescent. Leaves bipinnate; pinnæ 12—14 pairs; leaflets 10—22 pairs on each pinna, ½—¾ in. long, obliquely-oblong. Flowers bright yellow, in large, rusty, terminal panicles; petals 5, ¾ in. long, with long ferrugineous hairs at base and back; stamens 10. Pod flat, brownish, 2–4 in. long, resembling the blade of a paddle.

A littoral species found in coast forests. Middle Andaman; Long Island; Kyd Island; South Andaman; Rutland Island. Fl. May-July. Fr. Aug.-Dec. It resembles and is easily mistaken for *Albizzia stipulata* and is often called by the same vernacular name, *Bonmérá*. It has handsome and conspicuous flowers.

Poinciana regia, *Bojer*. *The Gold Mohur* or *Fleur de Paradis* of the West Indies. An ornamental tree with gorgeous scarlet flowers which come out about the month of December, and with long flat hanging pods. A native of Madagascar, introduced and planted in Port Blair. *Seinban*, Burm.

Sub-Fam. 3. MIMOSEÆ.

Trees, shrubs or climbers. Leaves equally bipinnate. Flowers small, white, yellowish or pink, usually collected together in tufts, globose heads or cylindrical spikes; petals joined at the base; stamens generally 10. Pods flat, sometimes twisting.

Native climbers.
- Unarmed. Common petiole ending in a tendril. Pod woody, large .. .. 1. Entada.
- Prickly. Flowers in globose heads. Pods thin and flat 2. Acacia.

Introduced shrubs.
- Unarmed. Flowers white. Pods flat ... Leucæna.
- Prickly. Flowers bright-yellow. Pod cylindric ... 2. Acacia.

Native forest trees.
- Leaflets alternate. Flowers in cylindrical spikes. Pod twisting ... . 3. Adenanthera.
- Leaflets opposite. Flowers in tufts or heads. Pods flat 4. Albizzia.
- Leaflets opposite. Branchlets angled. Pod twisting ... 5. Pithecolobium.

Introduced planted trees.
- Unarmed avenue tree. Flowers pinkish. Pods linear, sweetish ... ... Enterolobium.
- Armed with straight thorns. Leaflets 4. Pods twisted ... Pithecolobium.

1. ENTADA.

• 222. **E. scandens**, *Benth.*; H. ii. 287; Br. 261. *The Sword-bean of India* or *West Indian Cacoon*. Vern. *Gón-nyin*, Burm.

An enormous climber with twisted and angled stems, cut soft, reddish. Leaves bipinnate, the common petiole ending in a branched tendril; pinnæ, 2—5 pairs; leaflets 4—8 on each pinna, 1—3 in. long, obovate, glossy. Flowers pale yellow, in slender cylindrical spikes. Pod woody, 1—4 feet long, 3—4 in. wide, thickened along the edges and depressed and constricted between the seeds. Seeds 1½—2 in. diam., nearly orbicular, chocolate red.

Abundant in the islands and found in nearly all localities both in the interior and along the seashores. It is easily known by its angled stems, large pods and coloured seeds which are often found washed up on the beaches. In India the seeds are hollowed out and used as snuff boxes or tinder boxes, hence, it is sometimes given the name of *Match-box Bean*. In Burma they are used for gambling. The Andamanese eat the kernel. The leaves are eaten by elephants and it is sometimes called by mahauts, *Mandrassi bel*. Fl. H. S. Fr. R. S.

2. ACACIA.

Prickly shrubs or climbers. Leaves bipinnate with numerous small leaflets. Flowers white or yellow, in globose heads, with many stamens. Pods flat and linear, dry.

Native climbers.
Pinnæ 8—12 pairs. Leaflets 30—35 pairs ... ... A. pseudo-Intsia.
Pinnæ 20—40 pairs. Leaflets 35—40 pairs ... ... A. pennata.
Introduced shrub.
Pinnæ 4—8 pairs. Leaflets 10—20 pairs. Flowers bright-yellow ... ... A. Farnesiana.

223. **A. pseudo-Intsia**, *Miq.*; H. ii. 297; Br. 269. Vern. *Soo yit*, Burm.

A large scandent shrub armed with small, sharp, recurved, glossy and dark-coloured prickles. Pinnæ 8—12 pairs, 2½—3½ in. long; leaflets 30—35 pairs on each pinna, ⅛—¼ in long. Flowers yellowish-white, in round heads nearly ½ in. diam. Pod not seen.

Very common in the islands. Fl. at the beginning of the R. S. and coming out about the same time as those of the *Pyinma*.

224. **A. pennata**, *Willd.*; H. ii. 297; Br. 269.

A large climber ascending the tallest trees, armed with many sharp slightly recurved prickles. Leaves feathery; pinnæ 20—40 pairs, each with 35—40 pairs of sessile leaflets. Flower-heads cream-coloured or yellowish, clustered by 4 to 8 in panicles. Pod linear-oblong, thin, shining, 4—6 in. long.

Very common throughout the islands and easily known by its feathery leaves. Flowering at the same time as the preceding one and bearing the same vernacular name.

225. **A. Farnesiana**, *Willd.* *The West Indian Blackthorn.* A thorny shrub. Pinnæ 4—8 pairs; leaflets 10—20 pairs. Flowers golden-yellow, in globose heads. Pods 2—3 in. long, nearly cylindric, pointed at the ends. On Ross Island and other stations in Port Blair. Fl. H. S. It is a native of America and is sometimes called the *Sponge Tree*.

226. **Leucæna glauca**, *Benth.* An unarmed shrub. Pinnæ 5—7 pairs; leaflets 12—14 pairs, ¼ in. long. Flowers white, in round heads 1 in. diam. Pods brown, 6 in. long with thickened edges and many seeds. Very common everywhere in Port Blair in waste places and others and scrambling up fences, etc. Fl. at all times of the year.

3. ADENANTHERA.

227. **A. pavonina**, *Linn.*; H. ii. 287; Br. 262. Vern. *Yweygyi*, Burm.

A large unarmed tree (60—80 × 6—10) with a reddish-brown corky bark, finely fissured lengthwise and crosswise. Leaves bipinnate, with 4—6 pairs of rather distant pinnæ each 4—6 in. long; leaflets alternate, 20—40 on each pinna, elliptic-oblong, 1 in. long, glaucous beneath. Flowers yellow, in long cylindrical racemes. Pod linear, 4—8 in. long, curved and twisted when drying, with bright red, shining, compressed seeds.

Frequent everywhere in deciduous forests. Leafless in the H. S. Fl. at the beginning of the R. S., just after the new leaves. It is a graceful tree when it has had its new light-green delicate foliage, and is then one of the ornaments of these forests. It can easily be known by its slender reddish rachis and pinnae and by its alternate leaflets. The wood is reddish-brown, hard and close-grained and is sometimes called *Red Sandalwood*, and also known as *Coralwood* and *Condori wood*. The seeds are known as *Barricarri Seeds* and they "are used as weights by Indian goldsmiths as they are said to be a very constant weight, *viz.*, 4 grains"; those of *Arbus precatorius* are also said to be constant in weight, *i.e.*, 1 grain.

4. ALBIZZIA.

Large deciduous unarmed trees with bipinnate leaves. Flowers in tufts or globose heads, yellowish-white; corolla funnel-shaped; stamens many, with long filaments. Pod thin, flat and straight.

Leaflets less than ½ in. long.
  Pinnæ 6—20 pairs. Pod 5—6 in. long, ¾ in. broad ... A. stipulata.
Leaflets 1 in. long or longer.
  Pinnæ 2—3 pairs. Pod 4—12 in. long, 1—2 in. broad ... A. Lebbek.
  Pinnæ 2—6 pairs. Pod 4—8 in. long, ¾—1 in. broad ... A. procera.

A. moluccana, *Miq.* A native of the Moluccas, said to attain a colossal size, has been introduced and raised in 1905, at Wimberleygunj, from seed obtained from Singapore and Ceylon.

228. **A. stipulata,** *Boivin*; H. ii. 300; Br. 272. Vern. *Bônmèza*, Burm.

A large tree (60—100 × 6—10) with a flat-topped light crown, bark smooth, grey, with very fine longitudinal fissures and raised horizontal lines, thick; cut strongly and irregularly streaked dark chocolate and red, turning dark brown. Leaves with large membranous stipules; pinnæ 6—20 pairs, 2½—4 in. long; leaflets 25—45 pairs on each pinna, ⅛—⅓ in. long, pale beneath. Flower heads 1½ in. across. Pod 5—6 in. long, dull, pale-brown, about ¾ in. broad.

Fairly common in the islands and dispersed throughout the forests; frequent along streams. Leafless in the H. S. Fl. at the beginning of the R. S. Fr. Dec.-Febr.

229. **A. Lebbek,** *Benth.*; H. ii. 298; Br. 271. *The Siris Tree.* Vern. Koko, Burm.

A large tree (60—100 × 6—10) with a whitish bark and numerous horizontal short corky lines, in old trees dark coloured and rough. Pinnæ 2—3 pairs, 4—5 in. long; leaflets 5—9 pairs, 1—1½ in. long, elliptic-oblong, base oblique in the upper ones, apex rounded or emarginate.

Flowers silky, white turning pale yellow; stamens 1½ in. long, tinged with green. Pods straw-coloured, 4—12 in. long, 1—2 in. broad.

Common. Usually found everywhere in deciduous forests. Very common on Interview Island and apparently absent on Baratang. Leafless early in the H. S. New leaves and flowers at the end of the H. S. Fr. Nov.-Febr.

A very fine timber tree; wood dark-brown, with lighter and darker streaks, moderately hard, taking a fine polish and excellent to work. It is useful for house-building and makes fine furniture. Gamble says it is probably the *East Indian Walnut* of the European market.

230. *A. **procera**, *Benth.*; H. ii. 299; Br. 271. Vern. *Sit*, Burm

A large tree with pale-brown smooth bark. Rachis 12—18 in. long, pinnæ 2—6 pairs, 5—6 in. long; leaflets 6—12 pairs, 1—1½ in. long, obliquely ovate to ovate-oblong, dark-green and glabrous above, pale with scattered hairs beneath. Flower heads ¾ in. across; corolla yellowish-white with greenish-yellow stamens. Pod bright reddish-brown, glossy, 4—8 in. long and ¾ in. broad, with 6—12 seeds.

North Andaman and Coco Islands, *Prain*. Not seen on the South or Middle Andaman. Fl. May-Aug. Chiefly found growing near river-beds and in moist places. It is sometimes called the *Tali-tongue Pod*.

5. PITHECOLOBIUM.

231. **P. angulatum**, *Benth.*; H. ii. 306; Br. 275. Vern. *Thanthat*, Burm.

A small soft-wooded tree (25—30 × 1½—3) with sharply angled branchlets rachis and pinnæ. Leaves bipinnate; pinnæ usually 2 pairs; leaflets 2—3 pairs in the lower pinnæ, and 4—8 pairs in the upper pinnæ, ovate or rhomboid, pale beneath, glossy above, the smallest at the bottom of the lower pinnæ, about 1 in. long, the largest at the top of the upper pinnæ, about 6 in. long. Flowers creamy- or yellowish-white, in large terminal panicles. Pods spirally twisted, orange-red when ripe with bluish-black seeds.

Fairly frequent; usually in damp and open places alongside streams. Middle and South Andaman; Long and Havelock Islands. Fl. Febr.-March. Fr. July-Aug.

P. dulce, *Benth.* *The Manilla Tamarind.* Vern. *Kywedanyin*. Burm. A tree armed with straight thorns; branches drooping. Pinnæ 2, each with a pair of bluish-green leaflets 1—2 in. long. Flowers white. Pod twisted spirally, with shining black seeds embedded in a sweetish edible white pulp. Common in Port Blair as a moderate-sized tree and also trimmed as a hedge-plant along roads and around the tennis courts on Ross Island.

Enterolobium Saman, *Prain.* *The Rain Tree.* Vern. *Thinbaw-Kokko*, Burm. "A native of Guiana, introduced to the West Indies, whence it has been sent to Asia." Planted along roadsides and elsewhere in Port Blair and doing very well. Fl. H. S., white tinged with pink.

Fam. 34. ROSACEÆ.

The Rose Family.

Two Andaman plants with simple, alternate, stipulate leaves. Flowers usually with 5 imbricate sepals and 5 petals inserted with the stamens around the mouth of the calyx tube.

A large and well-known family of the temperate climes, notable for its beautiful flowers and many excellent fruits. Some varieties of the common cultivated Rose are grown in gardens in Port Blair.

Leaves with black dots on the under-surface. Petals 5, orbicular ; stamens 60—80 ... ... 1. Prunus.
Petals 6, oblanceolate ; stamens about 30 ... ... 2. Pygeum.

1. PRUNUS.

* 232. **P. martabanica,** *Kurz* ; H. ii. 316 ; Br. 281. *The Martaban Almond. The Red Thingan Tree.* Vern. *Lal Thingan.*

A large tree (50—90 × 6—10) with a dark chocolate-brown bark peeling easily from the sapwood, cut dark-red with a very pleasant smell like that of essence of almond. Leaves 3—6 in. long, 1¼—2½ in. broad, elliptic to ovate-oblong, acuminate, glabrous, lateral nerves faint, lower surface pale with numerous black dots ; petiole ⅓—½ in. long. Flowers ⅓ in. diam., white, fragrant and handsome, in racemes 2—3 in. long, from the scars of fallen leaves. Fruit ¾ in. long, ellipsoid-oblong, pointed.

Not common. Usually on evergreen hills associated with *Myristica andamanica* and *glaucescens* and *Dipterocarpus Griffithii.* Fl. in Jan. when nearly all its leaves fall off. Fr. April-May.

2. PYGEUM.

233. ***P. acuminatum,** *Colebr* ; H. ii. 318 ; Br. 282.

A tall tree, young branchlets ash grey. Leaves 4—6½ in. long, 1¼—3½ in. broad, elliptic to elliptic-oblong, shortly caudate-acuminate, base rounded and slightly cuneate and unequal, often with one or two obscure glands, glabrous and coriaceous ; petiole ⅓ in. long. Flowers white, in racemes 2—3 in. long ; sepals and petals 6 ; stamens about 30. Fruit transversely oblong, slightly compressed, apiculate, ½ in. long and ¾ in. broad.

Gopiakabang. Apparently rare.

Fam. 35. SAXIFRAGACEÆ.

Leaves simple, opposite or sub-opposite. Flowers 4-merous.

1. POLYOSMA.

234. **P. integrifolia**, *Blume*; H. ii. 409; Br. 298.

A small evergreen tree (25—30 × 2—3) with a pale bark, the youngest shoots tawny pubescent. Leaves nearly opposite, 4—8 in. long, ½—3 in. broad, oblanceolate, shortly caudate-acuminate, distantly toothed, glabrous, with 8—12 pairs of lateral nerves depressed on the upper surface and interarching; petiole ½—1 in. long. Flowers white, in terminal racemes; petals linear-valvate; stamens 4, with hairy filaments. Berry ovoid, tapering, crowned by the persistent calyx limb.

In evergreen forests; uncommon. South Andaman, Mt. Harriet and Mt. Augusta. Fl. April-May. Its leaves resemble a little those of *Helicia excelsa*.

Fam. 36. RHIZOPHORACEÆ.

THE MANGROVE FAMILY.

Littoral (except *Carallia*) trees or shrubs. Leaves simple, opposite, smooth and leathery, with large stipules. Flowers bisexual; calyx with few or many, valvate, pointed lobes, persistent; petals as many as the sepals, often lobed or laciniated; stamens usually twice as many. Fruit crowned by the calyx, usually germinating on the tree and sending down a long, pointed radicle.

The members of this family, except *Carallia*, are the *True Mangroves*. They are remarkable for their peculiar manner of growth and seeding; sending down a large number of fantastically arched branching roots, they are firmly anchored in the soft mud, and while thus securing for themselves stability and protection against storms, they protect the soil on which they grow from erosion by tidal currents. Some also send up from the roots, through the soft mud, *woody knees*, "believed to facilitate the access of air to the roots." The seed germinates on the tree, sending down a long, hard-pointed, pendulous radicle, which, dropping perpendicularly, point foremost, into the soft mud is firmly planted *in situ*, or, floating upright in the water, it drifts about until its hard submerged point touches the soft mud, where it soon strikes root and establishes itself. The popular name *Mangrove*, is indiscriminately given to many kinds of trees found growing in swamps and along the seashores, such as the littoral members of this family, and species of *Carapa*, *Sonneratia*, *Avicennia* *Scyphiphora*, *Aegiceras*, *Aegialitis*, *Lumnitzera*, *Excoecaria*, and others.

Littoral. Seed germinating on the tree.
- Leaves more or less elliptic, acute or tapering at both ends.
  - Sepals and petals 4; stamens 8 ... 1. Rhizophora.
  - Sepals and petals 8—14; petals lobed and emarginate; stamens 16—28 ... ... 2. Bruguiera.
- Leaves more or less oblong or obovate, rounded or notched at the top. Sepals and petals 5—6.
  - Shrub. Leaves 3—5 in. long. Stamens many ... 3. Kandelia.
  - Small tree. Leaves 2—4 in. long. Stamens 10—12 ... 4. Ceriops.

Inland. Seed not germinating on the tree. Flowers rather small ... ... 5. Carallia.

1. RHIZOPHORA.

Small or moderate-sized trees with numerous arched roots which support the stem. Leaves thick, with indistinct venation, mucronate. Flowers 4-merous; petals entire; stamens 8, with short filaments. Fruit with a long, smooth radicle.

Flowers pedicellate, in axillary cymes ... ... R. mucronata.
Flowers sessile; usually in twos .. .. R. conjugata.

235. **R. mucronata**, *Lamarck* : H. ii. 435; Br. 303. Vern *Pyu*, Burm.; *Khari lakri*, *Kala lakri*, Hind.

Usually irregularly grown and much branched (25—40 × 3—6) with a very rough bark. Leaves 4—7 in. long, 2—4 in. broad, elliptic, acute at both ends, mucronate, shining, pale beneath and with black dots; petioles 1—2 in. long. Flowers yellowish-white, nearly 1 in. across, on short pedicels in axillary cymes; petals hairy on the margins. Fruit dark-brown, with a radicle 1–3 feet long.

Very common, fringing all tidal creeks and also along the seashores. In some places it forms impenetrable belts of vegetation at the water's edge, many miles long and as much as a mile in depth, regularly inundated by the tides. It grows gregariously or mixed with the other kinds of mangroves Fl. and Fr. apparently at all times of the year. The wood is good for fuel and the bark gives a useful tannin and a dye which is used for dyeing and strengthening fishing nets, etc. It is also known as the *Black Mangrove*.

236. **R. conjugata**, *Linn*; H. ii. 436; Br. 304.

A tree very much like the preceding one, but with more lanceolate leaves. Flowers like those of the former, but usually in twos and sessile; petals glabrous.

In similar localities and mixed with *R. mucronata* and having the same vernacular names.

2. BRUGUIERA.

Base of stem supported by short aerial roots and sending up through the soft mud numerous woody *knees*. Leaves coriaceous and glossy, on slender petioles. Flowers solitary or 1—3 together; calyx lobes and petals 8—14; stamens twice as many. Radicle short, faintly ribbed.

Leaves 4—7 in. long. Flowers 1 in. long ... ... B. gymnorhiza.
Leaves 3—4½ in. long. Flowers ½ in. long ... ... B. parviflora.

237. **B. gymnorhiza**, *Lam*; H. ii. 437; Br. 305.

Straight-stemmed (30—85 × 2—7), with a dark-coloured bark cracked lengthwise and crosswise. Leaves crowded at the ends of the branchlets, 4—7 in. long, broadly lanceolate, finely pointed, pale beneath; petioles 1—3 in. long. Flowers solitary, on stalks about 1 in. long; calyx scarlet with pointed lobes; petals bifid with hairs at the base. Radicles about 8 in. long, and 1 in. diam., faintly ribbed.

The largest of the mangroves. Common in mangrove forest everywhere. It is seen growing at its best high up the large creeks, such as the Bomlungta, the Betapur, the Yeratil and others, where it forms small patches of pure forests. Fl. Oct.-Nov. and sometimes during other months. The wood, though hard, is of inferior quality and is chiefly used for fuel. The bark gives tannin. It is called the *Harpoon-handle Tree* or *Orange Mangrove* in Australia.

238. **B. parviflora**, *W. and A.*; H. ii. 438; Br. 305.

A small tree 15—20 feet high with a rough dark-coloured bark and light-coloured foliage. Leaves collected at the ends of the branchlets, 3—4½ in. long, 1¼—2 in. broad, elliptic-lanceolate, finely pointed, decurrent into the petiole. Flowers ⅓ in. diam., greenish-white, in 1—3 flowered cymes; calyx greenish, the lobes lanceolate and reflexed in fruit. Radicle 3—4 in. long, ¼ in. diam., faintly ribbed.

Not as common as the preceding one, but found in similar localities. Long Island; Havelock Island; Middle Andaman; Rutland Island; frequent along the Betapur. Fl. H. S.

3. KANDELIA.

239 ***K. Rheedii**, *W. and A.*; H. ii. 437; Br. 304.

A simple-stemmed shrub. Leaves 2—5 in. long, narrowly elliptic-oblong, obtuse, narrowed to the base, rather shortly petioled. Flowers large, whitish, in poor long-peduncled axillary cymes; petals 5—6. Fruit conically ovoid with a long radicle.

In mangrove swamps. Brandis gives this as an Andaman plant. I have not seen it nor any Andaman specimens.

4. CERIOPS.

240. **C. Candolleana**, *Arn.*; H. ii. 436; Br. 304.

A small straight-stemmed tree up to 20 feet high and usually 1—2 feet in girth but sometimes larger, bark whitish, cut brown. Leaves pointing upwards, 2-4 in. long, collected at the ends of the branchlets, obovate-oblong, narrowed downwards to the somewhat long petioles. Flowers white, in cymes; petals appendaged at the top. Fruit dark-brown, club-shaped, with a faintly-ribbed radicle about a foot long and thick towards the bottom.

Very common in mangrove swamps, often forming small patches and growing very densely together. Fl. and Fr. at various times of the year.

5. CARALLIA.

241. **C. lucida**, *Roxb.*; H. ii. 439; Br. 305. Vern. *Maniawga*, Burm.

A tall tree (50—80 × 3—5) with a dark grey patchy bark, cut light brown, streaked and watery near the sapwood. Leaves 3—6 in.

long, broadly elliptic or elliptic-oblong, bluntly apiculate, margins recurved, dark green and glossy above, pale with numerous black dots beneath, venation indistinct, lateral nerves fine and interarching. Flowers less than ¼ in. diam., sessile, in compact axillary cymes; calyx with 6—8 teeth; petals toothed; stamens twice as many as the petals, alternately longer and shorter. Fruit small.

Uncommon. Middle and South Andaman. Fl. Febr.

Fam. 37. COMBRETACEÆ.

THE TERMINALIA FAMILY.

Trees, shrubs or climbers. Leaves simple (3-foliolate in *Illigera*), alternate, opposite, or whorled, exstipulate. Flowers usually bisexual and rather small, white, yellow or reddish; calyx segments 4—5, valvate; petals small or absent; stamens 4—5 or 8—10. Fruit dry or fleshy, variously winged or angled.

Some of the largest timber trees of the Andaman forests belong to this important family. The members here mentioned are of varied habit, but by the many peculiarities of their leaves, flowers and fruits, they may be readily recognised.

Trees with alternate leaves.
- Deciduous. Leaves penninerved, tufted or scattered. Fruit fibrous, angled or winged ... 1. Terminalia.
- Evergreen littoral trees like mangroves. Leaves small, thick, crenulate, almost veinless . 2. Lumnitzera.
- Deciduous tall littoral tree. Leaves broad, palminerved. Fruit with 2 upright oblanceolate wings ... ... 3. Gyrocarpus.

Rambling or scandent shrubs and climbers.
- Leaves simple, opposite.
  - Diffuse shrub. Stamens 10. Flowers in panicles. Fruit crowned by the calyx .. 4. Calycopteris.
  - High scandent. Flowers arranged like bottle brushes. Fruit with lateral wings ... . 5. Combretum.
  - Garden climber with conspicuous pink or white, long-tubed flowers ... ... 6. Quisqualis.
- Leaves trifoliolate, alternate.
  - Climber with butterfly-shaped fruits ... ... 7. Illigera.

1. TERMINALIA.

Large trees with alternate or tufted leaves. Flowers white or yellowish-white, sessile, in long spikes or racemes; calyx 5 toothed, woolly within; stamens inflexed. Fruit dry or fleshy, angled or winged.

"The leaves are often collected at the ends of the branches, whence the generic name." *Nairne.*

Petioles short. Leaves crowded very closely at the ends of the branchlets.
- Leaves tapering to the petiole. Fruit obscurely angled ... ... T. procera.

Leaves small cordate or auricled at base. Fruit boldly angled. Littoral tree .. . T. Catappa.
Petioles long and slender. Leaves more or less scattered or crowded at the ends of the branchlets.
Leaves 6—9 in. long, not glandular. Fruit with 2 broad lateral wings ... ... T. bialata.
Leaves 4—8 in. long, glandular at the top of the petiole. Fruit ridged ... ... T. Manii.

242. **T. procera,** *Roxb.*; H. ii. 444; Br. 307. *The White Bombway Tree.* Vern. *Safed Bombway,* Hind.

A tall tree (80—120 × 7—10) with a long straight bole and a flat umbrella-shaped crown; in young trees branching in whorls. Leaves 5—10 in. long, 2—4 in. broad, obovate, usually tapering towards the petiole at base, the apex more or less rounded or shortly apiculate. Flowers white, star-shaped, woolly within, in slender racemes. Drupe about 1½ in. long, ellipsoidal, obscurely angled but not compressed or keeled.

Very common in all localities. One of the commonest trees in the deciduous and semi-deciduous forests of the islands. Leafless in the H. S., the leaves turning deep yellow or brown before they fall, about the months of Dec.-Jan., and making the tree very conspicuous. Fl. Mar.-April, with the new leaves. Fr. July-Sept. The wood is reddish-brown to light-brown, moderately hard and heavy and close-grained, but not very durable; used for planking in house-building and for making furniture of an inferior quality. The bark yields an excellent tannin.

243. **T. Catappa,** *Linn.*; H. ii. 444; Br. 307. *The Bengal Almond or Indian Almond Tree.* Vern. *Badām,* Hind.

A large tree (60—80×6—10) somewhat resembling, and often mistaken for the preceding one. Leaves 8—12 in. long, 5—8 in. broad, obovate, tapering to the small-cordate or auricled base, apex rounded or apiculate. Flowers like those of the former. Fruits 1—2 in. long, compressed and keeled all round.

Frequently along the seashores of all the islands and never found naturally growing in the interior. Leafless early in the H. S. Fl. profusely in March-April, and unlike the former, to a smaller extent at other times during the year. It lacks the long, clean, straight boles of *Terminalia procera*, and I have found the unmistakeable characters of leaf and fruit that distinguish it from that one to be constant. It is also known as the *Fijian Almond Tree*, and sometimes by the name of *Olive Bark Tree.* The bark gives tannin and the kernels of the nuts are edible. Often planted and common on Ross Island.

244. **T. bialata,** *Steudel*; H. ii. 449; Br. 310. *The Andaman Ash or White Chuglam Tree.* Vern. *Safed Chuglam.*

Very large and tall (100—160×8—15) with large, thin, curved and often branched buttresses; bark light brown, smooth and finely fissured. Leaves 6—9 in. long, 3—4 in. broad, obovate or oblanceolate, shortly acuminate, tapering at base; petioles slender, 2—3 in. long. Flowers yellowish-white. Fruit butterfly-shaped, about 2 in. long and 4 in. across, ellipsoid, with 2 broad, stiff, veined wings.

Frequent and usually associated with *Padauk* and *White Bombway* but not so common as the latter. Leafless in the H. S. Fl. with the new leaves in May-June. Fr. falls in Febr.-April. One of the largest and most magnificent trees of the islands; it does not perhaps attain the enormous girth of the other giants of these forests, such as *Dipterocarpus incanus*, the *Didu*, and the *Padauk*, but it surpasses them in height, in which however it has a rival in the next one, *T. Manii*. The fruits, which resemble moths or butterflies, are beautiful; the kernels are eaten.

The wood is grey, beautifully mottled and moderately hard. It is used for planking in house building and for making oars and furniture and has been well reported on for aeroplane work. The name *Chuglam* comes from the Andamanese.

245. **T. Manii,** *King*; Br. 308. *The Black Chuglam Tree.* Vern. *Kala Chuglam.*

A tall tree (100—150×7—12) with a straight clean bole, bark very smooth, whitish to yellowish-brown. Leaves scattered, 4—8 in. long, 1½—3 in. broad, ovate to elliptic-lanceolate; petioles about 1 in. long, glandular near the insertion of the leaf blade. Flowers yellowish or greenish-white. Fruit ¾ in. long, ovoid and pointed, obscurely ridged.

Frequent, and usually found associated with the preceding one. One of the tallest trees in the islands. Conspicuous and easily recognised by its smooth clean and whitish bole which somewhat resembles those of some *Eucalypts*. Leafless in the H. S. Fl. May-July. Fr. Nov.-Dec.

Wood dark grey with darker markings; it is harder, heavier and said to be of a better quality than that of the *White Chuglam* and may be used for similar purposes.

2. LUMNITZERA.

Evergreen littoral trees with the habit of mangroves. Leaves fleshy and small, almost sessile, collected at the ends of the branchlets; lateral nerves inconspicuous. Flowers 5-merous; stamens 5—10. Fruit a berry.

Flowers scarlet, in terminal racemes ... ... L. coccinea.
Flowers white, in axillary racemes ... ... L. racemosa.

246. **L. coccinea,** *W. and A.*; H. ii. 452; Br. 315.

A small, pretty tree (15—30×1—3) with a dark-coloured, rough, fissured bark, peeling in flakes. Leaves dark green, 2—3 in. long, ½—¾ in. broad, narrowly obovate to oblanceolate, crenate, apex rounded and slightly retuse. Flowers handsome, bright scarlet, in terminal racemes; petals ½ in. long; stamens usually 7. Fruit ½—1 in. long.

Found growing with mangroves but not common. Long Island; Middle Strait; Colebrooke Passage; Havelock Island. Fl. and Fr. Sept.-Febr.

247. **L. racemosa,** *Willd.*; H. ii. 452; Br. 314.

A small, often straight-stemmed tree, about the same size as the preceding one. Leaves 1½—3 in. long, ¾—1¼ in. broad, oval to obovate, faintly crenate. Flowers white, in axillary racemes which elongate in fruiting. Drupe ½ in. long, compressed.

In swampy places, especially those exposed to the south-west monsoon. West coast of the North and Middle Andaman; Havelock Island at Prince's Inlet; South Cinque Island. Fl. and Fr. Febr.-April.

3. GYROCARPUS.

248. **G. americanus**, *Jacq.*; H. ii. 461; Br. 542. Vern. *Pinlè-thitkauk*, Burm.

A large deciduous tree (60—100×5—10) with a whitish-grey thick bark, cut mealy, white with yellowish juice. Leaves collected at the ends of the branchlets, *in mature plants* 5—8 in. long and 4—6 in. broad, broadly ovate-rotund, acuminate, base broad truncate, palmi-nerved; *in young plants* larger and lobed; petiole slender, 2—6 in. long. Flowers small, cream-coloured, in large terminal many-flowered cymes. Fruit ½ in. long, ovoid, velvety, with 2 erect obovate tapering wings.

Fairly frequent along the seashores of all the islands, especially along the east coast. Leafless in the H. S. Fl. Dec.-Jan. Fr. April-May. It resembles *Tetrameles nudiflora*. Wood grey, soft and very light, about 22 pounds per cubic foot. Used in India for making toys and in Madras for making catamarans.

4. CALYCOPTERIS.

249. ***C. floribunda**, *Lamk.*; H. ii. 449; Br. 314.

A large diffuse scandent shrub with drooping branchlets. Leaves 2½—4 in. long, 1—2 in. broad, ovate, shortly acuminate, both surfaces minutely tomentose; petioles ¼ in. long. Flowers yellowish-green, in tomentose axillary and terminal panicles; stamens 10, unequal. Fruit ¼ in. long, 5-angled, villous, surrounded by the enlarged ½—1 in. calyx lobes.

Collected only once in the Andamans by King's collectors on Mt. Harriet. Fl. Jan-May. In Burma it is called *Ayut-ne-nwe*.

5. COMBRETUM.

Climbers with opposite or whorled leaves which usually turn red before falling. Flowers in cylindrical spikes looking like bottle brushes; petals small; stamens 8—10, exserted. Fruits usually with 4 lateral wings.

Leaves opposite or very nearly so.
  Leaves 4—10 in. long ... ... C. extensum.
  Leaves 3—5½ in. long. Most parts scaly ... ... C. squamosum.
Leaves often in whorls of threes ... ... C. chinense.

250. **C. extensum**, *Roxb.*; H. ii. 458; Br. 314. Vern. *Maung-maka-nwe*.

An extensive woody climber. Leaves 4—10 in. long, broadly elliptic or ovate, acute or shortly acuminate, base rounded and narrowed into the 1—1½ in. long, petioles. Flowers yellowish, the filaments of the stamens often scarlet; calyx segments triangular, usually 4. Fruit 1¼—1½ in. long, often reddish.

Very common. Dispersed in the Middle and the South Andaman and in the adjoining smaller islands. Also in the North Andaman. *Fl.* Feb.-March. *Fr.* May.

251. ***C. squamosum**, *Roxb.*; H. ii. 456; Br. 313.

A large climber. Young branchlets, like almost all the other parts of the plant, covered with pale-edged scales. Leaves 3—5½ in. long, 2—4 in. broad, broadly elliptic, abruptly acuminate; petioles ¼—½ in. long. Fl. yellowish; calyx segments 4, broadly triangular, the mouth villous. Fruit ¾—1½ in. long.

South Andaman.

252. **C. chinense**, *Roxb.*; H. ii. 457; Br. 318.

Branchlets rounded. Leaves about 5 in. long and 3 in. broad, elliptic to obovate, shortly acuminate, base acute, covered with minute scales and dots. Flowers in axillary solitary spikes. Fruit 1—1½ in. long, and nearly as broad, retuse at both ends.

Frequent. Middle Andaman in coast forests; South Andaman, Port Mouat and around Port Blair; Long Island. *Fl.* Sept. *Fr.* Dec.

6. QUISQUALIS.

253. **Q. indica**, *Linn.*; *The Rangoon Creeper.* Vern. *Dawe-hmaing*, Burm.; *Rangoon bel*, Hind.

A native of Java and the Malay Peninsula. A luxuriant creeper with usually opposite leaves, dark green foliage, and showy long-tubed flowers which vary from white to pink or scarlet. Common in gardens in Port Blair. Fl. Febr.-July.

7. ILLIGERA.

254. **I. appendiculata**, *Blume*; H. ii. 460; Br. 542.

A large climber; the petioles and peduncles often twining around supports. Leaves trifoliolate; common petiole 3—4 in. long; leaflets 3—4 in. long, elliptic, apiculate, small cordate at base, glabrous and dark green above, rough and pale beneath. Flowers ⅓ in. diam., in lax pendulous panicles; calyx lobes pink, valvate; petals white; stamens 5, with staminodes. Fruit butterfly-shaped, with 2 broad lateral striate wings 2—3 in. across.

Fairly common and seen in nearly all localities in damp places along streams, and often growing on *Pometia pinnata*. *Fl.* Nov.-Dec. *Fr.* Jan.-Febr. Its fruits resemble those of the *White Chuglam*, but are much smaller.

Fam. 38. MYRTACEÆ.

The Eugenia Family.

Trees with simple, opposite or alternate exstipulate leaves. Flowers usually showy, white or pinkish, bisexual; calyx with 4—5 segments; petals as many, imbricate; stamens very many. Fruit usually fleshy and crowned by the persistent calyx.

Leaves opposite, gland-dotted, usually with a conspicuous vein within the margin. Fl. usually white. Fruit a berry ... ... 1. Eugenia.
Leaves alternate, not gland-dotted. Flowers showy, pinkish.
  Littoral trees with entire or crenate leaves. Stamens united at the bottom. Fruit ridged or angled ... 2. Barringtonia.
  Inland trees.
    Large deciduous tree with crenate leaves. Inner series of stamens small and antherless ... 3. Planchonia.
    Small tree with entire lanceolate leaves Stamens of inner and outer series without anthers ... 4. Careya.

1. EUGENIA.

Usually evergreen trees with opposite, gland-dotted leaves, the lateral nerves often numerous and fine and joined by an intramarginal vein. Calyx cup-shaped with 4 persistent lobes; petals 4; stamens many, inserted at the mouth of the calyx tube. Fruit a berry.

Lateral nerves of leaves generally less than 12 pairs and not fine and close together.
  Leaves 6 in. or more in length.
    Lateral nerves 9—12 pairs; base of leaf almost cordate... E. javanica.
  Leaves usually not more than 6 in. long.
    Branchlets rounded. Lateral nerves 5—8 pairs; leaves with black dots below ... ... E. Manii.
    Branchlets whitish. Lateral nerves 8—12 pairs ... E. Kurzii.
    Cultivated tree with lanceolate leaves ... ... E. Jambos.
Lateral nerves about 20 pairs. Petals 5—6 .. .. E. acuminatissima.
Lateral nerves very numerous. Petals usually 4.
  Leaves attaining more than 4 in. in length.
    Leaves 4—8 in. long ... ... E. claviflora.
    Leaves 3—6 in. long ... ... E. Jambolana.
  Leaves never more than 4 in. long.
    Leaves 1¼—3 in. long, ovate to broadly elliptic ... E. andamanica.
    Leaves 2—3½ in. long, lanceolate to ovate-lanceolate ... E. grata.
    Leaves 2—4 in. long, elliptic-lanceolate caudate-acuminate ... ... E. cymosa.

255. E. javanica, *Lamk.*; H. ii. 454; Br. 318.

A moderate-sized shady tree (25—35 × 3—6) with a dark brown bark, often with white patches on it, cut dark brown. Leaves 6—10 in. long, 3—4 in. broad, ovate to oblong-lanceolate, blunt acuminate. base rounded to almost cordate, lateral nerves 9—12 pairs, not very strong and looping intramarginally; petiole short. Flowers white, 1—1½ in. diam., in twos or threes in short axillary or terminal corymbose racemes. Fruit 1—1½ in. diam., depressed turbinate, white and glossy.

Frequent along the seashores and often found growing among boulders in large streams. North, Middle and South Andaman, the Archipelago and Rutland Island. Fl. Febr.-May. Fr. R. S. The fruit is edible but is pithy and tasteless. It is also called *Jungli Jamun*, but this name is also given to other *Eugenias* as is the Burmese name *Tae thabye*.

256. **E. Manii,** *King*; Br. 322.

A moderate-sized tree with a light brown smooth bark, cut fibrous, dark brown, branchlets rounded. Leaves 3—5 in. long, 1¾ - 3 in. broad, elliptic, shortly acuminate, base acute, lateral nerves 5—8 pairs, joined by the intramarginal vein rather far from the margin; petiole ¼ in. long. Flowers ¼ in. diam., white, fragrant, in axillary panicles from the scars below the leaves. Fruit nearly ⅓ in. diam., depressed globular.

Middle Andaman, in evergreen forests near Bomlungta. Port Mouat and Mt. Harriet. Fl. Nov.

257. **E. Kurzii,** *Duthie*, var. andamanica, *King*; H. ii. 478; Br. 319.

A moderate-sized tree, (40—60 × 3 - 6) with a whitish-grey fairly smooth bark peeling in flakes, cut brownish, branchlets whitish. Leaves 4—6 in. long, 1½—2¼ in. broad, ovate to elliptic, acuminate, lateral nerves 8—12 pairs; petiole ¼—⅓ in. Flowers ⅜ in. diam., white, in short axillary panicles. Fruit globose, ½ in. diam.

Middle Andaman, Bomlungta; South Andaman, North Bay. Fl. Febr.

E. Jambos, *Linn*; *The Rose Apple*. Vern. *Thabye*, Burm.; *Gulab Jamun*, Hind. A moderate-sized tree. Leaves 4—6 in. long, lanceolate-acuminate. Flowers large, whitish. Fruit globose or pear-shaped, dull yellow or pinkish. Introduced and planted in Port Blair for its handsome edible fruit which has a rose-water perfume.

258. **E. acuminatissima,** *Kurz*; H. ii. 483; Kz. i. 487.

A moderate-sized tree with a pale brown bark peeling in vertical flakes. Leaves 2½—4 in. long, 1—1½ in. broad, lanceolate or oblong-lanceolate, caudate-acuminate, base cuneate; petiole ¼ in. long. Flowers white, by threes in terminal panicles; petals 5—6, clawed. Fruit depressed-globular.

Middle Andaman, on Mt. Baker, Amitlated, Bomlungta; South Andaman around Port Blair, Port Mouat. Fl. Febr.-April.

259. **E. claviflora,** *Roxb.*; H. ii. 484; Br. 319.

A moderate-sized tree (30—50 × 2—6) with a whitish-grey bark, cut brownish and dry, looking as if perished. Leaves 4—8 in. long, 1½ - 3 in.

broad, elliptic-lanceolate, acuminate, lateral nerves very fine, intra-marginal vein conspicuous. Flowers handsome, white, $\frac{1}{2}-\frac{3}{4}$ in. diam., clustered in short cymes, axillary or from the leaf scars, calyx about 1 in. long, slender, trumpet shaped. Fruit $\frac{3}{4}$ in. long, barrel-shaped, white and turning scarlet.

Coast forests and evergreen forests and often bordering mangrove swamps. Middle Andaman, in several localities, Baratang, South Andaman, Navy Bay, Macpherson Strait. Fl. Jan.-Febr. Fr. March. Visited by numerous honey-bees when in blossom.

260. **E. Jambolana,** *Lam*; H. ii. 499; Br. 323. *The Java Plum.* Vern. *Thabye*, Burm.; *Jamun*, Hind.

A deciduous tree (40—80 x 5—8) with a pale grey bark peeling in flakes, cut reddish. Leaves 3—6 in. long, elliptic to oblong, bluntish-acuminate, marginal vein distinct; petiole $\frac{3}{4}$ in. long, slender. Flowers $\frac{1}{4}$ in. long, creamy-yellow, slender, by threes in small panicles from the scars of the previous years fallen leaves; petals 4, orbicular. Fruit $\frac{1}{2}-1\frac{1}{2}$ in. long, ovoid-oblong, black or purplish and juicy when ripe.

Middle Andaman, east coast; South Andaman; Barren Island. Also planted in Port Blair. Deciduous in the H. S., the leaves turning red when falling. New leaves and flowers April-May. Fr. in the R. S., edible, but "fit only for boys and birds to eat."

261. ***E. andamanica,** *King*; Br. 319.

A small glabrous tree. Leaves $1\frac{1}{2}-3$ in. long, 1—2 in. broad, rotund-ovate to broadly elliptic, coriaceous: petioles $\frac{1}{4}$ in. long. Flowers white, in fasciculate compound cymes, terminal or axillary, the branches of the inflorescence 4-angled, with 3—4 flowers at the apexes; calyx tube nearly $\frac{1}{3}$ in. long, with 4 erect triangular teeth; petals orbicular.

South Andaman, Dhani Khari.

262. ***E. grata,** *Wight*; H. ii. 486; Br. 322.

A small evergreen glabrous tree. Leaves $2-3\frac{1}{2}$ in. long, $\frac{3}{4}-1\frac{1}{2}$ in. broad, lanceolate to ovate-lanceolate, acuminate, the base acute, coriaceous and somewhat glaucous-opaque beneath; petiole $\frac{1}{4}$ in., or shorter. Flowers rather small, white, sessile, in glabrous axillary or terminal panicles. Fruit ovoid, black when ripe, crowned by the small calyx lobes.

South Andaman, Dhani Khari.

263. **E. cymosa,** *Lamk.*; H. ii. 482; Br. 321.

A small tree with a fairly smooth greyish bark, cut light brown. Leaves 2—4 in. long, $\frac{3}{4}-1\frac{1}{2}$ in. broad, elliptic-lanceolate, caudate-acuminate, base cuneate, lateral nerves numerous and fine with a fine intra-marginal vein; petiole $\frac{1}{4}$ in. Flowers white, $\frac{1}{4}$ in. diam. in axillary and terminal panicles; calyx tube funnel-shaped; petals orbicular, 4. Fruit bluish-black, the size of a pea, nearly globose.

South Andaman, Mt. Harriet, Dhani Khari, Chiriatapu; Rutland Island, Woodmason Bay. Fl. Nov.-Jan.

2. BARRINGTONIA.

Littoral evergreen trees with alternate leaves. Flowers large and showy, pinkish and white; calyx splitting irregularly; petals usually 4; stamens very many, the slender filaments united in a ring at the bottom. Fruit fibrous-fleshy, more or less angular.

Leaves entire. Flowers 3—4 in. diam., in terminal erect racemes. Fruit 4—6 in. long, angled ...	B. speciosa.
Leaves crenulate. Flowers 2—2½ in. diam., in pendulous racemes. Fruit 2—2½ in. long, obscurely angled .	B. racemosa.

264. **B. speciosa,** *Forst*; H. ii. 507; Br. 330. *The Queen of the Seashores.*

A moderate-sized tree (30—50 × 4—8) with dark green shining foliage, bark smooth, mauve-grey, cut whitish, faintly streaked. Leaves sessile, 8—16 in. long, 4—8 in. broad, obovate, narrowed at the base, apex rounded to retuse, fleshy coriaceous, glabrous and glossy. Flowers like powder-puffs, very beautiful and conspicuous; petals white, 2½ in. long, concave; stamens 3½ in. long, tinged with pink. Fruit turbinate-pyramidal.

Frequent along the seashores of the islands and found growing at the water's edge together with *Calophyllum Inophyllum* and *Terminalia Catappa*. Fl. and Fr. Jan.-March. Easily recognised by its large dark green shining leaves with very often purplish petioles and midrib. In Australia it goes by the name of *Sea Island Fish-poison Tree.*

265. **B. racemosa.** *Blume*; H. ii. 507; Br. 330. Vern. *Kyee bin*, Burm.

A small or moderate-sized tree (20—40 × 2—4) with a brownish bark, cut brown, somewhat fibrous. Leaves 6—12 in. long, 2—4 in. broad, or larger in young trees, obovate to oblanceolate, shortly acuminate, base narrowed, margin crenulate, chartaceous, petioles short. Flowers handsome, pinkish and waxy, in pendulous racemes up to 3 feet long; petals cream-coloured with recurved margins. Fruit ovoid, about 2½ in. long, shallowly and bluntly ridged and grooved.

Common in mostly all localities in swampy places just bordering mangrove and also often found growing plentifully in brackish *jheels* and low places flooded during the rains. Fl. and Fr. apparently at all times.

3. PLANCHONIA.

266. **P. andamanica,** *King*; H. ii. 511; Br. 332. *The Red Bombway Tree.* Vern. *Lal Bombway*, Hind. P. valida

A large deciduous tree (80—120 × 6—10) with dense dark green foliage, bark dark brown, cut reddish, fibrous. Leaves collected at the ends of the branchlets, 4—8 in. long, 2—5 in. broad, obovate to broadly elliptic, acute or shortly acuminate, margins crenulate-serrate, base running into and along the flattened petioles, lateral nerves 9—14 pairs, prominent and interarching. Flowers 2 in. long, white tinged with pink, in short terminal racemes; stamens united into a tube at the bottom, the inner ones small and without anthers. Fruit a berry.

Frequent in evergreen forests. Leafless for a short time about Nov. or Dec. The leaves turn bright red before falling and for a short while the tree is very conspicuous and easily picked out amongst the dense and varied vegetation of these jungles. Fl. with the new leaves in January. Wood reddish-brown, hard and close-grained, used locally for house-building. The local name, *Bowbray*, comes from the Burmese name, *Bambwe*, of *Careya arborea*, a tree somewhat resembling this one but not found in these islands.

4. CAREYA.

267. **C. valida,** *Kurz.* J. A. S. B. xlvi. 1877. ii. 72.

A small tree (20—30 × 2—3) with a brownish-grey bark, cut cream-coloured, stringy. Leaves 6—9 in. long, 2½—4 in. broad, lanceolate to elliptic-lanceolate, acuminate, narrowed at the base, glabrous, lateral nerves 11-14 pairs, interarching; petioles about 1 in. long. Flowers pinkish. Fruit about 4 in. long, brownish, with numerous corky warts, 4-angled.

Havelock Island at the head of the Muralat jig; the only locality where I have seen and collected it. Found growing in a damp place with *Myristica Irya* and *Barringtonia racemosa* and somewhat resembling the latter. Fl. April. Fr. C. S.

Psidium Guayava, *Linn.*; *The Guava Tree*; a native of Mexico, has been introduced and is common in Port Blair. It has edible fruit which makes delicious jelly. Fl. April-May. Fr. R. S.

The following species of the genus *Eucalyptus*, the *Australian Gum Trees*, have recently been introduced to Port Blair. The seed was obtained from New South Wales.

E. botryoides, *Smith. The Australian Laurel-leaved Mahogany*, or *Bastard Mahogany*. Attains 60—80 feet. Flowers white.

E. resinifera, *Smith. The Red Mahogany* or *Australian Kino Gum Tree*. Attains 80—120 feet. Flowers white.

E. robusta, *Smith. Australian Brown Mahogany* or *Swamp Mahogany*. Attains 100—150 feet.

E. rostrata, *Schl.*; *Australian Red Gum*. Attains 80—100 feet. Flowers white.

E. tereticornis, *Smith. The Australian Forest Red Gum* or *Flooded Gum*. Attaining 80—100 feet. Flowers creamy white.

The three last named are doing well in the plantations at Wimberleygunj.

Fam. 39. MELASTOMACEÆ.

Shrubs or small trees with opposite exstipulate leaves. Flowers white, rose-coloured or bluish, regular, with 4—5 deciduous calyx segments and as many petals; stamens twice as many, inflexed in bud. Fruit enclosed in the calyx.

A family closely allied to the last one, but with definite stamens. The leaves of the genus *Memecylon* look like those of the *Eugenia*, but they are not gland-dotted nor have they the distinct intramarginal vein. "The name of the order arose from the trivial fact of the fruit of the early known species staining the mouth black." *Nairne.*

Bristly shrubs. Leaves strongly 3-nerved. Flowers large and conspicuous, rose-coloured ... ... 1. Melastoma.
Glabrous shrubs or small trees. Leaves with inconspicuous lateral nerves. Flowers small, bluish ... ... 2. Memecylon.

1. MELASTOMA.

268. **M. malabathricum,** *Linn.*; H. ii. 523; Br. 333. *The Malabar Gooseberry Laurel.* Vern. *Myetpyè*, Burm.

A beautiful shrub 4—6 feet high, all the parts covered with hairy bristles or scales. Leaves bright green and reddish when young, 2—6 in. long, elliptic or ovate-lanceolate, strongly 3-nerved; petioles about ½ in. long. Flowers 2—3 in diam., rose coloured to purplish, stamens 10, unequal, filaments yellow, 5 long and with purple anthers. Berry ½ in. diam.

Evergreen forests, especially frequent along the edges of open grassy places around Port Blair and Port Mouat. Fl. Jan.-July. Hooker calls it the *Indian Rhododendron.* It is sometimes coarse-looking, but nevertheless strikingly handsome and conspicuous.

2. MEMECYLON.

Evergreen glabrous shrubs with stiff branchlets. Leaves coriaceous, with many inconspicuous nerves and usually drying yellowish. Flowers 4-merous, bluish or white, in axillary fascicles; stamens 8, equal. Fruit a berry.

Leaves sessile, bases cordate, stem-clasping ... ... M. cæruleum.
Leaves petioled, bases narrow or rounded.
Branchlets cylindrical.
Flowers in cymes ... ... M. edule.
Flowers in umbels ... ... M. andamanicum.
Branchlets angled.
Leaves 1—2 in. long ... ... M. pauciflorum.
Leaves 3½—5½ in. long ... ... M. elegans.

269. **M. cæruleum,** *Jack*; H. ii. 559; Br. 337.

A small hard-wooded tree about 25—30 feet high, bark grey, thin, with numerous fine fissures. Leaves 2½—5 in. long, 1—1½ in. broad, oblong or ovate-oblong, obtuse, base cordate. Flowers steel blue, rather small, in dense cymes, axillary or from the scars of fallen leaves. Fruit black when ripe, succulent.

Uncommon. Middle Andaman, on the high hills above Amitlated and also on the South Cinque Island where it is of poor growth and the leaves smaller and more roundish. Fl. April.

270. **M. edule,** *Roxb.* var. ovata, *King*; H. ii. 563; Br. 335.

A small tree. Leaves 2—4½ in. long, elliptic or ovate, acute or acuminate, base rounded or cuneate, lateral nerves 5—8 pairs, inconspicuous, petioles about ¼ in. long. Flowers brilliant blue, in many-flowered cymes, axillary or from the scars of fallen leaves. Fruit black when ripe, succulent.

Uncommon. Long Island; Port Mouat. Fl. March-May. Fr. June.

271. ***M. andamanicum,** *King*; Br. 336.

A shrub. Leaves 2¼—3 in. long, ¾—1 in. broad, oblong-lanceolate, bluntly acuminate, base cuneate, chartaceous, lateral nerves 10—12 pairs, interarching near the edge; petioles about ⅛ in. long. Flowers blue, umbellate by 3—6 at the ends of peduncles which are in pairs in the axils of the leaves or from the scars of fallen ones.

Evidently rare. Mt. Harriet. Also from the Nicobars.

272. **M. pauciflorum,** *Blume*; H. ii. 555; Br. 336.

A small shrubby tree with stiff branchlets. Leaves distichous, 1—2 in. long, ¾—1¼ in. broad, broadly elliptic or elliptic-rhomboid, apex blunt, often notched, pale beneath; petioles short. Cymes 7—10 flowered, axillary, petals acuminate. Fruit ¼ in. diam., depressed-globular, on slender stalks.

Not uncommon. Usually in coast forests. Middle and South Andaman; Baratang and Havelock Islands; Tarmugli Island. Fl. R. S. Fr. Jan.-Febr.

273. **M. elegans,** *Kurz.*; H. ii. 554; Br. 336.

A glabrous shrub with angled and sometimes winged branchlets. Leaves 3½—5½ in. long, oblong to elliptic-acuminate, the base cuneate; petioles about ⅛ in. long. Flowers blue, in lax cymes, often in pairs. Fruit ⅓ in. diam., smooth, globular.

Fairly common. Middle and South Andaman in several localities. Fl. R. S., Fr. Nov.-Jan.

Fam. 40. LYTHRACEÆ.

Trees, seldom shrubs, often with angled branchlets. Leaves simple, generally opposite, entire and exstipulate. Flowers small or large and showy; calyx cup-shaped, persistent, with valvate segments; petals when present, usually crumpled in bud; stamens few or many with the filaments bent inwards. Fruit a capsule.

An interesting family to which belong some important forest trees. Many of its members are of great beauty, and most of them have striking characters which make them easy of identification. "It is characteristic of this order that the petals are inserted on the top of the calyx tube, and the stamens a little lower down." *Nairne.*

Littoral bushy tree with small silky leaves. Flowers white, solitary; stamens 12 ... ... 1. Pemphis.
Littoral trees like mangroves. Leaves thick with indistinct venation. Flowers large; stamens many, thread-like ... 2. Sonneratia.
Inland forest trees.
Flowers large, lilac, in terminal panicles; calyx ribbed ... 3. Lagerstrœmia.
Flowers large, white, in terminal corymbs; calyx not ribbed ... ... 4. Duabanga.
Flowers small, yellowish, in slender racemes; petals none 5. Crypteronia.
Cultivated shrubs or small trees, sometimes spinescent.
Leaves clustered. Flowers crimson ... ... Punica.
Leaves small. Flowers greenish-yellow ... ... Lawsonia.

1. PEMPHIS.

274. **P. acidula**, *Forst.*; H. ii. 573; Br. 339.

A littoral shrubby tree 10—20 feet high with numerous, fine, often yellowish and leafless, branchlets. Leaves ½—1½ in. long, elliptic or oblong, obtuse or rounded at both ends, thick, silky pubescent, almost sessile. Flowers solitary, white or pink, ½ in. diam., 6-merous; calyx ribbed; stamens 12. Capsule opening by the top coming off.

West coast of the islands in exposed rocky places; also on Havelock Island at Golugma, and very common on South Sentinel Island. Often associated with *Tournefortia argentea* and when seen from a distance it looks like a *Tamarix*. It is apparently absent along the east coast. Fl. and Fr. Oct.-April.

2. SONNERATIA.

Evergreen trees with the habit of mangroves and sending up through the mud from the roots conical pointed root branches. Leaves coriaceous, entire, with indistinct venation. Flowers large; calyx persistent, thickly coriaceous with triangular segments; stamens slender and long, arranged in a ring at the mouth of the calyx; style long.

Leaves broadly obovate Flower buds pointed ... S. acida.
Leaves almost orbicular. Flower buds not pointed ... S. alba.

275. **S. acida**, *Smith*; H. ii. 579; Br. 340. Vern. *Lamu*. Burm.

A moderate-sized or rather large tree (20—50 × 3—7) with a dark brown rough bark, cracked lengthwise in old trees, cut dark brown, dry. Leaves 2—4 in. long and about as broad, broadly obovate, base decurrent to the rather short petiole, apex rounded or retuse. Flowers 1½—2 in.

diam., buds pointed; calyx purplish inside; petals very narrow, white; filaments 1½ in. long, thread-like. Fruit fleshy.

Common in mangrove swamps along the coasts and often forming narrow belts of forest; generally associated with *Avicennia officinalis*. Fl. and Fr. April-July. Brandis says that the petals are purple; I have invariably found them to be white. Kurz gives the height of this and the next one as not exceeding 15 feet, but this does not agree with my experience; trees of the dimensions given above are by no means uncommon. It is sometimes confused with *Avicennia officinalis*, and the petals are very narrow and may easily be mistaken for, or missed among, the stamens.

276. **S. alba,** *Smith*; H. ii. 580; Br. 341. Vern. *Lamu*, Burm.

A moderate-sized tree (20—50 × 2—5) with a stem resembling that of the preceding one, cut yellowish-brown with fibres like those of a coconut tree. Leaves 2—4½ in. long, broadly ovate to almost orbicular, rounded at base and apex; petiole short. Flowers usually in threes at the ends of the branchlets, somewhat smaller than those of *S. acida*; buds not pointed, calyx greenish within; petals none; filaments 1—1½ in. long.

Uncommon. In mangrove swamps along the Betapur creek. Fl. April-May. Fr. April-June.

3. LAGERSTRŒMIA.

277. **L. hypoleuca,** *Kurz*; H. ii. 577; Br. 330. Vern. *Pyinma*, Burm.

A large deciduous tree (60—90 × 6—10) with a thin whitish bark, cut very light brown turning black or purple near the sapwood. Leaves sub-opposite, 5—8 in. long, elliptic to ovate-oblong or lanceolate, pale beneath; petioles short. Flowers handsome and conspicuous, lilac, 1½ in. diam., in long terminal panicles; calyx ribbed; 6 stamens large and pinkish, the rest finer and yellowish. Fruit ovoid, dark-brown, ¾ in. long, supported by the persistent calyx and splitting by valves.

Dispersed in deciduous and semi-deciduous forests. Leafless in the H. S., the leaves turning reddish when falling. New leaves at the beginning of the R. S., and soon followed by the conspicuous and beautiful flowers about the months of July or August. Fr. shed their seed Dec.-Jan. It is one of the chief timber trees of the Andamans. The wood is pinkish-brown, fairly hard and durable and seasoning well, but liable to split in the log. Used for house and boat-building.

L. indica, *Linn.*, is a shrub sometimes seen in gardens in Port Blair. It has pretty pink and white flowers, is a native of China, and is known as the *Indian Crepe-flower* or *Pride of India*. Vern. *Saoni*, Hind.

4. DUABANGA.

278. **D. sonneratioides,** *Ham.*; H. ii. 579; Br. 340. Vern. *Ma-u*, *Ma-u-lettan*, Burm.

A large and tall deciduous tree (80—120 × 7—12) with thin horizontal branches drooping with the weight of the leaves and flowers; bark brown, cut dry, dirty brown, darkening immediately near the sapwood like that of the *Pyinma*. Leaves distichous, 7—15 in. long, ovate-oblong, shortly acuminate, base cordate, glabrous and glaucous beneath. Flowers white, 2—3 in. diam., in corymbs at the ends of the long branches; petals and stamens falling off early. Capsule dry.

Not very common. Along stream beds in the Middle and South Andaman, the Archipelago and Rutland Island. Leafless in the H. S. Fl. Jan.-April. Fr. May-June. The wood, which is grey and soft and seasons well, is said to be a very suitable timber for tea-boxes, for which purpose it is used in Assam and is said to be admirably fitted. Its leaves resemble those of the *Pyinma*, and the slender branches with their rows of evenly spaced leaves look like gigantic pinnate leaves.

5. CRYPTERONIA.

279. **C. paniculata,** *Blume*; H. ii. 574; Br. 341.

A moderate-sized tree (40—60 × 3—6) with a brownish bark peeling in thin irregular flakes, cut light brown, watery, branchlets angled. Leaves 3—6 in. long, elliptic, bluntish acuminate, narrowed at the base, glabrous, petioles ¼ in. Flowers small, yellowish-green, numerous in cylindrical spiciform panicled racemes, appearing when the tree is leafless or with the new leaves; stamens exserted.

Middle and South Andaman, common around Port Blair in clearings. Fl. Dec.-Febr. Fr. Febr.-May. The wood is reddish-brown or pale brown, heavy, but uneven grained and useful for fuel. It is of uninteresting appearance and in determining its name one would hardly suspect that it belonged to this family.

The two next have been introduced and planted.

Punica Granatum, *Linn.*; *The Pomegranate*. Vern. *Anar*, Hind. A deciduous shrubby tree often with spinescent branches. Leaves 1—3 in. long, oblong-lanceolate, narrowed at base. Flowers large, bright red. Fruit 2—3 in. diam., with a coriaceous rind and numerous seeds embedded in a clear white or ruby-coloured pulp. Wild in Afghanistan and Baluchistan.

Lawsonia alba, *Lam.*; *The Henna Plant*. Vern. *Dan*, Burm; *Mehndi* Hind. A shrub with slender whitish branchlets. Leaves ½—1½ in. long, elliptic-lanceolate to oblanceolate. Flowers white, rather small. Capsule reddish, the size of a pea. Introduced and now growing wild in several places in Port Blair. Fl. and Fr. at all times of the year. The leaves are powdered and made into a paste which gives the dye used for staining the finger nails, beard and teeth. Its flowers yield a delightful essence known as *Henna*.

Fam. 41. SAMYDACEÆ.

Trees with simple alternate leaves. Flowers small, in axillary clusters or from the scars of the fallen leaves; sepals usually 5; petals none; stamens 10, with alternating villous staminodes.

1. CASEARIA.

280. **C. andamanica**, *King*; Br. 343.

A tree (30—50 × 3—4) with a yellowish-brown bark. Leaves 6—12 in. long, 2¼—4 in. broad, oblong to oblong-lanceolate, acute or shortly acuminate, faintly serrulate, base unequally rounded, glabrous, coriaceous and glossy on the upper surface, lateral nerves 11—18 pairs; petioles ¾—1 in. long. Flowers barely ¼ in. diam., greenish-white; sepals concave.

Uncommon. Middle Andaman, Amitbted, Palodina; South Andaman, Chiriatapu; in evergreen forests. Fl. Jan.-April. Interesting on account of its uncommonness.

To Passifloraceæ belongs **Carica Papaya**, *Linn. The Papaya.* Vern. *Thinbaw thee*, Burm. It has been introduced and grows well in these islands.

Fam. 42. DATISCACEÆ.

Leaves simple, alternate, palminerved. Flowers very small, dioecious, 4-merous, without petals. Capsule opening at the top and crowned by the persistent calyx.

1. TETRAMELES.

281. **T. nudiflora**, *R. Br.*; H. ii. 657; Br. 346. *The Andamanese Canoe Tree.* Vern. *Thitpók*, Burm.; *Jungli Irungy*, Hind.

A very large deciduous tree with enormous buttresses, (100—150 × 9—12), bark whitish-grey, smooth and polished, the outer layer papery, cut creamy-white, discolouring. Leaves 5—7 in. long, broadly ovate, acute or acuminate, irregularly serrate, 3-nerved at the cordate base; petioles 2—5 in. long, or longer. Flowers greenish, small, in pendulous racemes at the ends of the leafless branchlets. Capsule ⅛ in. diam.

Common everywhere in deciduous and semi-deciduous forests. Deciduous in the H. S. Fl. in March-April when the tree is leafless, and soon followed by the fruit which falls in April-June. Easily recognised by its immense size, smooth bark and enormous buttresses which are, I believe, larger than those of any other tree in the islands. The wood is light-coloured, soft and light. It is the tree used by the Andamanese for making their dug-out canoes.

Fam. 43. ARALIACEÆ.

Trees or scandent shrubs with alternate, simple, lobed or compound leaves. Flowers small, usually umbellate, 5-merous; petals triangular;

stamens inflexed in bud. Fruit drupaceous.

Trees.
 Leaves simple, large, palmately lobed, on long petioles ... 1. Brassaiopsis.
 Leaves tripinnate, 2–4 feet long ... 2. Heteropanax.
 Leaves usually imparipinnate, sometimes twice or thrice pinnate ... ... 3. Arthrophyllum.
Climber with digitate leaves ... ... 4. Heptapleurum.

1. BRASSAIOPSIS.

282. **B. palmata,** *Kurz* ; H. ii. 735 ; Br. 352. Vern. *Baw*, Burm.

A small tree (15—20 × 1—2) usually unbranched, with large lobed leaves collected at the top of the stem. Leaves 2–2½ feet across, orbicular, cordate and palminerved, with 7—9 lobes; petioles 2–3 feet long. Flowers in long, narrow, lax panicles. Fruit yellow or orange-coloured, the size of a small bullet.

Middle Andaman, near the mouth of the Betapur Creek and also at Bomlungta; Baratang; South Andaman, Port Mouat, Mount Harriet. Fl. Nov.-Dec. Fr. Febr.-March. The stem and branches contain a white pith which makes excellent bottle corks, and the tree resembles in appearance the cultivated *Papaya tree*.

2. HETEROPANAX.

283. **H. fragrans,** *Seem.* ; H. ii. 734 ; Br. 352. Vern. *Kyaungdauk*, Burm.

A moderate-sized deciduous tree (30—40 × 3—4) with a thick greyish bark, cut mealy, light yellow-brown with a little yellowish-red juice. Leaves tripinnate, 2–4 feet long; leaflets 3–6 in. long, ovate, glabrous. Flowers yellow, fragrant, in dense panicled racemes, the male flowers in heads, the bisexual in umbels. Fruit $\frac{1}{4}$–$\frac{1}{2}$ in. diam., laterally compressed.

Frequent and dispersed in nearly all localities. Leafless in the H. S. Fl. Dec.-Febr. Fr. soon after. Resembles, and is sometimes mistaken for *Oroxylum indicum*, which has opposite leaves, very different flowers, and the bark of which when cut is stringy and turns green.

3. ARTHROPHYLLUM.

284. **A. diversifolium,** *Blume* ; H. ii. 733 ; Br. 353.

A small or moderate-sized tree (25—40 × 1½–3½), usually simple stemmed, but often branched in old trees, bark grey, cut creamy-yellow with yellowish juice. Leaves collected at the top of the stem or branches, usually imparipinnate, with 7—8 pairs of leaflets and an odd one, often bipinnate, or the floral leaves 3-foliolate ; leaflets 3–4 in. long, obliquely-ovate, the rachis thickened at their insertion. Flowers white, umbellately clustered. Berries ovoid-oblong.

Unfrequent. Middle Andaman at the mouth of the Betapur ; also on Mt. Harriet and the west coast of the South Andaman. Fl. and Fr. March-April.

4. HEPTAPLEURUM.

285. **H. venulosum,** *Seem.*; H. ii. 729; Br. 348. *The Angelica Plant.* Vern. *Myauk-letwa, Taukte-letwa,* Burm.; *Kath Semal,* Hind.

A scandent shrub attaching itself to supports by rootlets from the branchlets. Leaves digitately 5–7 foliolate, the common petiole 4—6 in. long, stem-clasping at the base; leaflets 3—8 in. long, elliptic or elliptic-lanceolate, thick and glabrous. Flowers greenish-yellow, in umbels forming racemes and collected in panicles. Fruit ovoid, bluntly ridged, yellow when ripe.

Middle and South Andaman, often on *Padauk.* Fl. Febr. Fr. March.

Similar, but with wider reticulations on the leaves and the panicles often composed of compound umbels, is **H. ellipticum,** *Seem.* also found in the Andamans.

To this family belongs the following familiar shrub often seen in gardens in Port Blair.

Panax fruticosum, *Linn.*; 3—5 feet high with tripinnate leaves, the leaflets variable in shape and variously serrate and laciniate. The leaves are often used for the decoration of the breakfast table.

Fam. 44. CORNACEÆ.

Scandent. Leaves simple, alternate, exstipulate. Flowers bisexual, petals valvate 5—10, with twice as many stamens. Fruit a berry crowned by the calyx.

1. ALANGIUM.

286. **A. Lamarckii,** *Thw.* var. glandulosa, *Thw.*; H. ii. 741; Br. 354.

A large unarmed climber. Leaves 3—6 in. long, 2—3½ in. broad, elliptic to oblong or obovate, rounded and 3-nerved at the base, shortly acuminate, glabrous and with tufts of hairs in the axils of the 4–5 pairs of lateral nerves beneath; petioles ¼—½ in. long. Flowers white, very fragrant, in axillary fascicles; petals usually 6, linear, about 1 in. long; stamens usually 18, with flat filaments. Drupe ellipsoid, ½—⅝ in. long, black when ripe.

Middle Andaman, in evergreen and in deciduous forest, Austin Strait, Palkat Bay and Rongat Bay; South Andaman. Fl. May. In India it often grows armed with spines.

Fam. 45. RUBIACEÆ.

THE COFFEE FAMILY.

Trees, shrubs and sometimes climbers. Leaves opposite or whorled, with the stipules joined between the petioles and sometimes forming a sheath around the stem. Flowers gamopetalous; corolla usually 4—5 lobed, with as many stamens as lobes inserted on the corolla tube. Fruit various.

A large tropical family well represented in these islands, but of the members here mentioned, none are of great forest importance. *Coffea Liberica. The Liberian Coffee*, a native of west tropical Africa has been introduced and planted at Dhani Khari. To the family also belong the *Peruvian bark* or *Cinchona* trees, natives of the Andes of South America, and *Cephaelis Ipecacuanha*, a native of Brazil, from the roots of which the drug ipecacuanha is obtained.

Flowers more or less small and collected in small or large globose heads.
- Inland trees or shrubs.
  - Flower heads arranged in cymes ... ... 1. Stephegyne.
  - Flowers in large solitary heads ... ... 2. Anthocephalus.
  - Flower heads 1—3 together ... ... 3. Nauclea.
- Littoral small tree with yellow wood. Fruit a hard fleshy mass the result of several flowers .. ... 4. Morinda.
- Climbers with quadrangular branchlets armed with strong recurved hooks ... ... 5. Uncaria

Flowers in terminal cymes.
- Small trees.
  - Flowers orange-coloured with a conspicuous white leaf-like calyx lobe ... . 6 Mussaenda.
  - Flowers white, corolla lobes twisted ... ... 7. Webera.
- Small trees or shrubs.
  - Flowers long-tubed, in compound cymes; corolla lobes twisted ... ... 8. Ixora.
- Shrubs with rounded branchlets. Corolla lobes valvate ... 9. Psychotria.

Flowers in axillary fascicles, cymes or clusters.
- Littoral.
  - Tree with broadly ovate cordate leaves. Flowers white, long-tubed, fragrant ... ... 10. Guettarda.
  - Shrub like a mangrove. Flowers white. Fruit grooved fleshy ... ... 11. Scyphiphora.
- Inland.
  - Corolla lobes twisted ... ... 12. Randia.
  - Corolla lobes valvate.
    - Shrub with leaves in whorls of 3's, foetid when bruised. Fl. white ... ... 13. Saprosma.
    - Branchlets angled. Corolla throat villous, lobes reflexed ... ... 14. Canthium.
    - Branchlets slender, rounded. Fl. white. Fr. pulpy, globose ... . 15. Gynochthodes.
    - Small tree. Leaves shortly petioled. Fl. white. Fr. globose, ribbed ... ... 16. Timonius.
    - Shrubs, usually hairy, with distichous leaves. Branchlets rounded ... 17. Lasianthus.

Flowers solitary, axillary, large and with twisted corolla lobes.
- Inland tree. Buds resinous; stipules connate around the stem ... ... 18. Gardenia.

Hydnophytum formicarum, *Jack*, is a small epiphytic shrub with thick tuber-like stems several inches in diameter, in which ants make their nests. It is common in mangrove swamps on *Heritiera littoralis* and its associates, and is known as the *Ant-house Plant*.

1. STEPHEGYNE.

287. **S. diversifolia,** *Hook. fil.*; H. iii. 326; Br. 370. Vern. *Bingah*, Burm.

A moderate-sized deciduous tree (40—60 × 3—6) with a light grey bark, cut light brown, dry, mealy-fibrous. Leaves 3—10 in. long and nearly as broad, broadly ovate from a cordate base, obtuse, puberulous beneath, lateral nerves 7—10 pairs, strong; petioles ½—1¼ in. long. Flowers fragrant, yellowish, in heads ¾ in. diam., on divaricately branching trichotomous cymes. Capsules small, ovoid-oblong, dehiscing at the apex.

Fairly frequent and dispersed in the leaf-shedding forests of the Middle Andaman and South Andaman, Ritchie's Archipelago and Rutland Island. Leafless in the H. S. Fl. Sept.-Jan. Fr. Jan.-May. The wood is yellowish-brown, evenly grained and moderately hard.

2. ANTHOCEPHALUS.

288. **A. Cadamba,** *Miq.*; H. iii. 23; Br. 367. Vern. *Ma-u*, Burm.; *Kadam*, Hind.

A large deciduous tree (70—100 × 5—7) with a straight stem and numerous slender horizontal branches, bark dark grey with fissures lengthwise. Leaves 6—10 in. long, and about half as broad, ovate or elliptic oblong, more or less rounded at the base, coriaceous and glossy above; petioles 1—2 in. long. Flowers small, white and yellow, collected in handsome globular heads about 2 in. diam., on a stalk 1—2 in. long. Fruit a fleshy receptacle made up of numerous closely packed yellowish capsules.

Very common in all localities and mostly so in damp places along large streams. Leafless for a short while about the month of May. Fl. Dec.-July. Fr. Aug.-Sept. The fruit is edible. The leaves of young plants are larger than those of mature plants. It is said to be reverenced both by Hindus and Buddhists and the specific name comes from the vernacular. Its wood is soft, whitish and even-grained, weighing about 40 pounds per cubic foot, and is said to be useful for making tea-boxes.

3. NAUCLEA.

Deciduous trees with large obovate stipules. Flowers sessile, small, in pedunculate heads, single or in twos or threes. Seeds winged, the wing forked at the end.

Large tree. Leaves 6—12 in. long ... ... N. Gageana.
Small tree. Leaves 4½—8¼ in. long ... ... N. purpurascens.

289. **N. Gageana**, *King*; Br. 368. Vern. *Teinkala*, Burm.

A very large tree (80–120 × 6—10) with a bark resembling that of the *Red Bombway*, cut fibrous, pinkish turning brown. Leaves 6—12 in. long, and about half as broad, broadly ovate-elliptic, base somewhat rounded and tapering to the ½—¾ in. petiole, glabrous and with 8—10 pairs of lateral nerves. Flower heads 1½ in. diam., solitary or in pairs, on stalks 1 in. long and bearing bracts 1¼ in. long. Fruit villous.

Fairly frequent. Middle Andaman, Bomlungta and Rongat Bay; South Andaman; Long Island. Leafless in the H. S. Fl. and Fr. Nov.-March. The wood is useful and resembles that of *Adina cordifolia*.

290. ***N. purpurascens**, *Korth*; J. A. S. B. No. 4. 1903, page 124.

A small tree, the young branches purple when fresh. Leaves 4½—8½ in. long, 1⅓–2 in. broad, elliptic or oblong-lanceolate, attenuate at base, glabrous, lateral nerves 7—9 pairs; petioles ⅓—¾ in. long. Flower heads about 1⅓ in. diam.. solitary or in threes, peduncles 1½–3 in. long, with two boat-shaped bracts; anthers with a minute apical appendage. Fruit densely villous, ribbed.

South Andaman, Mt. Harriet and Port Mouat. Fl. July-October.

4. MORINDA.

291. **M. citrifolia**, *Linn.*; H. iii. 155; Br. 392. Vern. *Nibase*, Burm.

A small littoral tree (15—30 × 2—3) with a cracked bark, cut dirty brown, yellow near the sapwood. Leaves 6—10 in. long, elliptic to elliptic-lanceolate, attenuate at the base, acute, glabrous; petiole ½—¾ in. long. Flowers white, sessile, collected in a globose receptacle on a leaf-opposed peduncle. Fruit a green, succulent, fleshy head about 1½ in. diam.

Fairly frequent along the seashores of the islands and easily known by its bright yellow wood which gives it the name of the *Canary-wood Tree*, and by its peculiar fruits on account of which it is sometimes called the *Indian Mulberry Tree*. Fl. and Fr. April-July.

5. UNCARIA.

292. **U. pedicellata**, *Roxb.*; H. iii. 28; Br. 370.

A large scandent shrub with quadrangular branchlets bearing axillary tendrils which form stout recurved hooks, all the younger parts rusty pubescent. Leaves 4—6 in. long, with twisted petioles, elliptic or broadly so, dark green and glossy above, pale and sparsely rusty pubescent beneath, lateral nerves about 9 pairs, conspicuous. Flowers in peduncled globose heads, the pedicles lengthening in fruiting and bearing elongate capsules; seeds winged.

Frequent in the Middle Andaman, Baratang, the Archipelago and around Port Blair. Fl. R. S. and H. S.

6. MUSSAENDA.

293. **M. macrophylla**, *Wall.*; H. iii. 89; Br. 376. Vern. *Ywetkla*, Burm.

A soft-wooded fast-growing tree (15 – 25 × 1—1½) with thin bark. Leaves 3—7 in. long and about half as broad, elliptic, shortly acuminate, narrowed to the petiole, glabrous, lateral nerves about 15 pairs, strong and curved; petioles slender ½—2 in. long. Flowers orange-red, handsome, in terminal cymes with one of the calyx lobes enlarged and resembling a beautiful white leaf; corolla about ¾ in. long. Berry ovoid, ½—¾ in. long.

Very common in damp open places and making its appearance rapidly in clearings. During the dry months it is difficult to distinguish from amongst the other forest growth, but during the rainy season it becomes conspicuous on account of its orange-red flowers and white leaf-like calyx-lobes.

7. WEBERA.

294. **W. Kurzii**, *Hook. fil.*; Br. 378.

A small slender tree with thin rounded branchlets. Leaves 4 – 7 in. long, 1½—3 in. broad, elliptic-lanceolate, acuminate at both ends, glabrous and drying black, lateral nerves fine, with tufts of hairs in the nerve axils beneath; petioles rather short. Flowers small, white, in trichotomous cymes; corolla funnel-shaped with spreading or reflexed lobes. Berries the size of a pea.

Frequent in most localities, chiefly along the sea-shores and also in the interior. Fl. and Fr. at various times of the year.

8. IXORA.

Evergreen shrubs or small trees with rounded branchlets. Flowers usually white or pink, 4-merous, in terminal trichotomous compound cymes, the corolla salver-shaped with twisted lobes which overlap to the left in bud and the tubes long and slender. Fruit a slightly 2-lobed drupe.

Small trees.
- Littoral. Leaves almost sessile and cordate at the base ... I. brunnescens.
- Inland. Leaves petiolate, tapering at the base ... I. Finlaysoniana.

Shrubs.
- Flowers crowded, white or pale rose-coloured ... I. grandifolia.
- Flowers laxly arranged, white ... ... I. barbata.

I. coccinea, *Linn.*, is an ornamental plant often seen used as a hedge plant in gardens. It has conspicuous scarlet flowers in dense umbels or corymbs and is sometimes called the *Jungle Geranium* or *Flame of the Woods*.

295. **I. brunnescens,** *Kurz.*; H. iii. 148; Br. 389.

A small tree (15–30 × 1–3) with very hard wood. Leaves 4–8 in. long and almost half as broad, nearly sessile obovate or oblanceolate, obtuse or rounded at the apex, tapering to the rounded or almost cordate base, lateral nerves about a dozen pairs. Flowers white, fragrant, corolla ⅓ in. long with reflexed lobes. Fruit ¼ in. diam.

Frequent along the seashores of the islands and associated with *Mimusops littoralis* and *Ochrosia borbonica*, and somewhat resembling the latter, but from which it may be easily distinguished by its having no milky juice and by its almost sessile leaves. Fl. H. S. and R. S.

296. **I. Finlaysoniana,** *Wall.*; Gen. Syst. iii. 572 (1834).

A small tree 20 feet high. Leaves 5–7 in. long, and about half as broad, elliptic or oblong, apex pointed or blunt, base tapering and decurrent into the ¼–½ in. petiole, lateral nerves 8–10 pairs, interarching rather far from the edge. Flowers white, fragrant, conspicuous and handsome, the tube about ¾ in. long. Fruit about ½ in. long, ellipsoid.

Middle Andaman, in the forests around Bomlungta. Fl. H. S.

297. **I. grandifolia,** *Zoll. and Morr.*; Br. 389.

A shrub with variable leaves 4–10 in. long, elliptic to ovate or lanceolate, acute or blunt at base and apex, glabrous, with 8–12 pairs of lateral nerves. Flowers white or pale rose-coloured, crowded, with slender long corolla tubes. Fruit ¼–½ in. across, slightly 2-lobed.

Frequent in all localities among shrubbery. The most interesting variety is var. *rosella*, which is common everywhere and which may be easily distinguished by its rose-coloured flowers and the reddish branches of the inflorescence. Fl. and Fr. Cold and Hot season.

298. ***I. barbata,** *Roxb.*; H. iii. 148; Br. 389.

A large shrub. Leaves 5–8 in. long, oblong to ovate—oblong, the lower ones on petioles up to ½ in. long, the upper ones cordate-ovate and nearly sessile, shortly bluntish acuminate, glabrous. Flowers white, laxly arranged; corolla tube about an inch long, woolly at the throat.

Rather frequent, *Kurz.* Fl. May–June.

9. PSYCHOTRIA.

Shrubs with round stems and flowers in terminal corymbose or paniculate cymes. Flowers usually 5-merous with the corolla lobes valvate in bud.

These are shrubs of uninteresting appearance and of little importance to the Forester. The following are the principal Andaman species:—

***P. adenophylla,** *Wall.* A glabrous shrub. Leaves 4–8 in. long, elliptic-lanceolate, narrowed to the ½ in. petiole, lateral nerves 16–18 pairs, arching, stipules connate, sheathing. Flowers white or greenish. Fruit purplish or black. Fl. H. S.

*P. platyneura, *Kurz.* Leaves 6—7 in long, elliptic to lanceolate or obovate, lateral nerves 18—22 pairs. Flowers in terminal cymes. Fruit small, obovoid, black. Fl. May-June.

P. andamanica, *Kurz.* Leaves obovate to oblong-lanceolate, shortly acuminate, lateral nerves 8—10 pairs, remote. Flowers small, greenish-white. Fruit ¼ in. long. Fl. April-May.

*P. Helferiana, *Kurz.* Leaves 6—12 in. long, elliptic or oblong-elliptic, acuminate, rusty pubescent on both surfaces, lateral nerves 9—16 pairs; petioles 1—2 in. long, stipules about 1 in. long. Flowers in dense cymes. Fruit ovoid, boldly 8-ridged.

10. GUETTARDA.

299. **G. speciosa,** *Linn.*; H. iii. 126; Br. 386.

A small littoral evergreen tree attaining a height of 25—30 feet, bark fairly smooth, grey, often with dark-coloured patches. Leaves collected at the ends of the leaf-scarred branchlets. 6—10 in. long, broadly ovate to almost orbicular, rounded or small cordate at the base, puberulous beneath, petioles rounded, ⅓—1½ in. long. Flowers white, fragrant, in few-flowered axillary cymes on long peduncles; corolla tube 1—1½ in. long, hairy at the mouth. Drupe about 1 in. diam., almost globular.

Frequent along all the seashores of the islands and growing just above high-water mark with *Hibiscus tiliaceus* and the other plants of this zone. The flowers are fragrant after sundown and appear at all times of the year. It is known as the *Sea coast Teak.* There is a form with more acuminate leaves which may turn out to be a distinct species.

11. SCYPHIPHORA.

300. **S. hydrophyllacea,** *Gærtn.*; H. iii. 125; Br. 384.

A small shrubby treelet about 8 feet high, looking like a mangrove, with light green foliage. Leaves collected at the ends of the branchlets, 1½—3 in. long and about half as broad, obovate, apex rounded, tapering to the petioles, glossy above. Flowers white, in small axillary compact cymes; the corolla with 4—5 twisted lobes, hairy at the throat. Drupe about ½ in. long, grooved.

Frequent in swamps along mangrove creeks in most localities. Fl. and Fr. Dec.-March. It is sometimes confused with *Lumnitzera* which grows in similar places, but the latter has alternate leaves which are narrow and obscurely crenate.

12. RANDIA.

Trees, shrubs or climbers, with short, often connate stipules Flowers usually whitish; corolla lobes twisted and overlapping to the left in bud, throat hairy; anthers narrow with short filaments. Fruit usually a hard berry.

Trees.
- Small tree. Flowers ¼ in. long. Berry small ... R. densiflora.
- Tall tree. Flowers 2 in. long. Berry 2 in. diam. ... R. exaltata.

Shrub armed with sharp spines.
Flowers 1—1½ in. long, clustered ... ... R. longiflora.
Unarmed climber.
Flowers nearly 1 in. long, from the scars of fallen leaves R. Forbesii.

301. **R. densiflora**, *Benth.*; Br. 383.

A tree attaining a height of 15—25 feet. Leaves 4—6 in. long, elliptic-oblong to elliptic-lanceolate, shortly acuminate, glabrous, drying black, lateral nerves about 10 pairs, curved; petioles about ½ in. long. Flowers ½ in. long, numerous in axillary cymes, corolla lobes spreading in flower. Fruit small.

Fairly common. Middle Andaman; South Andaman, in several localities around Port Blair and Port Mouat. Fl. April-June. Fr. R. S. It has very hard and heavy wood.

302. **R. exaltata**, *Griff.*; H. iii. 114; Br. 383.

A moderate-sized but tall tree (50—80×2—3) with a thin, smooth, dark grey bark, often with dark and light coloured patches, cut reddish, brown, watery and immediately turning yellow near the sapwood. Leaves 3—6½ in. long, and about half as broad, broadly elliptic to elliptic-lanceolate, shortly acuminate, slightly unequal at the base, lateral nerves 8—10 pairs with glands beneath. Flowers nearly 2 in. long, tinged with green inside and with purple spots, funnel-shaped. Fruit 2 in. diam., woody, brown-coloured.

Middle Andaman, in several localities; Baratang; South Andaman. Not uncommon and usually in evergreen forests. Fl. during the R. S., the fallen corollas of which may often be found scattered below the tree.

303. **R. longiflora**, *Lamk.*; H. iii. 111; Br. 382.

A rambling shrub armed with strong sharp spines. Leaves 3—6 in. long, elliptic or ovate, tapering downwards into the channelled petioles, lateral nerves 5—8 pairs with tufts of hairs in the nerve axils beneath and obscure net-venation. Flowers 1—1½ in. long, in compact clusters. Fruit about ½ in. long, ovoid globose.

In all localities; common among the undergrowth of *Padauk* forest. Fl. March-May. Fr. June-July.

304. ***R. Forbesii**, *King and Gamble.*; J.A.S.B. No. 4. 1903, p. 207.

A climber 60—80 feet long. Leaves 4—7 in. long, 2—3 in. broad, elliptic to ovate, acute, base narrow and slightly oblique, glabrous, lateral nerves 5—7 pairs; petioles ½ in. long. Flowers nearly an inch long, in many-flowered cymes from the scars of fallen leaves; corolla with 5 long blunt lobes. Fruit small.

South Andaman.

13. SAPROSMA.

305. **S. ternatum,** *Hook. fil.*; H. iii. 192; Br. 396.

A shrub. Leaves usually in whorls of threes, smelling unpleasantly when bruised, 4—8 in. long and half as broad, elliptic-lanceolate, acuminate, narrowed to the short petiole, glabrous. Flowers white, on slender pedicels in axillary fascicled cymes; corolla ½ in. across, the lobes reflexed in flower. Fruit about ½ in. long, ellipsoid, succulent, black when ripe.

A shrub, as uninteresting in appearance as it is common, especially in damp places along streams; found in all localities. Fl. and Fr. Mar.-June. Easily known by its leaves which are in whorls of threes.

14. CANTHIUM.

Flowers small, in axillary fascicles or cymes; corolla with 4—5 valvate lobes, reflexed at length, throat hairy. Drupe with 1 or 2 seeds.

Small tree. Leaves 5—8 in. long. Fruit 1 in. long ...	C. glabrum.
Shrub. Leaves 1—3 in. long. Fruit small ...	C. gracilipes.

306. **C. glabrum,** *Blume*; H. iii. 133; Br. 385.

A small tree (15—20×1—1½) with thin pale-coloured bark and slender horizontal branches, the branchlets 4-angled. Leaves 5—8 in. long, 2—4 in. broad, elliptic or ovate-elliptic, acuminate, base broad and rounded, glabrous and glossy above, lateral nerves 6—8 pairs; petiole about ½ in. long. Flowers small, in cymes about an inch in diam. Fruit about an inch long, ovoid and somewhat angular, pulpy.

Middle Andaman, Paikat Bay; Long Island; Baratang; South Andaman. Fl. Jan.-Febr. Fr. H. S.

307. **C. gracilipes,** *Kurz*; H. iii. 134; Br. 385.

A small shrub with slender stiff branchlets. Leaves 1—3 in. long, ovate to elliptic or lanceolate, acuminate, dark green above, pale beneath with a few silky hairs, membranous, petioles short. Flowers greenish-white, on slender pedicels, axillary or from the scars of fallen leaves. Fruit smooth, bluish-black, somewhat compressed and 2-lobed.

Frequent among shrubbery in deciduous forests. Middle and South Andaman. Fl. April-May. Poor-looking.

15. GYNOCHTHODES.

308. ***G. macrophylla,** *Kurz*; H. iii. 160; Br. 393.

An evergreen glabrous climbing shrub with slender rounded branchlets. Leaves 4—6 in. long, and a little less than half as broad, elliptic or elliptic-oblong, shortly and abruptly acuminate, base cuneate, lateral nerves 6—7 pairs; petioles up to ½ in. long. Flowers unisexual, in short axillary compact cymes; corolla tube short, lobes valvate with inflexed tips, throat hairy. Fruit ⅓ in. diam., globose, pulpy.

Among shrubbery along the sea coast of the islands. Fl. May. *Kurz.*

16. TIMONIUS.

309. ***T. Jambosella,** *Thwaites*; H. iii. 127; Br. 386.

An evergreen tree 30—35 feet high. Leaves 2½—4 in. long, lanceolate or elliptic-lanceolate, acuminate, tapering to the short petiole, glabrous, margins recurved, pale and silky beneath, lateral nerves 5—6 pairs, curving upwards. Flowers small, white, 4-merous, bracteolate, polygamous, the males in 3—12 flowered cymes, the females solitary on long peduncles. Drupe small, globose, ribbed.

South Andaman, around Port Blair. Fl. April-May.

17. LASIANTHUS.

Hairy shrubs with terete branches and distichous caudate-acuminate leaves with numerous parallel tertiary nerves. Flowers in axillary clusters or cymes; corolla hairy at the throat, with valvate lobes. Drupe small, with 3-angled stones.

The following occur in the islands;—

***L. cyanocarpus,** *Jack.* Softly hirsute all over. Leaves 6—10 in. long, elliptic-lanceolate, lateral nerves 7—10 pairs. Flowers sessile, in cymes enveloped by bracts. Fruit ovoid-globular, blue. Fl. May-June.

***L. Wallichii,** *Wight.* Simple-stemmed. Leaves 2—6 in. long, oblong or oblong-lanceolate, unequal at the rounded or cordate base, lateral nerves 7—8 pairs; petiole very short. Flowers white, in clusters with bracts. Drupe ovoid, blue. Fl. and Fr. H. S.

***L Kurzii,** *Hook. fil.* Branchlets pale reddish-brown. Leaves 5—8 in. long, oblong-lanceolate, glabrous above, softly pubescent beneath, lateral nerves 6—9 pairs. Flowers in fascicles, calyx deeply 5—7 cleft, strigose. Drupe small. Fl. March April.

***L. andamanicus,** *Hook. fil.* Branches, petioles and leaves beneath with long, strigose hairs. Leaves 6—8 in. long, oblong-lanceolate, lateral nerves 9—10 pairs. Flowers in small ebracteate clusters, villous. Drupe small, globose.

18. GARDENIA.

310. **G. coronaria,** *Ham.*; H. iii. 117; Br 379. *The Garland Gardenia.* Vern. *Yingat*, Burm.

A small or moderate-sized tree (25—30×2—1) with a greyish discoloured bark, cut whitish, irregularly spotted and streaked, stipules connate around the stem, buds resinous. Leaves 4—10 in. long and half as broad, obovate, slightly acuminate, tapering downwards to the

½ in. petioles, lateral nerves prominent with hairy glands in the axils beneath. Flowers large, fragrant, usually solitary; corolla cream-coloured, turning yellow in withering, tube up to 2 in. long, lobes an inch long, twisted in bud. Berry ovoid, 1—2 in. long.

Not common. Middle Andaman; Baratang; South Andaman. Fl. H. S. Fr. R. S. The leaves resemble those of *Bassia butyracea*. It is easily known by its large flowers, opposite leaves with sheathing stipules, and resinous buds. seen in DP

Fam. 46. GOODENIACEÆ.

An evergreen shrub of a more or less succulent character. Leaves simple, alternate. Flowers with an oblique corolla split on one side; stamens 5. Fruit a drupe.

1. SCÆVOLA.

311. **S. Koenigii**, *Vahl.*; H. iii. 421; Br. 403. *The Fan Flower.*

A littoral shrub 5—15 feet high with light green fleshy foliage and soft pithy stems. Leaves 4—10 in. long, 2½—4 in. broad, obovate to obovate-oblong, rounded at apex and tapering downwards to the very short petiole, glossy. Flowers white, nearly an inch across; corolla split, with the lobes all on one side, villous within. Drupe about ½ in. diam., ovoid-globose, ribbed.

Extremely common along all the seashores of the islands and fringing the beaches at high-water mark. Easily recognised, even at long distances by its light green foliage. Fl. and Fr. all the year round. The Burmese name, *Pinle-tan*, is seldom used in the Andamans.

Fam. 47. PLUMBAGINACEÆ.

312. ***Aegialitis rotundifolia**, *Roxb.*; Br. 413. A simple-stemmed soft-wooded littoral shrub 4—8 feet high. Leaves simple, alternate, 2—3 in. diam., orbicular, thickly coriaceous with thin and close venation; petioles 2—3 in. long, stout, with prominently winged stem-clasping stipules leaving scars when falling. Flowers white or pale yellow; calyx ribbed, with 5 valvate lobes; corolla lobes 5, slightly adhering at the base and with 5 stamens opposite them. Fruit 3 in. long, linear-curved, angled.

Found in mangrove swamps and a native of the Andamans according to Kurz, Brandis and the Flora of British India. I have not had the good fortune of finding this in the Andamans, nor have I seen any Andaman specimens in the Kew or the Calcutta Herbariums. It ought to be quite easily recognised.

Fam. 48. MYRSINACEÆ.

Evergreen shrubs or small trees with simple, alternate, and often gland-dotted leaves without stipules. Flowers 5-merous, bisexual; calyx persistent and often enlarging in fruit; corolla with the lobes often twisted and overlapping to the right; stamens opposite the corolla lobes.

Leaves gland-dotted. Flowers pink ... ... 1. Ardisia.
Leaves not gland-dotted. Flowers white.
Small tree like a mangrove. Flowers in umbels; stamens exserted. Fruit linear-curved ... .. 2. Aegiceras.
Inland small trees or shrubs. Flowers in racemes; filaments short. Fruit small ... ... 3. Maesa.

1. ARDISIA.

Leaves entire with gland dots that usually dry black. Flowers pink, corolla waxy with black dots; filaments short.

Flowers in axillary umbellate racemes... ... ... A. humilis.
Flowers in lax panicles ... ... A. andamanica.

813. **A. humilis**, *Vahl.*; H. iii. 529; Br. 418. Vern. *Kyetmauk*, Burm.

A small tree 15—25 feet high with dark-brown bark and slender branchlets. Leaves 3—6 in. long, obovate to obovate-oblong, narrowed to the base, succulent-coriaceous, with indistinct lateral nerves; petiole ⅛-¼ in. long. Flowers waxy, ⅛—⅜ in. diam., in axillary umbellate racemes; petals acute. Fruit ¼ in. diam., globose-depressed, red and turning purplish-black when ripe.

Often along the coasts in *Mohwa* forests. Middle Andaman; Long Island, Havelock and Rutland Islands. Fl. March-July. Fr. Nov.-March.

814. ***A. andamanica**, *Kurz*; H. iii. 521; Br. 419. Vern. *Kyetmauk*, Burm.

A small tree with reddish-brown bark. Leaves 3—7 in. long, lanceolate or oblong-lanceolate, acuminate, membranous with many gland dots, lateral nerves about 20 pairs, thin and weak; petiole ⅛—⅜ in. long. Flowers rose-coloured, small, in lax panicles; corolla lobes gland-dotted and with ciliate margins. Fruit pear-shaped or round.

Tropical forests of the Andamans, *Kurz*. Fl. June.

2. AEGICERAS.

815. **A. majus**, *Gaertn.*; H. iii. 533; Br. 421. *The Black Mangrove* or *Estuary Tree*. Vern. *Butalet*, Burm.

A small tree (12—15 × 1—2) with the habit of a mangrove. Leaves scattered, 1½—3½ in. long, obovate, apex rounded, margins recurved, coriaceous and glabrous, lateral nerves about 10 pairs, rather inconspicuous. Flowers white, fragrant, about ⅜ in. long, on slender pedicels in umbels; petals pointed, reflexed in flower. Fruit 1—2 in. long, cylindric, curved and pointed.

In mangrove swamps, uncommon and difficult to recognise when without flower or fruit. Fl. Jan.-April. Fr. R. S.

3. MAESA.

Leaves without gland dots. Flowers small, in racemes.

Straggling shrub. Flowers in short axillary racemes ...	M. andamanica.
Small tree. Flowers in slender axillary racemes	M. ramentacea.

316. **M. andamanica,** *Kurz.*; H. iii 508; Br. 416.

A straggling shrub with fine warted branchlets. Leaves 2—4 in. long, 1—2 in. broad, ovate-acuminate, rounded at the base, entire or denticulate; petioles slender, ¼—½ in. long. Flowers small, cream-coloured or white, on slender pedicels in short axillary racemes. Fruit yellowish when ripe, the size of a small pea.

Frequent in all localities in open places and among shrubbery along dry stream-beds. Fl. and Fr. Jan.-May.

317. **M. ramentacea,** *A. DC*; H. iii. 518; Br. 414.

A small tree (25—30 × 1½—2). Leaves like those of the preceding one, 3—8 in. long, entire, lateral nerves 5—10 pairs; petiole ½ in. long. Flowers small, in axillary glabrous racemes as long as the leaves.

South Andaman, Port Blair. Fl. and Fr. Jan.-April.

Fam. 49. SAPOTACEÆ.

The Mohwa Family.

Trees, mostly evergreen with milky juice. Leaves simple, alternate, entire and penninerved and without stipules. Flowers usually axillary and often clustered; calyx of 4—8 imbricate segments; corolla segments 4—24, with as many or twice to thrice as many stamens. Fruit fleshy with a single or many seeds.

Leaves with many, fine and parallel lateral nerves and a fine intramarginal vein. Flowers usually large, axillary, solitary or a few clustered	1. Mimusops.
Leaves with strong lateral nerves. Flowers rather large, many collected in clusters at the ends of the branchlets	2. Bassia.
Leaves with prominent or strong lateral nerves. Flowers small and inconspicuous, axillary or from the scars of fallen leaves	3. Sideroxylon.

1. MIMUSOPS.

Large trees with dark green glossy leaves with many fine and parallel lateral nerves joined intramarginally. Flowers solitary or a few in a cluster; calyx with 6—8 lobes; corolla segments 18—24; stamens 6—8, with staminodes. Berry with few or many seeds.

Littoral. Leaves tufted, 5—8 in. long ... ... M. littoralis.
Inland. Leaves scattered, 3—5 in. long ... ... M. Elengi.

318. **M. littoralis,** *Kurz*; H. iii. 549; Br. 426. *The Andaman Bulletwood Tree.* Vern. *Mohwa, Pinlè-mohwa,* Burm. and Hind.

A large and magnificent tree (60–120 × 8—16), with a rough black bark, furrowed in old trees, cut dark reddish. Leaves 5–8 in. long, 2—4 in. broad, collected at the ends of the branchlets, obovate, apex blunt, dark green and glossy, coriaceous; petioles about an inch long. Flowers 1 in. diam., solitary and axillary, stalks 1—1¼ in. long; corolla greenish-white, fragrant, sweet and edible. Berry 1½ in diam., depressed globose.

Common along the seashores of the islands and forming on the level land just above the beaches, belts of more or less pure forest known as *Mohwa forest*. Fl. at the beginning of the R. S. Fr. Dec. The name *Katpali thit*, mentioned by Kurz, is now seldom, if ever, used. It is sometimes called *Khari Mohwa*. The wood is reddish-brown, very hard, heavy and durable, but difficult to work. It is suitable for girders and posts and is not eaten by white ants, but is attacked by toredo. The Andamanese eat the flowers which, to me, have a sickly sweet taste.

319. **M. Elengi,** *Roxb.*; H. iii. 548; Br. 425. *The Indian Medlar Tree.* Vern. *Khaya,* Burm.

A large tree (50–100 × 4—7) with dark grey bark fissured lengthwise and transversely, cut dark red with pale irregular streaks. Leaves scattered, 3—5 in long, and about half as broad, elliptic, shortly and bluntly acuminate, base somewhat rounded, dark green and glossy; petioles ¾ in. long. Flowers about ½ in. diam., fragrant, axillary, solitary or a few in a cluster, stalks ½–¾ in. long. Berry 1 in. long, ovoid, yellow when ripe.

Not common. In evergreen and semi-evergreen forests in several localities. Fl. Feb.-Sept. Fr. C. S. The wood is dark reddish-brown, very hard, durable and useful. It yields the *Pagoda Gum* of Madras, and is cultivated in India for its flowers.

2. BASSIA.

320. **B. butyracea,** *Roxb*; H. iii. 543; Br. 487. *The Indian Butter Tree.* Vern. *Pohar Mohwa, Jungli Mohwa,* Hind.

A tall graceful tree (70—120 × 5–8) with a brown, smooth, thinly fissured bark, cut pinkish. Leaves 5—9 in. long, elliptic to obovate, shortly acuminate, acute and tapering downwards at the base, glabrous, lateral nerves 14—18 pairs, strong; petiole ¾—1½ in. long. Flowers on slender stalks, in clusters at the ends of the leafless branchlets; corolla yellow, ¾ in. long, with a pungent smell. Berry about 1 in. diam., almost globular, rusty puberulous.

Frequent and dispersed in nearly all localities in semi-deciduous and sometimes in evergreen forests. Leafless about the month of April, the leaves all turning yellow before falling. Fl. Jan.-April. Fr. March-May. Wood reddish-brown, fairly hard and heavy. "The seeds yield a white vegetable butter of the consistence of fine lard." *Brandis.*

B. **caloneura**, *Kurz.* The specimens of this, which were collected by Kurz, and which are in the Kew and the Calcutta Herbariums, are incomplete. The flowers are not known, the fruits are detached from the leaves in the specimens, and the latter match exceedingly well with those of *Cleistanthus myrianthus*, a common tree in these islands. Kurz says that it is "Frequent in the tropical forests of the South Andaman," yet it has never been collected by subsequent collectors.

3. SIDEROXYLON.

Flowers small; calyx and corolla segments 5—6, imbricate; stamens equal in number and opposite to the corolla segments, with alternating staminodes.

Large tree. Leaves glabrous; petioles up to 2¼ in. long ... *S. longepetiolatum.*
Moderate-sized tree. Leaves rusty-pubescent; petioles up to ¾ in. long ... ... *S. ferrugineum.*

321. **S. longepetiolatum.** *King and Prain*; Br. 423. Vern. *Lamba pathi*, Hind. Planchonella

A large and tall tree (70—130×4—9), often with large buttresses, bark grey, cut pinkish-brown. Leaves *in young plants* up to 30 in. long and a foot broad, *in mature plants* 4—8 in. long, 1½—3 in broad, elliptic or ovate-lanceolate, shortly and bluntly acuminate, base narrowed, glabrous, lateral nerves about 10 pairs; petioles 1½—2¼ in. long. Flowers rather small, greenish-white, on slender pedicels in axillary fascicles. Fruit 1—2 in. long, ovoid, succulent, yellow and turning dark brown when ripe; seed hard, chocolate-coloured, compressed and pointed, with a grove along one edge.

Fairly frequent; usually found in evergreen forests and seen in many localities. Fl. July-Sept. Fr. Jan.-Feb. The wood is white, soft and perishable. The leaves are used for elephant fodder and the Andamanese bake fish and pork in the large leaves of young plants. It is a long tree, with long leaves, long petioles and a long name.

322. **S. ferrugineum.** *Hook. and Arn*; Br. 423.

A handsome tree (20—40×2—4) usually branching low, bark dark grey, cut streaked white and brown, branchlets and young leaves rusty or tawny silky pubescent. Leaves 3—6 in. long, 1—3 in. broad, obovate to oblong-lanceolate, base tapering, margins recurved, apex rounded or blunt, dark green and glossy above, ferruginous beneath; petioles ¾ in. long. Flowers inconspicuous, in axillary clusters. Berry ¾ in. long, oblong-ovoid, glossy.

Uncommon, but not rare. Along the seashores of the Middle and South Andaman and the adjacent islands, and also on the high hills of the Middle Andaman, on Mt. Harriet, Mt. Ford, and on the South Cinque Island. It somewhat resembles the *Jack Tree.*

Achras Sapota, *Linn.* *The Sapodilla Plum*, a native of Jamaica, deserves mention on account of its edible fruit of which it has been said that "a more luscious, cool and agreeable fruit is not to be met with in this or perhaps any country in the world" It is the size of an orange, with a rough, brown, thin and tender rind. It may be seen cultivated in the Haddo gardens. It is also called the *Bully Tree.*

Fam. 50. EBENACEÆ.

THE EBONY AND MARBLE-WOOD FAMILY.

Evergreen trees with alternate, exstipulate leaves, entire and with short petioles. Flowers white or yellow, axillary, with jointed pedicels and usually unisexual; corolla of 3—6 lobes, the lobes overlapping to the right; stamens various. Fruit a berry with the seeds embedded in a pulp.

"Ebony, from which this order takes its name, is the heartwood of different species of *Diospyros.*" The leaves of the members of this family resemble those of some Anonaceous plants, and on this account it will be seen that the members of these two families come together in the artificial key in this book.

Trees. Flowers usually 4-merous. Berries globular ... 1. Diospyros.
A shrub. Flowers 3-merous. Berries oblong and pointed ... ... 2. Maba.

1. DIOSPYROS

Trees with heartwood often hard and black. Flowers usually 4-merous, the male flowers in cymes or clusters, the females solitary; stamens generally 16, often in pairs.

Leaves perfectly glabrous.
  Leaves not attaining more than 5 in. in length.
    L. distichous, up to 3 in. long Flowers very small, white. Berry black and glossy ... .. D. Kurzii.
    L. scattered, up to 5 in. long. Flowers ¼ in. long, yellowish-white. Berry scarlet ... ... D. oocarpa.
  Leaves up to 8 in. long
    L. elliptic oblong with fine net venation. Berry 1½ in. diam. D. pyrrhocarpa.
    L. broadly elliptic-oblong with few nerves. Berry ¾ in. diam. D. undulata
Leaves pubescent or more or less hairy.
  Leaves 1—1½ in. long, with long hairs along the margin. Berry ¾ in. diam. ... ... D. pilosula.
  Leaves 2—5 in. long, pubescent. Berry 1—1½ in. diam. ... D. montana.

323. **D. Kurzii,** *Hiern*, II. iii. 559; Br. 435. Vern. *Moong*, Burm.

A graceful tree (20—40×1½—3) with a dark grey bark, cut dirty brown, then yellowish, turning black; branchlets slender. Leaves distichous, 2½—3 in. long, 1—1½ in. broad, elliptic-acuminate, lateral nerves fine, drying very black; petioles short. Flowers small, white. Fruit about ½ in. diam., globose, very black and glossy when ripe.

Frequent everywhere in deciduous and semi-deciduous forests. Fl. May-Aug. Fr. Nov.-March. The small leaves arranged in two rows on the straight thin branchlets, when seen from below, resemble pinnate leaves. It is unmistakeable on account of its cut, sapwood, leaves and fruits drying black. It has no heartwood.

324. **D. oocarpa**, *Thw.* H. iii 560. *The Andaman Marblewood* or *Zebrawood*. Vern. *Thitkya*, Burm.; *Kala lakri*, Hind.

A moderate-sized tree (40—70×3—6) with a blackish chocolate coloured bark, often with greenish-white patches and peeling in flakes, cut reddish-brown. Leaves 3—4½ in. long, 1½—2 in. broad, ovate or elliptic, bluntish-acuminate, base almost rounded, turning dark-coloured in drying, lateral nerves irregular and inconspicuous, breaking up towards the margin; petioles ¼—⅓ in. long. Flowers ⅓ in. long, yellowish-white, 3-4-merous. Fruit the size of a small lime, scarlet when ripe.

Fairly frequent and found in deciduous and semi-deciduous forests with *Padauk* and the preceding one. Fl. May-Oct. Fr. July-Nov. The heartwood, which is used for ornamental purposes, is dark grey, with darker and often quite black streaks. It is difficult to obtain in sizes more than 6 or 8 in. square, and from many trees none is obtained. The wood of this tree has been described by previous writers under *D. Kurzii*, an error which probably came about by the corresponding numbers of wood and botanic specimens being inadvertently mixed. It is interesting to note that this confusion can be traced as far back as the year 1867 in specimens that were sent to the Paris Exhibition, *vide* Kurz's Andaman Report, page 61. The identification of this tree is not yet quite certain. It differs somewhat from the published description of *D. oocarpa* and the matter requires further investigation.

325. **D. pyrrhocarpa**, *Miq.* var. andamanica, *Kurz*; H. iii, 571. *The Large-leaf Tendu.* Vern. *Te*, Burm; *Tendu*, Hind.

A moderate-sized tree (30—50×2½—5) with a dark grey or almost blackish bark, cut pinkish-brown, turning dark brown. Leaves 4—8 in. long, elliptic-oblong, bluntish acuminate, with fine but distinct venation; petiole ¼—½ in. long. Flowers creamy-white; calyx velvety; corolla salver-shaped. Fruit 1½ in. diam., almost globular, woody, yellow when ripe.

A common tree frequent in deciduous forests and often in evergreen. Fl. March-June. Fr. Febr.-April. The fruit is eaten by wild pigs. A tree occurs, similar to this in all respects, except the flowers which have a more globose corolla tube and leafy 4-folded calyces about ⅜ in. diam. These were collected on Long Island and on the Betapur boliu and matched well with specimens of *D. crumenata*, *Thw.* in the Calcutta Herbarium.

326. **D. undulata**, *Wall.*; H. iii. 568; Br. 433.

A small tree (20—30×1½—2) with a thin dark-coloured bark, cut creamy turning yellow. Leaves 4—8 in. long, 2—4 in. broad, oblong to ovate or elliptic, base rounded and slightly narrowed, shortly acuminate, lateral nerves few, interarching far from the edge; petioles ⅛ in. long. Flowers creamy-yellow. Fruit sessile, ¾ in. diam., globular slightly flattened and apiculate, supported by the woody cup-shaped calyx.

Frequently met with throughout the Middle and South Andaman, the Archipelago, Baratang and Rutland Island. Fl. R. S. Fr. Nov.-March. The wood when freshly cut is white and in a little while turns yellow.

327. **D. pilosula**, *Wall.*; H. iii. 554; Br. 436. *The Small-leaf Tendu*. Vern. *Tendu*, Hind.

A small tree (20–30 x 2–3) with a thin blackish-green bark, the branchlets with fine long hairs. Leaves 1–2½ in. long, elliptic to elliptic-lanceolate, base almost rounded, dark green and glossy above, pubescent on the nerves beneath and often with fine long hairs along the margins; petiole short. Flowers yellowish; calyx lobes lanceolate; corolla tube slender. Fruit ¾ in. diam., globular, supported by the persistent but not accrescent calyx.

Associated with *D. pyrrhocarpa* and the *Marble-wood* tree and dispersed in all localities. Fl. at the beginning of the R. S. Fr. falls Oct.-Nov. The wood is pinkish and is said by Burman convicts to be the best local wood for making axe handles. A small and very dark coloured heartwood is sometimes present.

328. **D. montana**, *Roxb.*; H. iii. 555; Br. 431. Vern. *Gyut*, Burm.

A small or moderate-sized tree (30–60 x 2–5) with a very black bark peeling in thin small flakes, cut cream-coloured, finely streaked and turning yellowish-brown. Leaves 2–5 in. long, and 1–2 in. broad, ovate-oblong, acuminate, often with a cordate base, pubescent, not firm in texture, petioles slender, ½ in. long. Flowers handsome, ¼ in. diam., calyx segments triangular, almost foliaceous; corolla white, turning yellow and then black, tube urceolate, ¼ in. long; stamens 8. Berry 1¼ in. diam., globular and glossy.

In deciduous forests with the other species of this genus but not as common. Fl. March-April. Fr. March-May. Wood light yellowish, often with a small black core.

2. MABA.

329. **M. andamanica**, *Kurz*; H. iii. 551; Br. 437.

An evergreen shrub 3–5 feet high, the branchlets pale yellow hirsute-tomentose. Leaves 4–8 in. long, elliptically to ovate-oblong, abruptly acuminate, glabrous above, adpressed tawny hairy on the midrib and nerves beneath; petiole short. Flowers 3-merous; calyx and corolla adpressed pubescent. Berries about 1 in. long, oblong and pointed, smooth, with three linear oblong seeds.

Upper mixed forests of the Andamans. Fl. April. *Kurz*. Also at Bomlungta but uncommon.

Fam. 51. STYRACEÆ.

Leaves simple, alternate and turning yellowish in drying. Flowers usually small and 5-merous. Fruit a succulent drupe.

1. SYMPLOCOS.

330. * **S. racemosa**, *Roxb.*; H. iii. 576.

An evergreen tree (20—25 × 1—1½) the young shoots more or less pubescent. Leaves 3—6 in. long, oblong to obovate-lanceolate or lanceolate, bluntish acuminate or apiculate, tapering downwards and more or less serrulate, coriaceous and almost glabrous with strong nerves. Flowers small, in axillary villous-tomentose racemes, yellow, calyx deeply 5 lobed; petals 5; stamens very many. Fruit cylindric, nearly ½ in. long, bluish-black when fully ripe.

Rare. Mt. Harriet. Fl. Jan.-Febr.

Fam. 52. OLEACEÆ.

THE JASMINE FAMILY.

Unarmed trees or climbing shrubs with opposite, simple or trifoliolate exstipulate leaves. Flowers usually white, in clusters or short cymes; calyx small; corolla usually 4—5 lobed; stamens 2. Fruit often in pairs.

Climbing shrubs with simple or trifoliolate petioled leaves. Flowers conspicuous ... ... 1. Jasminum.
Small trees with short-petioled simple leaves. Flowers small and inconspicuous ... ... 2. Linociera.

1. JASMINUM.

Straggling scandent shrubs. Flowers usually white; corolla salver-shaped with a long tube, the lobes spreading, twisted in bud; stamens 2, included. Berries often in pairs.

In the Andamans the Burmese name *Taw sabè-waw* is usually given to all the species mentioned here.

Leaves trifoliolate.
Leaflets 2—4 in. long, acuminate. Cymes puberulous ... J. caudatum.
Leaflets 1—3 in. long, shortly apiculate. Cymes glandular ... ... J. mauritianum.
Leaves simple.
Leaves 1—2 in. long, finely acute ... ... J. Ritchiei.
Leaves 2—4½ in. long, finely acuminate ... ... J. cordifolium.

331. **J. caudatum,** *Wall.*; Br. 451.

A scandent shrub. Leaves pinnately trifoliolate, the common petiole about an inch long, swollen at the base; leaflets 2—4 in. long, 1—2½ in. broad, ovate to elliptic and often broadly so, shortly acuminate, rounded at the base, glabrous, dark green, glossy, the centre leaflet the largest and on a long petiolule. Flowers handsome and very fragrant, in axillary puberulous cymes; corolla tube 1—1½ in. long, the limb ½—¾ in. across. Fruit ⅓—½ in. long, ellipsoid-ovoid, glossy, purple when ripe.

Middle Andaman, Cuthbert Bay, Bomlungta, Amitlated; Long Island; Baratang. Fl. Nov.-Jan. Fr. Febr.

332. **J. mauritianum,** *Boj.*; Hort. Maurit. 204.

Scandent. Leaves pinnately trifoliolate, the common petiole 1—1½ in. long; leaflets 1—3 in. long, and about half as broad, broadly elliptic to ovate, somewhat shortly and bluntly apiculate, lateral nerves fine, interarching rather far from the margin. Flowers white, in ample terminal corymbose glandular cymes; corolla tube 1—1½ in. long, the limb about ½ in. across.

Long Island. Fl. Dec.

J. Ritchiei, *C. B. Clarke*, **var. purpurascens,** *C. B. Clarke*. Scandent. Leaves simple, 1—2 in. long, ¾—1¼ in. broad, broadly ovate, acute and finely pointed, base rounded, glabrous, lateral veins fine; petiole short and slender. Flowers collected in threes, in few-flowered cymes, white; corolla tube about ¾ in. long, limb nearly 1 in. across. Fruit about ½ in. long. Middle Andaman. Fl. Febr.

333. **J. cordifolium,** *Wall.*; Br. 450.

Straggling and scandent. Leaves 2—4½ in. long, 1—2 in. broad, ovate or broadly so, finely acuminate, narrowed at the rounded or truncate base, dark green and glabrous, with few lateral nerves boldly interarching far from the margin; petioles ¼—½ in. long, jointed. Flowers 1 in. diam., in axillary or terminal trichotomous cymes; corolla tube ¾ in. long, lobes 6—8, ½ in. long. Fruit ovoid, ¾ in. long.

Not common. Middle Andaman, Betapur; South Andaman, Chiriatapu. Fl. Jan.

2. LINOCIERA.

Small trees with entire, more or less acuminate, very shortly petioled leaves. Flowers small; calyx 4-lobed; corolla of 4 petals cohering in pairs. Drupe globose or ellipsoid.

Shrubby tree. Leaves 2—4 in. long ... ... L. Parkinsonii.
Small tree. Leaves 3—6 in. long ... ... L. terniflora.

334. L. Parkinsonii, *Hutchinson* ; *Kew. Bull. 1919. p. 229.*

A shrubby tree 10—15 feet high and 2—3 in. diam., the bark and branchlets white, the latter slender. Leaves 2—4 in. long, elliptic to obovate, acuminate, glabrous, dark green and glossy above, lateral nerves 6—8 pairs, thin but distinct, looping far from the margin; petiole very short. Flowers small, in axillary clusters. Fruit ellipsoid.

Very common in deciduous forests; one of the commonest little trees in *Padauk* forest. It resembles at a glance *Murraya exotica* with which it is often found growing. *Fl.* at the beginning of the R. S. *Fr.* R. S.

335. L. terniflora, *Wall.*; H. iii. 610; Br. 449.

A small tree (15—20 × 1—2) with a greyish finely-fissured discoloured bark, cut mealy, light brown with spots, darkening slightly in a little while. Leaves 3—5 in. long, 1—2 in. broad, elliptic-obovate to lanceolate, with the margins slightly recurved, acuminate, tapering to the very short petiole, lateral nerves somewhat obscure. Flowers clustered by three or more in short stiff axillary racemes. Drupe ½ in. long, ovoid-oblong, bluish-black.

Middle Andaman, Mt. Baker, Bomlungta, Betapur, Bamtang; often near dry stream-beds. *Fl.* Dec.-Febr.

Fam. 53. APOCYNACEÆ.

THE OLEANDER FAMILY.

Trees, shrubs, or climbers, usually abounding in milky juice. Leaves generally opposite or whorled, sometimes alternate. Flowers white, yellow or pinkish, generally conspicuous; calyx 5-lobed; corolla with a short tube and 5 twisted segments, often with scales at the throat; stamens 5, often conniving in a cone. Fruit often paired, the seeds usually with tufts of long hairs.

An interesting family, several members of which have conspicuous and beautiful flowers. The milky juice of many is poisonous.

Trees
- Leaves whorled, more or less obovate, with many lateral nerves joined intramarginally. Flowers white, rather small.
  - Littoral. Fruit ovoid, spongy-fibrous ... 1. Ochrosia.
  - Inland. Fruit linear, 1—1½ ft. long ... 2. Alstonia.
- Leaves opposite.
  - L. 3—4 in. long, with many lateral nerves joined intramarginally. Flowers rather small. Fruit globose ... ... 3. Hunteria.
  - L. 3—7 in. long, with stem-clasping petioles. Fl. 1 in. diam. Fr. curved-oblong ... ... 4. Tabernæmontana.
  - L. 3—5 in. long, distichous. Fl. yellow, ¾—1 in. diam. Fr. linear, 6—12 in. long ... ... 5. Wrightia.

Leaves alternate.
  Native and littoral. Fl. white, 1½ inch diam. Fr. spongy-fibrous ... ... 6. Cerbera.
  Introduced.
    L. large, lanceolate. Fl. yellow and white ... Plumeria.
    L. 4—6 in. long, linear. Fl. yellow ... Thevetia.
Erect shrubs.
  Forest spiny shrub. Leaves ovate to rotund. Fl. white ... 7. Carissa.
  Garden shrub. Leaves linear. Fl. showy ... Nerium.
Scandent shrubs or climbers.
  Native forest climbers.
    Leaves not more than 6 in. in length.
      L. with hair tufts in the nerve axils beneath. Fl. white, rather small. Pod necklace shaped ... ... 8. Parameria.
      Fl. yellowish, rather large with linear twisted corolla segments ... ... 9. Strophanthus.
      L. with an intramarginal vein. Fl. white, with reflexed corolla lobes ... ... 10. Aganosma.
      Fl. rather small, in ample panicles ... 11. Anodendron.
    Leaves attaining 9 in. or a foot in length.
      L. pubescent beneath. Fl. 2—3 in. diam. Follicles linear-angled ... ... 12. Chonemorpha.
      Lateral nerves looping near the edge. Fl. 1 in. diam. Fr. linear ... ... 13. Rynchodia.
  Introduced garden climbers.
    Leaves whorled. Fl. large, yellow ... ... Allamanda.
    Leaves opposite, often rough. Fl. white, bell-shaped ... ... Vallaris.

1. OCHROSIA.

336. **O. borbonica**, *Gmel.*; H. iii. 638; Br. 458. *The Wedge Apple.*

A moderate-sized tree (30—60 × 2—4) with a straight stem and pale yellowish-grey bark, cut mealy, streaked brown and yellow, the branchlets marked by the prominent scars of fallen leaves. Leaves whorled, 4—10 in. long and 2—5 in. broad, obovate, obtuse or rounded, glabrous, the lateral nerves numerous and joined by a vein along the margin; petiole thick, up to 1½ in. long. Flowers white, ½ in. diam., in dichotomously branched panicles; corolla lobes narrow and overlapping to the right. Fruit usually in pairs, the size of a hen's egg, spongy fibrous, bright yellow when ripe.

Along the seashores. Fl. June-Nov. Fr. July-March. "This species is more frequent in the Andamans than *Cerbera Odollam*, and the fruits, especially when the outer skin is removed and only the fibrous endocarp is seen, resemble those of the latter species." *Prain.* They are smaller than those of *Cerbera.* Wood yellowish, moderately hard and splitting readily.

2. ALSTONIA.

337. **A. Kurzii**, *Hook. fil.*; H. iii. 643; Br. 459. Vern. *Taungmeok*, Burm.; *Chatiun*, Hind.

A large tree (60—100 × 5—10) with a yellowish bark full of acrid milky juice. Leaves elegant, in whorls of 5—10, 6—12 in. long, obovate-oblong, narrowed to the petiole, pale beneath with numerous lateral nerves joined by an intramarginal one; petiole ½ in. long. Flowers rather small, white, fragrant, in many-flowered cymes. Follicles in pairs, 1—1½ ft. long.

Usually in semi-deciduous forest, often near the sea-coast and along streams. North, Middle and South Andaman. Fl. Febr.

3. HUNTERIA.

338. **H. corymbosa,** *Roxb.*; H. iii. 637; Br. 457.

A small tree (20—40 × 1½—3) with a grey bark, cut dirty brown, then whitish with little milky juice. Leaves 3—4 in. long, 1—1½ in. broad, oblong or oblong-lanceolate, acuminate, glabrous, with many lateral nerves joined by an intramarginal vein; petiole slender. Flowers white, less than ½ in. diam., in poor terminal cymes; corolla tube ¼ in. long, the lobes twisted and overlapping to the left. Fruit globose, ½—¾ in. diam., orange-red when ripe.

Middle Andaman, in semi-deciduous forests. Not uncommon. Fl. March. Fr. May-June. The leaves resemble those of some *Eugenias* and the fruits are eaten by pigeons. The wood is yellowish-brown, hard and close-grained.

4. TABERNÆMONTANA.

339. **T. crispa,** *Roxb*; H. iii. 648; Br. 460.

A small tree 10—20 feet high with whitish branchlets. Leaves 3—7 in. long, 1—3 in. broad, oblong to obovate-lanceolate, acuminate and tapering to the base, lateral nerves 7—14 pairs; petioles ½ in. long, clasping the stem at the base. Flowers handsome, 1 in. diam., white; corolla lobes overlapping to the left, the margins crispy waved; tube ½—¾ in. long. Fruit in pairs, curved oblong, about 1 in. long.

Rather common in all localities both in the interior and along the seashores. Leafless in the H. S. Fl. April-July. Sometimes called *Tawzalat*.

5. WRIGHTIA.

340. **W. tomentosa,** *Roem. and Schl.*; H. iii. 653. Br. 461.

A small deciduous tree with stringy bark and a viscid milky juice. Leaves distichous, 3—5 in. long, elliptic to obovate, acuminate, softly tomentose and drying brown; petioles rather short. Flowers ¾—1 in. across, yellowish, showy but with an unpleasant smell, in erect tomentose corymbs; corolla lobes spreading, with 5—7 orange-red scales at the throat. Follicle 6—12 in. long, linear-cylindric, with numerous corky spots and a shallow furrow on each side.

Uncommon. Middle Andaman, Mt. Baker. Fl. H. S.

6. CERBERA.

341. **C. Odollam,** *Gaertn.*; H. iii. 638; Br. 457. *The Poison Nut of Madagascar.* Vern. *Pinlè-zalatgyi*, Burm.; *Kalwa*, Hind.

A small or moderate-sized littoral tree (25—50 × 2—4) with a grey bark, cut whitish with copious milky juice. **Leaves** crowded alternate, 5—10 in. long, 1—2¼ in. broad, obovate-lanceolate, shortly acuminate, with many lateral nerves joined by an intramarginal one; petioles 1—1½ in. long. **Flowers** conspicuous, white, 1½ in. diam.; calyx lobes lanceolate-reflexed; corolla tube ¾ in. long, the lobes overlapping to the left. **Fruit** 4—5 in. diam., oval, the outer skin bursting irregularly, the inside fibrous, splitting in two halves.

Along the seashores and bordering on mangrove; not very common but easily recognised. Fl. Febr.-May. The fruits are often found along the beaches washed up by the sea. The leaves and flowers turn very black in drying. The wood is soft and the seeds yield an oil which is used for burning. In Australia it is called the *Black's Poison Nut.*

Plumeria acutifolia, *Poiret. The Spanish Jasmine.* Vern. *Tayokzaga, Thinbawsaga*, Burm. A small much-branched tree with thick branchlets and large lanceolate leaves. Flowers funnel-shaped, white with a yellow centre, fragrant. A native of Central America and Mexico. Often planted in Port Blair. In India it is often planted near temples or pagodas and so gets the name of the *Temple* or *Pagoda Flower*, and some writers call it the *Frangipani Tree.*

Thevetia neriifolia, *Juss. The Yellow Oleander.* Vern. *Payaung ban*, Burm. A small tree with leaves resembling those of the *Oleander*, and with yellow funnel-shaped flowers 2—3 in. long. Fruit a green drupe. Planted in Port Blair, but not so common as the last. It possesses poisonous properties.

7. CARISSA.

342. **C. spinarum,** *A. DC.*; H. iii. 631; Br. 455.

A shrub 4—6 feet high with sharp spines, straight on the stem, forked or curved on the branches. **Leaves** 1—2½ in. long, ovate to ovate-rotund, blunt with a mucro, glabrous with rather indistinct lateral nerves; petioles less than ⅛ in. long, every other leaf with a spine at the base. **Flowers** white, fragrant, in few-flowered corymbiform cymes; corolla tube nearly ½ in. long. **Berry** dark purple, ¼ in. long.

Not common. South Andaman and Rutland Island. Also along the coast. Fl. and Fr. May.

Nerium odorum, *Sol. The Oleander.* A much-branched shrub with linear-lanceolate leaves in whorls of threes, and beautiful white, pink or yellow rose-like flowers. Commonly found in gardens in Port Blair. All parts of this plant are poisonous.

8. PARAMERIA.

343. **P. glandulifera**, *Benth.*; H. iii. 660; Br. 461.

Scandent with branchlets at right angles to the stem. Leaves 3—5 in. long, 1½—2 in. broad, elliptic to oblong or obovate-lanceolate, bluntish-acuminate, dark green and glossy above with 5—7 pairs of weak lateral nerves, each with a tuft of hairs in the axil beneath. Flowers less than ¼ in. diam., white, in axillary and terminal small panicles; corolla lobes overlapping to the left. Follicles necklace shaped, 6—12 in. long, slender and constricted between the seeds. Seeds with long silky hairs.

Interior and littoral forests. Fl. Nov.-Febr. Fr. April. It has handsome and fragrant flowers and yields a sort of caoutchouc or rubber.

9. STROPHANTHUS.

344. **S. Wallichii**, *A. DC.*; H. iii. 655; Br. 462.

A climber. Leaves 2—4 in. long, oblong or elliptic, shortly acuminate, entire and glabrous; petioles ¼ in. long. Flowers conspicuous; corolla yellowish with purple or brown streaks inside, the tube ½ in. long, the lobes 1—3 in. long, ending in long tails. Follicles in pairs, the seeds with silky hairs.

Middle Andaman, in several localities; Baratang; South Andaman. Fl. April.

10. AGANOSMA.

345. **A marginata**, *G. Don*; H. iii. 663; Br. 464. Vern. *Ka-aung-nwe*, Burm.

A climber as thick as a man's wrist, the juice yellowish milky. Leaves with a raised line on the stem between the petioles, 3—4 in. long and 1—2 in. broad, oblong or elliptic-oblong, shortly acuminate, more or less rounded at the base, glabrous and glossy above, the lateral nerves joined by a strong intramarginal vein; petioles short. Flowers white, tube ¼ in. long, corolla lobes overlapping to the right, recurved in flower. Follicles 6-18 in. long, cylindric.

Middle Andaman; Long Island. Fairly common but hardly noticeable except when in flower. Fl. at the beginning of the R. S.

11. ANODENDRON.

346. **A. paniculatum**, *A. DC.*; H. iii. 668; Br. 463. *The Andamanese Bow-string Plant.* Vern. *Jungli Shaw.*

A climber with watery milky juice. Leaves 3—5 in. long, 1—2 in. broad, oblong or elliptic-oblong, apiculate, glabrous and glossy, lateral nerves 10—14 pairs; petioles ¼—½ in. long. Flowers small, yellowish, in ample terminal and axillary lax panicles; corolla lobes hairy, linear, twisted to the left and overlapping to the right. Follicles woody, 5—6 in. long, the seeds with white hairs.

In nearly all localities. Fl. March-April. The stems give a strong fibre with which the Andamanese make their bow strings.

12. CHONEMORPHA.

347. C. macrophylla, *G. Don*; H. iii. 661; Br. 463.

A large evergreen scandent shrub with softly pubescent branchlets and copious milky juice. Leaves about a foot long, ovate, elliptic, or orbicular, membranous, pubescent beneath, with 8—12 pairs of irregular lateral nerves; petioles ½—2 in. long. Flowers 2—3 in. diam., white turning reddish or orange-coloured in withering; corolla lobes overlapping to the right. Follicles 12—18 in. long, boldly 3-angled.

Frequent in the tropical forests along the chaungs in the Andamans. *Kurz.* Wimberleygunj. Fl. in the R. S. Yields a kind of caoutchouc. Easily known by its large showy flowers.

Allamanda cathartica, *Linn.* *The Willow-leaved Allamanda.* Native of Central America and the West Indies. A shrub with dark green glossy whorled leaves and large showy campanulate yellow flowers. Common in Port Blair. Fl. R. S.

Vallaris Heynei, *Sprengl.* A climber with elliptic somewhat rough leaves and pure white fragrant bell-shaped blossoms. Common in gardens in Port Blair.

Vinca rosea, Linn. *The Periwinkle.* An undershrub often found in waste places. Flowers conspicuous, with a slender tube and broad lobes, rose-coloured, or white with a rose-coloured throat. Fl. Jan.-May. Sometimes called *Dead man's Flowers.*

Fam. 54. ASCLEPIADACEÆ.

Shrubs or climbers with milky juice. Leaves simple, opposite and without stipules. Flowers more or less umbelled, bisexual; calyx 5-lobed; corolla 5-parted, the lobes valvate or twisted in bud; stamens 5, at the base of the corolla, connate into a tube, appendaged and formed into a corona with the pollen in waxy masses beneath. Follicles 2, the seeds with tufts of long hairs attached.

A family of little importance to the forester in the Andamans. It is closely related to the preceding one, differing by its remarkable arrangement of the staminal tube and pollen.

Native forest climbers.
  Woody climber. Leaves 4—5 in. long. Corolla lobes overlapping to the left ... . 1. Toxocarpus.
  Scandent shrubs. Leaves 1—2 in. long. Corolla lobes overlapping to the right ... ... 2. Sarcolobus.
Introduced shrubs with thick downy leaves. Flowers white or purplish with valvate corolla lobes ... ... 3. Calotropis.

1. TOXOCARPUS.

348. *T. Kurzii, *Hook. fil.*; H. iv. 15; Br. 469.

A woody climber. Leaves 4—6 in. long, 2½—3 in. broad, broadly elliptic-ovate, cuspidate, coriaceous and glossy; petioles nearly ¾ in. long. Flowers yellow, few in small cymes, sessile; calyx nearly glabrous.

Middle Andaman, in the bamboo jungles at Middle Straits, *Kurz*.

2. SARCOLOBUS.

349. *S. carinatus, *Wall.*; H. iv. 28; Br. 470.

A scandent shrub. Leaves 1—3 in. long, elliptic-lanceolate or oblong, thick in texture with obscure nerves; petiole ¼ in. or less. Flowers in axillary cymes; corolla small, yellow with lines of brown dots. Fruit 3 in. long, curved and beaked with several narrow undulate keels, turgid, pale yellow and fleshy.

Sea coasts of the Andamans.

Hoya parasitica, *Wall*, deserves mention. It is a common twiner found in mangrove swamps. It has thick, fleshy, dead-looking, elliptic or lanceolate 3—5 nerved leaves, and waxy, white or pinkish, umbellate flowers with a pearly lustre. Follicles very slender.

350. **Calotropis gigantea**, *R. Br.*, is a much branched shrub, the young shoots inflorescence and underside of the leaves clothed with a soft white down. Leaves 4—6 in. long, ovate-cordate and stem-clasping at the base. Flowers conspicuous, ¾—1 in. across, white or purple with valvate reflexed lobes. Introduced and often found growing in waste places in Port Blair. It has a silky strong fibre. "The acrid juice is poisonous for human beings, but the leaves are eaten by goats with impunity." *Collett*.

FAM. 55. LOGANIACEÆ.

THE STRYCHNINE FAMILY.

Trees or scandent shrubs. Leaves simple and opposite, connected by a raised line on the stem, penninerved or palminerved. Flowers usually white, pentamerous; corolla lobes twisted or valvate in bud; stamens on the corolla tube. Fruit a berry.

Leaves strongly 3-nerved. Flowers rather small, the corolla lobes valvate. A climber .. .. 1. Strychnos.
Leaves large. Flowers large, the corolla lobes twisted in bud. A tree ... ... 2. Fagraea.

1 STRYCHNOS.

351. S. acuminata, *Wall.*; H. iv. 86; Br. 474. Vern. *Kabaung-nwe*, Burm.

A large climber with stout twisted irregular stems. Leaves 4—6 in. long, ovate-acuminate, entire, with 3 strong nerves and 2 finer marginal ones, glossy and drying black; petioles ¼ in. long. Flowers white, fragrant, rather small, in axillary compound cymes; petals united at the base, valvate. Berry ¾—1 in. diam., globular.

Very common in the islands in all localities. Fl. May-June. It possesses poisonous properties.

Strychnine is obtained from the seeds of *S. Nux-vomica*, *Linn*, a small tree of India and Burma.

2. FAGRÆA.

352. F. morindæfolia, *Blume*; H. iv. 84; Br. 477.

A moderate-sized elegant tree (30—50 × 2—4) with a dark-coloured bark fissured lengthwise, cut yellowish-white, branches slender. Leaves up to 10 in. long and 5 in. broad, broadly oblong to oblong-elliptic, apiculate, base broad, coriaceous, dark green and glossy above, pale beneath; petioles stout. Flowers ¾ in. diam., funnel-shaped, white tinged beneath with orange, fascicled in pendulous terminal racemes; calyx and pedicels glossy brown; corolla lobes overlapping to the right.

In evergreen forests, not uncommon. Middle Andaman, in many localities, Baratang; South Andaman, Rutland Island. Associated with *Calophyllum spectabile* and *Polocarpus neriifolia*. Fl. and Fr. Febr.-June. It is sometimes called *Thitbala* by Burmans. Brandis records the Andamans as a locality for *F. fragrans*, *Roxb*, a common tree in Tenasserim but not found here. The specimens in the Calcutta Herbarium are of Helfer's collections.

Fam. 56. BORAGINACEÆ.

Trees or shrubs, sometimes scandent. Leaves simple, usually alternate without stipules. Flowers large or small, usually 5-merous, often in one-sided spikes or racemes; stamens usually 5, on the corolla tube; style often twice forked or branched. Fruit a drupe.

Flowers in cymes; style twice forked.
  Trees with long petioled leaves. Drupe globose ... 1. Cordia.
  Tree. L. with short, channelled petiole. Drupe lobed 2. Ehretia.
Flowers in one-sided cymes; styles short.
  Littoral tree with thick silky leaves ... ... 3. Tournefortia.
Flowers in axillary corymbs; style long.
  Stiff riverine shrub with small spoon-shaped leaves ... 4. Rhabdia.

1. CORDIA.

Leaves entire with long petioles. Flowers white or orange-coloured; style twice-forked.

Littoral tree. Flowers large, bright orange-coloured ... C. subcordata.
Inland tree. Flowers rather small, white ... ... C. grandis.

353. **C. subcordata**, *Lamk.*; H. iv. 140; Br. 480.

A small littoral tree (15 – 30 × 2 – 3) with a cracked bark, cut pale pinkish, streaked. Leaves up to 8 in. long, and 5 in. broad, broadly ovate, acute or apiculate, base rounded or sub-cordate, lateral nerves 4—7 pairs, prominent, the lowest somewhat basal; petioles up to 3 in. long. Flowers handsome and conspicuous, 1¾ in. diam., funnel shaped with crumpled lobes; bright orange; stamens 6. Fruit 1 in. diam., hard, globose.

Fairly common along all seashores. Fl. and Fr. H. S. and R. S. Its flowers usually attract attention, otherwise, being commonplace looking it is usually passed by unnoticed.

354. **C. grandis**, *Roxb.*; H. iv. 137; Br. 479. Vern. *Thanat*, Burm.

A large tree (50 – 90 × 5 – 8) with a fairly smooth grey bark, cut pale coloured darkening to a dirty brown. Leaves 3—6 in. long, 2¼—4 in. broad, broadly ovate, acute or shortly acuminate to a fine point, somewhat rounded and 3—5 nerved at the base, lateral nerves 3—5 pairs; petioles slender 1—3 in. long. Flowers white, rather small, in large terminal panicles; stamens 4. Fruit ½ in. diam.

Not common. Middle Andaman; Long Island; Havelock Island; South Andaman. Leafless in the H. S. Fl. in the R. S.

2. EHRETIA.

355. **E. lævis**, *Roxb.*; H. iv. 141; Br. 481.

A tree (40—50 × 3—4) with whitish-grey branches. Leaves 3—7 in. long, ovate to elliptic-oblong, acuminate, with 5—8 pairs of lateral nerves depressed on the upper surface, glabrous and drying brown; petioles ½ in. long, channelled. Flowers small, white, in axillary or terminal small cymes; petals reflexed; stamens 5. Drupe small, nearly 2-lobed, red turning black.

South Andaman, in several localities; Guitar Island. Fl. Dec. A very variable tree of uninteresting appearance.

3. TOURNEFORTIA.

356. **T. argentea**, *Linn. fil.*; H. iv. 145; Br. 482. *The Silver Leaf Tree.*

A small tree 15 or 20 feet high with a dark-coloured, rough, furrowed bark. Leaves on short thick petioles, collected at the ends of the numerous thick branchlets, 3—8 in. long, obovate, obtuse or rounded, base narrowed, light-green and fleshy, both surfaces covered with a close silky tomentum, lateral nerves few. Flowers white, small and sessile, arranged unilaterally along the branches of terminal panicles. Fruit ¼ in. diam.

West coast of the islands along the seashores in places exposed to the south-west monsoon. Fl. and Fr. Dec.-April. Trimen describes it as "an extremely beautiful little tree" which undoubtedly it is. I always stopped when passing to look at it and in doing so looked about for its associates *Pemphis acidula* and *Sophora tomentosa*.

T. **ovata**, *Wall.*, is a weak climber with elliptic-lanceolate, acuminate leaves 3—6 in. long, and small white flowers arranged in unilateral cymes. Along the seashores among shrubbery. Fl. H. S.

3. RHABDIA.

357. **R. lycioides,** *Mart*; H. iv. 145; Br. 482.

A small shrub with stiff long branches. Leaves fasciculate, ½—1 in. long, spathulate, narrowed to the petiole. Flowers small, pink or reddish, in axillary few-flowered corymbs; stamens 5. Fruit orange-red, glossy.

In stony stream beds with *Homonoia riparia*, and submerged during the R. S. Fl. and Fr. H. S.

Fam. 57. CONVOLVULACEÆ.

THE CONVOLVULUS FAMILY.

Climbers with simple, alternate, exstipulate leaves. Flowers often large and showy, bisexual and pentamerous; calyx imbricate, enlarging sometimes in fruit; corolla rotate, bell-shaped or trumpet-shaped, often folded in bud. Fruit capsular.

Although of no importance to the forester, the family 'which can scarcely be mistaken for any other,' deserves mention on account of the conspicuous and showy flowers of some of its members. The flowers of *Erycibe* are unlike those of the others given here, and the beginner would hardly suspect that it belonged to this family.

Leaves glabrous. Flowers rather small, white to yellow; petals bifid and folded ... . 1. Erycibe.
Leaves silky beneath. Flowers purple, showy ... ... 2. Argyreia.

1. ERYCIBE.

358. **E. paniculata,** *Roxb.*; H. iv. 180; Br. 483.

A climber as thick as a man's arm with whitish branches, the branchlets, petioles and inflorescence covered with reddish-brown tomentum. Leaves 3—7 in. long, 1½—3 in. broad, ovate to elliptic-oblong, shortly acuminate, pale beneath, lateral nerves 6—8 pairs, thin; petioles ¾ in. long. Flowers in terminal panicles; corolla white, turning yellow when fading, ¾ in. diam., rotate, waxy and brown beneath, lobes bifid, one folded, overlapping to the right in bud. Fruit ½ in. long, ellipsoid, black and pulpy when ripe.

Fairly frequent. Middle Andaman; Havelock Island; South Andaman, in many localities. Fl. Oct.-Dec. Fr. Nov.-Febr.

2. ARGYREIA.

359. **A. Championii**, *Benth.*; Br. 485.

A large climber. Leaves 4—5 in. long, elliptic or obovate, narrowed at base, densely grey silky below, lateral nerves 9—11 pairs; petioles ¾—1¼ in. long. Flowers conspicuous, funnel-shaped, 1½ in. long, rose-purple, calyx reddish within, silky externally. Capsule ½ in. diam. globose.

Common in the Middle and the South Andaman. Fl. just before the R. S. Fr. May-June.

The following are less important climbers or twiners :—

IPOMOEA.

The first five are native.

I. denticulata, *Choisy*. Leaves 1—2½ in. long, ovate-cordate, petiole 1½ in. long. Flowers purple, 1½ in. long. Common along beaches.

I. illustris, *Prain*. Leaves 4—6 in. long, ovate, cordate or hastate; petiole 1½—2 in. long. Flowers purple, 4 in. long, wide campanulate. Common along the coasts.

I. biloba, *Forsk*. *The Goat's-foot Creeper*. Leaves deeply lobed. Flowers 2 in. long, purple. Very common on the sands along the coasts and found growing with *Vigna retusa* and *Clitoria Ternatea*.

I. cymosa, *Roem. and Schult.* Leaves 1—4 in. long, ovate-oblong. Flowers white with a yellow tinge, 1—1½ in. long. Often along streams.

I. petaloidea, *Choisy*. Leaves 2—6 in. long, or more, ovate or lanceolate with strong purplish venation beneath. Flowers 2 in. long, bright yellow. Often along streams. Fl. H. S.

I. bona-nox, *Linn.* *The Moon Flower.* Leaves 2—4 in. long, cordate acuminate; petiole 1—3 in. long. Flowers 2—3 in long, white, opening at nightfall and fading the next morning. Called by negroes in America *The Lady of the Night*. Introduced.

I. Batatas, *Lam.* *The Sweet Potato.* Leaves cordate, lobed, hairy. Flowers large, white tinged with red. Cultivated.

Porana spectabilis, *Kurz*; Br. 487. Leaves 2—4 in. long, ovate, velvety on both sides. Flowers white, bell-shaped, 1½ in. long, sepals unequally enlarged in fruit. Native.

Fam. 58. SOLANACEÆ.

THE TOBACCO FAMILY.

Shrubs or soft-wooded trees, sometimes prickly and with stellate hairs. Leaves alternate and often in pairs on the same side of the stem. Flowers often showy, 5-merous, corolla valvate, imbricate or twisted in bud; stamens often connivent into a cone. Fruit usually a berry.

All given here have been introduced.

3—8 in. long, ovate-lanceolate, shortly acuminate, base unequal, petiolules short. Flowers large, in ample erect panicles; corolla 2½ in. long, purple and yellow. Capsule 1—2 feet long, flat and broadly winged.

Frequent in all localities in deciduous and semi-deciduous forests. Leafless in the H S? Fl. Jan.-Feb. Fr. H. S. It is said to be immune from attack by white ants and is useful for planking and house-building. It smells like teak when freshly cut. Gamble says "It is used by the Andamanese for making canoes and has a fine wood which deserves to be better known."

4. OROXYLUM.

365. **O. indicum,** *Vent.*; H. iv. 378; Br. 496. *The Sword-fruit Tree.* Vern. *Kyaung ya,* Burm.

A moderate-sized tree (30—40 × 2—4), with a fairly thick grey bark, cut stringy, yellow turning green. Leaves very large, 3—5 feet long, bipinnate or tripinnate; leaflets 3—5 in. long, ovate or broadly so, shortly and bluntly acuminate, base rounded or cordate, glabrous. Flowers large, at the ends of long erect penduncles; corolla 2½ in. long, purple and yellow. Capsule 2—4 feet long and 3—4 in. broad, flat, sword-shaped, with numerous white-winged seeds.

Common in all localities in deciduous forests and often along streams. Fl. June-Nov. Fr. Nov.-Feb. "The tree loses its leaves in the cold weather, and then, with the large dark pods hanging from the leafless branchlets, has a very wierd effect." *Nairne.* The wood is yellowish-white and soft. The bark and fruits are used for tanning and dyeing. The young fruits are eaten as a vegetable by Burmans. The tree resembles *Heteropanax fragrans.*

Fam. 60. ACANTHACEÆ.

THE ACANTHUS FAMILY.

Shrubs or climbers with opposite exstipulate leaves; often spinous. Flowers white or bluish, conspicuous; corolla tubular and generally 2-lipped; stamens 4, didynamous, or 2, on the corolla. Fruit a capsule.

A family of little importance here, but a large tropical one.

1. ACANTHUS.

Littoral and often spiny. Flowers conspicuous; corolla lipped; stamens 4, didynamous.

Spiny shrubs.
- Flowers bright blue ... ... A. ilicifolius.
- Flowers white ... ... A. ebracteatus.

A slender climber. Flowers white ... ... A. volubilis.

366. **A. ilicifolius**, *Linn.*; H. iv. 481; Br. 497, Vern. *Khaya* Burm.

A shrub 1—5 feet high with stout, stiff, cylindrical spinescent branches. Leaves 4—10 in. long, 1—3 in. broad, elliptical to elongate-oblong, spinulous along the margins and ending in a sharp spine, glabrous, nearly sessile. Flowers conspicuous, in spikes; corolla $1\frac{1}{2}$ in. long, bright blue; anthers bearded. Capsule 1 in. long.

In mangrove swamps, often fringing small creeks and frequently found growing with *Brownlowia lanceolata*. Tidal streams of the Middle and South Andaman. Fl. and Fr. at various times of the year. The leaves resemble those of the holly and it is sometimes called the *Sea Holly*.

367. **A. ebracteatus**, *Vahl.*; H. iv. 481; Br. 497.

A shrub resembling the preceding one. Flowers about 1 in. long, white.

Same localities as the former. Fl. and Fr. at various times.

A. volubilis, *Wall.*, is a slender unnamed climber with oblong or obovate-oblong leaves. Flowers, 1 in. long, white. Uncommon. In tidal forests. Bomlungta and Yeratilajig. Fl. May.

The following deserve mention :—

Thunbergia laurifolia, *Lindl.*; Br. 497. A climber with palminerved, ovate-lanceolate, dentate leaves and large pale blue or lilac curved Convolvulus-like flowers. Very common in the islands.

Justicia Gendarussa, *Linn. fil.* A common-looking low shrub with lanceolate leaves 4—5 in. long. Flowers ½ in. long; corolla white stained with purple; stamens 2. Very common in waste places and along roadsides.

Fam. 61. VERBENACEÆ.

The Teak Family.

Trees, shrubs or climbers, often with 4-angled branchlets. Leaves opposite or whorled, simple, trifoliolate or digitately compound and without stipules. Flowers usually 4—5-merous; calyx persistent; corolla often irregular and 2-lipped; stamens usually 4, one pair longer than the other (5 in *Sphenodesme*). Fruit a drupe or a berry.

A family of some importance and interest to the forester. Many of its members have showy flowers and characters which enable them to be easily identified.

Leave simple.
  Trees.
    Small littoral tree with crenate-serrate leaves, aromatic when crushed. Flowers in corymbs ... ... 1. Premna.

Littoral tree like a mangrove. Leaves pale beneath. Flowers cream-coloured, in clusters ... ... 2. Avicennia.
Inland tree. Leaves palminerved with glands at the top of the petiole. Flowers large, yellowish ... ... 3. Gmelina.
Shrubs.
Native shrubs. Leaves dotted. Flowers long-tubed with exserted stamens ... ... 4. Clerodendron.
Introduced shrubs.
Prickly. Fl. pink or orange, in heads ... ... Lantana.
Unarmed. Fl. purple ... ... Duranta.
Climbers or scandent shrubs.
Flowers in involucred clusters ... ... 5. Sphenodesma.
Flowers in compact corymbs ... ... 1. Premna.
Leaves trifoliolate or digitately 5-foliolate.
Flowers lipped, bluish ... ... 6. Vitex.

1. PREMNA.

368. **P. integrifolia**, *Linn.*; H. iv. 575; Br. 510. Vern. *Taungtangyi*, Burm.

A small tree of irregular growth. Leaves 2—5 in. long, 1—3 in. broad, broadly ovate or elliptic, base narrowed or rounded, crenate-serrate in the upper part and acute with a fine point, lateral nerves few, the lowest basal and looping intramarginally; petiole ⅓—1 in. long. Flowers very small, white or yellow, in many-flowered corymbs; corolla 2-lipped, hairy at the throat. Fruit small, ribbed.

Common along the coasts. Fl. H. S. and R. S. The wood is fragrant and the leaves have a lemon-like smell when bruised.

369. **P. divaricata**, *Wall.*; H. iv. 575; Br. 510.

Has the general appearance of the former but is a climber. Leaves 3—5 in. long, ovate or elliptic, acuminate, puberulous beneath. Flowers white, like those of the former. Drupe ¼ in. long, smooth.

Interior forests, Bomlungta and the South Andaman. Not common. Fl. May.

2. AVICENNIA.

370. **A. officinalis**, *Linn.*; H. iv. 604; Br. 514. *The White Mangrove.* Vern. *Thame*, Burm.

An evergreen littoral tree (15—40 × 2—6) like a mangrove and branching low, the branches crooked and spreading, bark smooth, yellowish-grey, cut bright green, then yellowish-white. Leaves 2—4 in. long, obovate to elliptic, acute or rounded, with a very fine silvery-white tomentum beneath, petioles ¼ in. long. Flowers ¼ in. diam., yellow, sessile, collected in small clusters and arranged in lax corymbs. Capsule velvety, compressed, ovate and pointed, opening into 2 valves.

Very frequent along the seashores, in tidal forests and on muddy flats and often forming small pure patches. Flowers at the beginning of the R. S. Fr. July-Aug. It is sometimes confounded with the *Sonneratias*, which are much less common than this one and from which it can easily be distinguished by its smoother bark, the pale undersurface of its leaves, its smaller flowers, and the numerous small flexible root branches it sends up through the soft mud.

3. GMELINA.

371. ***G. arborea**, *Linn.*; H. iv. 581; Br. 509. Vern. *Yemane*, Burm.

A deciduous tree (50—60 × 6—9) with a brownish-grey bark, rather smooth, cut mealy, light greenish, then pale yellow, darkening slightly. Leaves 4—9 in. long, 3—5 in. broad, broadly ovate, acuminate, base rounded with 3—5 basal nerves and 2 large glands at the insertion of the slender 3—6 in. long petiole, almost glabrous above, pale and softly pubescent beneath. Flowers 1½ in. long, dull brown with a bright yellow lip and yellow inside, in narrow panicles; stamens 4, didynamous. Drupe 1 in. long, glossy, yellow when ripe.

Andamans, in upper mixed forests, *Kurz.* The Andaman specimens have been collected only in Port Blair where it may have been introduced and planted. I do not think it is a native of the islands. *Fl.* March-May.

Tectona grandis, *Linn. fil. The Teak Tree.* Vern. *Kyun*, Burm. *Sagwan*, Hind. A native of India, Burma, Siam and Java. Renowned on account of its splendid timber. It has been introduced to the Andamans and is doing well. *Fl.* beginning of the R. S. *Fr.* Nov.-Jan.

4. CLERODENDRON.

Shrubs with opposite or whorled dotted leaves. Flowers showy; calyx enlarging and sometimes coloured in fruit; corolla tube slender, with 5 spreading lobes; stamens exserted. Drupe succulent or dry.

An erect shrub with large serrate leaves ... ... C. infortunatum.
A straggling shrub with small entire leaves ... ... C. inerme.

372. **C. infortunatum**, *Gaertn.*; H. iv. 594; Br. 507. Vern. *Kaaung-gyi*, Burm.

A shrub 5—8 feet high, branchlets, petioles and underside of leaves hairy. Leaves 5—9 in. long, ovate, dentate-serrate, base rounded or cordate, undersurface with numerous minute black dots; petioles 2—6 in. long. Flowers in large terminal panicles, conspicuous; corolla white tinged with pink; stamens white, 1½ in. long. Drupe bluish-black, enclosed in the red calyx which opens when ripe.

Frequent everywhere, especially in damp evergreen forests and in rubbishy places. There are two kinds of flowers, the one with red calyx and white corolla tinged with pink, the other with green calyx and pure white corolla. *Fl.* H. S.

373. **C. inerme**, *Gaertn.*; H. iv. 589; Br. 507. *The Thornless Chance Tree of Australia.*

A straggling shrub with pale branches at right angles to the stem. Leaves 1—3 in. long, ovate to obovate, entire, strong-smelling when crushed, lateral nerves impressed; petiole short. Flowers white with a long corolla tube, the stamens purple. Drupe pear-shaped.

Very common; frequently along the seashores and often near mangrove. Used in Port Blair as a hedge plant. Fl. R. S. An exquisite perfume is said to be obtained from this somewhat commonplace-looking plant. When without flowers or fruits it resembles *Pisonia aculeata*, with which it is often found growing.

Duranta Plumieri, *Jacq.*, is a shrub often used as a hedge plant in Port Blair. It is sometimes armed and has leaves 1—2 in. long, often crenate-serrate. Flowers pale purple, in racemes. Fruit glossy, yellow.

Lantana aculeata, *Linn.* A shrub, the branchlets armed with recurved prickles. Leaves ovate, acute, crenate and harsh. Flowers collected in small clusters or heads, the corolla lilac, pink or orange. A native of Brazil, common in the settlement and sometimes used as a hedge plant.

5. SPHENODESME.

374. **S. unguiculata**, *Schauer.*; H. iv. 601; Br. 513. Vern. *Ka-nwe*, Burm.

A large climber with twisted stems. Leaves 4—7 in. long and half as broad, ovate to lanceolate, glabrous, lateral nerves 5—7 pairs; petioles strong. Flowers very fragrant, cream-coloured, in involucred clusters, usually by 7, at the ends of the slender branchlets of lax tawny-pubescent panicles; corolla ⅜ in. diam., trumpet-shaped with obovate lobes. Fruits supported by the enlarged, leafy, spathulate-lanceolate bracts which are 1—1½ in. long.

Very common in all localities. Fl. profusely Jan.-Febr. In March or April its fruits may be found strewn about the jungles. Its fragrant flowers and unique fruits are perhaps its only points of interest.

Petræa volubilis, *Linn. The Twining Petrea.* A scandent shrub with beautiful deep violet flowers and pale violet leafy calyces. A native of the West Indies. It may be seen on Ross Island along the road below Government House on the north side. Fl. March.

6. VITEX.

Trees or shrubs with digitately 3—5 foliolate compound leaves. Flowers bluish; calyx 5-toothed; corolla 2-lipped, the lower lip usually bearded; stamens 4, didynamous.

Leaves usually 3-foliolate, rarely 1-foliolate.
- Leaflets 1—3 in. long, white-tomentose beneath ... V. trifolia.
- Leaflets 2—5 in. long, slightly pubescent beneath ... V. diversifolia.

Leaves 3—5 foliolate.
- Leaflets entire with tufts of hairs in the nerve axils beneath. Fl. in lax cymes ... ... V. glabrata.
- Leaflets sometimes crenate-serrate, glabrous. Fl. in dense terminal panicles ... ... V. urceolata.

375. **V. trifolia**, *Linn. fil.*; H. iv. 583; Br. 504. *The Three leaved Chaste Tree.* Vern. *Kyaungban*, Burm.

A shrub. Leaves 3-foliolate; leaflets 1—3 in. long, ⅜—1¼ in. wide, the centre the largest, elliptic or obovate, glabrous above, densely white tomentose beneath, almost sessile; common petiole up to 1¼ in. long. Flowers ½ in. long, lilac or pale-blue, in terminal panicles. Drupe about ¼ in. diam., globose, purplish-black.

Very common in Port Blair and used as a hedge plant. Also along the seacoast at Havelock Island. Fl. March.

376. **V. diversifolia**, *Kurz*; H. iv. 585; Br. 504.

A small tree. Leaves usually 3-foliolate, sometimes 1-foliolate; leaflets 2—5 in. long, ovate to elliptic, slightly acuminate, base rounded, glabrous above, somewhat pubescent beneath along the midrib, lateral nerves 8—9 pairs; common petiole about 1½ in. long. Flowers ¼ in. across, in terminal panicles, white with the lower lip violet-blue. Fruit ¼ in. diam., globose, slightly depressed.

Middle Andaman, Mt. Baker, Rongat Bay, Bomlungta; South Andaman, in several localities. Usually in open places and along streams, but not common. Fl. and Fr. Nov.

377. **V. glabrata**, *R. Brown*; H. iv. 588; Br. 505. Vern. *Tauksha*, Burm.; *Jungli Pyinma*, Hind.

A moderate-sized tree (25—40 × 2—4) with a thin, white, smooth bark resembling that of the *Pyinma*, cut whitish. Leaves 3—5 foliolate, on slender petioles 2—5 in. long; leaflets 2—6 in. long, 1½—2 in. broad, elliptic to ovate or oblanceolate, acuminate, tapering at the base, glabrous, with small tufts of hairs in the nerve axils beneath. Flowers ⅓ in. across, in axillary lax cymes, white with the lower lip violet-blue; stamens exserted. Drupe ⅓ in. diam.

Middle and South Andaman; Long Island. In deciduous forest. Leafless in the H. S. Fl. at the beginning of the R. S.

378. **V. urceolata**, *Clarke*; H. iv. 585.

A moderate-sized tree (20—40 × 2—4) with a light grey thin bark very much like that of the preceding one. Leaves 3—5-foliolate, the common petiole 3—5 in. long; leaflets up to 6 in. long, oblong-lanceolate to obovate, acuminate, often coarsely crenate-serrate. Flowers tinged with purple, in dense terminal panicles.

Long Island and South Andaman. Fl. July.

Fam. 62. NYCTAGINACEÆ.

Trees or scandent shrubs with opposite leaves without stipules. Flowers (*in native plants*) small and unattractive, bisexual or unisexual, with a 5—10-toothed perianth; stamens 6—12, exserted. Fruit more or less angled, prickly or sticky.

To this family the following well-known introduced garden plants belong and deserve mention :—

Bougainvillæa spectabilis, *Willd. The Showy Bougainvillea.* A scrambling shrub, native of South America, with conspicuous bright purple floral leaves which are in threes and enclose the small yellowish-white flowers.

Mirabilis dichotoma, *Linn. The Marvel of Peru.* A shrub with bright purple or yellowish-white flowers opening towards evening and so called the *Four o'clock Plant*, or *Char-baje*, Hind.

1. PISONIA.

Characters the same as under the family.

An armed straggling shrub.	Leaves 1—3 in. long	...	P. aculeata.
An unarmed soft-wooded tree.	Leaves 9—14 in. long	...	P. excelsa.

379. P. aculeata, *Linn.*; H. iv. 711; Br. 517.

A straggling shrub with whitish stems and armed with strong recurved sharp thorns, branchlets decussate and at right angles to the stem. Leaves 1—3 in. long, ovate to oblong or lanceolate, decurrent at the base, glabrous or softly pubescent below. Flowers small, greenish-white, in compact axillary cymes. Fruit club-shaped, ½ in. long, 5-ridged, the ridges with small glandular sticky prickles.

Frequent along the seashores of the islands and often forming small thickets. Along streams on the east coast of the Middle Andaman and on Long Island; Ritchie's Archipelago and the South Andaman. Fl. Dec.-Jan. Fr. March-April. It resembles and is often found growing with *Clerodendron inerme.*

380. P. excelsa, *Blume*; H. iv. 711; Br. 517. Vern. *Bania*, Hind.

A large evergreen soft-wooded tree (30—60 × 4—12) with a dark-coloured stem. Leaves often in whorls of threes, 9—12 in. long, obovate to elliptic or oblong-lanceolate, glabrous, lateral nerves 9—12 pairs; petiole ½—1 in., stout. Flowers yellowish white, barely ¼ in. diam., in terminal cymes; perianth funnel-shaped with reflexed triangular segments. Fruit 1½—2 in. long, with 5 raised lines of a very tenacious matter.

Frequent in the islands and usually, if not always, found growing in damp places near streams. The wood is white, soft and full of sap and is eaten with relish by elephants. The fruits are covered with a matter as sticky as bird-lime. Fl. Jan.-Febr. Fr. April-May.

*P. alba, *Spanoghe*; is an evergreen tree with leaves 6—10 in. long and linear club-shaped fruit ½ in long with 5 corners, each of which has a line of recurved prickles. It is said by Kurz to be found in the beach forests of the islands and to be rare. I have seen no Andaman specimens of this tree and those from Narcondam look just like the preceding one. It is an interesting plant which is said to bear white leaves which turn darker away from the light. It is called the *Lettuce Tree* and is found in the Malay and Pacific Archipelagos.

To **Polygonaceæ**, a family consisting mostly of herbs, belongs **Antigonon leptopus**, *H. and A. The Sandwich Island or Honolulu Creeper.* It is a lovely plant with delicate pink flowers and light green leaves and is found in gardens in Port Blair. It is often used to decorate homes and I have heard of it as the *Bower Creeper*.

Fam. 63. MYRISTICACEÆ.

THE NUTMEG FAMILY.

Aromatic evergreen trees, their bark abounding in a viscid reddish juice. Leaves simple, alternate, without stipules and penninerved. Flowers small, diœcious, the perianth valvately 3–4-lobed; stamens several, united at the base. Fruit fleshy, the covering splitting into halves and exposing a nut-like bright red seed.

1. MYRISTICA.

Characters as given above. The vernacular name *Jaiphal* is given to nearly all mentioned here.

Leaves glaucous beneath. Flowers axillary fascicle ... **M. glaucescens.**
Leaves pale silvery or coppery beneath. Flowers axillary fasciculate ... ... **M. andamanica.**
Leaves not glaucous or pale beneath. Flowers in branched panicles.
  L. 6—15 in. long, oblong lanceolate ... ... **M. Irya.**
  L. 6—12 in. long, elliptic to oblong ... ... **M. Prainii.**
  L. 4—8 in. long, oblong-lanceolate ... ... **M. glabra.**

M. fragrans, *Houtt. The True Nutmeg*, is a native of the Moluccas.

381. **M. glaucescens**, *Hook. fil.*; H. v. 111; Br. 526.

A small or moderate-sized pretty tree (30—50 × 2—4) with a dark-coloured bark peeling in flakes, cut reddish with copious blood-red juice. Leaves 6—12 in. long, $1\frac{1}{2}$—3 in. broad, lanceolate to linear-lanceolate, shortly acuminate, dark green above, glaucous beneath with 15—20 pairs of lateral nerves; petiole strong, $\frac{1}{2}$—$\frac{3}{4}$ in. long. Flowers small, pinkish inside, in axillary clusters. Fruit ellipsoid or ovoid, about 1 in. long, covered with a brown tomentum and with a blood-red seed.

Very common everywhere especially in evergreen forests. Fl. Nov.-Febr. Fr. R. S., eaten by pigeons. There are, I believe, two varieties of this: the one with leaves up to a foot long and rather common, the other with narrower leaves up to 7 in. long, less common and found only on evergreen hills with, though distinct from, the former.

382. **M. andamanica.** *Hook. fil.*; H. v. 103; Br. 524.

A slender handsome tree (30—50 × 2—4) with slender horizontal branches and often with curved stilt-like roots at the base, bark blackish green, cut dark red with blood-red juice. Leaves 8—15 in. long and 3—7 in. broad, oblong to elliptic-lanceolate, dark green and glossy above, silvery or coppery beneath, lateral nerves 12-15 pairs, rather distant and wavy; petiole strong, 1—1½ in. long. Flowers few, in the leaf axils, small urceolate-globular, whitish. Fruit about the size and shape of a hen's egg or larger, pointed, pericarp thick, brown; seed blood-red, slashed.

Not uncommon, usually on evergreen hills. Middle Andaman in several localities; Porlob Island and South Andaman. Fl. July-Aug. Fr. Dec.-Febr. It is not a large tree, but is, I think, one of the most graceful of those that ornament these forests. The fruits resemble peaches.

383. **M. Irya,** *Gaertn.*; Fl. v. 109; Br. 525.

A tall tree (60—100 × 4—8), the bark coming off in flakes, yellowish-brown with white or greenish patches, cut pinkish, darkening in a little while. Leaves distichous, 6—15 in. long, 1½—4 in. broad, lanceolate or oblong-lanceolate, acuminate, base rounded or cuneate, glabrous, lateral nerves 9—20 pairs. Flowers very small, yellowish, in axillary compound panicles. Fruit almost globose, about 1 in. long.

Rather frequent on flat low damp ground, especially that bordering on mangrove creeks, but not in places reached by the sea. Usually found with *Barringtonia racemosa* and *Calophyllum spectabile*. Fl. Dec.-Febr. Fr. R. S. Wood light and soft, pinkish.

384. **M. Prainii,** *King*; Br. 525.

A tall straight-stemmed tree (60—90 × 5—7) with a high crown and slender branches, bark dark grey, smooth, cut reddish-brown with thin pinkish juice. Leaves 6—12 in. long, 3—5 in. broad, elliptic-oblong to broadly elliptic, acute, base broad and somewhat rounded, lateral nerves 15—18 pairs. Flowers small, in lax much-branched panicles. Fruit ovoid, 1½ in. long, with a thick pericarp, the seed red laciniated.

Fairly frequent in semi-deciduous and evergreen forests. Middle Andaman; Long Island, frequent; Baratang and Rutland Island; South Andaman and Havelock Island. Fl. R. S. Fr. Dec.-Jan. It somewhat resembles *Anthocephalus Cadamba*, and is often given the same Burmese name, *Mau*, but can easily be distinguished by its alternate leaves and coloured juice.

385. **M. glabra,** *Blume*; Br. 525.

A moderate-sized tree (30—70 × 3—6) with brownish bark, cut reddish brown with pink juice. Leaves 4—8 in. long, oblong-lanceolate, shortly acuminate, narrowed at the base, glabrous, lateral nerves 14—20 pairs, spreading and not evenly parallel. Flowers small, yellowish inside, in small panicles below the leaves. Fruit ¾—1¼ inch long, ellipsoid or ovoid-globose.

Uncommon. Middle Andaman at Bomlungta and South Andaman on Mt. Lethbridge. Fl. Nov.-Jan.

Fam. 64. LAURACEÆ.

The Cinnamon Family.

Evergreen trees or shrubs with simple alternate or opposite gland-dotted leaves, usually pale glaucous beneath and without stipules. Flowers small, regular, with a tubular 6-cleft perianth; stamens generally 9, often more, in multiples of threes, with flattened filaments. Fruit a drupe.

Leaves opposite or nearly so, strongly 3-nerved. All parts aromatic ... ... 1. Cinnamomum.
Leaves alternate, penninerved.
  Flowers small, collected together and enclosed in concave bracts. Fruit on the enlarged perianth ... 2. Litsæa.
  Flowers solitary, in panicles. Fruit enclosed in the accrescent perianth ... ... 3. Cryptocarya.
Leaves in tufts at the ends of the branchlets. Drupe seated on the thickened coloured stalk ... ... 4. Dehaasia.

1. CINNAMOMUM.

386. **C. obtusifolium**, *Nees*; H. v. 128; Br. 533, Vern. *Thitkyabo, Nalingyaw*, Burm.

A moderate-sized tree (40—50 × 3—5) with a grey bark, cut brownish, very aromatic. Leaves opposite or nearly so, 6—10 in. long, oblong to oblong-lanceolate, obtuse or rounded and strongly 3-nerved at the base, rigidly coriaceous, glossy above and pale glaucous below; petiole ¼—¾ in. long. Flowers greenish-white, in large panicles from between the terminal pair of leaflets. Fruit ½ in. long, glossy oblong, supported by the persistent calyx lobes.

Not common. Middle Andaman, along the streams between Cuthbert and Rongat Bays; also on the South Andaman and near Mt. Ford on Rutland Island. Fl. and Fr. March. Strongly aromatic in all its parts.

C. zeylanicum, *Breyn*; *The Cinnamon Tree*. Vern. *Hmanthein*; Burm.; *Dalchini*. Hind. Has been introduced and may be seen in the Haddo gardens.

2. LITSÆA.

Trees with alternate penninerved leaves, usually pale glaucous beneath. Flowers small, sessile, diœcious, 4—6 enclosed by as many concave bracts; stamens 9—12 or more. Fruit seated on the often enlarged perianth tube.

Leaves glabrous beneath or nearly so.
  Petioles up to 2 in. long.
    Leaves 5—10 in long, ovate or elliptic-lanceolate ... L. chinensis.
    Leaves 4—6 in. long, obovate or oblong... ... L. leiantha.
  Petiole seldom more than ½ in. long
    Leaves 6—10 in. long, oblong-lanceolate ... L. Panamonja.
Leaves pubescent or tomentose beneath.
  Leaves 5—9 in. long, broadly elliptic ... ... L. Kurzii.

387. **L. chinensis**, *Lam.*; H. v. 157; Br. 536.

A small tree (15—30 × 1—2½) with dark greenish-grey often discoloured bark, cut dirty brown, streaked, somewhat mealy. Leaves 5—10 in long, ovate to elliptic lanceolate, pale green above, almost glaucous beneath, with 8—12 pairs of somewhat irregular lateral nerves; petioles up to 2 in. long. Flowers heads white, handsome and very fragrant. Fruit ½ in. diam.

Not common. Middle Andaman, Mt. Baker, Bomlungta; Long Island; Baratang; South Cinque Island. Fl. July.

388. **L. leiantha**, *Kurz.*; H. v. 170; Br. 538.

An evergreen tree 30—40 feet high, all parts glabrous. Leaves 4—6 in. long, obovate to obvate-oblong, acute or bluntish at both ends, coriaceous, turning black in drying; petioles 1½—2 in. long. Flower heads umbellately arising from above the scars of the fallen leaves.

South Andaman. Brandis says the leaves are broadly-elliptic.

389. **L. Panamonja**, *Ham.*; H. v. 175; Br. 538.

A moderate-sized tree (35—60 × 3—6) with a dark brownish-grey bark, cut dirty yellowish-brown. Leaves 6—10 in. long, 1½—3 in. broad, oblong-lanceolate, acute, dark green and glaucous above, pale glaucous beneath, aromatic when crushed, lateral nerves 9—11 pairs, rather weak; petiole ½—¾ in. long. Flower heads ½ in. diam., in axillary racemes.

Middle Andaman, frequent in low moist forests along the Bomlungta and Betapur streams. Fl. April. Fruit not seen. Its leaves resemble those of *Myristica glaucescens*.

390. **L. Kurzii**, *King*; H. v. 164; Br. 537.

A moderate-sized tree (40—60 × 3—5) with a rough and somewhat discoloured bark. Leaves 5—9 in long, 3—4 in. broad, elliptic or broadly so, more or less rounded at base and apex, velvety brown tomentose beneath, aromatic when bruised, with 8—12 lateral nerves, the reticulate veins distinct on the undersurface; petioles ½—¾ in. long. Flower heads many, from the old leaf scars below the leaves.

Middle and South Andaman. In moist evergreen forests and often found growing with *L. Panamonja*. It is sometimes called *Tamaák*, Burm. Fl. March.

Another *Litsea*, which is often found growing with *L. Panamonja* and *L. Kurzii*, occurs in these islands.

3. CRYPTOCARYA.

Shrubs or small trees. Leaves alternate, penninerved, usually coriaceous and drying brown. Flowers small, in panicles. Fruit wholly enclosed by the accrescent perianth tube.

Differing from *Litsaea* in having its flowers in panicles and its stamens with 2-celled anthers. The leaves are usually brown tomentose and pale beneath and the inflorescence pale pubescent.

Leaves rusty pubescent beneath.
Tree. Leaves 3—9 in. long ... ... C. andamanica.
Shrub. Leaves 6—9 in. long ... ... C. Ferrarsi.
Leaves glabrous beneath
Fruit ⅓ in. diam., globose ... ... C. caesia.
Fruit ⅔ in. long, ellipsoid, pointed ... ... C. amygdalina.

391. **C. andamanica**, *Hook. fil.*; H. v. 118; Br. 527.

A small tree 15—30 feet high, with rusty-pubescent young branchlets. Leaves 3—9 in. long, and about a third as broad, elliptic or oblong, shortly and finely acuminate, dark green above, drying brown, pale glaucous and rusty pubescent beneath, lateral nerves 10—15 pairs, prominent beneath; petiole ½ in. long. Flowers small, in axillary and terminal panicles. Fruit 1 in. long, narrowly ellipsoid.

Middle Andaman, on the east coast near Amitlated and at Bomlungta; South Andaman. Fl. April.

392. **C. Ferrarsi**, *King*; H. v. 118; Br. 528.

A shrub with elongated branches. Leaves 6—9 in. long and about 2 in. broad, narrowly linear-oblong, acuminate, narrowed down to the petiole, thinly coriaceous, pale and glabrous above, almost glaucous and finely rusty pubescent beneath. Panicles long-peduncled. Fruit ⅓ in. long, smooth, obtuse.

Uncommon. Middle Andaman, on the high hills in the east. Fl. H. S.

393. **C. caesia**, *Blume*; H. v. 119; Br. 528.

A small tree (25—35 × 2—3). Leaves 5—8 in. long, ovate-oblong to ovate-lanceolate, bluntish acuminate, glabrous, dark green and glossy above, pale and dull below, lateral nerves 6—10 pairs, weak and somewhat irregular, petiole ¼—⅓ in. long. Flowers small, white, in axillary or terminal panicles. Fruit about ⅓ in. diam., globose.

Uncommon. Havelock Island and Long Island. Fl. Febr.

394. ***C. amygdalina**, *Nees*; H. v. 118; Br. 527.

A tree attaining 40 feet in height. Leaves 3—8 in. long, oblong-lanceolate, acute or obtuse, glabrous and glossy above, lateral nerves 6—12 pairs, oblique and nearly straight. Panicles as long as the leaves, long peduncled, the pedicels jointed; flowers small. Fruit ⅔ in. long, ellipsoid, pointed at the ends, black.

Andamans. The description is taken from the Flora of British India and Brandis' Indian Trees. Hooker says that the Andaman specimens may prove specifically distinct.

4. DEHAASIA.

395. **D. Kurzii,** *King*; Br. 528.

A small tree attaining 30 feet in height and 3 feet in girth, bark thin, dirty greenish-grey, cut light brown. Leaves collected at the ends of the branchlets on slender petioles up to 2 in. long, 5—9 in. long, 2—4 in. broad, obovate, rounded at the top and suddenly ending in a sharp point, tapering at the base, dark green above, glaucous beneath, lateral nerves 8—12 pairs. Flowers in lax axillary panicles. Fruit 1—1½ in. long, ellipsoid, glossy, bluish-black, seated on the swollen reddish pedicel.

Middle Andaman, Bomlungta and north of Rongat Bay: Long Island; South Andaman. Uncommon. Fr. Dec. The leaves and the fruits are very suggestive of the family *Anacardiaceae*.

Fam. 65. HERNANDIACEÆ.

A littoral tree with simple alternate, peltate leaves. Flowers small. Fruit a drupe in a globose fleshy receptacle.

1. HERNANDIA.

336. **H. peltata.** *Meissn.*; H. v. 188; Br. 542.

A moderate-sized tree with thick grey bark and thick branchlets marked with leaf-scars. Leaves 4—9 in. long, 3—6 in. broad, peltate, broadly ovate, truncate or sub-cordate at the base, glabrous, with entire but slightly recurved margins, with 5—7 conspicuous basal nerves; petioles stout, terete, up to 9 in. long. Flowers white, crowded in panicles, small. Fruit a dark-coloured ribbed drupe inside a greenish-white globular receptacle about 1½ in. diam., with a circular opening at the top.

Common along all the seashores of the islands and growing at the water's edge. Fl. and Fr. Jan.-May. It has soft and light-coloured wood. Its singular fruits earn for it the appropriate name of *Jack-in-the-box Plant*.

Fam. 66. PROTEACEÆ.

397. ***Helicia excelsa,** *Blume*; H. v. 191; Br. 543.

A moderate-sized tree with simple alternate leaves. Leaves 4—10 in. long, oblanceolate, serrate in the upper portion, base narrowed down to the petiole, light green, glabrous, lateral nerves ascending, coriaceous, petiole ½—1½ in. long. Flowers small, about ¼ in. long, in slender racemes clothed with a deciduous reddish or rusty tomentum; perianth segments 4, valvate; stamens 4. Fruit $\frac{1}{3}$—$\frac{3}{4}$ in. diam., smooth, nearly globose.

Rare. Hopetown. Fl. Dec.

Fam. 67. THYMELÆACEÆ.

398. **Linostoma andamanica,** *Hutchinson.*

A woody climber as thick as a man's arm and climbing over the tallest trees, stems hooked. Leaves opposite or nearly so, 2—3 in. long, ovate- or elliptic-lanceolate, glabrous with numerous fine and nearly parallel lateral nerves. Flowers small, greenish-white, fragrant; perianth lobes 5; stamens 10, with scales above them at the mouth of the perianth tube. Nut pointed, about $\frac{1}{3}$ in. long, at the end of a slender stalk to which is attached a pair of brown, veined, membranous, concave and outstretched wings.

Middle Andaman in several localities; Baratang and Havelock Island. Dispersed but very uncommon. Fl. and Fr. H. S. The fruit is attractive and the delicate veined wings, spread out like those of a bird, are attached by the slender stalk to the nut like the arrangement of a parachute.

Fam. 68. ELAEAGNACEÆ.

399. **Elaeagnus latifolia,** *Linn*; H. v. 202; Br. 547. *The Wild Olive*. Vern. *Hmangu*, Burm.; *Kataphal*, Hind.

A straggling shrub, often spinescent, the branchlets, leaves and other parts covered with minute silvery or coppery scales. Leaves alternate, 3—5 in. long, elliptic, acuminate, base more or less rounded, silvery white or coppery beneath; petiole $\frac{1}{4}$—$\frac{1}{2}$ in. long. Flowers small, in axillary clusters. Fruit about an inch long, ovoid-oblong, succulent, red when ripe.

Fairly frequent and seen in many localities. Fl. Dec.-Jan. Fr. Febr.-March. Its silvery leaves make it easy of recognition and it is known to nearly all Burmans on account of its acid fruit which is eaten.

Fam. 69. LORANTHACEÆ.

THE MISTLETOE FAMILY.

Parasitic shrubs found growing and living on other trees. Leaves opposite or alternate, entire, thick or fleshy; calyx with a truncate limb;

petals 4—8; stamens as many as the petals or perianth lobes and inserted on and opposite to them. Fruit a berry or drupe.

The vernacular name *Kyibaung*, is often given to all mentioned here. They have opposite leaves except *Loranthus coccineus*.

Leaves palminerved. Flowers small and inconspicuous	...	1. Viscum.
Leaves penninerved with obscure venation. Flowers often conspicuous and coloured	... ...	2. Loranthus.

1. VISCUM.

400. ***V. ovalifolium.** *Wall.*; H. v. 214; Br. 552.

Evergreen and glabrous. Leaves opposite, 2—3 in. long, ovate-oblong, blunt, tapering into a short thick petiole, 3—5 nerved at the base, coriaceous and glabrous. Flowers unisexual, crowded in axillary, frequently spicate clusters. Berry (unripe) smooth, ovoid-oblong.

Andamans, *Brandis*.

2. LORANTHUS.

Flowers bisexual; petals spreading or reflexed at the apex.

Leaves opposite. Flowers rather large.		
Flowers scarlet, 1—1½ in. long	... ...	L. longiflorus.
Flowers yellow, ¾ in. long	... ...	L. globosus.
Leaves usually alternate. Flowers small	... ...	L. coccineus.

401. **L. longiflorus,** *Des.*; H. v. 214; Br. 549.

Leaves usually opposite, 3—5 in. long, broadly ovate, coriaceous, with obscure venation; petiole short and thick. Flowers scarlet, 1—1½ in. long, linear-curved; petals and stamens 5. Fruit oblong, ½ in. long.

Frequent in the Andamans. Fl. Febr.-July. Often on *Padauk*.

402. **L. globosus,** *Roxb.*; Br. 551.

Branchlets whitish-grey. Leaves opposite 2—3½ in. long, ¾—2 in. broad, ovate-lanceolate, acuminate, thickly coriaceous, light green and glabrous with obscure venation. Flowers in peduncled clusters, axillary or from the scars of fallen leaves, yellow, ¾ in. long; petals and stamens 6, the latter exserted. Fruit globular, yellow.

Very common. Usually, if not always found on *Sterculia campanulata* (*Papita*). Very conspicuous and flowering in Febr. or March when the host tree is leafless.

403. **L. coccineus,** *Jack*; H. v. 206; Br. 519.

Branchlets rusty tomentose. Leaves usually alternate, 3—5 in. long, 2—3 in. broad, broadly ovate, base rounded, coriaceous and with weak and somewhat obscure net venation. Flowers rusty-tomentose, 4-merous, small, in simple axillary racemes. Fruit ovoid, prolonged into a narrow neck.

Not uncommon. Middle and South Andaman and Rutland Island. Fl. Nov.-March.

Fam. 70. SANTALACEÆ.

THE SANDALWOOD FAMILY.

404. **Champereia Griffithiana**, *Planch.*; H. v. 236; Br. 555. Vern. *Sanni, Sansiywet.* Burm.

A straight tree (30—50 × 2—3) with a dark grey bark, cut greenish then pale-yellow, branchlets dark-coloured. Leaves 3—7 in. long, 1—2 in. broad, ovate to ovate-lanceolate, finely acute, more or less rounded at the base, glabrous, dark green and glossy above with few lateral nerves; petiole very short. Flowers very small, greenish, in axillary cymes or from the branches and stem. Fruit ½—¾ in. long, ellipsoidal, orange or red when ripe.

Fairly frequent in the interior and also along the coasts in *Mohwa* forests. Middle and South Andaman; Baratang Island; Ritchie's Archipelago; Little Andaman, "a common tree in the coast zone" *Prain.* The leaves are cooked and eaten as a vegetable by Burmans. When without its very small flowers or fruits it has no striking characters by which it may be readily recognised.

Fam. 71. EUPHORBIACEÆ.

THE CROTON OR CASTOR BEAN FAMILY.

Trees or shrubs, sometimes with milky or watery juice. Leaves generally alternate and simple, often lobed, and 3-foliolate in *Bischofia*, stipulate. Flowers small, usually unisexual, perianth calycine, simple or with an inner whorl; stamens various; carpels usually 3. Fruit generally 3-celled, drupaceous or of cocci splitting from a persistent axis.

A large family, chiefly tropical, and although well represented in these islands, none of the native members are of any great importance to the forester. The Para and Ceara rubber trees, which have been introduced, are natives of Brazil.

Soft-wooded trees or shrubs, abounding in milky juice, with angled or flattened branches and fleshy leaves. Flowers small, clustered ... ... 1. **Euphorbia.**
Trees or shrubs with normal branches and leaves.
  Leaves simple, the margins entire or almost so.
    Petioles usually less than 1 in. long.
      Leaves not more than 2 in. long.
        L. distichous, pale beneath. Fl. clustered on the branches below the leaves ... ... 2. **Phyllanthus.**
        Shrub. L. pale beneath. Fl. in axillary few-flowered clusters ... ... 3. **Breynia.**
      Leaves attaining more than 2 in., but not more than 4 in. in length.
        L. usually distichous, pale beneath. Fl. usually clustered in the leaf axils ... ... 4. **Bridelia.**
        Branchlets angular and compressed. L. distichous, glaucous beneath. Fl. in axillary clusters ... 5. **Glochidion.**

Leaves attaining more than 4 in., but not more than 6 in. in length.
L. coriaceous. Fl. in dense axillary clusters or from the leaf scars. Fruit grooved ... ... 6. Cyclostemon.
Shrub. Fl. in umbel or corymb-like racemes; sepals enlarged in fruit ... ... 7. Blachia.
Tree. Leaves turning yellow or brown in drying. Fl. in sessile clusters opposite the leaves ... 8. Gelonium.
Leaves attaining more than 6 in. in length.
L. distichous. Fl. in small fascicles usually from the leaf axils ... ... 5. Glochidion.
L. coppery beneath. Fl. in axillary fascicles or from the leaf scars ... ... 9. Cleistanthus.
Petioles thickened at the top. Fl. in tassel-like catkins ... 10. Aporosa.
L. coriaceous. Fl. in fascicled racemes opposite the leaves ... ... 8. Gelonium.
Petioles more than 1 in. long, often up to a foot or more in length.
Leaves peltate and palminerved.
L. about a foot across; petiole 4—8 in. long. Juice reddish ... ... 11. Macaranga.
L. more than a foot across; petioles more than a foot long. Juice reddish ... ... 11. Macaranga.
L. 5—12 in. across with 2 conspicuous glands at the top of the petiole ... ... 12. Endospermum.
Leaves not peltate.
Leaves with penninerved venation.
Shrubs with 3-lobed capsules on long stalks ... 13. Actephila.
Tree. Petiole bent and thickened at the top. Fruit in handsome hanging clusters ... ... 14. Baccaurea.
Large tree. L. pointed, on slender petioles ... 15. Sapium.
Leaves with palminerved venation.
Shrubby trees with stellate hairs. L. glandular near the petiole ... 16. Croton.
Small tree. L. with pale hairs and minute red glands beneath ... ... 17. Mallotus.
A tree. L. glabrous. Capsules 1—1½ in. across. 17. Mallotus.
Leaves simple, the margins crenate, serrate, dentate or lobed.
Leaves lobed. Introduced plants with watery juice.
Shrubby tree. L. 4—6 in. across. Capsule lobed ... Jatropha.
Small tree. L. about a foot across. Capsule prickly ... Ricinis.
Leaves serrate, crenate or dentate.
Petioles short, rarely over an inch long.
Littoral tree full of acrid milky juice Fl. in tassels ... 18. Excoecaria.
Straight-stemmed tree. L. faintly serrate ... 19. Hemicyclia.
Small straight-stemmed tree. L. broad, wavy-serrate. Fr. lobed ... ... 20. Cleidion.
Willow-like riverine shrub. L. narrow, pale beneath. 21. Homonoia.
Common shrub with opposite leaves with minute glistening glands beneath ... ... 17. Mallotus.
Petioles up to 2 in. or more in length.
A common shrub. L. cordate and slightly peltate, acuminate. Capsule bristly ... ... 17. Mallotus.
A tree with hollow branchlets. L. wavy-toothed. Seed scarlet ... ... 22. Claoxylon.
A small tree. L. elliptic to lanceolate with a fine mucro. Capsule 2-lobed, compressed ... ... 20. Cleidion.

A small tree. Petioles thickened and bent at the top.
L. with black dots beneath ... ... 11. Macaranga.
Large tree with trifoliolate leaves and reddish juice ... 23. Bischofia.

1. EUPHORBIA.

Soft-wooded shrubs or small trees with angular fleshy branches abounding in milky juice. Leaves alternate on the stems, opposite on the flowering branches. Flowers small, collected together in heads.

Branches 3—5 angled ... ... E. trigona.
Branches flat ... ... E. epiphylloides.

405. **E. trigona**, *Hawort* ; H. v. 256 ; Br. 558. Vern. *Shazaung*, *Zizaung*, Burm.

A tree (15—30×1—2½) having a light-coloured bark with raised vertical lines of protuberances ; branches 3—5-angled, fleshy, the wings repand sinuate. Flower heads yellowish.

Common in the deciduous forests of the islands especially in the northern islands in dry places. Fl. H. S.

406. **E. epiphylloides**, *Kurz* ; H. v. 254 ; Br. 558. Vern. *Zizaung*, Burm. ; *Sabar*, Hind.

A small simple-stemmed tree 8—15 feet high, with horizontal dark green, flat and spreading, fleshy branches, the edges sinuate. Flowers ¼ in. diam., pink or yellowish, arising in the sinuses. Capsule glabrous.

In several localities, both in the interior and along the seashores. Fl. Febr.

E. antiquorum, *Linn.* ; has been introduced and may be seen growing as a hedge plant in some localities in Port Blair.

2. PHYLLANTHUS.

Trees or shrubs with alternate, short petioled, entire and distichous leaves. Flowers small, apetalous ; sepals 4—6 in 2 series, disc distinct ; stamens 3—5. Fruit a capsule or a berry.

Deciduous tree .. .. P. columnaris.
Straggling climbing shrub ... ... P. reticulatus.

407. ***P. columnaris**, *Muell. Arg.* ; H. v. 291 ; Br. 571.

A deciduous tree 20—25 feet high with finely tomentose branchlets. Leaves 1—2 in. long, oblong to elliptic, acute at both ends, thin, glaucous and pubescent beneath, lateral nerves 5—7 pairs, slender. Flowers small, in clusters from the leafless branchlets or below the leaves. Capsule the size of a large pea, 3-valved.

South Andaman and Rutland Island

408. ***P. reticulatus,** *Poiret*; H. v. 288; Br. 570.

A straggling climbing shrub with numerous drooping branchlets. Leaves 1—2 in. long, oblong or elliptic, base and apex blunt or acute, thin, glabrous above, glaucescent and sparingly puberulous beneath. Flowers usually clustered, also solitary, on slender axillary peduncles. Fruit the size of a small pea, purple when ripe.

South Andaman, usually along streams.

P. Emblica, *Linn.*, has been introduced. It has very small leaves that look like the leaflets of a pinnate leaf, and its acid, astringent, pale green and smooth berries are the *Emblic Myrabolams* of commerce. Vern. *Zibyu*, Burm.; *Amla*, Hind.

3. BREYNIA.

409. ***B. rhamnoides,** *Muell. Arg.*; H. v. 330; Br. 568.

A small deciduous glabrous shrub. Leaves 1—1½ in. long, distichous and close together, very shortly petioled, elliptic to elliptic-ovate, base acute or obtuse, membranous and more or less glaucescent beneath. Flowers small, yellowish, on pedicels thickened upwards, in axillary few-flowered clusters. Berries ¼ in. diam.

Beach forests, chiefly in the neighbourhood of the sea, especially behind mangrove. Fl. Nov.-May.

4. BRIDELIA.

Branchlets slender. Leaves alternate, shortly petioled and entire. Flowers in clusters; calyx 5—cleft; stamens 5; styles 2—forked. Fruit a berry.

Small tree. Leaves pubescent beneath ... ... B. tomentosa.
Scandent shrub. Leaves glabrous ... ... B. Griffithii.

410. **B. tomentosa,** *Blume*; H. v. 271; Br. 560.

A small tree (15—20×1—1½) with thin brownish bark, cut reddish-brown, branchlets slender and long. Leaves 1—3 in. long, elliptic to lanceolate, bluntish acuminate, base rounded, dark green and glabrous above, glaucous and pubescent beneath, lateral nerves 7—12 pairs, prominent and slightly curved. Flowers small, greenish, in axillary clusters. Berry the size of a pea, globular, bluish-black.

Very common in all localities, especially along streams, creeks and the seashores. Fl. Oct.-March. Fr. R. S. Variable in the size of its leaves.

411. ***B. Griffithii,** *Hook. fil.*; H. v. 272; Br. 561.

Scandent with slender drooping branchlets. Leaves 2—4 in. long, elliptic-oblong, acuminate, base rounded, glabrous, thinly coriaceous, lateral nerves 5—7 pairs, arching. Flowers in small axillary clusters.

South Andaman *Kurz.* Fr. Febr.

5. GLOCHIDION.

Small, usually deciduous, trees with distichous short-petioled leaves. Flowers small, in axillary clusters; sepals 6, in two series; stamens 3—8, connate; styles connate into a column; disc none. Fruit a capsule.

Leaves glabrous
- Leaves 4—7 in. long, somewhat oblique ... ... G. calocarpum.
- Leaves 3—4 in. long, glaucous beneath ... ... G. andamanicum.

Leaves, petioles and branchlets softly tomentose ... ... G. hirsutum.

412. *G. calocarpum, *Kurz*; H. v. 309; Br. 573.

A small evergreen tree 20—25 feet high. Leaves 4—7 in. long, ovate to ovate-oblong, somewhat oblique, softly acuminate with a mucro, base rounded, glabrous and glossy; petioles stout. Flowers small, fascicled, pedicelled. Capsules about ¼ in. diam., purple.

In the interior forests and along the streams and seashores. Fl. and Fr. Febr.-March.

413. G. andamanicum, *Kurz*; H. v. 322; Br. 575.

A small deciduous tree (15—25×1—2) with compressed and angular branchlets. Leaves 3—4 in. long, broadly elliptic, bluntish acuminate, lateral nerves 5—7 pairs, slender, glabrous and glaucous beneath. Flowers yellowish, sessile, in small clusters. Fruit depressed globular, ½ in. diam., puberulous, with glossy red seeds.

South Andaman, Mt. Harriet. Fl. and Fr. April-May.

414. G. hirsutum. *Muell. Arg.*; H. v. 311; Br. 573.

A small or moderate-sized deciduous tree (20—40×2—3½), the branchlets, petioles and undersurface of the leaves densely and softly tomentose. Leaves 5—7 in. long, elliptic-oblong, base rounded or cordate. Flowers yellowish, in axillary clusters, hirsute. Capsule globose, obscurely lobed.

Middle Andaman; Long Island; South Andaman. Fl. Febr.-March.

6. CYCLOSTEMON.

Trees with shortly petioled leaves. Flowers small, in clusters, usually in the leaf axils; sepals 4—5, imbricate, the two outer larger; petals none; stamens many. Fruit a drupe.

- Flowers in axillary clusters ... ... C. assamicus.
- Flowers from the stem or branches ... ... C. macrophyllus.

415. C. assamicus, *Hook. fil.*; H. v. 342; Br. 567.

A small evergreen tree with numerous slender branches. Leaves 3—6 in. long and about half as broad elliptic to elongate-elliptic, acuminate, base more or less rounded, glabrous, dark green and glossy, with 8—12 pairs of rather weak lateral nerves. Flowers clustered in the axils, greenish, stigmas 2. Fruit scarlet, ½—¾ in. long, ovoid with 2 furrows, velvety pubescent.

Fairly common in the South Andaman in various localities. Fl. Nov.-Dec. Fr. April.

416. **C. macrophyllus,** *Blume*; H. v. 340; Br. 567.

A small tree (15–25×2—3) often crookedly grown, bark light brown. Leaves 4–6 in. long, 1½—2½ in. broad, elliptic to elliptic-oblong, more or less acute at both ends and with rather weak nerves; petioles ¼—⅓ in. long. Flowers small, tawny velvety, from the stems or old branchlets. Fruit yellow or red when ripe, ½—¾ in. long, oblong-ovoid, slightly 2-grooved.

In several localities in the Middle and the South Andaman and on Long Island; often along the beds of streams among boulders. Fl. and Fr. Dec.-May.

7. BLACHIA.

417. **B. andamanica.** *Hook. fil.*; H. v. 403; Br. 581.

A large evergreen shrub. Leaves 3—6 in. long, elliptic to obovate-oblong, shortly and bluntish acuminate, base acute or obtuse, entire, glabrous. Flowers small, in umbel- or corymb-like racemes; stamens many; styles 3, divided. Capsules globular, of 3 cocci, the size of a cherry, rough.

Frequent in the tropical forests of the South Andaman, *Kurz*; also in the Middle Andaman. Fl. and Fr. April-June.

8. GELONIUM.

Small trees with short-petioled entire leaves. Flowers small, in leaf-opposed clusters; petals none; stamens numerous.

Flowers in fascicled racemes	...	...	... G. multiflorum.
Flowers in sessile fascicles ...	...	...	... G. bifarium.

418. ***G. multiflorum,** *A. Juss.*; H. v. 459; Br. 582.

An evergreen tree 30—40 feet high. Leaves 3—7 in. long, bright green, oblong or oblong-lanceolate, obtuse, narrowed down to the petiole, coriaceous. Flowers greenish-yellow, rather small, fragrant, on glabrous pedicels in fascicled racemes opposite the leaves. Fruit ⅓—½ in. diam., globose, obscurely 3-lobed.

Andamans, *Brandis*. Exudes a yellow resin from the buds.

419. **G. bifarium,** *Roxb.*; H. v. 459; Br. 582.

A straight-stemmed tree (25—40×1½—2½) with a dark greyish bark. Leaves 5—6 in. long, coriaceous, obovate or elliptic-oblong, apex blunt, base acute, entire, glabrous, with a few lateral nerves and turning yellowish or reddish-brown in drying. Flowers small, on slender pedicels, forming sessile clusters opposite the leaves. Capsule of 3 cocci, the size of a pea.

A fairly common tree both in the interior forests and along the coast, especially the latter. Middle and South Andaman; Rutland and the South Cinque Island. Fl. Febr.-April. Fr. April-May. "It has the habit and foliage of *Gelonium multiflorum*, but the flowers are much smaller and are always in sessile fascicles and longer pedicelled." *Hooker.*

9. CLEISTANTHUS.

420. **C. myrianthus,** *Kurz,* var. attenuatus, *Tabl.*; H. v. 275; Br. 561.

A small or moderate-sized tree (40—70×2—4) with a dark-coloured greenish-brown bark, cut reddish-brown. Leaves 4—7 in. long and hardly half as broad, elliptic to elliptic-lanceolate, acuminate, base acute, dark green and glossy above with a pale coppery appearance beneath, lateral nerves about 10 pairs, ascending, petiole ¼—½ in. Flowers greenish-yellow, barely ¼ in. diam., in clusters from the axils of the leaves or from the scars of the fallen ones; calyx teeth triangular; stamens 5. Fruit nearly ½ in. long, 3-lobed.

A common, but pretty tree, found in nearly all localities in semi-deciduous forests; easily known by the pale copper-coloured appearance of the undersurface of the leaves. Fl. Dec.-Febr. Fr. April-May.

10. APOROSA.

421. **A. villosula,** *Kurz*; H. v. 347; Br. 563.

A small tree (15—30×1½—3) with a discoloured bark. Leaves 6—10 in. long, 3—4 in. broad, oblong-elliptic, bluntly acuminate, base obtuse, glabrous or nearly so, with about 8 pairs of distinct interarching lateral nerves; petioles about ¾ in. long, thickened at the top. Flowers very small, in tassel-like catkins up to 4 in. long, which arise from the axils of the leaves or the scars of the fallen ones. Fruit ¼ in. long, ovoid, apiculate, hairy.

Fairly frequent and seen in several localities in the Middle and the South Andaman, on Long Island and the Archipelago. Fl. Dec.-April. Fr. March-June. It has a very common-place appearance and is unlikely to attract notice.

11. MACARANGA.

Fast growing and soft-wooded trees, often with large peltate orbicular leaves on long petioles. Flowers minute, usually enclosed by large bracts. Fruit a capsule, often with bristles. Juice often reddish.

Leaves not peltate, oblong or elliptic-oblong ... ... **M. andamanica.**
Leaves peltate, more or less orbicular.
  Leaves up to a foot across ... ... **M. indica.**
  Leaves more than a foot across ... ... **M. Tanarius.**

422. M. andamanica, *Kurz*; Kz. ii. 389.

A small tree 15—20 feet high and a foot or more in girth, bark light grey with dark patches, cut dark chocolate-red. Leaves up to 7 in. long and 3 in. broad, oblong to elliptic-oblong, acuminate, distantly wavy dentate, base rounded and minutely cordate, glabrous with numerous black dots on the lower surface, lateral nerves 8—10 pairs, fine, curving and looping; petioles up to 2½ in. long, thickened and bent at the apex. Flowers usually enclosed within two leafy ovate bracts about an inch long.

Not rare. Usually in evergreen places along streams. South and Middle Andaman in several localities. Fl. R. S.

423. M. indica, *Wight*; H. v. 446; Br. 592.

An evergreen tree (30—50 × 2—4) with a pale grey bark, cut dark reddish, branchlets glaucescent, exuding a clear pale-reddish gum-resin when broken, stipules large. Leaves peltate, up to a foot across, orbicular or nearly so, many nerved at the insertion of the 4—8 in. long petiole, shortly and softly pubescent and brown gland-dotted beneath. Flowers yellowish, the males in sessile panicled clusters in the axil of a glandular bract, the females in short panicles with minute bracts. Capsule ¼ in. diam.

Frequent in damp places, both in the interior forests and on the flat low ground along streams. Middle and South Andaman. Fl. Mar.-May.

424. M. Tanarius, *Muell. Arg.*; H. v. 447; Br. 592. Vern. *Petwainq*, Burm.; *Golpapita*, Hind.

A tree very much resembling the previous one but not growing to such a large size. Leaves often much more than a foot across and with petioles up to a foot long. Bracts of male flowers large and concealing the flowers clusters. Capsules beset with soft prickles.

Very common and picturesque; in all localities along large streams and in open places, often found with the preceding one, which is usually given the same vernacular names, and with *Anthocephalus Cadamba* and *Leea acuminata*. Fl. and Fr. Febr.-May. The large leaves are used for wrapping up articles.

12. ENDOSPERMUM.

425. E. malaccense, *Benth*, ex *Muell. Arg.* in flora xlvii (1864) 469.

A large deciduous tree (80—120 × 8—12) with a smooth yellowish bark, cut brownish, mealy, with watery sap. Leaves crowded at the ends of the thick branchlets, 5—12 in. across, broadly ovate, peltate, with 7—9 basal nerves and two swollen glands at the insertion of the

4—8 in. long petiole, and also often with glands where the nerves branch, glabrous above, pale and softly pubescent beneath. Flowers small, yellow, appearing with the new leaves.

In evergreen forests on hills. Not very common and usually associated with *Myristica andamanica* and *Fagraea morindaefolia*. Middle and South Andaman. Leafless in the H. S., the leaves turning bright yellow when falling. Fl. April-May. An interesting tree of the Malayan Peninsula which, I believe, has not been reported before this from these islands. It somewhat resembles *Gmelina arborea*.

13. ACTEPHILA.

426. A. excelsa, *Muell. Arg.*; H. v. 282; Br. 561.

A common shrub with leaves at irregular intervals on the branches. Leaves 3—8 in. long, elliptic-oblong to obovate, shortly acuminate, narrowed to the base, glabrous, dark green above and paler beneath, lateral nerves 6—8 pairs, looping near the margin; petioles up to 2 in. long, thickened at the insertion of the blade. Flowers; male, several and shortly pedicelled; females, solitary on slender pedicels, styles 3, divided. Capsule ¾—1½ in. diam., 3-lobed, depressed globose, on a 2 in. stalk.

Very common in all localities, but unattractive and with inconspicuous flowers. Fl. and Fr. Dec.-Jan.

A. puberula, *Kurz*, is a shrub much resembling the former and almost equally as common, but with the base of the leaf rounded or almost cordate and with orange-coloured flowers. Middle and South Andaman, on Neill Island and on Barren Island.

14. BACCAUREA.

427. B. sapida, *Muell. Arg.*; H. v. 371; Br. 562. Vern. *Kanazo*, Burm.; *Kataphal*, Hind.

An evergreen tree (20—50 × 2—5) with a light-coloured brownish-grey bark. Leaves 4—8 in. long, and about half as broad, elliptic to obovate-lanceolate, abruptly bluntish acuminate, almost entire, base narrowed to the 1—3 in. long petioles which are thickened and bent at their apices. Flowers creamy-yellow, numerous and small, in slender pendulous racemes from the branchlets below the leaves. Berries globular, less than 1 in. diam., velvety, yellow when ripe and containing a clear pale rose-coloured pulp.

Fairly frequent in evergreen forests on the hills or along streams and seen in many localities. Fl. Jan.-March. Fr. May-June. This, on account of its handsome bunches of edible berries, which have a pleasantly acid taste, but require to be eaten with caution, is one of the few trees in which interest is taken, and consequently the vernacular name is usually correctly given, although the name *Kataphal* is given to some other plants in these islands.

15. SAPIUM.

428. **S. baccatum,** *Roxb.*; H. v. 470; Br. 584.

A large deciduous tree (50—90 × 5—8) with a dark-coloured rough and deeply cracked bark. Leaves 3—7 in. long, ovate to ovate-lanceolate, base rounded, acuminate, thin, glabrous and pale beneath; petioles slender, 1—3 in. long. Flowers small, yellowish, in spiciform racemes, the bracts having a large gland at each side; stamens 2—3, with red anthers. Fruit up to half inch diam., smooth, red or purple.

Evergreen forests with *Endospermum malaccense* and the *Lamba pathi*. Middle Andaman, on the evergreen hills. Leafless in the H. S. The old leaves turn bright yellow before falling and the young shoots are orange-red. Fl. April, just after the new leaves come out. Its Burmese name, *Leisa*, is not well known in the Andamans. Its bark resembles that of the *White Thingan*.

16. CROTON.

Small trees or shrubs with stellate hairs or scales. Leaves with long petioles, palminerved and glandular at base. Sepals and petals 4—5; stamens 4—6, on hairy receptacles. Fruit a 3-valved cocci.

Small tree. Leaves with silvery or coppery scales beneath ...	C. argyratus.
Shrub. Leaves with stellate hairs beneath	C. sublyratus.

429. **C. argyratus,** *Blume*; H. v. 385; Br. 577.

A small tree, the young branchlets, petioles, inflorescence and undersurface of the leaves covered with silvery or coppery scales. Leaves 4—8 in. long, and about half as broad, ovate to elliptic-lanceolate, rounded and 3-nerved at the 2-glandular base; petioles ½—2 in. long, slender. Flowers white, rather small, in axillary or terminal racemes; petals and filaments villous. Capsule globular, slightly 3-lobed.

Not uncommon. Middle Andaman, on the high hills in the east; South Andaman; Rutland Island; South Cinque Island. Fl. Jan. The leaves turn orange-red when falling.

430. **C. sublyratus,** *Kurz*; H. v. 370; Br. 578.

A deciduous shrub with rusty stellate hairs and scales. Leaves 4—8 in. long, 1½—3 in. broad, elongate-elliptic to oblanceolate, acuminate, base rounded or cordate and glandular, margin usually minutely wavy-serrate with few stellate hairs on the undersurface; petiole slender, up to 3 in. long. Flowers small, in rusty stellate-tomentose racemes. Capsule 3-lobed, the size of a small pea.

Frequent in most localities in deciduous forests, both in the interior and along the seashores. The leaves turn orange-red before falling and are usually aromatic when crushed. Fl. and Fr. Febr.-June.

Codiaeum variegatum, *Blume*, is a garden shrub with leaves very variable in size form, and colour, and commonly called a *Croton*. It is a native of the Moluccas and is common in gardens.

17. MALLOTUS.

Shrubs or small trees with opposite or alternate leaves, usually palminerved and with minute scales on the undersurface. Flowers usually in slender racemes, the males in clusters, the females solitary and in bracts; stamens few or many.

Leaves alternate.
- Shrub with peltate leaves. Capsule covered with soft bristles ... ... M. acuminatus.
- Small tree. Leaves with minute red glands on the pale undersurface. Capsule covered with red powder ... M. philippinensis.

Leaves opposite or whorled.
- Petioles rather short. Leaves with minute golden glands beneath. Capsule prickly ... ... M. andamanicus.
- Petioles longish. Leaves palminerved. Capsule woody ... M. Kurzii.

431. **M. acuminatus**, *Muell. Arg.*; H. v. 431; Br. 588.

A common shrub 8—12 feet high. Leaves alternate, 3—8 in. long, ovate-oblong to broadly oblong, acuminate, usually peltate at the rounded or almost cordate palminerved base, dark green above, paler below, lateral nerves about 7 pairs, petiole slender and long. Flowers yellowish white in terminal racemes. Capsule about the size of a pea, covered with soft bristles.

Very common everywhere especially in low open places. Fl. and Fr. at various times during the year.

432. **M. philippinensis**, *Muell. Arg.*; H. v. 422; Br. 717. *The Kamela Dye Plant.* Vern. *Taw-thidin* Burm.; *Raini*, Hind.

A small tree (15—25 × 1½—2½) with a dark-coloured bark. Leaves 4—9 in. long, ovate-lanceolate, acuminate, 3-nerved at the base and with distinct venation beneath, dark green above, pale pubescent with numerous minute red glands beneath; petioles up to 3 in. long, slender and thickened at the apex. Flowers rather small, in terminal rusty-pubescent spikes. Fruit the size of a pea, covered with a red powder.

Not common. Seen at Long Island on the east coast and at Golugma on Havelock Island. Fl. July-Jan. The red powder which covers the capsules gives the Kamela dye which is used for dyeing silk. It is also called the *Monkey-face Tree.*

433. **M. andamanicus**, *Hook. fil.*; H. v. 439; Br. 589.

A shrub 8—12 feet high. Leaves opposite, 4—12 in. long and nearly half as broad, obovate, acuminate, margin wavy serrate, narrowed downwards to the rather short petioles, glabrous, with numerous minute golden glistening glands on the undersurface, lateral nerves 8—14 pairs. Flowers small, greenish, the males sessile and in catkin-like spikes. Capsule ¾ in. diam., with stiff scattered prickles.

A common shrub found in all localities and dispersed throughout the jungles and frequent along the coast in *Mohwa* forest. Fl. March-April. Fr. May-June.

434. *M. Kurzii, *Hook. fil.*; H. v. 427; Br. 590.

An evergreen tree (40—60 × 4—6) with opposite or whorled leaves. Leaves 6—9 in. long, obovate to elliptic, acuminate or apiculate, 3-nerved at the base, glabrous, lateral nerves 4—6 pairs, prominent beneath; petiole 1—2 in. long, jointed and thickened at the apex. Male flowers small, in short racemes, filaments free. Capsules 1—1½ in. across, 2—3 coccous, almost globose, brown and glossy, woody; seeds purple with a thick covering.

Rather frequent in the tropical forests of the islands. Fr. March-April. *Kurz.*

435. **Jatropha Curcas,** *Linn.*; Vern.; *Thinbaw-kyetsu*, Burm.; *Safed Arand*, Hind. A shrub with thick crooked branches and thin, smooth, grey bark. Leaves about 6 in. across, broadly cordate, 3—5-lobed, glabrous, 3—7-nerved at the base; petiole 3—6 in. long. Flowers yellowish-green. Capsule 1—1½ in. long. It has a pale watery tenacious juice. It is used as a hedge plant in some of the villages in Port Blair. The seed is known as the *Physic Nut*.

Ricinus communis, *Linn.*; *Palma Christi* or the *Castor Oil Plant*, Vern., *Kyetsu*, Burm.; *Erandi*, Hind. A small soft-wooded tree 15—20 feet high with peltate leaves up to 2 feet in diam., palmately lobed, the lobes oblong-lanceolate, petioles long. Capsules prickly. The seeds yield the well-known and valuable oil. It is said to be a native of Africa.

18. EXCŒCARIA.

436. **E. Agallocha,** *Linn*; H. v. 472; Br. 585. *The Milky Mangrove* or *The Blinding Tree.* Vern. *Tayaw*, Burm.

A small tree (15—20×2—4), full of acrid milky juice. Leaves 2—4 in. long, and about half as broad, elliptic, acuminate, with indistinct lateral nerves looping intramarginally, glabrous and glossy, margin crenate; petioles ½—1½ in. long. Flowers yellowish-green, minute, in catkin-like spikes about 2 in. long. Capsule ½—1 in. diam., deeply 3-lobed.

Frequent near, or in mangrove swamps, and often along creeks with leaning stems sending up straight vertical branches. Leafless in April or May, the leaves just before falling turning bright yellow or red and for a short time making the tree very conspicuous. It is quite a pretty little tree when it has put on its new foliage. Fl. and Fr. June-Dec. The acrid milky juice, which is poisonous, blisters the skin and is said to cause blindness if it enters the eye.

19. HEMICYCLIA.

437. **H. andamanica,** *Kurz*; H. v. 388; Br. 567.

A moderate-sized straight-stemmed pretty tree (40—60×3—7), with a thin and somewhat smooth grey bark with light and dark markings, cut greenish, then creamy-yellow and faintly streaked. Leaves 3—3½ in. long, 1—1½ in. broad, ovate-oblong, unequal at the rounded base, margin faintly serrate, acuminate, glabrous, with fine indistinct venation; petioles rather short. Flowers small, in clusters from the axils of the leaves or from the scars of the fallen ones. Fruit about $\frac{3}{4}$ in. long, smooth, red when ripe.

A frequent tree found in mostly all localities both in damp and dry places, and often an associate of Padauk. Fl. Febr.-March. Fr. May-June. The wood is light-coloured but hard and makes a good charcoal. The fruit is sometimes eaten.

20. CLEIDION.

Small trees. Leaves with long petioles. Flowers in racemes with numerous stamens.

Fruit 2-lobed, 1 in. across	C. javanicum.
Fruit 3-lobed, $\frac{1}{2}$ in. across	C. nitidum.

438. **C javanicum**, *Blume*; H. v. 442; Br. 592.

A small tree (20—30 × 1—1½), with a light brownish bark, cut dirty brown, mealy and watery near the sapwood, branchlets pithy inside. Leaves 5—8 in. long, 1½—2 in. broad, elliptic to lanceolate or oblong, apiculate with a mucro, bluntly and distantly serrate, glabrous, lateral nerves rather distant; petiole slender, 1½—2 in. long. Flowers white, less than $\frac{1}{4}$ in. diam., in axillary racemes; stamens collected in a head. Fruit of 2 cocci, 1 in. across, crowned by the slender styles.

A common tree usually found in all localities growing along the banks of streams. Fl. Febr.-March. Fr. May-June.

439. **C. nitidum**, *Thwaites*; H .v. 442; Br. 593.

A small tree (20—25 × 1—3), with a brownish-green bark like that of the *Letauk*, cut brown. Leaves 4—7 in. long and about half as broad, obovate or elliptic-lanceolate, acute or apiculate, base acute or rounded, margin coarsely and distantly wavy serrate, glabrous, dark green above and somewhat pale beneath, lateral nerves about 6 pairs, looping rather far from the margin. Flowers white, fasciculate in slender spike-like racemes. Fruit $\frac{1}{2}$ in. diam., 3-lobed.

A common tree usually found in deciduous forests and seen in all localities, and often forming small patches where the forest is more or less free of undergrowth. Fl. and Fr. Dec.-May.

21. HOMONOIA.

440. **H. riparia**, *Lour*; H. v. 455; Br. 593. Vern. *Momaka*, Burm.

A shrub 4—10 feet high resembling in appearance a willow. Leaves 3—8 in. long, $\frac{1}{4}$—$\frac{3}{4}$ in. broad, linear or linear-lanceolate, acuminate, finely serrate, pale beneath with numerous minute scales; petioles $\frac{1}{4}$—$\frac{1}{2}$ in. long. Flowers reddish-brown, small, in axillary spikes. Capsules small.

Very common, growing in the sand and shingle of stream beds with *Rhabdia lycioides*. Fl. Jan.-April. Fr. March-May. It is said to be leafless for a short period during the R. S.

22. CLAOXYLON.

441. **C. indicum,** *Hassk.*; H. v. 410; Br. 586.

A small tree (20—30×1—2½), with hollow branchlets. Leaves 6—10 in. long and half as broad, oblong-lanceolate or lanceolate, abruptly acuminate, base acute, margin repand toothed, minutely puberulous beneath; petioles 2—5 in. long. Male flowers minutely clustered in long racemes, the females in short racemes. Capsule nearly ⅓ in. diam., tomentose; seeds scarlet.

Frequent in the Andamans, *Kurz.* Betapur bolin, Spike Island. Fl. Jan.-April. Fr. March-May.

23. BISCHOFIA.

442. **B. javanica,** *Blume*; H. v. 345; Br. 558. Vern. *Ye Padauk*, Burm.

A large deciduous tree (80—120×7—10), with a dark-coloured rough bark exfoliating in flakes, cut reddish with blood-red juice. Leaves trifoliolate, on a common petiole 3—8 in. long; leaflets as long as the common petiole, elliptic, acuminate, with crenate margins. Flowers yellowish, very small, in panicles. Fruit globose, ¼—⅓ in. diam.

Uncommon. Middle Andaman, Betapur and Rongat. Leafless in the H. S., the new leaves in April to May with the flowers. Wood reddish, moderately hard and of good quality.

The following rubber trees which have been introduced, deserve mention:—

Hevea brasiliensis, *Muell. Arg. The Para Rubber Tree.* It has trifoliolate leaves on long petioles. A native of the Province of Para on the Amazon river.

Manihot Glasiovii, *Muell. Arg. The Ceara Rubber* or *Scrap Rubber Tree.* It has peltate leaves with 3—7 deeply divided elliptic or obovate lobes and petioles 2—6 in. long. A native of Brazil.

Fam. 72. ULMACEÆ.

Trees with watery sap. Leaves simple, alternate, penninerved or palminerved, stipulate. Flowers small, usually unisexual and with 4—5 perianth lobes and as many stamens opposite to them.

Leaves palminerved, margins serrate (except *C. Wightii*).
- Leaves glabrous. Sepals imbricate ... ... 1. Celtis.
- Leaves softly tomentose beneath. Sepals induplicate-valvate ... ... 2. Trema.

Leaves penninerved, with entire margins ... ... 3. Gironniera.

1. CELTIS.

Leaves bifarious, strongly triplinerved, entire or serrate, net venation weak. Sepals imbricate.

Leaves entire, 4—9 in. long ... ... C. Wightii.
Leaves crenate-serrate, 3½—4½ in. long ... ... C. cinnamomea.

443. **C. Wightii**, *Planch.*; H. v. 483; Br. 596.

A handsome evergreen tree (40—60 × 3—5), with a thin grey bark, cut mealy. Leaves 4—9 in. long and about half as broad, elliptic to elliptic-oblong, acute or shortly acuminate, base obtuse or rounded, glabrous, rigidly chartaceous, with 3 strong nerves running nearly the whole length of the blade; petioles ⅓—⅔ in. long. Flowers whitish, small. Drupe ¼—½ in. long, scarlet.

A common tree in deciduous and semi-deciduous forests. Fl. Dec.-Jan. Fr. March-May. It has a stem and bark like that of *Hemicyclia andamanica* which it also somewhat generally resembles. Wood creamy-white, fairly hard, and said to make a good charcoal. It is sometimes given the vernacular names *Thitlindat*, Burm., and *Chamma*, Hind., but these are not well-known.

444. **C. cinnamomea**, *Lindl.*; H. v. 482; Br. 596.

An evergreen tree (30—40 × 2½—3), somewhat resembling the preceding one. Leaves 3½—4½ in. long, obliquely ovate, acuminate, rounded at the base, crenate-serrate or remotely so, glabrous, strongly 3-nerved; petioles ¼ in. long. Flowers in short cymes. Drupe ovoid, narrowed at the truncate apex, smooth.

In similar localities but not so frequent as the last one. Middle Andaman; Long Island; Baratang; Havelock Island; Rutland Island. Fl. May. The heartwood, which is said to be used medicinally by Burmans, has, when freshly cut, a dirty brown colour and a very offensive smell.

2. TREMA.

445. **T. amboinensis**. *Blume*; H. v. 484; Br. 597. Vern. *Seiksa*, Burm.; *Buckri pathi*, Hind.

A small or moderate-sized soft-wooded tree of rapid growth and having a light crown, bark grey. Leaves 4—6 in. long, 1½—3 in. broad, ovate, finely acuminate, deeply cordate and unequal at the 3—7 nerved base, margin serrulate, softly whitish-grey tomentose beneath. Flowers in small axillary clusters. Fruit small.

Frequent everywhere, especially in open places and sometimes along streams. One of the first trees to make its appearance in new clearings and spreading very rapidly. It resembles *Grewia laevigata*, and its leaves are used for feeding goats, hence its vernacular name. Fl. Dec.-March.

3. GIRONNIERA.

Leaves coriaceous, penninerved, with connate convolute stipules. Flowers small; males in cymes; females axillary and usually solitary.

Leaves elliptic to elliptic-oblong, lateral nerves 5—8 pairs. ... G. subæqualis.
Leaves ovate to elliptic-lanceolate, lateral nerves 10—15 pairs. ... G. lucida.

446. ***G. subæqualis,** *Planch.*; H. v. 48; Br. 596.

An evergreen tree 30 to 40 feet high, the branchlets, petioles and stipules pubescent. Leaves 4—8 in. long, elliptic to elliptic-oblong, acuminate, base unequal, rigidly chartaceous, rough beneath, lateral nerves 5—8 pairs, ascending, with fine reticulations; petioles ¼—½ in. long. Drupe about ⅓ in. long, compressed, ellipsoid, minutely hispid.

Andamans, *King*, Fr. August.

447. **G. lucida,** *Kurz*: H. v. 483; Br. 593.

A moderate-sized evergreen tree with a dark brown rough bark, cut reddish-brown with irregular white streaks. Leaves 5—8 in. long, 1½—2½ in. broad, ovate to elliptic-lanceolate, long acuminate to a fine point, dark green and glossy, chartaceous, lateral nerves 10—15 pairs, strong and slightly curved. Female flowers on slender stalks, the stigmas slender and brush-like. Drupe ⅓ in. long, ovoid and glabrous.

Middle and South Andaman. Fl. Febr. Fr. August.

Fam. 73. MORACEÆ.

THE FIG FAMILY.

Trees, shrubs or climbers abounding in milky juice. Leaves simple, usually alternate, often lobed in young trees; stipules large, generally convolute. Flowers very small and numerous, collected on globose cylindric or hollow receptacles which often enlarge and bear the fruits with them.

A family of some importance to the Forester, as of the members here mentioned some are important timber-yielding trees and the leaves of many are used as elephant fodder.

All mentioned here have alternate leaves except *Ficus hispida*.

Mostly trees and unarmed.
Leaves entire (except *F. hispida* and *F. brevicuspis*).
Flowers minute, contained in hollow fleshy receptacles ... 1. Ficus.
Flowers minute on globose receptacles which enlarge in fruiting ... ... 2. Artocarpus.
Flowers minute, borne on mushroom-shaped receptacles or inside pear-shaped ones ... ... 3. Antiaris.

Leaves serrate.
Deciduous tree. Leaves large with long-petioled cordate leaves. Fl. in tassel-like catkins ... 4. Morus.
Evergreen tree. Leaves small, short petioled and rough. Fl. in axillary clusters ... ... 5. Streblus.
Shrubby tree or climber armed with strong and sharp spines.
Shrubby tree with serrate leaves ... ... 6. Phyllochlamys.
Woody climber with entire leaves ... ... 7. Plecospermum.

1. FICUS. Fig Trees.

Trees or shrubs, often scandent or epiphytical. Leaves alternate (except in *F. hispida*). Figs sessile or stalked, in the axils of the leaves or from the scars of the fallen ones, or from the branches or the stem.

Leaves dentate or serrate, rough or harsh to the touch.
L. opposite, palminerved; petiole 3—4 in. long. Figs usually clustered on the stem ... ... F. hispida.
L. alternate, penninerved; petiole 1—2 in. long. Figs solitary, from the leaf axils or the scars of fallen ones ... F. brevicuspis.
Leaves entire and mostly glabrous.
Leaves broadly ovate (width more than half the length), with cordate or rounded strongly palminerved bases and long petioles.
Figs sessile, paired, from the leaf axils or scars of fallen ones.
L. 3—6 in. long, white-dotted on the upper surface F. Rumphii.
Figs in clusters from the stem or branches.
L. 6—9 in. long; petiole 2—5 in. long ... F. glomerata.
L. 4—7 in. long; petiole 1—1½ in. long ... F. variegata.
Leaves more or less ovate, elliptic or oblong (about twice as long as broad).
Leaves up to 4 in. long; petioles not more than 1 in. long. Figs sessile, single or paired in the leaf axils.
Lateral nerves very many, distinct and joined intramarginally ... . F. Benjamina.
Lateral nerves many with finer intermediate ones.
L. weakly basal-nerved, apex blunt ... F. retusa.
L. shortly acuminate, nerves looping ... F. glabella.
Leaves up to 8 in. long, often weakly 3-nerved at base, the two lateral nerves running along the margin.
Petioles not more than 1 in. long
L. ovate, rhomboid or elliptic, rough, lateral nerves 4—5 pairs. Figs solitary, on slender stalks F. gibbosa.
Scandent. L. ovate to elliptic, strongly 3-nerved. Figs solitary or paired, stalked ... F. scandens.
Stem-clasping. L. oblong, elliptic or obovate. Figs sessile, in pairs ... ... F. obtusifolia.
Petioles up to 4 in. long.
L. 3—6 in. long; petioles 1—2 in. long, flattened. Figs sessile, from the leaf axils ... F. indica.
L. 4—7 in. long; petioles slender, up to 4 in. long. Figs sessile, from the leaf scars or axils. F. infectoria.
L. 4—7 in. long; petioles ¾—1½ in. long, thick. Figs sessile, paired, axillary ... .. F. altissima.
Epiphytic climber. L. 3—8 in. long; petioles ¾—1½ in. long. Figs axillary or on the stem ... F. ramentacea.

L. 4—8 in. long, strongly 3-nerved; petioles slender. Figs on slender stalks from the leaf axils or scars ... ... **F. sp.**

Leaves attaining more than 8 in. in length.

L. up to 12 in. long, oblong or elliptic; petiole up to 3 in. long. Figs solitary, axillary, on stalks **F. callosa.**

Leaves more or less lanceolate, penninerved, (the length about thrice the width).

L. 5—8 in. long, lateral nerves 12—14 pairs; petioles ½—1½ in. long, channelled. Figs axillary and stalked. **F. nervosa.**

L. 5—7 in. long, lateral nerves 8—10 pairs; petioles ½—1½ in. long. Figs axillary .. ... **F. glaberrima.**

The vernacular names *Nyaung*, Burm., and *Gular*, Hind., are often indiscriminately given to Fig trees in the Andamans.

448. **F. hispida,** *Linn. fil.*; H. v. 522; Br. 606. Vern. *Ka-aung*, Burm.; *Gular*, Hind.

A small tree (20—30×3—4), with low branches, the stems and branches marked with raised rings, the young branchlets hollow, bark greyish-white. Leaves opposite, with rough hairs, 6—10 in. long, ovate to elliptic or obovate, apiculate, base rounded or cordate with 3—5 nerves, irregular and shallow dentate; petioles 3—4 in. long. Figs 1 in. diam., in dense clusters hanging from the stem and branches, or in the leaf axils singly or by pairs, obovoid, yellowish when ripe.

Frequent in the islands in nearly all localities and usually found along streams. *Fr.* Nov.-Jan. It is easily known by its opposite leaves and hollow branchlets.

449. **F. brevicuspis,** *Miq*; Br. 604.

A small tree. Leaves 4—12 in. long, elliptic to oblong or obovate, shortly cuspidate, narrowed to the small rounded base, margin in the upper half slightly denticulate, rough and harsh to the touch, lateral nerves 7—12 pairs; petiole ½—2 in. long. Figs ½ in. diam., on stalks about as long, solitary, from the leaf axils or scars of fallen ones.

Middle Andaman, Betapur, Amitlated, Bomlungta; Long Island; Havelock Island; South Andaman, Ali Masjid Reserve. *Fr.* March-April.

450. **F. Rumphii,** *Blume*; H. v. 512; Br. 601. Vern. *Nyaung byu*, Burm.

A large tree (50—80×5—8) often epiphytic and stem-clasping, bark smooth, whitish-grey, cut light pinkish. Leaves 3—6 in. long, 2½—4 in. broad, broadly ovate, acuminate, base truncate or sub-cordate, margins wavy folded, lateral nerves fine, interarching near the edge; petiole 2—4 in. long, slender. Figs ½ in. diam., or less, sessile, in pairs from the leaf axils or the leaf scars on the branchlets.

Fairly frequent in deciduous forests. Middle Andaman, in several localities; Long Island; Havelock Island; South Andaman and Rutland Island. Leafless in the H. S. *Fr.* Dec.-March. Often mistaken for *F. religiosa*, and Prain writes that it has been largely planted on roadsides at Aberdeen under the impression that it was the *Pipal*. Its leaves have not the slender tails that terminate those of the *Pipal* and are not so glossy.

F. religiosa, *Linn.* *The Peepul Tree.* Vern. *Nyaung-bawdi*, Burm.; *Pipal*, Hind. A large tree resembling the preceding one, but more handsome and not so common here. Leaves with slender petioles, the blade glossy and ending in a slender tail 1—3 in. long. Figs black, in axillary pairs. A native of India and planted in the Andamans. It is sacred to Hindus and Buddhists.

451. **F. glomerata**, *Roxb.*; H. v. 535; Br. 609. *The Cluster Fig Tree.* Vern. *Thapan, Ye Thapan.* Burm.; *Lal Gular*, Hind.

A large tree (60—90×5—8) with a smooth brownish-grey bark, cut dark reddish. Leaves 6—9 in. long, 4—6 in. broad, broadly ovate, acuminate, cordate and strongly 3-nerved at the base, glabrous, lateral nerves 5—7 pairs, strong and looping near the margin; petiole 2—5 in. long. Figs about an inch in diam., pear-shaped, depressed, purplish-red, on slender stalks in dense clusters from the stem and branches.

Middle Andaman; Havelock Island; South Andaman. Not common. Often near streams. Fr. Febr.-March. The figs are edible and it is sometimes called the *Wild Fig Tree*. The leaves are often covered with galls.

452. **F. variegata**, *Blume*; H. v. 535; Br. 609.

A tree (30—40×3—4) with a smooth grey bark. Leaves 4—7 in. long, 2—4 in. broad, ovate, acuminate, more or less rounded and 3—5 nerved at the base, glabrous, with 3—5 pairs of lateral nerves looping intramarginally; petiole 1—2½ in. long. Figs 1 in. diam., globose, slightly depressed, smooth and reddish when ripe, on 1 in. stalks, in clusters from the woody tubercles on the stem.

South Andaman, Mt. Harriet, Chiriatapu. Fr. Jan. The leaves are very rarely denticulate.

453. **F. Benjamina**, *Linn.*; H. v. 508; Br. 604. *The Willow Fig Tree.* Vern. *Nyaung-thabye*, Burm.

A large tree with a spreading crown and drooping branches. Leaves 2—3 in. long, and half as broad, ovate to elliptic, bluntly acuminate, base acute or rounded, glabrous, lateral nerves numerous and fine, joined near the edge by a conspicuous intramarginal vein; petiole ½—¾ in. long. Figs ¼—¾ in. diam., sessile, axillary or from the leaf scars, globular, narrowed to the base, yellow or red when ripe.

Middle and South Andaman; Havelock and Rutland Islands. Also planted on Ross Island. Fr. Nov.-April. The leaves are like those of some *Eugenias*.

454. **F. retusa**, *Linn.*; H. v. 511; Br. 603. Vern. *Nyaung-ok*, Burm.

A large evergreen shady tree, often stem-clasping and with numerous aerial roots. Leaves 2—4 in. long and half as broad, elliptic to ovate or obovate, base and apex rounded to acute or very shortly and bluntly acuminate, dark green, lateral nerves many, thin, with finer intermediate ones, the basal running along the margin; petioles ¼—½ in. long. Figs about ¼ in. diam., sessile, usually in axillary pairs, white or pinkish when ripe.

Common, especially along creeks and the seashores, and most frequent on low ground bordering swamps where it grows as a spreading tree with numerous stout aerial roots. *Fr.* Nov.-Dec. It is also called, like the next one, the *Swamp Fig Tree.*

455. **F. glabella,** *Blume*; H. v. 511; Br. 603. *The Swamp Fig Tree.*

A small tree with a greyish bark, cut brown. Leaves 2½—4 in. long and about half as broad, elliptic to elliptic-oblong, suddenly and shortly acuminate, base rounded, glabrous, lateral nerves 12—16 pairs, looping intramarginally; petioles ½—1 in. long, slender. Figs less than ¼ in. diam., solitary or paired, from the leaf axils or scars below the leaves, sessile or shortly stalked, white with red spots.

Uncommon. Long Island and Havelock Island; South Andaman. Fr. Febr.-March. The figs are eaten by pigeons.

456. **F. gibbosa,** *Blume*; H. v. 469; Br. 599. Vern. *Nyaung-thabye,* Burm.

A small tree, often epiphytic and enclosing the stems of trees in a network of branches, bark light grey. Leaves 3—5 in. long, and about half as broad, ovate to rhomboid or elliptic, more or less acuminate, often unequal sided, dark green and glossy above, yellowish green and rough to the touch beneath, lateral nerves 4—6 pairs, looping near the margin, the lowest basal, all white on the undersurface; petiole short. Figs ¼—⅜ in. diam., solitary and axillary, on short stalks, yellow when ripe.

Not common. Long Island and Havelock Island; South Andaman. Fr. Jan.-May.

457.* **F. scandens,** *Roxb.*; H. v. 526; Br. 609.

An evergreen scandent shrub trailing on rocks and ascending tall trees. Leaves 2—5 in. long, ovate to elliptically ovate, acute, base rounded and strongly 3-nerved, glabrous; petioles ¼—1 in. long. Figs about ¼ in. diam., solitary or in pairs, from the leaf axils or the scars of fallen ones, globular, depressed, shortly stalked, yellow to crimson and rough when ripe.

South Andaman, Port Mouat, Goplakabang, Namunaghar. Fr. March-April.

458. **F. obtusifolia,** *Roxb.* H. v. 507; Br. 603. Vern. *Nyaung-gyat,* Burm.

An evergreen tree (50—70 × 6—12) often epiphytic, with a thin grey bark, cut reddish. Leaves 4—8 in. long, elongate-elliptic or obovate, rounded or blunt, base somewhat unequal and weakly 3-nerved, thick coriaceous, dark green and glossy, lateral nerves 15—18 pairs, slender with intermediate ones. Figs ½ in. diam., sessile, in the leaf axils or from the scars of fallen ones, triangular-globose, with 3 large bracts, yellow when ripe.

South Andaman, Mt. Harriet. A doubtful native of the islands. Fr. Nov.-April.

459. **F. indica,** *Linn.*; H. v. 506; Br. 603. Vern. *Nyaung-thabye*, Burm.

A large stem-clasping tree with spreading branches and a large crown. Leaves 3—6 in. long, and half as broad, elliptic to elongate-elliptic, acute or blunt at base and apex, sometimes bluntly apiculate, coriaceous, dark green and glossy, lateral nerves 6—8 pairs, with many slender intermediate ones, joined intramarginally, the lowest basal; petiole 1—2 in. long, flattened. Figs ¾—1 in. long, sessile, by pairs in the leaf axils or from the leaf scars, cylindric or globular, bright red or yellow when ripe.

In many localities. At first epiphytic, often on *Padauk* or on *Mimusops littoralis*, and eventually forming an independent stem, often of enormous size. Fr. Jan.-Febr. and July-Aug. When the fruit is ripe it is, like some of the other fig trees, the rendezvous of pigeons, minahs and birds of many other kinds.

460. **F. infectoria,** *Roxb.*; H. v. 515; Br. 602. Vern. *Nyaung-gyin*, Burm.

A large deciduous tree with spreading branches, bark grey, cut brownish. Leaves 4—7 in. long, 2½—4½ in. broad, oblong or elliptic to ovate-oblong, shortly acuminate, margin wavy, glabrous, lateral nerves 8—10 pairs, the lowest from the base, thin but distinct and looping along the margins, chartaceous, petiole 1—4 in. long, slender. Figs ¼ in. diam., almost sessile, from the leaf axils or the scars of fallen leaves, yellowish-white when ripe.

In various localities and not uncommon. Leafless Dec.-Jan. New leaves and fruit Febr.-June. The figs are eaten by pigeons.

461. ***F. altissima,** *Blume*; H. v. 504; Br. 600.

A large spreading tree with few aerial roots. Leaves 4—7 in. long, broadly ovate-elliptic, shortly and obtusely cuspidate, base rounded and sometimes slightly unequal, glabrous and coriaceous, weakly 3-nerved above the base with 5—6 pairs of distinct lateral nerves; petioles 1—3 in. long, thick and channelled. Figs ¾—1 in. long, globular, sessile and paired in the leaf axils, orange-red or yellow when ripe.

Andamans, Port Mouat. Fr. March-April.

462. *F. ramentacea, *Roxb.*; H. v. 528; Br. 609.

A powerful epiphytic climber often becoming an independent tree. Leaves 3—8 in. long, ovate to ovate-elliptic, acute or shortly acuminate, rounded to cordate at base, bright green, glossy and nearly glabrous, with 3—5 basal nerves and 4—8 pairs of lateral nerves, prominent beneath; petiole ¾—1½ in. long. Figs ¼—½ in. diam., axillary or clustered on the stem below the leaves, sessile or on short stalks, orange or orange-red and smooth when ripe.

South Andaman, North Bay, Port Mouat, Ranguchang. Fr. Dec.-Jan.

463. F. sp.

A moderate-sized deciduous tree with a very smooth whitish-grey thin bark, cut creamy-yellow, mealy. Leaves 4—8 in. long, 1¾—2½ in. broad, obovate or elliptic, shortly cuspidate, slightly narrowed to the rounded 3-nerved base, lateral nerves few, glabrous; petioles about an inch long, slender. Figs ½ in. diam., on stalks ½—1 in. long, one or two from the leaf axils or from the scars of the fallen ones, globular, smooth, yellowish when ripe.

Bomlungta; Havelock Island and Long Island. Fr. in December, appearing when the tree is leafless or with the new leaves.

464. F. callosa, *Willd.*; H. v. 516; Br. 601.

A large deciduous tree (40—80×4—8) with a light grey smooth bark. Leaves 6—12 in. long and about half as broad, oblong to elliptic, blunt or apiculate, base rounded to almost cordate with weak basal nerves and 10—12 pairs of prominent lateral ones and distinct venation, glabrous and rough to the touch; petiole up to 3 in. long. Figs ¾ in. diam., on ½ in. stalks, usually solitary in the leaf axils, globular, depressed above, puberulous, green or yellow when ripe.

Middle and South Andaman; Long Island; Havelock and Rutland Islands, also around Port Blair and on Ross Island. Fr. Jan. It resembles *F. bengalensis* and is sometimes given its vernacular name *Bargat*.

465. F. nervosa, *Roth.*; H. v. 512; Br. 600.

A large tree up to 8 feet in girth and often with large buttresses and with dark-coloured fairly smooth bark, cut mealy, yellowish. Leaves 5—8 in. long, 1½—3 in. broad, oblong to obovate-lanceolate, shortly and finely acuminate, dark green and glossy, drying dark brown, lateral nerves 12—14 pairs, prominent, looping near the margin; petiole ½—1½ in. long, channelled. Figs ¾ in. diam., on slender stalks, single or in pairs from the leaf axils, orange-coloured.

In many localities on evergreen hills and in low evergreen forest. The leaves are used for elephant fodder in the Andamans and the vernacular name *Thapon* is sometimes used. Fr. Feb.

466. **F. glaberrima,** *Blume*; H. v. 506; Br. 600.

A large tree. Leaves 5—7 in. long, oblong-lanceolate, acuminate, base acute, glabrous, lateral nerves 8—10 pairs, the lowest from the base and running along the margin, rather distant; petioles up to 2 in. long, slender and channelled. Figs ⅜ in. diam., usually sessile, numerous at the ends of the branchlets and by pairs in the axils of the leaves, apiculate, purple or orange-coloured when ripe.

Middle Andaman; Port Blair. Fr. Nov.-Febr. The leaves resemble those of *Ficus nervosa*.

2. ARTOCARPUS.

Milky juice thick and tenacious. Leaves usually entire in mature trees, pinnately lobed in young plants. Fruit fleshy, composed of the enlarged receptacle together with the perianths and the carpels which enclose the seeds.

Evergreen trees. Leaves perfectly glabrous.
Native. Leaves large, oblong or ovate ... ... A. Gomeziana.
Introduced. Leaves elliptic or obovate ... ... A. integrifolia.
Deciduous trees. Leaves soft or rough pubescent.
Leaves soft pubescent ... ... A. Lakoocha.
Leaves harsh with stiff hairs ... ... A. Chaplasha.

467. **A. Gomeziana,** *Wall.*; H. v. 544; Br. 612. Vern. *Kala Lakuch, Bara Lakuch*, Hind.

A moderate-sized or large tree (50—90×4 - 8) with a dark-coloured bark. Leaves 7—10 in. long, and about half as broad, oblong to ovate-oblong, very shortly acuminate or cuspidate, bases broad, dark green, glabrous and glossy with about 12 pairs of strong looping lateral nerves; petiole 1 in. long, strong. Receptacles ¾ in. diam. Fruit ovoid or obovoid, 2 in. long.

In nearly all localities in evergreen or semi-evergreen forests. Fr. July-Nov. The wood is yellowish, hard and durable, and very useful for house-posts. The leaves are used for elephant fodder. The vernacular names of this and *A. Lakoocha* are usually hopelessly confused. The dark green glossy leaves distinguish it.

A. integrifolia, *Linn. The Jack Tree.* Vern. *Peinne*, Burm.; *Kathar*, Hind. Leaves 4—8 in. long, elliptic or obovate; stipules amplexicaul leaving scars. Fruit up to 2½ feet long. Introduced and cultivated for its fruit which is said to be the largest edible fruit in the world. A yellow dye, used for dyeing silk, is obtained from the wood which is sometimes called *Orange wood*.

468. **A. Lakoocha,** *Roxb.*; H. v. 543; Br. 612. Vern. *Myauk-lôk* Burm.; *Barhal*, Hind.

A moderate-sized deciduous tree (30—60×3—6) with a dark-coloured bark. Leaves 8—12 in. long and 4—8 in. broad, broadly ovate or oblong.

apiculate, base rounded and unequal, coriaceous, with 14—16 pairs of strong lateral nerves, the lower surface clothed with soft velvety-grey or rusty pubescence; petiole strong, ¾—1½ in. long. Male receptacles 2 in. long, spongy, depressed-oblong, yellow; female ¾—1½ in. long, globular, greenish, 2—4 in. long and velvety when ripe.

In many localities but not so common as *A. Gomeziana*. Fl. Nov.-Febr. Fr. R. S. Leafless for a short while during the H. S. or the C. S. Its large pubescent leaves which have a tendency to fold inwards on the strong curved midrib distinguish it. It is sometimes called the *Monkey Jack Tree*.

469. **A. Chaplasha**, *Roxb.*; H. v. 543; Br. 611. Vern. *Taung-peinnè*, Burm.

A large deciduous tree (80—120 × 8—12) with a dark-coloured bark peeling in flakes, the young branchlets and stipules with stiff hairs, the branchlets marked with the ring-like scars of fallen stipules. Leaves up to a foot long and 8 in. broad, broadly ovate or elliptic, the base rounded to almost cordate, lateral nerves prominent, about 12 pairs, rough with minute stiff hairs; petioles about an inch long, strong, rusty pubescent. Flower heads globular, 1 in. long, on a 1—2 in. long stalk. Fruit 3—4 in. diam., yellow when ripe.

Frequent in all localities. Leafless in the H. S. Fl. Febr.-April. Fr. at the beginning of the R. S. Wood yellow, turning brown, moderately hard and seasoning well; a useful timber used for house and boat building and for making common furniture and packing cases. The leaves are used for elephant fodder and the fruit is edible.

A. incisa, *Linn. fl.* *The Breadfruit Tree* of the South Sea Islands, has been introduced. The leaves are 1—3 feet long and deeply pinnately lobed.

3. ANTIARIS.

470. **A. toxicaria**, *Leschen.*; H. v. 537; Br. 614. *The Upas Tree of Java.* Vern. *Hmyaseik*, Burm.; *Jungli Lakuch*, Hind.

A large tall tree (90—140 × 6—9) with a straight stem, bark grey with light patches, cut greenish, then yellowish, faintly streaked, with pale yellow juice. Leaves 4—9 in. long, 1¾—4 in. broad, oblong to ovate-oblong, acuminate, base broad rounded, dark green and glabrous, lateral nerves 9—12 pairs, distinct and looping near the margin; petioles short. Flowers when the tree is leafless, greenish, on mushroom-shaped receptacles ½ in. across. Fruit pear-shaped.

Middle and South Andaman; Baratang; Long Island and Havelock Island. Leafless in the H. S. Fl. Febr. This, the notorious *Upas Tree*, to which such deadly effects were once ascribed, bears no bad reputation in these islands. The tree is frequently felled for its leaves which are used for elephant fodder, and the juice has apparently no harmful effect on the skin but 'hardens into a white resin which is said to be used to prepare the upas poison for arrows.' Its bark is fibrous and tough and is said to be used in Ceylon for making sacks.

4. MORUS.

471. **M. laevigata**, *Wall.*; H. v. 492; Br. 613.

A deciduous tree (40—60×4—7), the bark in old trees dark-coloured, rough and furrowed, cut finely streaked brown and white. Leaves 4—8 in. long, 3—6 in. broad, or larger in young plants, broadly ovate, acuminate, base rounded or cordate and strongly 3-nerved, margins finely serrate, ultimately glabrous; petiole 1—2 in. long, slender. Flowers very small, in drooping spikes 2-4 in. long, from the axils of the fallen leaves.

Great Andaman and the adjoining islands. Leafless in the H. S. Fl. March-April when the tree is leafless. Wood yellowish-brown darkening to reddish-brown, hard, close-grained and durable with distinct annual rings; useful for house-posts.

5. STREBLUS.

472. **S. asper**, *Lour.*; H. v. 489; Br. 615. Vern. *Ôkhnè*, Burm.; *Cheroot pathi*, Hind.

A scraggy tree (20—30 × 1½—3), the bark greenish-grey and somewhat discoloured, cut whitish with thin cream-coloured juice. Leaves 2—4 in. long, elliptic to obovate, narrowed to the rounded base, margin coarsely serrate, apex acuminate to a fine point, rough to the touch, lateral nerves distinct; petiole very short. Flowers small, in axillary clusters. Fruit yellow, enclosed by the enlarged sepals.

Frequent in all localities in deciduous and semi-deciduous forests. Fl. Jan.-Febr. Fr. March-May. The wood is cut up into small pieces and, mixed with tobacco, is used for making Burmese cheroots.

6. PHYLLOCHLAMYS.

473. **P. spinosa**, *Bureau*; H. v. 488; Br. 615.

A small gnarled shrubby tree 5—8 feet high, armed with sharp spines which often bear leaves; juice cream-coloured. Leaves 1—2 in. long, acuminate to a fine point, rhomboid-elliptic to obovate or oblanceolate; margin irregularly serrate; petiole very short. Male flowers clustered; female flowers solitary; sepals enlarged in fruit.

Very common everywhere in deciduous and semi-deciduous forests. Fl. May. The leaves resemble those of *Streblus asper*.

7. PLECOSPERMUM.

474. **P. andamanicum**, *King*; H. v. 491; Br. 614. Vern. *Badmash kanta*. Hind.

A large woody climber up to 5 or 6 in. in diam., with yellowish furrowed stems and armed with straight sharp spines up to 3 in. long, bark peeling in small flakes. Leaves 3—6 in. long and about half as broad, elliptic to obovate, apex suddenly and finely short acuminate, glabrous lateral nerves 3—8 pairs the lowest almost basal. Flowers yellowish-white, in heads ½ in. diam., black tomentose when young.

Frequent in all localities in deciduous and semi-deciduous forests. Fl. Dec.-Jan. Among those working in the forests, this, as its name indicates, is of ill repute, on account of its sharp spines which cause wounds that fester and take a long while to heal. The wood is very hard.

FAM. 74. URTICACEÆ.

Juice watery. Leaves simple, alternate, palminerved, with stipules and usually with long petioles. Flowers small, unisexual, clustered in globose heads or in spikes.

1. PIPTURUS.

475. **P. velutinus,** *Wedd.*; H. v. 589; Br. 617.

A small much-branched tree the branchlets, petioles and underside of the leaves grey or silvery pubescent. Leaves 4—8 in. long, broadly ovate, base rounded or cordate and strongly 3-nerved, crenate-serrate, dark green above, pale beneath; petioles slender 2—5 in. long. Flowers small, clustered in axillary spikes.

Uncommon. Sometimes seen along the seashores. Long Island and Portman Bay. Fl. Dec.-Febr.

476. **Debregeasia sp.** is a large climber with almost orbicular or ovate leaves on long petioles, the young leaves have a border of white silky hairs along the margin on the under surface, and the flower-heads, which resemble raspberries and are reddish, appear during the hot season when the plant is leafless. It is frequently found on *Padauk* and when cut rapidly sends out many thread-like roots.

FAM. 75. CASUARINACEÆ.

THE CASUARINA FAMILY.

477. **Casuarina equisetifolia,** *Forst.*; Br. 620. *The Swamp Oak, or Beefwood Tree of Australia.* Vern. *Tinyu, Pinlè kabwè*, Burm.

A tall straight-stemmed evergreen tree with a rough bark and drooping branches, the branchlets needle-like, scaly, greenish and performing the function of leaves. Fruit ¾ in. diam., globose, woody and resembling a cone.

Indigenous on the west coast of the North Andaman and on the Little Andaman, and planted in Port Blair. "It has, or had, the reputation of improving the climate of malarious places." It is also known as the *Cassowary Tree.*

FAM. 76. GNETACEÆ.

478. **Gnetum scandens,** *Roxb.*; V. v. 642; Br. 683. Vern. *Gyut-nwe, Subrut,* Burm.

A large evergreen climber with flattened and twisted stems. **Leaves** simple, opposite, 3—9 in. long, elliptic to ovate-oblong, apiculate, glabrous and glossy, dark green, drying black, lateral nerves 9—10 pairs, looping near the margin; petioles ¼—½ in. long. Flowers in green cylindrical catkins. Fruit orange-coloured, edible when ripe.

Common in many localities; usually in evergreen forests. Fl. and Fr. C. S. and H. S. "The fallen catkins look exactly like green caterpillars with black rings and legs all round." *Nairne.*

FAM. 77. CONIFERÆ.

479. **Podocarpus neriifolia,** *Don.*; H. v. 649; Br. 695. Vern. *Thitmin* (*Prince of Woods*), Burm.; *Halis*, Hind.

A graceful evergreen tree (30—50 × 3—6) with dark green drooping foliage, bark thin and smooth, brown, cut pinkish, somewhat stringy. **Leaves** scattered, 4—10 in. long, ⅓—¾ in. broad, linear, nearly sessile, glabrous, rigidly coriaceous, the midrib prominent, the venation inconspicuous. Flowers in axillary catkins. Fruit globose, ¼—½ in. diam.

Rather uncommon; usually scattered in evergreen forests; rather plentiful on the high hills of the Middle Andaman, but here, like the surrounding growth, it remains stunted and hardly attains any useful size. The wood is light-coloured, even grained and moderately hard, working easily and very useful for boat-building, planking, oars and masts, and for making camp furniture. It bears little resemblance to the other well-known members of this family, the Pines, Cedars, and Firs.

Araucaria Cunninghami, *Sweet*, a native of Queensland, and known as the *Moreton Bay Pine*, has been introduced to the islands. It is a graceful tree with feathery branches bearing short sharp-pointed needles.

FAM. 78. CYCADACEÆ.

THE CYCAD FAMILY.

480. **Cycas Rumphii,** *Miq.*; H. v. 657; Br. 698. Vern. *Mondaing*, Burm.

An elegant evergreen palm-like tree 10—25 feet high with a rough simple or sometimes forked stem. **Leaves** 3—6 feet long, collected at the top of the stem, dark green and glossy; leaflets very many, 6—10 in. long, confluent in the upper part of the leaf. Flowers in orange-coloured scaly cones. Fruit globular, about 2 in. diam., woody, smooth, orange-coloured when ripe.

Common in the littoral zone along the coasts of the islands. Fl. C. S. Fr. H. S. and R. S. The fruit, which is edible when cooked but poisonous when raw, is eaten by the Andamanese. Kurz writes "Exudes a good sort of resin which is applied to malignant ulcers and which excites suppuration in an incredibly short time." It is often planted as an ornamental tree in gardens in Port Blair.

FAM. 79. AMARYLLIDACEÆ.

The Aloe Family.

Plants with long fleshy leaves tufted from near the ground. Flowers usually white, sometimes pink or yellow, often large and handsome; stamens 6, long. Fruit a capsule.

1. CRINUM.

481. **C. asiaticum,** *Linn.*; H. vi. 280. *The Antidote Lily* or *Asiatic Poison Bulb.*

A littoral herbaceous shrub 3—6 feet high, with very many smooth and light green, long and narrow fleshy leaves 3—5 feet long and 5—7 in. broad. Flowers white, conspicuous, on a long stalk up to 3 feet long; perianth tube 3—4 in. long, segments recurved. Fruit 1—2 in. diam.

Common along the seashores above the beaches. Fl. Febr.-May, fragrant at night. "The leaves are said to be equal as an emetic to the finest Ipecacuanha." *Nairne.* It somewhat resembles the Aloe Plant.

The following members of this family deserve mention:—

Agave sisalana, *Perrine. The Sisal Hemp of America,* has been introduced but has not been very successfully grown.

The next two are garden plants with handsome flowers often used to decorate homes:—

Zephyranthes rosea, and **Z. carinata,** *Swamp Lilies.* Leaves grass-like. Flowers lily-like, rose-coloured, on long stalks appearing during the rains.

The plant with beautiful white lily-like flowers with slender stamens joined by a thin membrane is a species of *Pancratium.*

FAM. 80. SCITAMINACEÆ.

The Banana Family.

Shrubs or trees, usually with herbaceous stems. Leaves long and broad, with numerous fine nerves pinnately arranged from the strong midrib. Flowers irregular, with coloured bracts and most of the stamens petaloid, only one normally developed and with an anther.

Leaves long and large with the lateral nerves nearly at right angles to the midrib ... ... 1. Musa.
Leaves not very large, with ascending lateral nerves. Stems dark-green and polished ... ... 2. Clinogyne.

1. MUSA.

482. **M. sapientum,** *Linn.*, var. simiarum, *Kurz*; H. vi. 262. *The Wild Plantain.* Vern. *Hnget-pyaw*, Burm.; *Jungli Kela*, Hind. Frequently seen along large streams and in damp places in the islands. Several varieties of the Banana have been introduced and are successfully cultivated.

M. textilis, *Nees. The Manilla Hemp*, a native of the Phillipines, has also been introduced to Port Blair. It is like the common banana in appearance.

Ravenala madagascariensis, *Gmel. The Traveller's Palm* of Madagascar, or *Water Tree* of the Dutch. An elegant palm-like tree with long-petioled leaves like those of the banana arranged in the shape of a large open fan. It has been introduced and a few trees are to be seen in Port Blair. Water is obtained from the tree by piercing the base of the leaf stalks.

2. CLINOGYNE.

483. **C. grandis,** *Benth.*; H. vi. 258. Vern. *Yông*, Burm.; *Kala pathi*, Hind.

A shrub 5—15 feet high with straight, cylindrical, dark green polished stems about 1 in. diam., pithy inside and thickened at the nodes. Leaves up to a foot long and 8 in. broad, ovate or broadly so, dark green above, pale beneath. Flowers white, ¾ in. long. Fruit globose.

Very common in moist places near streams in all localities. Fl. Febr.-May. Easily known by its polished dark green stems.

Canna indica, *Linn. The Indian Shot Plant*, is a common herb with variegated flowers frequent in gardens in Port Blair.

Several other less important but interesting members of this family, with beautiful flowers, are natives of the Andamans; they are mostly herbaceous and do not come within the scope of this work.

FAM. 81. FLAGELLARIACEÆ.

484. **Flagellaria indica,** *Linn.*, H. vi. 391. Vern. *Myauk-kyein*, Burm.

A glabrous climber with greenish hollow stems often as thick as the little finger. Leaves with sheating petioles, 6—10 in. long, lanceolate and ending in a fine slender spiral tendril. Flowers white, fragrant.

Frequent in the islands, especially near the sea-coast; seen in many localities. The stems resemble those of canes.

To the family BROMELIACEÆ, belongs the *Pine Apple*, **Ananas sativus,** *Schult.* Vern. *Ananas*, Hind. Introduced and cultivated in Port Blair. "The fruit consists of numerous flowers and bracts grown together in a mass, and the crown of leaves, which looks so out of place, growing apparently out of the fruit, belongs really to the flowerless top of the spike." *Nairne.*

FAM. 82. PANDANACEÆ.

THE SCREW-PINE FAMILY.

Trees or climbers (*Freycinetia*) with linear ensiform leaves arranged in whorls, spinulous along the edges and at the back of the midrib. Flowers many and small, on a spadix enclosed in a leafy spathe. Fruit, a mass of united fleshy drupes.

Trees with leaves 3 feet or more in length	...	... 1. Pandanus.
Climber with leaves 1 to 3 feet in length	...	... 2. Freycinetia.

1. PANDANUS.

Characters—the same as under the family.

Small littoral tree. Leaves 3—6 feet long	...	... P. tectorius.
Moderate-sized. Leaves 15—18 feet long	...	... P. andamanensium.

485. **P. tectorius**, *Solander*; H. vi. 485; Br. 659. *The Fragrant Screw-pine.* Vern. *Sathapu*, Burm.; *Keora*, Hind.

A much-branched tree 15—20 feet high with numerous, stout, aerial roots. Leaves 3—6 feet long, sword-shaped, caudate-acuminate, spinulous. Flowers very fragrant with white spinulous spathes. Fruit 6—10 in. long, scarlet when ripe.

Common along seashores and often forming belts which fringe the beaches just above high-water mark. Fl. R. S. This is *P. laevis*, *Kurz*.

486. **P. andamanensium**, *Kurz*; H. vi. 485; Br. 659. Vern. *Kasan*, Burm.; *Keora*, Hind.

An elegant tree (30—50 × 1½—3), simple-stemmed or branched, the stem smooth with numerous short sharp prickles, supported at the base by stilt-like roots. Leaves 15—18 feet long, 3—4 in. broad, sword-shaped, spinulous. Fruit scarlet, the size of a man's head.

In all localities, especially in low moist swampy places which are flooded during the rains.

Also ascribed to these islands by Kurz who says "Marshy places in the coast forests of the Andamans," is *P. Leram*, *Jones*, the *Nicobar Breadfruit Tree*.

2. FREYCINETIA.

487. **F. insignis**, *Blume*; H. vi. 488; Br. 660.

A climber ascending large trees, stems 1—2 in. diam., straight, whitish, marked with rings. Leaves in three-rowed spirals, 1—3 feet long, ½—1 in. broad, spinulous-serrate. Fruit 2½ in. long.

Middle Andaman, Bomlungta; South Andaman. It is sometimes called the *Climbing Screw-pine*.

FAM. 83. LILIACEÆ.

THE LILY FAMILY.

Trees or shrubs with various leaves. Flowers as a rule bisexual, the perianth petal-like, with 6 divisions in two series; stamens usually 6. Fruit a capsule or berry.

The flowers of the members given here look very unlike *Lilies*, those of the family *Amaryllidaceae* resembling them more.

Trees with linear tufted leaves, parallel-nerved and with stem-clasping petioles	1. Dracæna.
Scandent and prickly. Leaves palmately and reticulately veined	2. Smilax.
Shrub with needle-like leaves	3. Asparagus.

1. DRACÆNA.

Soft-wooded trees with lanceolate, longitudinally veined leaves, crowded at the ends of the branchlets; petioles almost stem-clasping, leaving ring-like scars on the branchlets. Flowers white, or yellowish-white, in terminal panicles.

Leaves linear-lanceolate. Flowers yellowish, nearly an inch long	D. angustifolia.
Leaves broadly lanceolate. Flowers greenish-yellow, rather small	D. spicata.

488. **D. angustifolia**, *Roxb.*; H. vi. 327; Br. 641. Vern. *Seiksa*, Burm.; *Buckripathi*, Hind.

A slender tree attaining a height of 20 feet and a girth of about 2 feet. Leaves 1—2 feet long, 1—1½ in. broad, lanceolate or linear-lanceolate. Flowers yellowish, nearly an inch long, in raceme-like panicles. Fruit orange-coloured when ripe.

Common in the islands in many localities and rather frequent along the coast. Fl. and Fr. March-June. The leaves are used for goat fodder, hence the vernacular names.

489. **D. spicata**, *Roxb.*; H. vi. 328; Br. 461.

A tree (10—15×1—1½). Leaves 1—1½ feet long, 1½—2 in. broad, elliptic-lanceolate or broadly lanceolate. Flowers greenish-yellow, rather small, filaments white. Berries crimson when ripe.

South Andaman. Fl. April-May. It is given the same vernacular names as the preceding one.

2. SMILAX.

490. **S. aspericaulis**, *Wall.*; H. vi. 306. Vern. *Seinnabaw*, Burm.; *Ram datūn*, Hind.

A climber with stems about an inch in diam., and armed with numerous sharp prickles. Leaves 4—8 in. long and about half as broad, ovate or oblong, apiculate, strongly 3-nerved from the base to the apex, with fine and distinct reticulations; petioles ½—1 in. long, channelled and stems-clasping with tendril-like stipules. Flowers greenish-white, small, in umbels. Berry ⅓ in. diam.

Very common in many localities. Fl. Febr.-March. The stems are used for making tooth-sticks.

3. ASPARAGUS.

491. **A. racemosus,** *Willd.*; H. vi. 316; Br. 642.

A delicate shrub, sometimes straggling, the leaves minute and bearing in their axils feathery needle-like light-green branchlets. Flowers white, small, fragrant, in racemes. Berries red.

Middle and South Andaman, not common; often among shrubbery in rocky places near the sea.

Gloriosa superba, *Linn.* A climber with lanceolate leaves ending in a fine curl. Flowers with long, scarlet and yellow, narrow, wavy petals and very long yellow stamens. The roots are poisonous. Middle Andaman and Rutland Island, among shrubbery, near the sea.

Fam. 84. PALMÆ.

The Palm and Cane Family.

Erect trees (palms) or climbers (canes), with unbranched stems, smooth and marked with ring-like scars or covered by the persistent bases of the petioles. Flowers small, in spikes or panicles, and enclosed in spathes; perianth 6, divided, in two whorls; stamens 3 or 6. Fruit with a fibrous or scaly covering.

A large tropical family of great economic importance; many of its members are ornamental as well as useful, while some of the products yielded by them are of the greatest utility. To the forester in these islands, canes and the leaves of many palms are useful. Several palms ornament our gardens in Port Blair and the cocoanut palm, which grows so well here, furnishes several valuable products.

Erect palms, with pinnate leaves and numerous linear sword shaped leaflets.
- Leaflets folded inwards lengthwise, glaucous beneath, the lowest transformed into spines ... 1. Phœnix.
- Littoral with underground stems. Leaves 15-30 feet long; leaflets 4—5 feet long, glaucous beneath ... 2. Nipa.
- Stems slender, annulate. Leaflets often confluent, especially in the upper part of the leaf ... ... { 3. Areca. 4. Pinanga.

Scandent, with pinnate leaves often ending in a slender whip-like appendage; leaflets many, sword-shaped or lanceolate. Fruit scaly ... ... { 5. Calamus. 6. Dæmonorops.

Scandent with pinnate leaves ending in a spinous tendril; leaflets rhomboid or wedge-shaped, glaucous beneath. Fruit scaly ... ... 7. Korthalsia.

Erect unarmed palms with bipinnate leaves, the leaflets rhomboid or wedge-shaped. Fruit fibrous ... ... 8. Caryota.
Erect palms with fan-shaped leaves, the petioles armed with recurved spines. Fruit fibrous.
Leaves 8—16 feet across, cleft into 80—100 segments to about the middle ... ... 9. Corypha.
Leaves 2—6 feet across, divided into 12—25 wedge-shaped segments down to the base ... ... 10. Licuala.

1. PHŒNIX.

Slender palms, the bases of the petioles adhering to the stem below the leaves. Leaflets with no midrib, folded inwards longitudinally, ending in a sharp point, the lowest ones transformed into long sharp spines.

492. **P. paludosa,** *Roxb.*; H. vi. 427; Br. 646. *The Sea Date Palm.* Vern. *Thinbaung*, Burm.; *Khajur*, Hind.

A slender palm (20—30×1—3) with annular stems. Leaves 4—6 feet long; leaflets 1—2 feet long, usually arranged in pairs, sword-shaped, glossy above, glaucescent beneath, entire, with fine distinct veins; spines 1—2½ in. long. Flowers yellow, handsome, in compact spikes. Fruit ½ in. diam., orange-red and turning black when ripe.

Frequently along mangrove creeks and in mangrove swamps and often forming small clumps. Fl. Febr.-April. Fr. June-Dec. Its specific name signifies its habit of growing in swamps.

On the Cinque Islands and on the eastern slopes of Mt. Ford on Rutland Island above Portman Bay, a species of *Phœnix* is frequent. Stem single, not annulate. Leaves bifarious; base of petioles with much dark brown fibre. Spadix and fruit orange coloured. *Brandis.*

2. NIPA.

493. **N. fruticans,** *Wurmb*; H. vi. 424; Br. 648. *The Water Coconut or Dani Palm.* Vern. *Dani*, Burm.

A palm with underground stems. Leaves 15—30 feet long, unarmed, somewhat resembling those of the coconut palm; leaflets 4—5 feet long, rigid, glaucous beneath; petiole very strong and thick. Fruit 4-6 in. long, turbinate, compressed and angular, fibrous, with a large white seed.

Along many tidal creeks in the Andamans and usually making them very picturesque. Its leaves are used for thatching. The nuts may often be found washed up on the seashores. 'The seeds might be used as vegetable ivory.' *Kurz.*

Cocos nucifera, *Linn.* *The Coconut Palm.* Vern. *On*, Burm.; *Naryal*, Hind. Indigenous to the Coco Islands but introduced and extensively planted at Port Blair and on some of the outlying islands. It is one of the ornaments of the Settlement. Kurz says it is really wild along the north-western coast of the North Andaman. Single trees or small groves may be found at many places along the coasts, but these have either been planted or have sprung up from nuts washed up by the sea. It is extensively grown in the Nicobar Islands and its original home is said to be unknown. The wood is commercially known as *Porcupine Wood*, and has been so named because of quill-like growths therein.

3. ARECA.

494. **A. triandra**, *Roxb.*; H. vi. 406; Br. 646. *The Wild Areca Palm.* Vern. *Tawkun.*, Burm.; *Jungli Supari*, Hind.

A slender palm 15—25 feet high and 1—3 in. diam., with annulate stems. Leaves 4—6 feet long; leaflets 1½—3 feet long, solitary or 2-3 joined together especially in the upper part of the leaf, falcate-acuminate. Fruit ¾ in. long, oblong, smooth, orange-coloured turning scarlet.

Evergreen forests, on hills or in low places in nearly all localities. Fl. H. S. and R. S. Fr. the following year. The fruits are used for chewing with betel leaf like those of the true areca.

A. Catechu, *Linn.* *The Areca* or *Betelnut Palm.* Vern. *Kun*, Burm.; *Supari* Hind. A slender palm attaining a height of 80 feet and 8 inches diameter, the leaves collected in a tuft at the top. Introduced and cultivated in Port Blair.

4. PINANGA.

Resembles *Areca* and is difficult to distinguish from it.

495.* **P. Manii**, *Becc.*; H. vi. 409; Br. 647.

A slender palm attaining a height of 50 feet and a diameter of 6 inches. Leaves 15—20 feet long, with leaflets 2—3 feet long and 3 in. wide; leaf sheaths 4 feet long, clasping the stem. Spikes numerous, slender, pendulous. Fruit ½ in. long, broadly ovoid.

No Andaman specimens seen.

496. **P. Kuhlii**, *Blume*; H. vi. 409; Br. 647.

A slender palm 20—30 feet high and about 3 in. diam. Leaves 3—4 feet long with many falcate-linear to linear-lanceolate leaflets 1—2 feet long, finely acuminate. Spikes 6—15 in. long, numerous, on a stout spadix 3—10 in. long. Fruit ½ in. long.

This is *P. costata, Blume*, of Kurz's Forest Flora and he writes "In the tropical forests of the South Andaman. Fr. June." I rather think this is the one called *Kumpak*, Burm., a common palm in many localities and much resembling *Areca triandra.* Its dimensions do not satisfactorily agree with those of either of the *Pinangas* given here as its leaves attain as much as 8 feet in length. These I find difficult to place satisfactorily.

There is another stately palm with pinnate leaves found in some gardens in Port Blair and on Mt. Harriet. It has smooth stems 30—50 feet high. It is, I think, a species of *Oreodoxa*.

5. CALAMUS.

Scandent and spinescent, the stems annulate. Leaves pinnate with many linear leaflets, the midrib or rachis in some species prolonged into a slender spinous whip-like tail (the flagellum or cirrhus). Fruit scaly.

Note.—In those species whose leaves are prolonged into armed whip-like tails, this is the case only in stem leaves. The radical leaves (those which spring from the ground) are usually not so prolonged. Only the stem leaves should be used to determine a species by the following analysis.

Dæmonorops very closely resembles *Calamus* and it has been included in the following analysis :—

Leaflets arranged equidistantly along the rachis.
  Rachis prolonged into a long armed whip-like appendage.
    Leaflets 2-3 feet long ... ... **C. andamanicus.**
    Leaflets 1-2 feet long ... ... **D. Kurzianus.**
    Leaflets 8-12 in. long ... ... **D. Manii.**
  Rachis not prolonged into a whip-like appendage.
    Leaflets up to a foot long ... ... **C. pseudorivalis.**
Leaflets not arranged equidistantly along the rachis, *i.e.*, two or more together or fascicled.
  Rachis prolonged into a whip-like appendage.
    Leaflets 1—1½ feet long, broadly lanceolate ... **C. palustris.**
  Rachis not prolonged into a whip-like appendage.
    Leaves 10—14 feet long; leaflets 1½—2 feet long ... **C. longisetus.**
    Leaves 3—5 feet long; leaflets up to a foot long ... **C. viminalis.**

497. **C. andamanicus,** *Kurz*; H. vi. 457; Br. 653. *The Thick Cane.* Vern. *Thaing Kyein*, Burm.; *Mota bet*, Hind.

Very large and high scandent, the naked stems up to 2 in. diam., with nodes 10—16 in. apart, sheathed stems up to 5 in. diam. Leaves very large, 6—10 feet long and terminated by a flagellum 6—8 feet long; leaf-sheaths armed with rows or crests of spines or spiculæ, the rachis armed with groups of stout recurved black-tipped claws; the flagellum stout and armed with ½-whorls of recurved sharp claws; leaflets very many, alternate, 2—3 feet long and 1 in. broad, with spinescent bristles along the margin and along the nerves beneath. Fruit ¾ in. long, ovoid-ellipsoid, conically beaked.

Common in the islands both in deciduous forests and in evergreen. Fl. Nov.-Dec. Fr. April-July. The rows or crests of spines, which break off easily, on the leaf sheaths and petioles distinguish it. It is also the largest cane in the islands and attains a great length, often forming large loops on the ground and climbing over the highest trees. The thick stems are used for shoulder poles and for making the frames of cane furniture and also for making baskets. The leaves are used for thatching. When cut the stem yields a fair amount of good water.

498. **C. pseudorivalis,** *Becc.*; Br. 719. *The White Cane.* Vern. *Kyeinbyu*, Burm.; *China bet*, *Safed bet*, Hind.

Scandent and of moderate size with dark green handsome foliage; naked stems up to ¾ in. diam.; sheathed stems up to 2 in. diam. Leaves 3½—4 feet long, not prolonged into a cirrhus, the leaf sheaths armed sparingly with flat, rather short, brownish or blackish spines; rachis armed below in the upper portion with strong recurved spines; leaflets about 28 pairs, sword-shaped, up to a foot long, spinulous along the edges, sparingly if at all with bristles above or below along the midrib. Fruit ½ in. long.

Frequent in many localities. Fl. Nov.-Dec. Fr. April-June. It is the most useful cane in the islands. The sheathed stems have a white polished surface and, split and trimmed, are used extensively for making cane furniture, boxes, baskets, etc., and the canes are also used as walking rattans. The naked stems are greenish and strong and are used for rafting timber. According to Mr. C. G. Rogers there are several varieties of this species but they are all imperfectly known.

499. **C. palustris**, *Griff.*; H. vi. 458; Br. 654. Vern. *Yamata, Nagata*, Burm.; *Malai bet*, Hind.

Scandent and of moderate or fairly large size, the naked stems up to an inch in diam. Leaves about 8 feet long with a flagellum 4—5 feet long; leaf sheaths armed with not very many broad based and flat deflexed brown spines 1—1½ in. long, rachis armed with single spines at the sides in the lower portion and half-whorls of recurved black-tipped spines above; leaflets few, 1—1½ ft. long, broadly lanceolate, acuminate to a bristle, concavo-convex, 5—7 ribbed with entire or sparsely serrulate edges, pale beneath. Fruit ½ in. long, ovoid-ellipsoid, apiculate.

Frequent, especially in evergreen forests. Fl. Nov.-Febr. This is the easiest cane to recognise in forests on account of its broad, rather distantly grouped and concave leaves which are pale beneath. It is sometimes used for making baskets and also as walking canes but not for making cane furniture.

500. **C. longisetus**, *Griff.*; H. vi. 440; Br. 653. Vern. *Jungli Kyein*, Burm.; *Jungli bet*, Hind.

Large and high scandent, the naked canes up to 1½ in. diam. Leaves 10—14 feet long, the leaf sheaths fearfully armed with many whorls of long or short, flat, blackish and glossy sharp spines up to 1½ or 2 in. long, the petiole armed below with spines similar to those on the sheath and in the upper portion with solitary black deflexed spines beneath; leaflets 1½—2 feet long, sword-shaped, spinulous along the edges and with few bristles above and beneath along the nerves. Fruit 1 in. long, ovoid, mottled like a leopard's skin.

Very common everywhere in the islands. Fl. Nov.-Jan. Fr. May-July. The canes are not used as they split unevenly and break easily, and the leaves are unfit for thatching. It is easily distinguished from the other large canes by its long black spines of uneven length on the sheath, its leaves without a flagellum and the leaflets not evenly spaced on the rachis.

501. **C. viminalis**, *Willd.*; var. fasciculatus, *Becc.*, sub-var. andamanicus, *Becc.*; H. vi. 444; Br. 652. Vern. *Kyein-ga.*, Burm.

Small or moderate-sized, the naked stems ⅓—⅔ in. diam., the younger parts and sheaths covered with a pale powder. Leaves 3—5 feet long, sheaths sparingly armed, the petiole and rachis armed at the sides with straight ⅓—1½ in. long spines; leaflets up to a foot long, fasciculate and pointing many ways, narrowly lanceolate, distantly spinulose serrate. Spadix ending in a long slender armed appendage Fruit globose ¼—⅓ in. diam.

Frequent in clearings around Port Blair, also in the forests of the Middle and South Andaman. Fl. Nov.-Jan.

There is also another small cane in the islands known as *Hasali bet*. It has leaves 3½ ft. long, not prolonged into a cirrhus, the leaf sheaths armed with flat blackish-brown spines up to 2 in. long; leaflets 20—25 pairs, the upper ones confluent, and from the sheaths just below the insertion of the petioles are long fine spinous whip-like appendages.

6. DÆMONOROPS.

Closely resembles *Calamus*, the difference being of a technical nature which hardly concerns us here. It has been included under the analysis of the genus *Calamus* in this book.

502. **D. Kurzianus,** *Becc.*; H. vi. 463; Br. 650. Vern. *Ye-thaing-kyein*, Burm.

A large scandent cane the naked stems up to 1½ in. diam., the sheathed ones as thick as the arm. Leaves 6—12 feet long, with a flagellum 6—8 feet long; leaf sheaths fearfully armed with numerous flat black spines about an inch long, the rachis armed below along the centre with, at first solitary, then paired, and higher up 3—5 nate, and in the flagellum whorled, recurved claws; leaflets very many, 1—2 feet long, narrowly sword-shaped, spinulous along the edges with black spinescent bristles along the nerves. Fruit ¾ in. long, globular, apiculate.

Frequent in all localities in low damp places and along large streams. Fl. Nov.-Jan. Fr. May-July. It closely resembles *C. andamanicus* but is not so large and it has longer flat black spines on the sheaths. The radical leaves are extensively used for thatching and are called *Bet pathi* or *Kyein pet*. It exudes a red resin which is the *Dragon's Blood* referred to by Kurz under *C. grandis*.

503. ***D. Manii,** *Becc.*; H. vi. 463; Br. 650.

Moderate-sized and scandent. Leaves 4½—6 feet long, ending in a strongly clawed flagellum, the rachis armed below with single spines low down, double above, and higher up with whorls of clawed spines; leaflets 8—12 in. long, numerous, sword-shaped, the midrib and side nerves with spinescent bristles above and fewer below. Fruit spherical with a mucro, ½—¾ in. diam.

The leaves are said to be used for thatching.

7. KORTHALSIA.

504. **K. laciniosa,** *Mart.*; H. vi. 475; Br. 654. ***The Red Cane.*** Vern. *Kyeians*, Burm.; *Lal bet, Lal kubri bet,* Hind.

A large armed scandent conspicuous cane-palm, the canes up to ¾ in. diam. Leaves pinnate, 2—4 feet long, terminating in a long thorny whip-like tendril, the rachis sparingly armed with short spines; leaflets equidistant, ovate or cuneate-rhomboid, narrowed to the short petiole, irregularly toothed, dark green above, pale below, 4—8 in. long. Fruit scaly up to ½ in. long.

Common in all localities and very conspicuous. The canes are reddish and are used for walking sticks. The leaves are eaten by elephants. The smaller variety (Br. 719) reported by Mr. C. G. Rogers was found at Havelock Island. Fr. Feb.

8. CARYOTA.

505. **C. mitis,** *Lour.*; H. vi. 423; Br. 654. Vern. *Minbaw*, Burm.; *Mari Supari*, Hind.

An elegant palm 8—10 feet high and 4—5 in. diam. with a tufted crown. Leaves 8—10 feet long and 6—8 feet across, the leaflets obversely cuneate-deltoid, oblique, irregularly toothed on the outer margin, 4—8 in. long. Flowers in dense pendulous spikes from the stem. Drupes globular or nearly so, smooth, bluish-black.

Frequent in all localities and usually in evergreen forests. Fl. and Fr. H. S. Frequently planted in gardens in Port Blair as an ornamental palm.

9. CORYPHA.

506. **C. umbraculifera,** *Linn.*; H. vi. 428; Br. 657. *The Talipot Palm of Ceylon* or *Fan Palm of Southern India.* Vern. *Pe, Pelin*, Burm.

A large palm 30—60 feet high with a straight cylindrical stem 1—2 feet in diam. Leaves very large, 8—16 feet across, fan-shaped, cleft to about the middle into 80 or 100 segments; petiole large and strong, 18—25 feet long, armed along the margins with stout dark-coloured spines. Drupes 1½ in. diam., globular.

Not common. Middle Andaman, Mt. Wimberley; South Andaman, Port Mouat, Wimberleygunj, Tarmugli Island. I found an old Jarawa encampment among a little group of these palms on Baratang Island. It is "the largest and most imposing of Eastern Palms." It flowers and fruits when about 40 years old and then dies. The leaves are used for making fans, umbrellas and for writing upon. "The seeds have the hardness of ivory and are known as *Baryarbata Nuts*, they are used as beads in Ceylon and in the manufacture of buttons in Europe."

The two next mentioned fan-palms have been introduced :—

Borassus flabellifer, *Linn.* *The Palmyra Palm.* A native of tropical Africa. Vern. *Tan*, Burm; *Tal*, Hind. A large palm attaining 100 feet or more with leaves 3-4 feet diam., and spinous petioles 2—4 feet long. It yields toddy and the fruit is roasted and eaten. It is also known as the *Brab Tree*. It grows extensively in Southern India, and "an ancient Tamil song in praise of the palm enumerates 801 uses that can be made of it."

Livistona chinensis, *R. Brown*, is a handsome palm grown in gardens in Port Blair. It attains 15—30 feet in height, has leaves 3-4 feet in diam., and petioles armed with short recurved spines. It is a native of China and Japan.

10. LICUALA.

Conspicuous and handsome small palms with rough stems and fan-shaped leaves divided to the base into numerous wedge-shaped segments; petioles armed with strong recurved sharp spines. Flowers in drooping spikes from an erect spadix.

Leaves 3-6 ft. across; petioles 4-12 ft. long ... ... L. peltata.
Leaves 2-4 feet across; petioles 2-4 ft. long ... ... L. spinosa.

507. **L. peltata**, *Roxb.*; H. vi. 430; Br. 656. Vern. *Salu*, Burm.; *Selai pathi*, *Mota pathi*, Hind.

Stem 8—10 feet high. Leaves 3—6 feet across; petioles 4—12 feet long. Flowers yellowish, in pendulous spikes. Fruit orange-coloured.

Frequent in the islands in nearly all localities, but said to be absent on Ritchie's Archipelago. Fl. and Fr. Febr.-March. The leaves are extensively used for thatching, and for this purpose they may be just spread out and laid on the roof, or, as in better class of work, the leaflets are stripped off the petioles and folded crosswise on to strips of bamboo, to which they are stitched or fastened with finely split bamboo, hence the vernacular name. The leaves are also used for various other purposes such as for making hats and umbrellas, for wrapping up articles, etc. Owing to the unrestricted cutting of the palms to obtain the useful leaves, the plants have nearly all disappeared in the vicinity of Port Blair, and the leaves have now to be brought from Baratang and Long Island.

508. **L. spinosa**, *Wurmb.*; H. vi. 431; Br. 656. Vern. *Jungli Selai*, Hind.

Stem 8—15 feet high. Leaves 2—4 feet across; petioles 2—4 feet long. Flowers smaller than those of the preceding one. Fruit orange-coloured.

Usually in damp swampy places near mangrove and often growing in small patches. Fl. Dec.-Jan. Fr. April-May. The leaves are sometimes used like those of the preceding one, but being smaller and heavier they are not preferred.

Fam. 85. GRAMINEÆ.

THE GRASS AND BAMBOO FAMILY.

Grasses or bamboos with hollow stems interrupted by joints or nodes. Leaves usually linear, oblong, or lanceolate, with numerous, fine, parallel veins, the blade being joined to the sheath by a short petiole.

Flowers in spikelets, usually arranged in large terminal panicles, racemes or spikes.

Grasses usually attaining a height of not more than 15 feet; stems not woody.	
Native. Leaves up to 20 in. long	1. Phragmites.
Native. Leaves up to 5 feet long	2. Saccharum.
Introduced. Leaves up to 18 in. long	3. Thysanolæna.
Bamboos with woody stems attaining more than 15 feet in height.	
Stems up to 50 ft. long and 4 in. diam., sheaths clothed with black hairs. Leaves 3—16 in. long	4. Oxytenanthera.
Stems attaining 30 feet	5. Bambusa. 6. Schizostachyum.
Scandent bamboo with stems up to 300 feet long, bent at the nodes	7. Dinochloa.

1. PHRAGMITES.

509. **P. Karka,** *Trin*; H. vii. 304. Vern. *Wagyu*, Burm.

Attaining 10 to 12 feet in height with stems a little thicker than a pencil. Leaf blade up to 20 in. long and 1½ in. broad. Panicles about a foot long.

Fairly plentiful along the Bomlungta and Betapur streams in the Middle Andaman. Fl. April. The vernacular name of this and those of the other grasses given here are purely local.

2. SACCHARUM.

510. **S. arundinaceum,** *Retz.*; H. vii. 119. Vern. *Paung*, Burm.; *Jungli Ganna*, Hind.

Attains a height of 12 to 15 feet with stems pithy inside. Leaf blade 4—5 feet long and 2 in. broad. Flowers in handsome panicles 1—2 feet long, silky, greyish-brown.

Very common along the large streams in the Middle Andaman and growing very thickly and luxuriantly. Fl. in the H. S. Elephants love to browse in it.

S. officinarum, *Linn.* *The Sugar Cane*, which the preceding one, though not so stout, somewhat resembles, has been introduced and is cultivated in Port Blair.

S. Munja, *Roxb.* *The Munj Grass*, has also been introduced and may be found growing in patches at Haddo in Port Blair.

3. THYSANOLÆNA.

511. **T. Agrostis,** *Nees*; H. vii. 61.

A large handsome grass 8—12 feet high with polished glabrous stems. Leaves 1—2 feet long and 2—4 in. broad, linear-lanceolate, cordate, tapering to a fine point. Panicles 1—2 feet long, dense and slender.

Introduced and running wild in Port Blair where it may be seen growing in small clumps; plentiful at Wimberleygunj, Mt. Harriet and other places. It is locally called *Nurval* and is called by some writers the *Broom Grass*. In India the stems furnish the reed pens used in vernacular writing.

The following also deserve mention:—

Zea Mays, *Linn.* *The Maize or Indian Corn.* Vern. *Buta, Maka,* Hind., is cultivated in Port Blair.

Arundo versicolor, *Mill.* *The Ribbon Grass,* is sometimes seen in gardens in Port Blair.

There are many other grasses found in these islands but these are beyond the scope of this work and my powers to treat of.

4. OXYTENANTHERA.

512. **O. nigrociliata,** *Monro*; H. vii. 401; Br. 674. Vern. *We,* Burm.; *Bans, Bamboo,* Hind.

Attains a height of 30 to 50 feet; stems hollow with rather thin walls, internodes 18—30 in. long and 2—4 in. diam., dark green. Leaves lanceolate, 8—18 in. long. Culm sheaths 6—16 in. long, densely clothed with black hairs. Flowers in leafy panicles.

Very common and often gregarious. It is one of the commonest bamboos in the islands and is locally put to very many uses, such as for building huts and barracks, for making fishing stakes and baskets, and for mat work.

5. BAMBUSA.

Arboraceous tufted bamboos with unarmed, more or less alternately fasciculate, or single, branches. Usually dying rapidly or slowly after flowering.

Stems ½—1 in. diam.	Leaves 10-15 in. long	... ...	B. lineata.
Stems 3-4 in diam.	Leaves 4-7 in. long	... ...	B. schizostachyoides.

513. ***B. lineata,** *Monro*; Br. 670.

Internodes 16—24 in. long and ½—1 in. diam., walls thin, branches single, culm-sheaths about 6 in. long, clothed when young with golden-brown hairs. Leaves 10—15 in. long and 1—3 in. broad, pale beneath; leaf-sheaths ribbed, keeled, fringed with long stiff bristles at the mouth. Flowers in leafy panicles.

Rutland Island. Fl. annually.

514. **B. schizostachyoides,** *Kurz*; Br. 670.

Attaining 20—30 feet with very hollow green and glossy stems 3—4 in. diam.; internodes 18—24 in. long. Leaves 4—7 in. long, lanceolate to linear-lanceolate; leaf sheaths hispid, soon glabrescent, ciliate on the margins. Flowers in clustered spikes.

South Andaman, Kurz. Fl. and Fr. April-May. If I am right in its determination it is, I think, common in the Middle Andaman.

6. SCHIZOSTACHYUM.

515. *S. **Rogersii**, *Brandis*; Br. 679.

Tufted. Culms weak, up to 30 feet long and ¾ in. diam., with thin walls; culm-sheaths 3—4 in. long. Leaves 7—9 in. long and 1—1½ in. broad. Flowers in long spikes terminating leafy branchlets.

Andamans, *Brandis*.

7. DINOCHLOA.

516. **D. andamanica**, *Kurz*; Br. 681. *The Climbing Bamboo.* Vern. *Wanwè*, Burm.; *Bel Bamboo*, Hind.

Scandent and attaining 300 feet in length with zig-zag branches, internodes 9—18 in. long and up to 1 in. diam., dark green. Leaves 9—12 in. long and 2—3 in. broad. Flowers in narrow terminal panicles.

Very common and forming impenetrable tangled thickets and often climbing on the tallest trees.

Dendrocalamus Brandisii, *Kurz*, is a picturesque bamboo forming large dense clumps, attaining a height of 80-100 feet and with bamboos 5—7 in. diam. It has been introduced and may be seen in the Haddo gardens.

APPENDIX.

Lists of the Principal Evergreen, Deciduous, Littoral and Introduced Plants.

List of the Principal Evergreen Trees.

Aglaia andamanica.
Aglaia Ganggo.
Alstonia Kurzii.
Amoora Rohituka.
Areca triandra.
Atalantia monophylla.
Baccaurea sapida.
Barringtonia racemosa.
Barringtonia speciosa.
Bouea burmanica.
Buchanania platyneura.
Calophyllum amoenum.
Calophyllum Inophyllum.
Calophyllum spectabile.
Carallia lucida.
Caryota mitis.
Celtis Wightii.
Champereia Griffithiana.
Cleistanthus myrianthus.
Cyclostemon assamicus.
Cyclostemon macrophyllus.
Dehaasia Kurzii.
Diospyros Kurzii.
Diospyros montana.
Diospyros oocarpa.
Diospyros pilosula.
Diospyros pyrrhocarpa.
Diospyros undulata.
Drimycarpus racemosus.
Dysoxylum thyrsoideum.
Elaeocarpus aristatus.
Elaeocarpus robustus.
Eugenia javanica.
Fagraea morindaefolia.
Ficus Benjamina.
Ficus indica.
Ficus retusa.
Garcinia andamanica.
Garcinia Cowa.
Garcinia speciosa.
Garcinia Xanthochymus.
Gelonium bifarium.
Grewia calophylla.
Hemicyclia andamanica.
Heritiera littoralis.
Hopea odorata.
Hydnocarpus castanea.
Licuala peltata.
Litsaea Kurzii.
Litsaea Panamonja.
Macaranga indica.
Macaranga Tanarius.
Melodorum macranthum.
Mesua ferrea.
Mimusops Elengi.
Mimusops littoralis.
Mitrephora Prainii.
Murraya exotica.
Myristica andamanica.
Myristica glaucescens.
Myristica Irya.
Myristica Prainii.
Pandanus andamanensium.
Picrasma javanica.
Pisonia excelsa.
Podocarpus neriifolia.
Polyalthia Parkinsonii.
Pometia pinnata.
Pterospermum aceroides.
Randia exaltata.
Ryparosa Kurzii.
Sageraea elliptica.
Semecarpus Kurzii.

Semecarpus Prainii.
Sideroxylon longepetiolatum.
Talauma andamanica.
Ternstroemia penangiana.
Xanthophyllum andamanicum.

List of the Principal Deciduous Trees.

Adenanthera pavonina.
Ailanthus Kurzii.
Albizzia Lebbek.
Albizzia procera.
Albizzia stipulata.
Anthocephalus Cadamba.
Antiaris toxicaria.
Artocarpus Chaplasha.
Artocarpus Lakoocha.
Bassia butyracea.
Berrya Ammonilla.
Bischofia javanica.
Bombax insigne.
Canarium euphyllum.
Canarium Manii.
Chukrasia tabularis.
Cordia grandis.
Crypteronia paniculata.
Dipterocarpus costatus.
Dipterocarpus Griffithii.
Dipterocarpus incanus.
Dipterocarpus turbinatus.
Dracontomelum mangiferum.
Duabanga sonneratioides.
Endospermum malaccense.
Erythrina indica.
Excoecaria Agallocha.
Ficus callosa.
Ficus infectoria.
Ficus Rumphii.
Garuga pinnata.
Gyrocarpus americanus.
Heteropanax fragrans.
Heterophragma adenophyllum.
Lagerstroemia hypoleuca.
Morus lævigata.
Nauclea Gageana.
Ochna Wallichii.
Odina Wodier.
Oroxylum indicum.
Pajanelia Rheedii.
Parishia insignis.
Planchonia andamanica.
Prunus martabanica
Pterocarpus dalbergioides.
Sapium baccatum.
Spondias mangifera.
Sterculia alata.
Sterculia campanulata.
Sterculia colorata.
Sterculia parviflora.
Sterculia rubiginosa.
Sterculia villosa.
Terminalia bialata.
Terminalia Catappa.
Terminalia Manii.
Terminalia procera.
Tetrameles nudiflora.
Vitex glabrata.
Walsura Candollei.
Walsura robusta.
Zanthoxylum Budrunga.

List of Littoral Plants (excluding Mangroves), i.e., those that naturally confine themselves to littoral tracts in the Andamans.

Acanthus ebracteatus.
Acanthus ilicifolius.
Afzelia bijuga.
Aphania Danura.
Ardisia humilis.
Arytera littoralis.

Barringtonia speciosa.
Brownlowia lanceolata.
Cæsalpinia Bonducella.
Cæsalpinia Nuga.
Canavalia turgida.
Carapa moluccensis.
Cerbera Odollam.
Clerodendron inerme.
Colubrina asiatica.
Cordia subcordata.
Crinum asiaticum.
Cycas Rumphii.
Cynometra ramiflora.
Dalbergia monosperma.
Derris andamanica.
Derris uliginosa.
Desmodium umbellatum.
Dodonæa viscosa.
Dolichandrone Rheedii.
Erythrina indica.
Ganophyllum falcatum.
Glyptopetalum calocarpum.
Guettarda speciosa.
Gyrocarpus americanus.
Heritiera littoralis.
Hernandia peltata.
Hibiscus tiliaceus.
Hydnophytum formicarum.
Ixora brunnescens.
Licuala spinosa.
Mimusops littoralis.
Morinda citrifolia.
Mucuna gigantea.
Ochrosia borbonica.
Pandanus tectorius.
Peltophorum ferrugineum.
Pemphis acidula.
Phœnix paludosa.
Pipturus velutinus.
Pisonia aculeata.
Pongamia glabra.
Premna integrifolia.
Salacia latifolia.
Salacia prinoides.
Scævola Kœnigii.
Smythea calpicarpa.
Sophora tomentosa.
Sterculia rubiginosa.
Terminalia Catappa.
Thespesia populnea.
Tournefortia argentea.
Ximenia americana.

List of Plants found growing in swamps, and which may be classed as Mangroves.

Ægialitis rotundifolia.
Ægiceras majus.
Avicennia officinalis.
Bruguiera gymnorhiza.
Bruguiera parviflora.
Carapa obovata.
Ceriops Candolleana.
Kandelia Rheedii.
Lumnitzera coccinea.
Lumnitzera racemosa.
Nipa fruticans.
Phœnix paludosa.
Rhizophora conjugata.
Rhizophora mucronata.
Scyphiphora hydrophyllacea.
Sonneratia acida.
Sonneratia alba.

List of the Principal Non-indigenous Plants of the Andaman Islands.

Acacia arabica.
Acacia Farnesiana.
Achras Sapota.
Aegle Marmelos.

Afzelia palembanica.
Agave sisalana.
Albizzia moluccana.
Allamanda cathartica.
Amherstia nobilis.
Anacardium occidentale.
Ananas sativus.
Anona reticulata.
Anona squamosa.
Antigonon leptopus.
Araucaria Cunninghami.
Areca Catechu.
Artocarpus incisa.
Artocarpus integrifolia.
Arundo versicolor.
Averrhoa Carambola.
Azadirachta indica.
Bixa orellana.
Bombax malabaricum.
Borassus flabellifer.
Bougainvillæa spectabilis.
Brownea Ariza.
Cæsalpinia pulcherrima.
Calotropis gigantea.
Canna indica.
Capsicum frutescens.
Carica Papaya.
Cassia alata.
Cassia Fistula.
Cassia siamea.
Cinnamomum zeylanicum.
Citrus decumana.
Citrus medica.
Cocus nucifera.
Codiæum variegatum.
Coffea liberica.
Dendrocalamus Brandisii.
Durio zibethinus.
Enterolobium Saman.
Eriodendron anfractuosum.
Eucalyptus botryoides.
Eucalyptus resinifera.
Eucalyptus robusta.
Eucalyptus rostrata.
Eucalyptus tereticornis.
Eugenia Jambos.
Euphorbia antiquorum.
Ficus religiosa.
Garcinia Mangostana.
Gmelina arborea.
Hevea brasiliensis.
Hibiscus esculentus.
Hibiscus mutabilis.
Hibiscus Rosa sinensis.
Hibiscus Sabdariffa.
Hibiscus schizopetalus.
Ipomoea Batatas.
Ipomoea bona-nox.
Ixora coccinea.
Jatropha Curcas.
Justicia Gendarussa.
Kigelia pinnata.
Lagetstrœmia indica.
Lantana indica.
Lawsonia alba.
Leucæna glauca.
Livistona chinensis.
Mangifera indica.
Manihot Glaziovii.
Mirabilis dichotoma.
Moringa pterygosperma.
Murraya Kœnigii.
Nerium odorum.
Nicotiana Tabacum.
Oreodoxa sp.
Panax fruticosum.
Pancratium sp.
Phyllanthus Emblica.
Pithecolobium dulce.
Plumeria acutifolia.
Poinciana regia.
Psidium Guayava.
Punica Granatum.
Quisqualis indica.

Ravenala madagascariensis.
Ricinis communis.
Saccharum Munja.
Saccharum officinarum.
Sandoricum indicum.
Saraca indica.
Sesbania grandiflora.
Solanum ferox.
Solanum lycopersicum.
Solanum Melongena.
Solanum torvum.
Solanum verbascifolium.
Swietenia Mahagoni.
Tamarindus indica.
Tectona grandis.
Theobroma Cacao.
Thevetia neriifolia.
Thysanolæna Agrostis.
Vallaris Heynei.
Vinca rosea.
Zea Mays.
Zephyranthes carinata.
Zephyranthes rosea.
Zizyphus Jujuba.

KEY TO PLATE 1.

All drawings are one-third natural size.

1. Winged seed of Sterculia alata, p. 99.
2. Reddish winged fruit of Pterolobium macropterum, p. 155.
3. Winged fruit of Ventilago madraspatana, p. 129.
4. Winged seed of Pterospermum aceroides, p. 102.
5. Winged seed of Hippocratea macrantha, p. 128.
6. Jointed pod of Desmodium umbellatum, p. 151.
7. Pod of Dalbergia volubilis, p. 149.
8. Flattened pod of Peltophorum ferrugineum, p. 157.
9. Beaked pod of Pongamia glabra, p. 152.
10. Thin samara of Ailanthus Kurzii, p. 113.
11. Pod with narrow wing along one edge of Derris scandens, p. 148.
12. Membranous pod of Spatholobus acuminatus, p. 146.
13. Pod of Derris andamanica winged along both edges, p. 148.
14. Pod with papery wing along one edge of Mezoneurum cucullatum, p. 156,
15. Flattened pod of Caesalpinia Nuga, p. 157.
16. Membranous follicle of Sterculia colorata, p. 101.
17. Membranous follicle of Sterculia campanulata, p. 100.
18. Samara of Pterocarpus dalbergioides, p. 152.
19. Pod with narrow wing along one edge of Derris uliginosa, p. 147.
20. Butterfly-shaped fruit of Illigera appendiculata, p. 170.
21. Membranous samaras, in threes, of Aspidopterys andamanica, p. 107.
22. Butterfly-shaped fruit of Terminalia bialata, p. 167.
23. Nut of Parishia insignis, with four weak reddish wings, p. 142.
24. Nut of Hopea odorata with two stiff wings, p. 94.
25. Fruit of Hiptage Madablota with three wings, p. 106.
26. Nut with two erect stiff wings of Gyrocarpus americanus, p. 169.

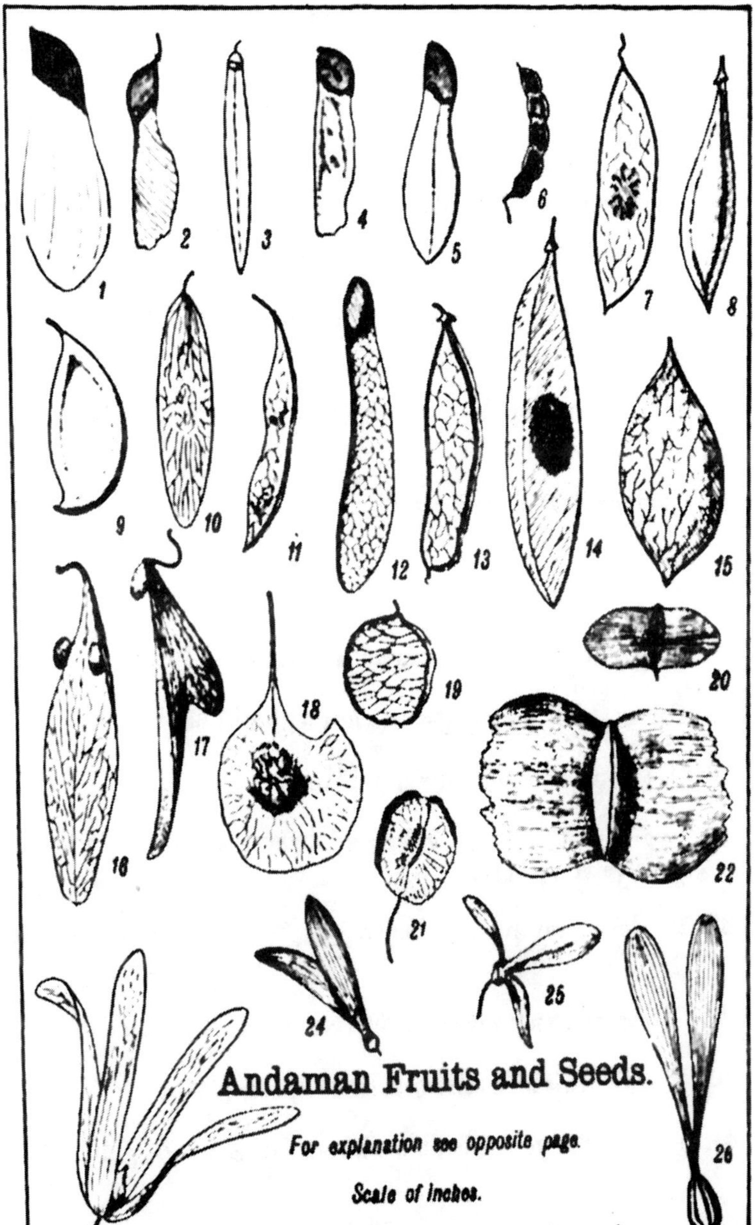
1
2
3
4
5
6
7
8
9
10
11
12
13
14
15
16
17
18
19
20
21
22
23
24
25
26
Andaman Fruits and Seeds.
For explanation see opposite page.
Scale of inches.
0 1 2 3 4 5 6

KEY TO PLATE 2.

All drawings are one-third natural size.

27. Woody pod of Afzelia bijuga, p. 154.

28. Dark brown pod of Albizzia stipulata, p. 160.

29. Straw-coloured pod of Albizzia Lebbek, p. 160.

30. Two-valved capsule of Hippocratea macrantha with winged seeds inside, p. 128.

31. Blackish pod of Mucuna gigantea, double-winged along both edges, p. 145.

32. Orange-coloured two-lobed fruit of Harpullia cupanioides, p 136.

33. Keeled fruit of Heritiera littoralis, p. 102.

34. Prickly fruit of Buettneria andamanensis, p. 102.

35. Capsule of Hibiscus Abelmoschus with stiff hairs, p. 96.

36. Pod of Sophora tomentosa, p. 151.

37. Egg-shaped fruit of Chukrasia tabularis, splitting into three or four valves, p. 119.

38. Bracteate involucral clusters of Sphenodesme unguiculata, p. 220.

39. Compressed and ridged nut of Terminalia Catappa, p. 167.

40. Winged fruit of Ancistrocladus extensus, p. 95.

41. Fruit of Berrya Ammonilla with radiating wings, p. 103.

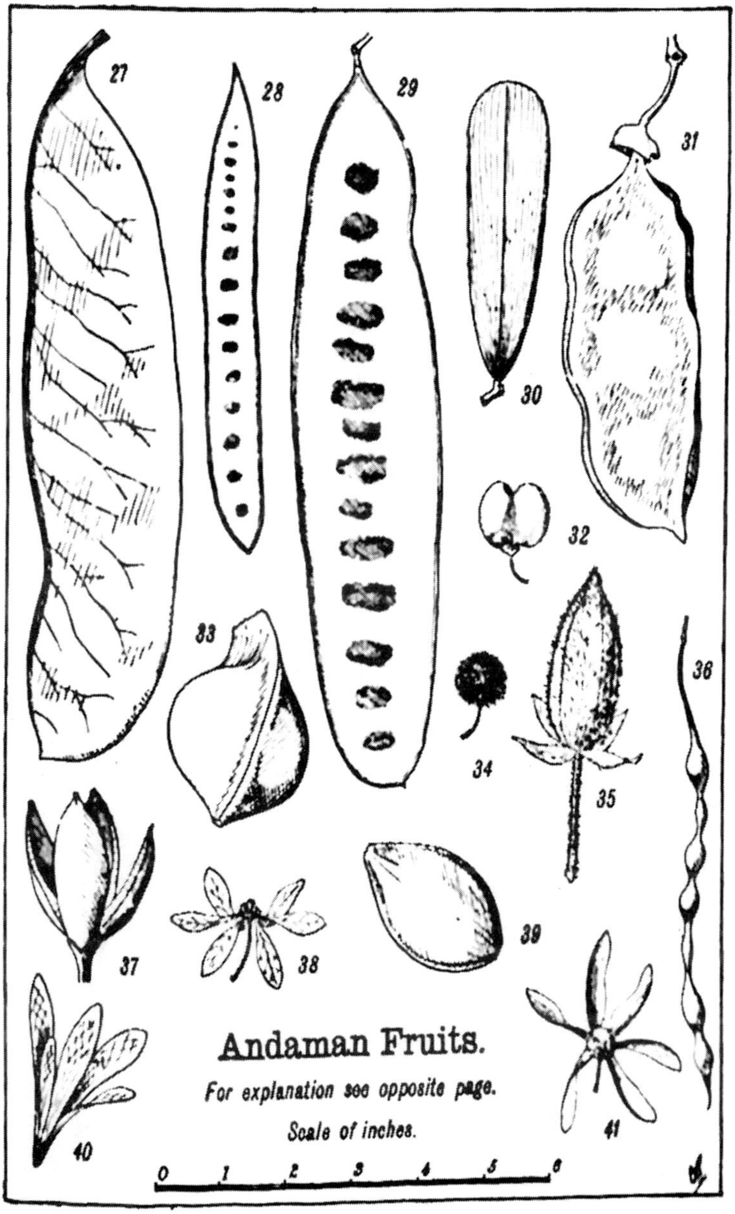

Andaman Fruits.

For explanation see opposite page.

Scale of inches.

KEY TO PLATE 3.

All drawings are one-third natural size.

42. Fruit of Bruguiera gymnorhiza, with pointed radlcle, p. 164.

43. Fruit of Unona Dasymaschala, p. 77.

44. Fruit consisting of several fruitlets of Mitrephora Prainii, p. 76.

45. Fruit of Ceriops Candolleana, with long, pointed radicle, p. 165.

46. Bluish-black fruit of Dehaasia Kurzii, seated on swollen reddish pedicel, p. 228.

47. Fibrous fruit of Nipa fruticans, p. 263.

48. Fruit of Sonneratia acida, p. 178.

49. Fruit of Thespesia populnea, p. 97.

50. Curved and pointed fruit of Aegiceras majus, p. 194.

51. Four-winged fruit of Combretum extensum, p. 169.

52. Follicle of Sterculia alata, p. 99.

53. Nut of Myristica andamanica, splitting in halves, p. 223.

54. Scarlet follicle of Sterculia villosa, p. 101.

PLATE 8.

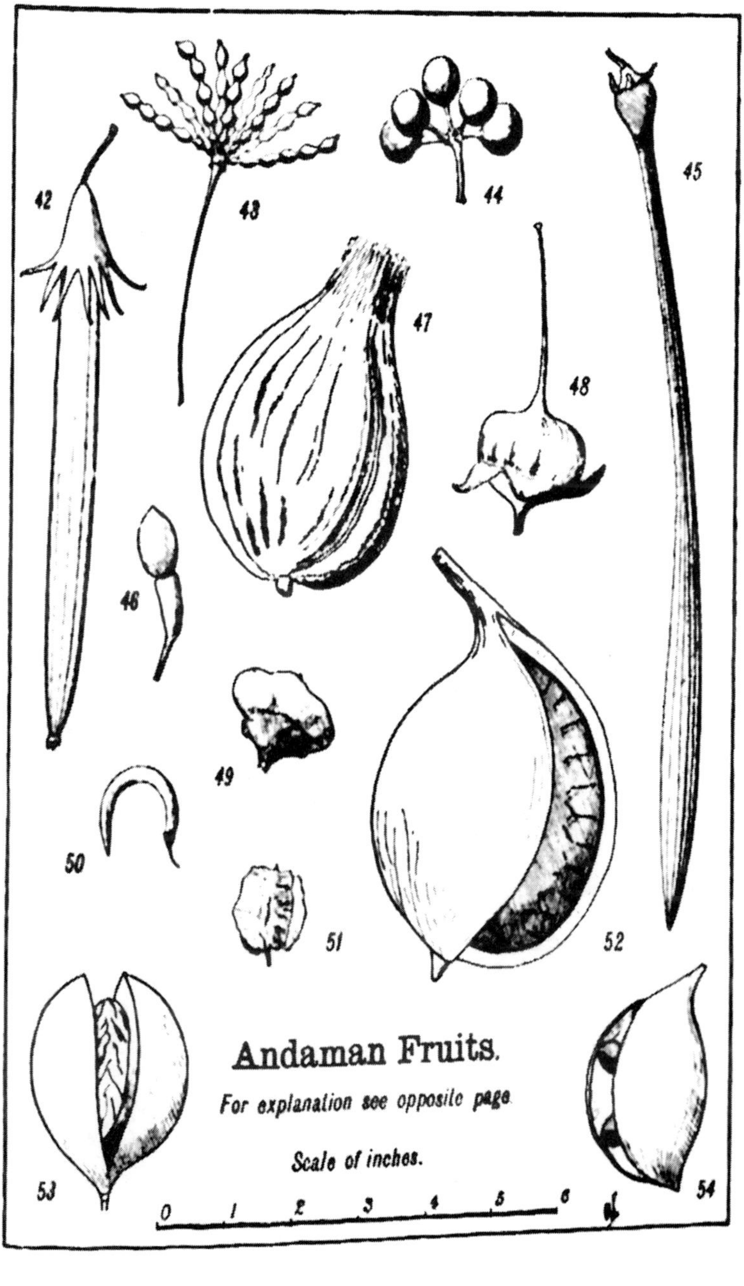

Andaman Fruits.

For explanation see opposite page.

PLATE 4.

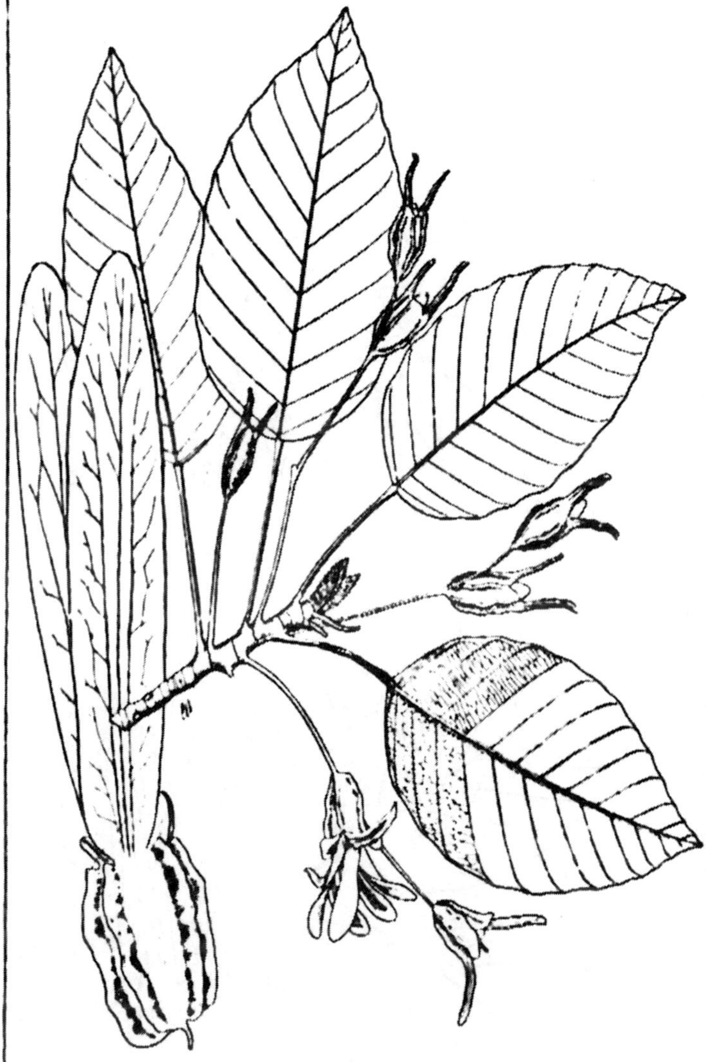

Dipterocarpus Griffithii, Miq

Scale of inches.

0 1 2 3 4 5 6 7 8

PLATE 5.

Dipterocarpus turbinatus, Gaertn. f.
var andamanica

Dipterocarpus Kerrii, King

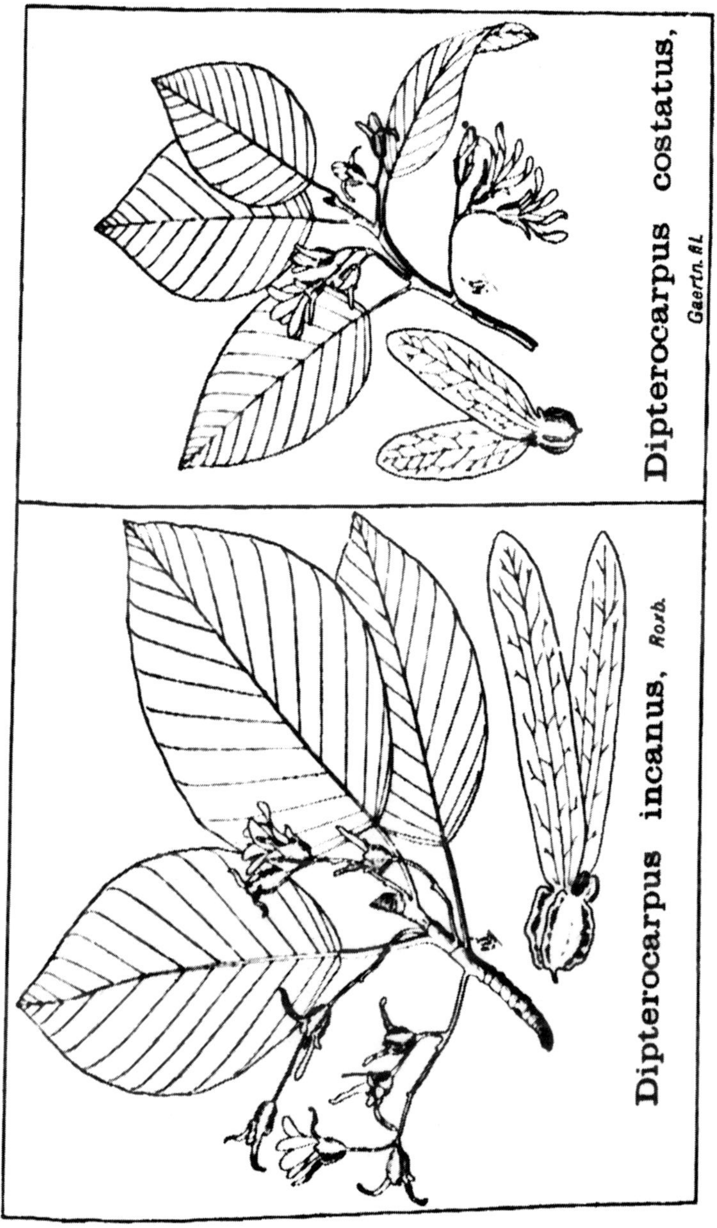

Dipterocarpus costatus, Gaertn. fil.

Dipterocarpus incanus, Roxb.

A GLOSSARY OF BOTANICAL TERMS.

Accrescent.—Said of parts that persist and increase in size after flowering, as the two calyx lobes of the *Dipterocarps*.

Acumen.—A sharp somewhat prolonged point, as the apex of the leaves of *Ficus religiosa*.

Acuminate.—Tapering to a point, as the apex of the leaves of *Brownlowia lanceolata*.

Acute.—Ending in an acute angle.

Adnate.—Said of the union of organs of a different nature, as the stamens and corolla of *Randia exaltata*.

Adpressed.—Said of hairs lying close against the surface.

Aerial.—Said of roots produced in the air, as those of *Rhizophora mucronata*.

Alternate.—One above the other at different intervals, as the leaves of the *Dipterocarps* on the branchlets, or between each other, as the sepals and petals of *Ochna Wallichii*.

Ample.—Abundant, not scanty, as the inflorescence of the *Padauk*.

Amplexicaul.—Clasping the stem, as the petioles of *Dracæna*.

Angled.—Said of stems, as those of *Memecylon elegans*, or of fruits as those of *Barringtonia speciosa*

Annular.—Marked by rings, as the stems of canes.

Anther.—That part of the stamen in which the pollen is generated.

Apetalous.—Without petals, as the flowers of *Sonneratia alba*.

Apiculate.—With a short point.

Apocarpous.—With the carpels distinct from each other, as in the fruit of the *Chai*.

Appendage.—An added part, as the wings of *Illigera appendiculata*.

Armed.—Provided with prickles, spines or thorns.

Aromatic.—Having a fragrance, as the bark of *Cinnamomum*, or the resin of *Canarium Manii*.

Attenuate.—Narrowed and gradually tapering, as the leaves of *Ancistrocladus attenuatus*.

Ascending.—Directed upwards obliquely.

Auriculate.—Said of leaves having small rounded lobes at the base.

Axil.—The upper angle formed by a leaf and the supporting stems.

Axillary.—In, or relating to, the axil, as the flowers of *Mimusops littoralis.*

Axis.—The centre line or support about which the other parts are arranged.

Base.—The lower part, or the part attached to the support.

Basal-nerved.—With the main nerves proceeding from the base, as in the leaves of *Sterculia villosa.*

Berry.—A simple fruit, succulent or fleshy throughout, and usually with many seeds immersed in the pulp, as a *lime*, or the fruit of *Mimusops littoralis.*

Bifid.—Divided to about the middle into two segments by a narrow sinus, as the petals of *Bruguiera gymnorhiza.*

Bipinnate.—Twice pinnate, as the leaves of *Adenanthera pavonina* and the *Koko.*

Bisexual.—Having both stamens and pistils in the same flower.

Bole.—The main stem of a tree.

Bract.—A modified leaf, usually smaller than and differing from other leaves in shape and colour, borne on the flowering shoots and from the axils of which flowers spring. A small or secondary bract of the individual flowers of a many-flowered inflorescence is called a *bracteole.*

Bristle.—A stiff hair, as those on the fruits of *Buettneria.*

Buttressed.—The vertical woody projections at the base of the stems of trees, as those of *Tetrameles nudiflora* or the *Padauk.*

Caducous.—Falling off very early, as the petals of *Duabanga sonneratioides.*

Calyx.—The outer whorl, usually greenish, of floral envelopes; the sepals.

Calycine.—Resembling or relating to the calyx.

Campanulate.—Bell-shaped, as the flowers of *Sterculia campanulata* or those of *Fagræa morindæfolia.*

Capsule.—A dry fruit of several united carpels splitting open when ripe to discharge the seeds, as those of the *Didu* and *Pyinma.*

Carpel.—A single infolded pistil-leaf or seed-vessel which bears ovules on its inner margins.

Catkin.—An inflorescence resembling a cat's tail; a slender pendulous and usually deciduous spike of unisexual flowers; see the catkins of *Gnetum scandens*, and the catkin-like spikes of *Excoecaria Agallocha*.

Caudate.—With a long slender tail-like appendage as the apices of the leaves of the *Pipal*.

Chartaceous.—Of the texture of writing paper, as the leaves of *Grewia Microcos*.

Ciliate.—With a fringe of hairs on the margin like those of an eyelash.

Cirrhus.—A tendril or slender whip-like process, as those which terminate some canes and as in *Gouania andamanica*.

Clavate.—Club-shaped, as the fruits of *Anaxagorea luzoniensis*.

Claw.—The narrow base of many petals, as those of *Mitrephora Prainii*.

Cleft.—Narrowly divided to about halfway down.

Climber.—A plant that ascends upon supports or other plants by means of supports.

Cluster.—A general term for a collection of flowers or fruits, as the flowers of *Bassia butyracea* or the fruits of *Baccaurea sapida*.

Coccous.—A seed-like lobe of a dry fruit which breaks up or separates when mature; pl. Cocci.

Cohesion.—Said of the union of parts of a similar nature, as the petals in pairs in *Linociera terniflora*.

Compound.—Composed of several parts, as the leaf of the *Padauk* or the *Didu*.

Connate.—Said of the union of similar organs; see Cohesion.

Connivent.—Having the parts converging at the apex, as the calyx segments of *Sterculia parviflora*.

Contorted.—Said of petals twisted upon their axis, so that every one has one margin covered and one uncovered, as those of the *Shoe Flower* and of the *Gurjans*.

Convolute.—Rolled lengthwise upon itself, as the stipules of *Artocarpus Chaplasha*.

Cordate.—Heart-shaped, also said of the base of a leaf when lobed like a heart as those of *Sterculia alata*.

Coriaceous.—Having a texture like that of leather, as the leaves of the *Mango* tree.

Corolla.—The inner whorl of floral members, the petals, whether joined together or not.

Corona.—A process from the inner face of petals or from the throat of a corolla resembling in arrangement a crown.

Corymb.—A raceme in which the main axis is short and the lower pedicels longer than the upper ones, the top of the inflorescence being more or less flattened and with a convex outline, as in *Duabanga sonneratioides.*

Corymbiform.—Resembling in appearance a corymb.

Crenate.—With rounded teeth ; scalloped, as the leaflets of *Zanthoxylum Budrunga.*

Crenulate.—Finely crenate, as the leaves of *Barringtonia racemosa.*

Culm.—The hollow and jointed stem of bamboos and grasses.

Cuneate.—Shaped like a wedge, as the leaves of *Ancistrocladus attenuatus.*

Cyme.—An irregular inflorescence in which the flowering proceeds from the centre outwards as in *Eugenia claviflora.*

Deciduous.—Said of trees that shed all their leaves annually and are leafless for a short time before the new leaves appear ; also said of petals when they fall off early as those of *Dillenia pilosa.*

Decurrent.—Produced down, as the blade of the leaves of *Planchonia andamanica.*

Dehiscence.—The manner of the opening or splitting of dry fruits to shed their seeds, or the anthers to shed their pollen.

Deltoid.—Triangular in outline, as the leaflets of *Caryota mitis.*

Dense.—Compact ; grown close together.

Dentate.—With triangular teeth pointing outwards.

Denticulate.—Finely dentate.

Diadelphous.—Said of stamens when joined by their filaments into two sets or groups as those of *Dalbergia volubilis.*

Dichotomous.—When the branches fork in pairs.

Didynamous.—With two long and two short stamens as those of *Acanthus.*

Digitate.—Said of a compound leaf when all the leaflets start from the same point from the apex of the petiole, as those of *Bombax insigne.*

Diœcious.—When the flowers are unisexual, the male and female being borne on separate plants such as *Tetrameles nudiflora.*

Disc.—The name given to growths, ring-like or glandular, from the receptacle between the corolla and stamens, or the stamens and ovary.

Distichous.—Arranged in two vertical and opposite ranks, as the leaves of *Duabanga sonneratioides.*

Divaricate.—Spreading widely apart as the branches of the inflorescence of *Stephegyne diversifolia.*

Dorsal.—Pertaining to the back or the part away from the axis, as the keel in the boat-shaped follicles of *Sterculia colorata.*

Drupe.—A fleshy fruit with a succulent outer portion and a hard inner portion, as the mango and the fruits of *Sideroxylon longepetiolatum.*

Ellipsoid.—A solid with an elliptic outline, as the fruits of *Bouea burmanica.*

Emarginate.—With a notch at the apex, as the leaflets of the *Koko.*

Endocarp.—The inner layer of the pericarp of a drupe, which is hard and forms the so-called stone, as in a mango.

Ensiform.—Sword-shaped, like the leaves of *Pandanus tectorius.*

Entire.—Having an unbroken margin, as the leaves of *Rhizophora.*

Epipetalous.—Said of stamens inserted on the petals, as those of *Gardenia coronaria.*

Evergreen.—Said of plants that are never wholly devoid of green leaves.

Epiphyte.—A plant that grows upon another but draws no nourishment from it.

Exotic.—Not native, belonging to another country.

Exserted.—Said of stamens when they project beyond the mouth of the limb of the corolla.

Exstipulate.—Not having stipules.

Falcate.—Shaped like a sickle.

Family.—A group of allied genera.

Fascicle.—A compact cluster, like the flowers of *Garcinia andamanica.*

Ferrugineous.—Of the colour of rust, as the undersurface of the leaves of *Sideroxylon ferrugineum*.

Fertile.—Fruitful; productive of anything.

Fibrous.—Composed of fibres, like the outer covering of the coco-nut.

Filament.—The stalk of an anther.

Filiform.—Like a thread, as the filaments of the stamens of *Sonneratia alba*.

Fimbriate.—Fringed, having the edge with thread-like processes as the petals of *Hiptage Madablota*.

Flabelliform.—Fan-shaped, as the leaves of *Borassus flabellifer*.

Flagellum.—A whip-like process frequent in canes.

Fleshy.—Thick and succulent.

Follicle.—A dry usually one-celled and many-seeded pod opening along one side only, as the fruits of *Sterculia alata*.

Free.—Said of organs not united to one another.

Fugacious.—Falling off very early.

Gamopetalous.—Having the petals joined to one another as those of *Ipomoea biloba*.

Gamosepalous.—Having the sepals joined to one another.

Glabrous.—Smooth, without hairs.

Glabrescent.—Becoming glabrous.

Gland.—A swelling or excrescence, as those at the top of the petiole of *Endospermum malaccense*, and those between the sets of stamens in *Cratoxylon formosum*.

Gland-dotted.—Dotted with translucent glands, as the leaves of *Limonia alata*.

Glaucous.—Of a pale bluish-green colour, as the undersurface of the leaves of *Myristica glaucescens*.

Globose.—Almost spherical, like the fruits of *Garuga pinnata*.

Habit.—The general appearance of a plant.

Head.—A close cluster of sessile flowers at the apex of a main axis, an usually having an involucre of bracts below the flowers, as the *Sunflower*.

Hirsute.—Rough with long and somewhat stiff hairs.

Hispid.—With stiff hairs or bristles, like those of *Ficus hispida.*

Imbricate.—With the edges overlapping like the tiles on a roof.

Imparipinnate.—Pinnate with an odd leaflet at the end of the common petiole, as in the *Dhup.*

Inland.—Belonging to the interior ; remote from the sea.

Indefinite.—Very numerous ; usually more than ten, as the stamens of *Bombax insigne.*

Indehiscent.—Not splitting open to shed the seeds, as the fruits of the *Padauk.*

Indigenous.—Native ; belonging naturally to a locality.

Inflexed.—Bent inwards, like the stamens of the *Pyinma.*

Inflorescence.—A collective term to denote the manner in which flowers are arranged and supported by the floral stalks and branches.

Internode.—That portion of a stem between the places where leaves are borne, or in bamboos between the joints.

Interpetiolar.—Situated between the petioles as the stipules of *Nauclea Gageana.*

Intramarginal.—Within the margin.

Introduced.—Not originally native and brought in by some other agency, as the *Teak* tree to the Andamans.

Involucre.—A whorl of bracts, often found at the apex of the peduncle below the pedicels or rays.

Irregular.—Said of a flower when it has petals, or perianth lobes, unequal in size and shape, as those of *Acanthus.*

Keel.—A ridge ; also the lowest petals of a papilionaceous corolla which enclose the stamens.

Laciniate.—Irregularly cleft into narrow segments.

Lanceolate.—Shaped like the head of a lance, as the leaves of *Brownlowia lanceolata.*

Lateral.—Referring to, or on, the side.

Lax.—Not dense or compact, as the inflorescence of *Ancistrocladus extensus.*

Leaflet.—One of the distinct blades of a compound leaf.

Legume.—A pod, characteristic of the Family *Leguminoseæ,* opening along both edges when ripe.

Lepidote.—Scaly, as the leaves of *Elaeagnus latifolia.*

Limb.—The expanded part of a gamopetalous corolla, as in the flowers of *Guettarda speciosa.*

Linear.—Narrow and long, at least five times as long as broad.

Littoral.—Inhabiting the seashores.

Lobe.—A rounded, sometimes pointed, division of a leaf or petal.

Loculicidal.—Splitting through the cells of a dry fruit as in the *Pyinma.*

Male.—Said of a flower with stamens but no pistil

Membranous.—Thin and translucent as the fruits of *Sterculia campanulata.*

Midrib.—The central main nerve of a leaf that forms the continuation of the petiole.

Monadelphous.—Having the stamens united into one set or group, as those of the *Chinese Shoe Flower.*

Monaecious.—Having unisexual flowers and both male and female on the same plant, as in *Ficus.*

Mucronate.—Abruptly ending in a short straight sharp point, as the leaves of *Rhizophora mucronata.*

Net-veined.—With the veins of the leaf forming a net-work.

Node.—The portion of the stem where leaves are produced.

Ob.—A prefix meaning reversed.

Obcordate.—Said of a heart-shaped leaf with the two lobes at the apex.

Oblanceolate.—Said of a lanceolate leaf with the broader portion near the apex.

Oblique.—Slanting; unequal-sided, as the lateral leaflets of *Parishia insignis.*

Oblong.—Two or three times as long as broad with almost parallel sides.

Obovate.—Ovate in outline with the broader end towards the apex, as the leaves of *Mimusops littoralis.*

Obovoid.—Said of an egg-shaped fruit with the stalk attached to the narrower end.

Obtuse.—Blunt or somewhat rounded at the top.

Opposite.—Said of a pair of leaves at a node, one on either side of the stem, as those of the *Gangaw*; also of leaflets as those of *Carapa obovata*.

Orbicular.—Circular in outline, or nearly so.

Ovate.—Egg-shaped, the broader portion near the base.

Ovary.—The portion of the seed vessel in which the ovules or young seeds are contained.

Ovoid.—A solid with an egg-shaped outline, as the fruits of *Elaeocarpus robustus*.

Palmate.—With the main nerves or leaflets all meeting and radiating from the top of the petiole; digitate; see the leaves of *Sterculia villosa* and those of the *Didu*.

Palminerved.—With the main nerves diverging from the top of the petiole as in the leaves of *Macaranga Tanarius* or *Grewia calophylla*.

Panicle.—A compound or much-branched inflorescence in which the first branchings from the main axis are racemose, as in the *Pyinma* and *Berrya Ammonilla*.

Parallel-veined.—With simple veins running close and almost parallel to each other, as in the leaves of *Calophyllum Inophyllum* and in the *Bamboos*.

Parasite.—Said of a plant which grows upon another plant and draws nourishment from it.

Paripinnate.—Pinnate, with a pair of leaflets terminating the common petiole, as in *Carapa obovata* and *Pometia pinnata*.

Pedicel.—The stalk of an individual flower in an inflorescence.

Peduncle.—The stalk of a solitary flower, or the main stalk of a flower cluster or inflorescence; also the stalk of a fruit or fruit cluster.

Peltate.—Like a shield; said of a leaf with the stalk attached to the undersurface at some part away from the margin as in *Macaranga Tanarius* and *Hernandia peltata*.

Penninerved.—With the lateral or secondary veins running from the midrib to the margin in a pinnate manner.

Pentamerous.—With the floral members in whorls of fives.

Perianth.—The floral envelopes; also a term applied to calyx or corolla when there is little or no difference between them.

Pericarp.—The wall of the ovary which, in ripening, becomes the wall of the fruit and which immediately surrounds the seeds. It may be in two or three distinct layers, the skin of which is the *epicarp*, the pulp the *mesocarp*, and the stone the *endocarp*.

Persistent.—Said of parts which remain attached to their support longer than their usual season, as petals or sepals in the case of fruits until mature.

Petal.—One of the floral leaves of the corolla, whether distinct or united.

Petaloid, resembling a petal.

Petiole.—The stalk of a leaf; *petiolule*, the stalk of a leaflet.

Pinna.—The primary branches of a bipinnate or tripinnate leaf.

Pinnate.—Said of a compound leaf with leaflets arranged on either side of the rachis, as in *Pometia pinnata.*

Pinnately.—Said of veins when arranged on either side of the midrib as in a feather, or of lobes or divisions arranged in a pinnate manner.

Pinnule.—The secondary branches of a tripinnate leaf.

Pistil.—The female organ of a flower consisting of an ovary and stigma, with or without the style.

Pod.—The common name given to many dry dehiscent fruits as the *Cotton Pod*, but especially to those of the Pea Family, as of the *Koko* or *Entada scandens.*

Polygamous.—Bearing bisexual and unisexual flowers on the same or on different individual plants.

Pore.—A small opening.

Puberulous.—With very short, soft and straight hairs.

Pubescent.—With short, soft and straight hairs.

Pyrene.—One of the small stones of a drupaceous fruit.

Quadrangular.—Four cornered.

Raceme.—An inflorescence with a simple axis bearing stalked flowers, the youngest flowers being at the top, as in *Barringtonia racemosa* and *Terminalia procera.*

Rachis.—The prolongation of the petiole in a pinnate or bipinnate leaf on which the leaflets or pinnae are borne. Also the prolongation of the peduncle of the inflorescence.

Receptacle.—The part of the floral axis, often enlarged, on which the floral organs are borne, well seen in *Ochna Wallichii* in fruiting; also the enlarged axis which bears flowers as in the *Figs* or *Artocarpus Chaplasha.*

Reflexed.—Bent backwards and downwards.

Regular.—When the members of each whorl of floral organs are alike in size and shape.

Repand.—With a wavy margin.

Reticulate.—Said of veins when arranged like net-work.

Retuse.—With a shallow notch in a rounded apex.

Rotund.—Circular in outline or nearly so.

Rugose.—Wrinkled, as the fruits of *Cynometra ramiflora.*

Rusty.—Like rust.

Samara.—A dry, winged, indehiscent fruit as those of the *Padauk.*

Scandent.—Climbing.

Scattered.—Said of leaves when disposed at distant intervals on the stem, as those of the *Black Chuglam.*

Secondary.—Said of nerves that proceed from the main or primary ones.

Sepal.—One of the floral leaves of the calyx.

Serrate.—Notched like the teeth of a saw.

Serrulate.—Finely serrate, like the leave of *Alsodeia bengalensis.*

Sessile.—Without a stalk.

Shrub.—Plants usually not exceeding 15 feet in height and generally having a distinct woody stem or stems and branching near the ground.

Simple.—Said of a leaf when consisting of one undivided piece, or of a fruit when it is the result of the ripening of a single pistil.

Sinuate.—Strongly wavy.

Sinus.—The indentation between the lobes or other divisions in a leaf.

Solitary.—Singly.

Spadix.—An inflorescence in which sessile flowers are arranged on a thick fleshy axis and enclosed by a spathe, as in the *Screw-pine.*

Spathe.—A large leafy or membranous sheath-like bract, well seen in *Pandanus tectorius.*

Spathulate.—Spoon-shaped, as the leaves of *Rhabdia lycioides.*

Spherical.—Globular, like the fruits of *Calophyllum Inophyllum.*

Spiciform.—Like a spike ; spicate.

Spike.—An inflorescence with a slender simple axis bearing stalkless flowers as that of the *White Chuglam.*

Spinulous.—Armed with small spines.

Stamen.—The male organ of a flower composed of the anther, which contains the pollen, and of the filament or stalk, or of anthers only.

Staminode.—A stamen without an anther.

Stellate.—Arranged in the form of a star, as the hairs on the leaves of *Pterospermum aceroides.*

Stigma.—The upper extremity of the style which receives the pollen.

Stipule.—Small appendages usually found in pairs at the base of the leaf.

Stipel.—The appendage of a leaflet.

Style.—The stalk bearing the stigma ; see the flowers of *Sonneratia.*

Sub.—A prefix meaning almost.

Supra-axillary.—Inserted on the stem just above the leaf axil, as flowers of *Capparis horrida.*

Superior.—Said of the ovary when it is free from the calyx or other parts of the flower.

Suture.—A seam ; the united margins of the carpel or the line in a dehiscent fruit where the valves unite.

Tail.—A long slender appendage as those terminating the leaves of *Ficus religiosa.*

Tapering.—Gradually narrowing to a point.

Tawny.—Of a dark yellowish colour as the hairs on the buds of *Dipterocarpus Griffithii.*

Tendril.—A slender thread-like body, simple or branched, which attaches itself to a support by coiling around it or adhering to it.

Terminal.—Relating to, or forming, the end, as the inflorescence at the end of the branchlets of *Fagraea morindæfolia.*

Tetramerous.—Having the parts in fours.

Tomentose.—Closely covered with short, soft and matted hairs.

Tomentum.—A covering of tomentose hairs.

Tree.—A woody plant with a distinct main stem and usually attaining a height of more than 15 feet.

Trichotomous.—With the branchings in threes.

Trifoliolate.—Having three leaflets. Pinnately-trifoliolate, when the insertion of the centre leaflet is above that of the lateral leaflets. Digitately trifoliolate, when all three leaflets are inserted together at the apex of the petiole.

Trigonous.—Three angled, as the fruits of the *Dhup.*

Trimerous.—Having the parts in threes, as the flowers of *Talauma.*

Tripinnate.—Thrice pinnate, as the leaves of *Moringa pterygosperma.*

Turgid.—Swollen, as the fruits of *Strongylodon ruber.*

Umbel.—An inflorescence in which the flowers stalks are of nearly all the same length and proceed from the top of a common peduncle, as in *Aegiceras majus.* *Umbellule*, a small umbel.

Umbelliform.—Resembling in appearance an umbel.

Unarmed.—Without prickles, spines or thorns.

Undulate.—Wavy, as the margins of the leaves of the *Dipterocarps.*

Unisexual.—Having only stamens or only pistil.

Valvate.—Said of sepals and petals when their margins are in contact and there is no overlapping, and of fruits which split open by valves or along the lines that correspond to the sutures.

Vaulted.—Arching over, as the petals of *Mitrephora Prainii.*

Venation.—A collective term for the veins of a leaf and the manner of their arrangement.

Versatile.—Swinging freely on its support.

Villous.—Having long and soft hairs.

Whorl.—A ring of leaves or other organs all at the same node and at equal distances apart, as the leaves of *Alstonia scholaris.*

Wing.—A membranous appendage as those of the fruits of *Gurjans*, and the seeds of *Sterculia alata.*

Zygomorphic.—Said of flowers such as many of the *Pea Family*, which are capable of being bisected into two similar halves only in one plane.

INDEX OF THE FAMILIES, GENERA AND SPECIES.

INDEX OF VERNACULAR AND COMMON NAMES.